The
Social
Web

THE SOCIAL WEB

An Introduction to Sociology

FIFTH EDITION

JOHN A. PERRY
CUYAHOGA COMMUNITY COLLEGE

ERNA K. PERRY

HARPER & ROW, PUBLISHERS, New York
Cambridge, Philadelphia, San Francisco, Washington,
London, Mexico City, São Paulo, Singapore, Sydney

Sponsoring Editor: Alan McClare
Project Editor: Lauren G. Shafer
Text Design: Graphnick Design
Cover Illustration: Detail from Willem de Kooning,
Easter Monday. Oil and newspaper transfer on canvas.
H. 96″W. 74″. 1955–56.
The Metropolitan Museum of Art, Rogers Fund, 1956.
Text Art: Fineline Illustrations, Inc.
Photo Research: Mira Schachne
Production Manager: Jeanie Berke
Production Assistant: Paula Roppolo
Compositor: Ruttle, Shaw & Wetherill, Inc.
Printer and Binder: R. R. Donnelley & Sons Company
Photograph credits begin on page 389.

The Social Web: An Introduction to Sociology   Fifth Edition
Copyright © 1988 by Harper & Row, Publishers, Inc.

Library of Congress Cataloging in Publication Data

Perry, John A. (John Ambrose), 1931–
    The social web.

    Includes bibliographies and index.
    1. Sociology.   I. Perry, Erna.   II. Title.
HM51.P44   1988   301   87–9295
ISBN 0-06-045123-8

87 88 89 90 9 8 7 6 5 4 3 2 1

Brief
Contents

Contents

Perspectives and Concepts of Sociology

PART ONE

1

What should the aims of sociology be? Should the discipline pursue a rigidly scientific course, or turn a sympathetic ear to human problems and suffering? The author argues for a balance between these two extremes.

A report on a survey undertaken to discover how women are coping with the new statuses and roles they occupy as a result of the success of the feminist movement.

x

CONTENTS

Socialization: Successes and Failures 96

The Chapter in Brief 96

Terms to Remember 97

Suggestions for Further Reading 99

Reading: Sharon Begley, "What Shapes the Child?" Newsweek (October 1, 1984). 99

The past is not necessarily a prelude to the future, nor is an individual's personality cast in stone.

CHAPTER 5 | DEVIANCE AND DEVIANTS 103

Social Control 104
Sanctions 105

Deviance 105
The Relative Nature of Deviance 106

Functions of Deviance 107
Reinforcement of Group Norms 108 | Adaptation to Social Change 108

Attempts to Explain Deviance 108
Biological Explanations 109 | Psychological Explanations 109

Sociological Explanations of Deviance 110
Anomie Theory 110 | Cultural Transmission (Differential Association) Theory 113 | Labeling Theory 114

New Trends in Criminology 116
Crime: Deviance that Hurts 117
Classification of Crimes 118 | Crime Statistics 119
The Criminal Justice System 119

The Chapter in Brief 122

Terms to Remember 123

Suggestions for Further Reading 124

Reading: David Kelley, "Stalking the Criminal Mind," Harper's (August 1985), pp. 53–59. 125

Do criminals *know* that they are breaking the bond that makes society possible? Or are they victims of circumstances who cannot control their deviant actions?

We are born with unequal life chances, some destined to become
life's anointed, others its hollow-eyed "Skunk Hollowers" of one
type or another.

Social Change:
Processes and Results

PART THREE

225

The colliding worlds of the past and the present are nowhere so shocking as when a preliterate hunting and gathering society comes in contact with the technology of an urban industrial one.

What makes an organized crowd, gathered for a pleasurable afternoon of spectator sport, become a mindless mob intent on maiming and killing?

Cultural Patterns: Pivotal Institutions

PART FOUR

297

The transition into a post-industrial era poses serious problems for
industrial workers, but the young American worker of this generation seems ready to accept the challenge.

Study Guide

Preface

To the Instructor

We have completely rewritten the fifth edition of *The Social Web* to give you a concise, streamlined text. *The Social Web* now contains twelve chapters that examine chief sociological concepts, including a completely new chapter on social differentiation based on gender, age, and handicaps. Five pivotal social institutions are also explored: family, religion, education, economy, and government. While all of the text has been revised, we have retained the lively, journalistic style that made earlier editions popular. In addition, we have chosen all new selected readings, again taken from the popular press, including the *New York Times, Fortune,* the *Washington Post, The New Republic, Science,* and *Newsweek,* among others. As in previous editions, each chapter concludes with a summary and definitions of key terms.

To reinforce what students learn in the text chapters and readings, we have added a *Study Guide* that is bound into the back of the book. It gives students the opportunity to study and review what they have learned without imposing the added expense of buying an extra workbook. Students can use the study guide on their own, either individually or together, or you may assign parts as you feel appropriate.

Many people have contributed to making *The Social Web,* Fifth Edition a complete and effective teaching package for students. Our reviewers have been instrumental in suggesting how to improve each edition, and we want to thank all who worked on this edition as well as on the first four: Jacqueline Wiseman, University of California—San Diego; Chaim I. Waxman, Central

Connecticut State College; Irving Witt, College of San Mateo; Albert Chabot, Macomb County Community College; Peter Chroman, College of San Mateo; Marybeth Collins, Central Piedmont Community College; Mary H. Donovan, Springfield Technical Community College; Glenna Teti, Monterey Peninsula College; Domenic A. Vavala, Johnson and Wales College; Gregory Staatz, Emporia State University; Martin Epstein, Middlesex Community College; Norman Goldner, University of Detroit; William J. Brindle, Monroe Community College; John Dumitru, Foothill College; Ruby Lewis, Dekalb Community College; Douglas B. McGaw, Emporia State University; Thomas F. Cravens, St. Louis Community College; R. E. Dorsett, Austin Community College; Roger Branch, Georgia Southern College; Darryl Chubin, Georgia Technical University; Al Garbin, University of Georgia; Dennis W. Teitge, Valparaiso University; Kenrick S. Thompson, Northern Michigan University; W. Clinton Terry, University of Florida; Gerald Meyers, Lakeland Community College; Otto Sampson, Norfolk State University; Gerald Friedman, Broome Community College; Tinuel Black, Loop College—City Colleges of Chicago; and Stephen A. Green, North Adams State College.

As usual, the staff at Harper & Row have been most helpful and supportive. We would like to single out Alan McClare, our Sponsoring Editor, and Lauren Shafer, the Project Editor, without forgetting those who worked behind the scenes to produce an attractive book.

To the Student

We wrote this book for you as an introduction to the fascinating subject of sociology. We have made it easy and enjoyable to read by using examples that apply to your lives. We have made our chapters manageable in length and have defined our terms clearly and repeated them often. We have tried not to overwhelm you with footnotes and scholarly references, but instead have concentrated on leading you to a clearer understanding of the essence of sociology. We have chosen the readings that end each chapter from the popular press to show how sociology applies to your life and career.

To help you do well in your course we have included a *Study Guide* that is bound into the text at the back. You can use it to review for quizzes and exams and to identify key ideas and terms for each chapter. You can review on your own or by working with your fellow students.

J.A.P.
E.K.P.

Perspectives and Concepts of Sociology

PART

One

Sociology: Science and Art

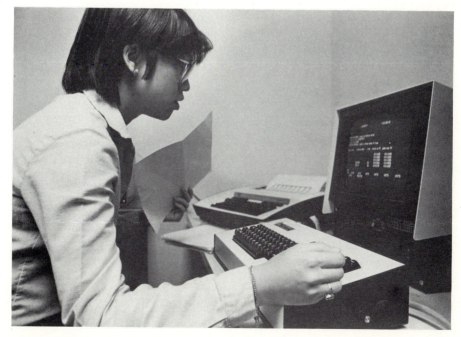

*A*t birth, each of us enters a physical world that is not of our own making. Some have the ocean in their backyard; some face a majestic mountain range as they get up each morning; still others survey a panorama of flat prairie, desert-brush vegetation, or tropical palm fronds. For some, brick and cement stretch out as far as the eye can see. Although we can eventually leave our birthplaces, we cannot change their nature except in minor ways—the desert can be made to bloom, roads and passes can be built through mountains, the prairie can become a chain of residential suburbs. These alterations, however, are only cosmetic; the basic physical environment remains. In sum, all living organisms exist in an environment shaped by forces and governed by laws only partially, and imperfectly, understood and controlled.

But each newly born human also enters a *social* world, one that has been shaped by our predecessors. This social world has traditions and rules for behavior, as well as patterns for getting things done, that each of us must learn or acquire before being considered, by ourselves and others, as being human.

The physical world that we encounter at birth has long been studied by those whose endless curiosity has driven them to observe phenomena and make deductions regarding cause and effect. The disciplines that eventually evolved into the study of the world's various aspects are known as the *physical sciences*. Much later in human history, such investigators turned their attention to the world of their own making, the social world, of which they were becoming increasingly conscious. This was the beginning of the *social sciences*.

The purpose of the social sciences is to offer a systematic study of all aspects of human behavior and the human condition, using, wherever possible, a methodology borrowed from the physical sciences. This insistence on a systematic and methodical approach distinguishes the social sciences from philosophy and art, which comment and reflect on the human condition and human behavior in less structured, less scientific ways.

Science: A New Tool of Inquiry

In defining the social sciences, key words to keep in mind are *systematically* and *methodically*. In other words, social scientists organize knowledge that has accumulated about how humans live in their world according to definite theories, concepts, and research rather than random, subjective (and thus possibly biased) observation.

As noted above, insights into the nature of human behavior and the characteristics of various societies have been expressed by artists and philosophers since time immemorial. But artists and philosophers avail themselves of such tools as intuition, authority, tradition, and common sense, methods available to and widely used by us all. Unfortunately these tools, while necessary and useful, are not always accurate or thorough, and are often colored by individual prejudices.

The modern era is distinguished from the past primarily by a new tool of inquiry, namely the **scientific method.** It is this method, rather than a particular body of knowledge, that gives scientists a unique way of looking at things. The purpose of the scientific method is to obtain evidence, verifiable and subject to replication, making no judgment about even the most obvious "facts" until original suppositions are overwhelmingly supported by proof.

The Scientific Spirit

Underlying the scientific method is an attitude best described as the **scientific spirit.** The most important principle of the scientific spirit is that of approaching the world with **doubt** and skepticism, taking no "truths" for granted. This attitude must be maintained even in regard to the scientist's own findings, which are always subject to change after further analysis.

Another necessary principle is that of **objectivity.** When confronting data intended to support a finding, scientists must try to rid themselves of all personal attitudes, desires, beliefs, values, and tendencies. They must strive to be totally dispassionate, allowing no individual biases to affect their judgment. Of course, such a degree of objectivity is only an ideal toward which scientists aspire: no human can be objective all the time. The issue of objectivity has been especially polemical in the social sciences, which deal with the often unsystematic relationships and behavior of people.

Closely related to objectivity is a third principle of the scientific spirit, **ethical neutrality.** According to this principle, scientists must not make value judgments about their findings; they must not pronounce their conclusions good or bad, right or wrong. They must only be concerned about whether their findings are true or false.

Finally, scientific conclusions must never be considered final, absolute, or universal truths. Rather, they should be seen as relative to the time and place in which they are obtained, and always subject to change or revision.

The Scientific Method

The basic technique of the scientific method is a special kind of investigation which we will call **scientific observation.** Scientific observation must not be confused with everyday "looking around." Most of us look at things all the time but seldom arrive at scientific conclusions. We obtain evidence from our senses, but to be reliable such evidence must first be confirmed by the scientific method.

Scientific observation must proceed systematically. The scientist must select and define a problem and then make an organized plan for collecting data.

Scientific observation must be accurate and precise. Collected data must be subjected to careful checking, rechecking, and cross-checking, as well as

Topics such as human sexuality could hardly be studied without the underpinnings of the scientific method.

accurate measurement. For instance, a scientist cannot say: "Large universities are full of men and women living together." Instead, such a hypothetical finding would have to be expressed as: "In universities with enrollments of 15,000 and over, 60.5 percent of the male students and 37 percent of the female students had lived together at some time during their college experience."

Scientific observation should take place under controlled conditions. Researchers should be able to keep particular features of the environment constant. Then, when other features change, specific causes can be linked to specific effects. In the social sciences this requirement is difficult to achieve; research on people cannot always be performed in a laboratory.

Finally, scientific observation must be made by a trained observer who knows which data are relevant and which are peripherally important.

Steps of the Scientific Method

The steps in the scientific method, illustrated in Figure 1.1, may be summarized as follows:

Forming a Hypothesis   In defining a problem for investigation, the scientist must first form a **hypothesis** that is subject to testing and verification. The hypothesis is a tentative statement, in clearly expressed terms, predicting a relationship between two or more factors (called **variables,** which vary or differ in individual cases), and/or the effect these factors may have on a given phenomenon (the **constant,** or characteristic that does not change). A hypothesis may be based on a mere hunch or educated guess of the researcher

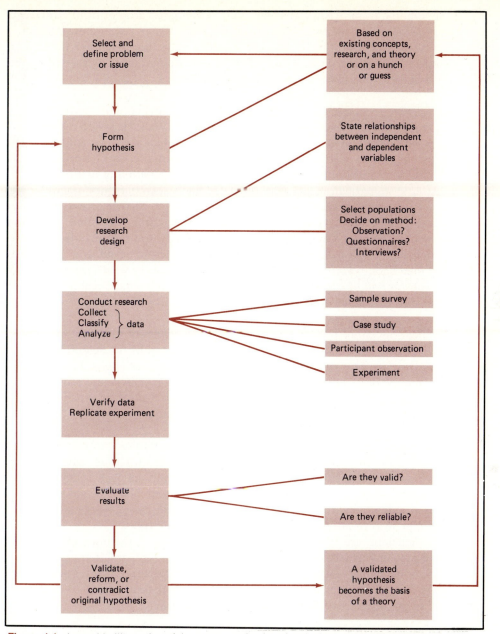

Figure 1.1 A graphic illustration of the steps a scientist takes in the pursuit of facts through the scientific method.

(the researcher may speculate, for instance, that social class influences the way one votes). Subsequent steps of the scientific method may prove the hypothesis valid (yes, social class affects voting behavior), reform it (yes, but only if the voter is in a specific age bracket), or contradict it altogether (no, social class has nothing to do with voting behavior). A hypothesis may also derive from commonsense deductions, or curiosity, or traditional wisdom; it may emerge from existing theories and previous research or from a review of the literature on an issue that interests a particular researcher. (In fact, a review of the literature is an important step in the scientific method: It connects new research with old, allows the accumulation of ideas, and directs the scientist toward the right variables to pursue.)

Developing a Research Design (Collecting, Classifying, and Analyzing Data)

The research plan that is developed after the hypothesis is stated must specify from what group or groups and in what manner data are to be collected. The researcher must also decide how best to obtain the data (through direct observation, questionnaires, interviews, or a combination of methods).

After systematically collecting the data, the researcher must classify, organize, and record them. Data must be made public, so that others may have access to both findings and procedures. In most scientific disciplines, including the social sciences, computers are used to classify and organize data.

Analysis of the data follows, in which the researcher subjects previously classified data to various statistical methods to discover whether relationships are substantial, or so small as to be caused by chance. Statistical computation determines whether or not the data support the hypothesis.

Verification Since most research is subject to error—of which the researcher may or may not be aware—the next important step in the scientific method is verification. This step consists of repeating the research project (replication) and may be done either by the original researcher or by some other investigator. In order for research to be considered valid, it must be capable of being repeated by another scientist with the same results.

Generalization Finally, conclusions must be drawn from the analysis of data. Do the data substantiate the original hypothesis? Do they refute it? Are alterations to the hypothesis in order? Too cautious researchers tend to undergeneralize, which can keep their work from being useful to others. Overconfident researchers, on the other hand, often make overgeneralizations that may lead to false hypotheses and wrong conclusions.

Conclusions are usually summarized in reports, sometimes published in professional journals or as monographs. The researcher attempts to relate these conclusions to existing theories or current research, making suggestions about the necessity of altering accepted theoretical assumptions or examining new hypotheses that have emerged from the work.

The Social Sciences and Sociology

As mentioned above, the social sciences emerged to study human behavior and the social worlds humans erect to simplify their lives. But why so many social science disciplines? Is one not sufficient?

Initially, of course, one was sufficient, and knowledge about people and their behavior accumulated under the heading "social philosophy." With time and the accelerating growth of knowledge, social philosophy evolved into separate disciplines. This process was much helped by certain ideas prevalent in the eighteenth century during the era commonly called the Enlightenment, a period characterized by an increasing faith in the power of reason. Among scholars and philosophers the idea took hold that just as natural scientists had been using the scientific method to discover universal laws of nature, similar laws applicable to human behavior could be uncovered by the same approach. Once the principles of social life were known, moreover, a more perfect society could be attained.

Conditions resulting from the Industrial Revolution gave further impetus to social thinkers, who felt compelled to seek solutions to the many new problems assailing individuals and societies. In fact, industrialization had created two new social classes, the owners of manufacturing machinery and the industrial workers who operated it. Vast discrepancies in standards of living existed between these two classes, with the workers enduring long hours, difficult working conditions, and frequent layoffs. Furthermore, people were increasingly flocking to cities in search of factory jobs. As a result urban centers suffered from overcrowding and lack of hygiene and soon became breeding grounds of poverty and crime. It was primarily these problems that early social scientists attempted to address by applying the scientific method to human behavior.

To the extent that all social sciences are studies of the same subjects—human behavior and the social environment—the boundaries between them are artificial. But each discipline focuses on a specific facet of that world and behavior, allowing the social scientist to specialize. Aware of the overlapping nature of their disciplines, social scientists often borrow from one another, their differences being, in short, a matter of emphasis.

Sociology

Sociology is the most recent of the social sciences, emerging long after history, geography, anthropology, economics, political science, and even psychology were already established. The climate for a science that was to study human groups did not arise until nearly the middle of the nineteenth century, when French philosopher Auguste Comte coined the term sociology in his *Positive Philosophy* (1838), a treatise in which he repudiated authority and speculation in favor of systematic observation and classification as the bases of all scientific inquiry. He was followed by Herbert Spencer in England (*Principles of Sociology*, 1876), Lester F. Ward in America (*Dynamic Sociology*, 1883), and most notably the French social philosopher Émile Durkheim. Durkheim (*Suicide*, 1897) demonstrated his use of scientific methodology by outlining the steps in his study of suicide: planning a research design, collecting masses of data, and deriving a theory from his findings about which kinds of individuals are likely to commit suicide.

Definition Contemporary sociology may be defined as the systematic and scientific study of human social relationships and the social systems that such behavior creates. In more popular terms, sociology is defined as the study of interacting human groups, the scientific approach to human society and human behavior. While psychology also analyzes human behavior, its focus is on the individual; the focus of sociology, conversely, is on the individual in interaction with others, moving within the social environment.

A distinguishing characteristic of sociology is its empiricism, its concern with what is rather than with what ought to be. In this sense the discipline has evolved from its beginnings, when it was seen, particularly by American sociologists, as a beacon for social progress. Another noticeable shift over the years has been sociology's movement from an initial status of pure science (its goal being solely the acquisition of knowledge, and not the use of that knowledge), to that of applied science as well, with sociological knowledge now widely used by professionals in such fields as social work, diplomacy, administration, advertising, and education.

Sociological Perspectives

All social sciences attempt to examine a distinct facet of human existence. Sociologists focus on the entire spectrum of this experience, but do so in a special way. Specifically, the sociologist's goal is to uncover the structure, or regular pattern, of social relationships that individuals create and recreate to give order to their lives. As Peter Berger states: "The fascination of sociology lies in the fact that its perspective makes us see in a new light the very world in which we have lived all our lives. . . . The sociologist does not look at phenomena that nobody is aware of. But he looks at the same phenomena in a different way" (1963, 28).

The "different way" Berger refers to is commonly known as the sociological perspective. That perspective goes beyond commonly accepted or officially defined explanations of reality. It recognizes that reality may be interpreted differently by different people at different times, or even by the same people at different times. Part of this approach also involves the realization that official interpretations are subjective and may be self-serving. The sociologist's view of reality can be aptly defined as painful awareness that things are seldom as they appear.

Individually, sociologists approach the study of their field from specific perspectives. It is impossible to study any phenomenon without a certain set of assumptions, and these assumptions are very important. (As long as people assumed that the earth was flat, for example, no attempt was made to sail around it: People were afraid of falling off the edge.) Sociological perspectives, also called paradigms or theoretical models, are frameworks, basic points of view from which the sociologist begins a journey of discovery, using the scientific method. While perspective is necessary in order to conduct any kind of research, it also often determines which elements are considered in reaching conclusions. In short, one must be aware of the researcher's perspective, for different points of departure may and do yield different conclusions. Table 1.1 demonstrates the perspectives most relevant in sociological inquiry today.

The Evolutionary Perspective

The earliest perspective in sociology was the **evolutionary perspective,** patterned on the biological example. According to this view, societies develop through a series of fixed stages. Like living organisms, societies proceed from simple to complex forms (hence, in an evolutionary fashion), and, since evolution theoretically leads to an improved product, the final stage of a society should represent its most perfect form.

In this century, however, it has become evident that not all societies pass through a fixed set of stages. In addition, the chaotic nature of twentieth-century societies does not support the notion that social evolution leads to superior development. The evolutionary perspective, therefore, has lost some credibility, although it has not been totally abandoned.

Certain sociologists maintain that because societies differ to begin with, their stages of development will vary accordingly. Even when they undergo similar stages, the results may differ. This slightly altered approach is known as the perspective of *multilinear evolution*. General patterns, multilinear evolutionists maintain, are visible in all societies. For instance, all societies tend to evolve from large extended families into smaller nuclear ones, and industrialization and urbanization generally result in liberalized attitudes and reduced levels of discrimination.

The Functionalist Perspective

Presently, three perspectives hold sway in sociology—structural functionalism (called functionalism for short), conflict theory, and symbolic interactionism—although a host of new ones are making inroads. Functionalism has been the dominant theoretical point of departure for the past 50 years, but conflict theory and symbolic interactionism now claim an equal number of adherents. Sociologists tend to rely on the theoretical approach that best explains the phenomena under analysis. The tendency has been to employ functionalism and conflict theory in studying *macro* processes (that is, in looking at societies on a large scale, from above), and symbolic interactionism in studying *micro* processes (focusing on a small facet of social life, from below). When dealing with complementary theoretical approaches, the use of more than one often results in a fuller understanding of a phenomenon. At other times, however, perspectives may prove contradictory, leaving the sociologist to decide which approach is more plausible.

The **functionalist perspective** incorporates aspects of evolutionary theory in its analogous view of societies and living organisms. As a living organism is made up of parts that contribute to the maintenance and survival of the whole, a particular society, functionalists claim, will similarly consist of a number of systems that contribute to the maintenance and survival of the whole. This

Sociological Paradigms (Theoretical Models) at a Glance

TABLE 1.1

(Structural) Functionalism	Conflict	Symbolic interactionism
Issue: What Is the Nature of Societies?		
Societies are similar to live organisms, with parts that are interdependent. These parts must be kept in balance if societies are to function.	Societies are competitive arenas in which social groups struggle for dominance or for specific rewards.	Societies are made up of numbers of small groups in which, as in a theater, people act out roles they have learned to play according to a standard script provided by society.
Issue: What Is the Nature of Life in Societies?		
Harmonious, as long as consensus and cooperation are pursued and conflict is avoided.	Full of conflict, since groups display divided interests and opposing goals. About the only agreement one can hope for is on the rules of the game.	Varied, depending on how individuals (actors) understand their roles, how they play their roles, and to which audiences they play.
Issue: What Is the Effect of Change on Society?		
Rapid change is disruptive because it disturbs the balance in a static society. To remain healthy, a society must soon reestablish balance, adjusting to change.	Change in general is productive and characteristic of societies that are in a continual state of flux, with power changing hands among competing groups. Conflict, and the change it produces, ultimately benefits societies.	New scripts come into existence, so new roles must be learned. Change occurs because some people refuse to play the roles according to the accepted script; they prefer to improvise.
Issue: What Causes Problems in Social Life?		
Rapid social change, which prevents society from making the necessary adjustments toward stability, creates social disorganization.	The fact that the groups that are in power oppress and exploit those who are not.	There is support given by groups and individuals to behavior that the majority considers deviant and dysfunctional.
Issue: What Is the Basic Question Sociology Should Answer?		
What does a social pattern do for individuals and/or groups?	Which individuals or groups benefit from a specific social pattern?	How do actors (individuals) interpret the playing of different roles?
Issue: What Is the Role of the Sociologist?		
To explain the elements of society, to show how they are related, and to explain how they affect each other.	To point out the groups in conflict, show which have power, and illustrate the way in which power is maintained.	To observe and record, methodically and in detail, the social drama: that is, individuals in society.
Issue: What Is the Cement that Holds Societies Together?		
The fact that most individuals agree on fundamental values and ways of behavior.	Power, authority, force, and coercion.	The fact that people interact and develop symbols whose meanings they come to share.

contribution represents their function, just as the function of the circulatory system in a biological organism is to provide oxygen and nourishment to tissues and carry off waste material.

From the functionalist perspective, the totality of systems called society exists in a delicate balance: if something happens to one of its parts, all other parts are affected. The system no longer functions properly and social problems arise. Although an occasional malfunction stimulates change, stability will generally be restored. Stability and change are in fact the two primary characteristics of a social system.

In addition to function, functionalists stress structure, the various parts of the system (leading to the use of the term structural functionalism). The chief structures in societies are institutions: the family, education, economy, government, religion, and so on. Each structure persists because it is functional, playing a particular part in helping the society survive. When a structure ceases to be functional it declines, bringing with it frequently disruptive social change. But a new balance is soon reestablished. The focus of analysis in structural functionalism is the interrelationship among various societal structures.

The structural-functionalist perspective was popularized by British anthropologists Bronislaw Malinowski and A. R. Radcliffe-Brown. In the United States, its best-known exponent was the late sociologist Talcott Parsons (1902–1979). The predominant perspective in the period following World War II, structural functionalism still claims a large majority of sociologists as adherents. The perspective does have its critics, however, particularly among those sympathetic to the conflict perspective.

The Conflict Perspective

The **conflict perspective** draws on the idea that conflict is the most important universal characteristic of societies, as well as the prime source of social change. A number of theorists have contributed to the development of this perspective. German sociologist Georg Simmel (1858–1918) believed that social order results from competing forces of harmony and disharmony and that conflict is an important social factor. Karl Marx (1818–1883), the theoretician of communism, saw history as progressing through stages, each of which was essentially the resolution of conflict between the haves and have-nots. Change in society, Marx believed, must occur through revolution, when the have-nots remove the haves and institute new systems. Such change is inevitable in any system based on inequality; when the deprived become aware of their deprivation, eventually they will rebel against it.

Although many of Marx's predictions failed to materialize, the Marxist perspective has continued to gather followers. Numerous American sociologists have expanded and kept it alive through several decades, even in the face of the popularity of structural functionalism. Among them are such noted figures as C. Wright Mills (1956, 1959), Lewis Coser (1956), and contemporary German sociologist Ralf Dahrendorf (1959, 1964). Conflict theorists point out that functionalists fail to consider a crucial question when analyzing social structures: "For *whom* are these structures functional?" The answer, according to conflict theorists, is that many structures are functional to specific dominant groups and these groups, possessing power, are thus able to maintain the status quo. The balance in society is therefore not based on a real consensus, but is forced on the powerless by the powerful. Analysis from the conflict perspective focuses on questions such as "Who gets what, why, and how?" in society.

The Symbolic-Interactionist Perspective

The theoretical perspective of **symbolic interactionism** grew out of attempts to explain socialization (how one becomes a member of society), specifically the development of the self. George Herbert Mead (1863–1931) is credited with having popularized this perspective in the United States during his tenure at the University of Chicago in the 1920s, although many facets originated in the works of Max Weber (1864–1930), Sigmund Freud (1856–1939), and Charles Horton Cooley (1846–1929). Mead termed the perspective "symbolic behaviorism"; "symbolic interactionism" was coined by contemporary sociologist Herbert Blumer. Other prominent modern interactionists include Erving Goffman (1959), Peter Berger, and Thomas Luckmann (1966).

Basic to interactionism is the observation that humans, like other animals, are constantly active and engage in gesturing—making movements or sounds to which others react. Unlike other animals, humans assign meanings to their gestures, which then become symbolic; that is, each action or sound comes to stand for some element understood by both the person making it and the person reacting. Shared symbols are significant because through them it is possible to develop common values and definitions.

Because people communicate through commonly shared symbols—language, for instance,—when a person reacts to a symbolic gesture or speech, he or she is in effect interpreting it socially, along the same lines as other members of the group. For instance, describing an unforgettable sunset, a speaker might use words such as sun, beautiful, red, disk, orange, and so on. All English-speaking listeners would understand these symbols; thus, the speaker would have interpreted an individual experience through social means. What is personally perceived, in short, can only be expressed in terms of shared—that is, social—meanings. Even thinking is done in social terms, thought being largely a consequence of language. Thinking, according to symbolic interactionists, is little more than a conversation between individual and self.

Another facet of symbolic interactionism is its view of reality. Reality is objective, existing apart from how any one person views it. But it is also subjective; each person views reality according to perceptions based on personal experiences and perhaps on temperament. Modern societies have governments (objective reality), but the same government may be viewed as either beneficial or oppressive by different individuals (subjective reality). Similarly, people do not respond to others directly, but rather to what they imagine the other to be. Reality, then, is as much constructed in the human mind as it is from external sources. The person sitting next to you in class is a friend, if you so perceive her, or a stuck-up so-and-so if you see her in another way. In either case, neither characteristic is really a part of that person; it is you who have attributed the friendship or enmity. You, then, have created your individual reality of that person, just as we all create the reality of those with whom we interact. Reality, in short, is a social construction, even though objective reality also exists in the universe. But objective reality has no meaning until we assign it one.

Symbolic interactionists tend to approach the analysis of society from the point of view of individuals interacting within small groups. Society is viewed as the sum of the interactions of individuals and groups, and its relative orderliness is attributed to the symbolic communication in which people continually engage. Through this type of communication, we learn the roles we are expected to play and the behavior we are expected to exhibit; we try to succeed in both our behavior and our role-playing because we want to be able to count on others to do the same.

Other Perspectives

The perspectives detailed above are prevalent in what may be regarded as mainstream sociology. A number of sociologists, however, choose to march to different drummers. **Ethnomethodology** does not assume that common sense or conventional rules are operative in specific situations; instead, this perspective attempts to discover what formal rules are genuinely operational in group life. **Sociobiology** is defined as the systematic study of the biological basis for social behavior in all organisms, including the human. **Humanistic sociology** has as its purpose the search for solutions through the application of sociological knowledge.

The scientific method would not be a valid tool of inquiry if it did not foster the development of explanatory theories. Yet the use of the method in sociology has failed to yield a grand, sweeping theory that could tell us, once and for all, how to achieve the perfect society. It has only offered a number of general orientations, or perspectives. None of these paradigms completely explains human societal interaction and organization. Each one, however, contributes to our understanding of social processes, and some explain specific facets of social life better than others. Although certain perspectives are contradictory in specific areas (for instance, functionalism and conflict theory differ on the subject of social classes and inequality), in general they are complementary and overlapping. At different times, one perspective is favored over another, and most individual sociologists are committed to a particular perspective, although some eclectically pick and choose. With as unpredictable a subject as human beings, perhaps that is the best we can expect to do.

The Scientific Method in Sociology

Sociology is considered a science because it relies on the scientific method as its system of inquiry. As a social science, it cannot employ exactly the same methodology as the physical sciences do; sociology's investigative method does, however, share with other sciences the use of concepts, theory, and research.

Concepts

A **concept** is a generalized idea about interrelated people, objects, and processes. Concepts are abstractions, ways of classifying similar things. For instance, the concept of chair includes all those objects that people sit on, although each person interprets the concept in his or her own way. In short, we all know what a chair is, but to some the word suggests a gilded Louis XIV antique, to others a chrome and vinyl creation.

Sociological concepts are the building blocks of theories sociologists use to generalize about aspects of human interaction. They are guidelines that direct investigators as they try to interpret and analyze reality. Concepts are, in essence, the technical vocabulary of sociology. Sociological concepts have precise meanings that differ considerably from generally understood versions. A student of sociology must therefore become acquainted with these concepts, understanding that they are generalized and abstract rather than concrete and real. When sociologists speak of "group," for example, they have no particular group in mind, but are instead referring to a generalized abstraction.

Theories

Concepts form the basis of theories. A **theory** is a set of concepts and generalizations so arranged as to explain and predict possible and probable relationships among phenomena. In sociology, theories are formulations of principles of behavior through which sociologists attempt to increase their knowledge of human interaction. Theories are founded on observation and analysis. Their intent is to explain the connections among human interactive occurrences. Without theories, the accumulation of sociological knowledge would be impossible, just as the formulation of theories would be impossible without concepts.

A theory does not have the force of a scientific law, an explanation of unchanging relationships among events. According to the law of gravity, for instance, an object always falls in the same direction under given conditions. Sociology, which deals with people who are unpredictable and subject to myriad variables, has no such laws. Theories are always open to change, even to total rejection, if new evidence is presented to challenge them.

Research

Research tests and bolsters theories. Research may be defined as scientific inquiry conducted under controlled conditions in which data are carefully observed for the purpose of determining the relationship between one factor (for example, income) and one or more other factors (for example, child-rearing techniques). As previously noted, the factors whose relationship sociologists try to uncover are known as *variables*. Variables are characteristics that vary or differ in individual cases—from person to person, from group to group, from time to time, from place to place. The opposite of a variable is a *constant*—a characteristic that does not vary. Age, education, income, religion, and political affiliation are some of the frequently used variables in sociological research. Independent variables exert influence on dependent variables: thus, income (an independent variable) may be found to influence child-rearing techniques (a dependent variable). Every scientific experiment consists of (1) keeping all variables constant except one, (2) changing that one variable, and (3) discovering what happens.

Sociological Research Methods

In the search for meaningful facts to bolster their hypotheses and assist in the formulation of valid theories, sociologists use a number of research methods. These include the perusal of public records, newspapers, legal codes, court records, minutes of committees, and annual reports of corporations. In addition, social researchers may refer to complicated calculations based on mathematical and statistical principles. Increasingly, computers are becoming a staple in sociological research, but frequently a combination of methods and sources is used: public and private documents are analyzed, the artistic output of a specific historical period is scrutinized, the literature is studied, and statistical information like birth and death rates is compiled. Such a mixture of methods was used by Philippe Ariès, author of *Centuries of Childhood* (1962), a now-classic illustration of changes in attitudes toward childhood and children over a number of centuries.

Most contemporary sociologists, however, shy away from research methods that are subject to personal interpretation, preferring instead those that appear more objective, that is, in which personal biases are eliminated as much as possible. This is not to say that descriptive, subjectively interpreted work is not being produced, nor that such work lacks meaning. But the most common research methods used by sociologists today, as outlined in Table 1.2, are as follows:

The Sample Survey

The **sample survey** is a research design consisting of two separate features, the sample and the survey. The researcher decides to study a specific group, called the *population,* a statistical concept referring to the totality of the phenomenon under investigation. The population may consist of any group from middle-aged professionals to newly registered voters to college students enrolled in four-year private schools. Since it is impossible to study every member of a chosen population, the researcher will select a statistically valid sample. Certain procedures are followed in such a selection, for only if the

Common Methods of Sociological Research

TABLE 1.2

Method	Subject of Research	Procedure	Use	Criticism
Sample survey	Statistically valid sample of a population.	Collect data; have sample fill out questionnaires; conduct personal interviews; obtain factual information; probe attitudes; establish relationships among variables.	Establishing facts.	Not always 100% accurate in reflecting attitudes and opinions.
Case study	Total behavior of a particular unit of people.	Gain confidence of members; obtain biographies of members; learn each member's views; establish hypotheses or relationships that can be tested by other means.	Studying a particular unit (family, gang, ethnic group) in depth, or several units for comparison.	Most useful when events under consideration are relatively unique; often cannot be used as a basis for generalization; expensive and difficult to compute quantitatively.
Participant observation	Members of specific group.	Researchers take part in life of group members, sometimes without revealing their identities.	Studying all or some aspects of a group's culture from the inside out.	Depends on personality of researcher; researcher may be biased; researcher may try to overgeneralize.
Experiment	In laboratory, people volunteer or are paid to be subjects. In the field, researcher studies an existing group.	Subjects undergo a number of tests, and their responses are recorded. Researchers control or hold constant one variable and systematically observe or measure the results.	Establishing facts that cannot be established in any other way.	Very expensive if many people are involved; physical safety and dignity of people must be considered; people may change their behavior when they know they are being observed.

sample is truly representative can larger generalizations about the results of research be made.

Next, the researcher must survey his chosen sample. This involves collecting data by means of questionnaires, personal interviews, statistical information, and/or probing of attitudes. Most importantly, relationships among variables are analyzed. If a broad spectrum of the population is being surveyed at a specific point in time, the study is called *cross-sectional*. If, on the other hand, the study continues over a longer period engaging in contrasts and comparisons, it is referred to as *longitudinal*.

The sample survey is an accurate tool for only certain investigative questions. While establishing factual information with this technique is comparatively easy, any survey of attitudes and opinions involves a greater margin for error.

The Case Study

This research design is especially helpful when a particular unit must be studied in depth, or several units examined for purposes of comparison. The unit may be a single person, a family, a group of residents in a retirement community, employees of a particular corporation, members of a religious movement, and so forth. The researcher must obtain a complete, detailed account of the behavior of the unit under consideration. In the **case study,** the entire population of the unit is studied, as opposed to the sample survey, in which only a representative portion is examined.

Many classic case studies in sociology have dealt with the problem of juvenile delinquency. After gaining the confidence of one or a group of delinquents, the researcher obtains a detailed account of experiences, written or dictated in the form of autobiographies. Such accounts provide a first-hand picture of the subject's family background, childhood, early contacts with peer groups, and attitudes toward society, as well as offering clues to the development of patterns leading to delinquency.

The value of case studies lies not in their individual accuracy but in their suggestion of hypotheses that can subsequently be tested by other methods. They are most helpful when the unit being analyzed is relatively unique, as in the case of a brainwashed group of prisoners of war or converts to an authoritarian religion.

Participant Observation

Somewhere between the techniques of case study and sample survey lies a method known as **participant observation.** Here the researcher tries to take part in the lives of the members of a group by associating with them as closely as possible and sharing in their experiences and life-styles. A number of sociologists and anthropologists have used this technique to study ethnic and black street-corner culture.

The participant observation technique has its shortcomings. Much depends on the personality of the researcher, who must cultivate the trust and friendship of his or her subjects. There is the danger of the researcher becoming too involved with the group, thereby losing objectivity, or of overgeneralizing in the belief that the findings obtained from a particular study apply to all similar groups. At the same time, this method, like the case study, can yield many useful insights to be tested and verified later on by more quantitative techniques.

There are obvious shortcomings in using the method of participant observation in researching the bar scene.

The Experiment

The experimental method is used in all scientific disciplines. In sociology, the **experiment** may take place either in a laboratory or in the field. In a laboratory experiment, subjects are recruited either as volunteers or paid participants. The researcher then administers a number of tests and records their responses. In the field experiment, the researcher goes out to the subjects instead of the subjects coming to him. But in both field and laboratory, one variable is controlled or held constant by setting up control groups, and systematic observation and measurement of the results are made.

Experimentation as a method of sociological research is also subject to shortcomings and pitfalls. Wide-ranging experiments involving thousands of subjects can be expensive and difficult to organize. The physical safety as well as the personal dignity of the group must be safeguarded. People cannot be forced to act as experimental subjects, and the ethics of tricking them into cooperating are certainly questionable. Finally, when men and women are aware of their participation in an experiment, their behavior often shifts from the norm, thus rendering the experiment invalid. Experiments are most reliable when the subjects, while knowing that some type of test is being conducted, are not aware of its true goals. Nevertheless, even harmless deception can lead to accusations of intellectual dishonesty; the technique is therefore not widely used.

In summarizing, it must be said that none of the research methods available to sociologists is 100 percent effective or error proof. Conducting research is difficult in all sciences; in the social sciences the task is compounded by problems of subjectivity, logistics, and the unpredictability of human behavior, as well as the great number of variables to be controlled.

As a result, sociologists often employ whatever techniques best fit the needs of their research designs. For instance, the historical, or impressionistic study, which consists of describing and analyzing observations according to informal but coherent and purposeful guidelines, is still popular. A classic impressionistic study was done by the Lynds, who described the functioning and power structure of small-town America in the early decades of this century (1929, 1937). The authors lived in a small midwestern community in whose life they participated; they interviewed in depth all persons of authority and conducted research in the local library on the background of the town and its inhabitants. Ultimately they produced a vivid portrayal of the community and most of their insights were probably valid. Still, their conclusions were unverifiable, and while the study remains interesting, it cannot be used to predict future behavior.

The demographic method has also proved an effective tool of sociological research. Émile Durkheim's work on suicide, previously mentioned, has become a classic. Durkheim compared the suicide rates of several European countries and linked suicide with three variables: religion, family, and political environment. He concluded that a lack of social integration (a fitting into society) resulted in the largest number of suicides.

In spite of the use of the scientific method, social scientists invariably have more difficulty obtaining verifiable data than do physical scientists. Examining fossil remains in the laboratory is very different from examining people as they relate to one another. Not only do human beings not lend themselves to many of the experiments that can be performed on the inert fossil, they also evoke a reaction from the researcher that the fossil does not. The researcher cannot help reacting to people—finding an individual likable, or disagreeable, or good-looking, or dumb—whereas in analyzing a fossil, such judgments do not enter one's mind. Thus, much as sociologists wish to further objectivity, their conclusions are often inevitably tinged by bias. In the study of human societies there can be no absolute conclusions, no absolutely objective interpretations.

Sociology and Sociologists

At this point, the student might well ask the question, "But what good is sociology? What do sociologists actually do?"

As noted earlier, sociology began as a pure science but has increasingly found practical applications. The distinction between pure and applied science is this: a **pure science** is concerned with the search for knowledge for its own sake, disregarding any practical considerations. An **applied science** is goal-oriented; specifically, it seeks to solve practical problems through the use of scientific findings. Astronomy, or the study of the planets, is a pure science. But when the United States government uses its findings to send explorers to the moon, then astronomy becomes an applied science. Similarly, a sociologist researching the causes of criminality is, for the moment, interested only in uncovering the factors that lead to such deviant behavior. But when a government agency sets up drop-in centers in crime-prone neighborhoods so that troubled individuals may obtain financial aid, training, or counseling, then sociological findings acquire a practical application.

The question of what sociologists actually do is relevant in a society that is materialistic, pragmatic, and achievement-oriented. Very briefly stated, sociologists may be involved in research, consulting, advising, and/or teaching, as illustrated in Table 1.3.

Research

The focus of the discipline of sociology is to train sociologists to be scientists engaged in research. As such, their goal is to uncover and organize knowledge about the structure and function of society and the interaction of its members. Research, in its search for the truth, attempts to correct false beliefs and assumptions based on unscientific common sense, such as the notions that some races are superior to others, that one sex is inferior to the other, or that rural residents have a moral edge over urban dwellers. All these commonsense "truths" have been reappraised and altered as a result of sociological research.

Sociological research also functions to predict behavior. This particular task is complicated by human behavior being continually subject to myriad factors with unpredictable effects. However, as long as a margin of safety is maintained, sociologists are able to forecast general trends and patterns. Social research successfully predicted, for instance, that a majority of modern women would enter the work force and remain there for most of their married lives; that the monogamous, nuclear family unit would continue to be the fundamental family structure in the United States; and that the pendulum would swing back to conservatism in politics, education, and even certain fashions.

Sociologists: What They Do

TABLE 1.3			
Research	Consulting	Technical advising	Teaching
Conduct scientific research for the sake of uncovering the truth. Correct false assumptions. Make predictions about human behavior.	Predict the probable outcome of specific public policies and social action programs.	Employed by government and private corporations to plan and conduct community-action programs, advise on public relations, deal with employer-employee relations, etc.	Pass on research findings in discipline, acquaint students with discipline, conduct research, publish results of research.

Consulting and Advising

Sociologists may hold jobs as consultants, technical experts, and advisers, especially in the public sector of the economy. A sociologist working as consultant to a government agency may be called on to suggest what effects a particular social policy may have on a specific constituency, which type of community-action program is likely to succeed, how best to structure employee-employer relations for maximum productivity and minimum stress, or whether federal grants to education will indeed narrow the gap between students of divergent backgrounds.

Sociologists are employed in this capacity at all levels of government, as well as by private firms. In government, they most often aid representatives in drafting legislation that will be effective, acceptable, and likely to be voted in. In the areas of criminology and race relations, the work of sociologists has been especially visible. And private organizations now often include a staff sociologist who may have specialized in social psychology, urban or rural sociology, industrial sociology, or the sociology of groups.

Academia

The great majority of sociologists are engaged in teaching. At universities, sociologists are expected to do research, publish their results, and pass on to students the findings and methods with which these results were gathered. In two-year colleges, introductory sociology courses offer students a taste of the scientific study of society and human interaction, possibly interesting some in pursuing sociology as a career.

The Chapter in Brief

Sociology is the scientific study of how people interact in groups—how we are all connected within a social web. The discipline is relatively new, although its subject matter has occupied philosophers and artists for thousands of years. What distinguishes the sociological approach is its use of the **scientific method** to formulate generalizations and theories about human behavior in society.

Sociology is concerned with what is, not with what ought to be; it is a **pure,** rather than an **applied science,** although it has developed practical applications; it is abstract rather than concrete; it deals with generalities rather than with particulars.

There are no grand theories to explain human interaction in society. When sociologists attempt to formulate a particular theory, they do so within the framework of a specific perspective. The **evolutionary perspective** assumes that society goes through a fixed and progressive number of stages similar to those experienced by living organisms. The **functionalist perspective** views society as existing in a delicate balance between stability and change, with stability continuously reinstated after the disruption of change, and patterns persisting if they are functional, disappearing if they are not. The **conflict perspective** sees society as undergoing constant conflict between individuals or groups, leading to necessary social change. **Symbolic interactionism** posits that all experience is socially interpreted; that people play specific roles and behave in an orderly fashion in response to the expectations of others. **Ethnomethodology, humanistic sociology,** and **sociobiology** are other less-established sociological perspectives.

Sociology uses the scientific method as a tool for building theories. The scientific method implies a set of attitudes including **doubt, objectivity,** and **ethical neutrality.** It also involves a specific technique based on precise, systematic observation and recording of data. This technique includes the selection and definition of problems, as well as a plan for collecting data; a statement of **hypothesis;** the actual collection of data; its classification, analysis, and verification (replication); and final generalization. Controlled conditions and trained observers are essential.

In sociology, the scientific method consists of **concepts** (abstract ways of classifying similar things); **theories** (sets of concepts arranged so as to explain and predict possible and probable relationships among phenomena); and **research** (to test and bolster these theories). Sociological research employs methods such as the **sample survey,** the **case study, participant observation,** and field and laboratory **experiments.** In addition the historical, impressionistic, and demographic methods are also used.

The scientific method, although vastly superior to superficial observation, insight, or other traditional methods, is especially difficult to apply in the social science disciplines, where it requires a degree of objectivity, skepticism, and ethical neutrality that the study of inert matter does not.

Sociology, which originated as a pure science, has lately found many pragmatic applications. Modern sociologists may be employed as researchers, consultants, advisers, and teachers. Sociological research has corrected many erroneous beliefs formerly based on common sense and misperceptions of reality.

Terms to Remember

Applied science   Science that is goal oriented in that it seeks to solve practical problems through the use of scientific findings.

Case study   A method of research consisting of a detailed investigation of a single social unit.

Concept   A generalized idea about people, objects, or processes that are related to one another; abstract ways of classifying similar things.

Conflict perspective   A theoretical perspective viewing society as a product of the conflicts and stresses in the relationships of individuals and groups which underlie all social change.

Constant   The characteristic that does not vary in the relationship between two or more factors, or variables.

Doubt   The most important principle of the scientific spirit, that is, that nothing is to be taken for granted.

Ethical neutrality   An attitude of the scientific method in the social sciences, requiring that scientists not pass moral judgment on their findings.

Ethnomethodology   A theoretical perspective emphasizing the everyday world and the formal rules operational in commonsense contexts.

Evolutionary perspective   A theoretical perspective that assumes that society, like biological organisms, progresses through a series of fixed stages of development.

Experiment   A method of research in which the researcher controls one variable and observes and records the results.

Functionalist perspective   A theoretical perspective that assumes that society exists in a delicate balance between stability and change, and that societal structures either function to maintain stability or disappear.

Humanistic sociology   A branch of sociology that attempts to promote the understanding of social problems and the search for solutions through the application of sociological knowledge.

Hypothesis   A tentative statement, in clearly defined terms, predicting a relationship between variables.

Objectivity   A principle of the scientific method, especially in the social sciences, requiring researchers to divest themselves of personal attitudes, desires, beliefs, values, and tendencies when confronting data.

Participant observation   A method of research in which researchers take part in the lives of the members of the group under analysis, sometimes without revealing their purpose.

Pure science   Science that is concerned with the search for knowledge for its own sake, disregarding any practical considerations.

Research   An aspect of scientific methodology that bolsters and complements theories. In sociology, four fundamental formats are used: the sample survey, the case study, the experiment, and participant observation.

Sample survey   A method of research consisting of an attempt to determine the occurrence of a given act or opinion within a particular sample group.

Scientific method   A tool of inquiry whose purpose is to obtain evidence that is verifiable and subject to replication so that suppositions are overwhelmingly supported by proof.

Scientific observation   The basic technique of the scientific method ensuring that procedures are systematic, accurate, and precise, and that they occur under controlled conditions and by trained observers.

Scientific spirit   The attitude underlying the scientific method.

Sociobiology   A theoretical perspective based on the systematic study of the biological basis of social behavior in all organisms.

Symbolic interactionism   A theoretical perspective focusing on the importance of communication through shared symbols for objects and events. Society represents the sum of interactions between individuals or groups behaving in an orderly fashion and fulfilling assigned roles in accordance with others' expectations.

Theory   A set of concepts arranged so as to explain and/or predict possible and probable relationships.

Variables   Factors whose relationships researchers try to uncover; characteristics that differ (vary) in each individual case, as opposed to a constant, a characteristic that remains the same.

Suggestions for Further Reading

Berger, Peter L.   1963. *Invitation to Sociology: A Humanistic Perspective.* New York: Doubleday-Anchor. In spite of its age, this remains the most stimulating introduction to the discipline.

Collins, Randall.   1985. *Three Sociological Traditions.* New York: Oxford University Press. A lucid exposition of the conflict, Durkheimian, and microinteractionist traditions in sociology. A prologue describing the rise of the social sciences is particularly helpful to the student with an insufficient background in the field.

Gardner, Martin.   1981. *Science: Good, Bad and Bogus.* Buffalo, N. Y.: Prometheus Books. A book that entertains while it illustrates how science and pseudoscience differ.

Matter of Balance

NEIL SMELSER

The average person stopped in the street and questioned as to the nature and function of sociology would be hard put to produce a correct definition of the discipline. Nor would such a person be very clear about what a sociologist does. It may come as a shock, however, to realize that sociologists themselves are divided, not so much about what their discipline is, as about what it ought to be. The division is not new and may have as much to do with temperament and personal inclination as with ideological or theoretical disagreement. Professor Neil Smelser of the University of California at Berkeley argues for a middle ground between the survey-takers and the dreamers.

Sociology came on the field somewhat later than economics and psychology, and it has a problem legitimizing itself as a science. There still is a very, very strong impulse to present itself as a legitimate science, encouraged by many of the research agencies that fund us, particularly

Source: From "Sociologists Examine an Issue That's Very Close to Home," in the *New York Times* (Week in Review), April 28, 1985, p. E7. Copyright © 1985 by The New York Times Company. Reprinted by permission.

the National Science Foundation, but others as well. So that impulse toward being a science is rewarded by those who, in many respects, are responsible for our sustenance.

But there's still a large portion of the field that is basically sympathetic to human problems and human suffering, and in that sense it is more humanistic in character. There are sociologists who are committed to a more human understanding of a subject than you can get by experimentation or the application of standardized survey questions. You get a more qualitative understanding of the human condition by doing field work and participant observation, getting in and mixing with people and understanding their situations, which the more scientific mode obviously does not do.

An example (of the scientific approach) is the work on status attainment that was initiated by Peter Blau and Otis Dudley Duncan in their monumental "The American Occupational Structure," published in 1967. It had to do with the conditions which stimulated or maximized a person's chances of improving his occupation and the conditions which held him back. The researchers looked at individuals' education and race, their fathers' occupations and education and so on, in a very, very elegant quantitative way based on an excellent national sample. Using highly sophisticated mathematical techniques, they came up with really exciting findings as to what it was that seemed to inhibit and what seemed to promote social mobility.

An example of the more humanistic side would be the work of Elliot Liebow, who wrote "Tally's Corner." He went out and lived among black males in Washington, D.C., for about a year, until he really came to understand their situation.

Rather than talk about the divisions, I would talk about the diversity and catholicity of sociology. There's a general understanding that there are a variety of research styles, a variety of kinds of topics to be pursued, and that in most departments and the profession as a whole these are regarded as valuable. There has to be a representation and diversity of approaches, just from the standpoint of the discipline's intellectual health and quality of research as well as the capacity to train and direct graduate students. If you look at practically any other social science, you will find it as internally divided as you find us. Economics has experienced it, political science, history, and in the life sciences I'm sure you find competition among approaches. That's healthy.

I happen to think that if you get too tied up with technique and method it is likely to be harmful to the imagination. There is the danger of what you might call a fetishism of technique, the danger of an overemphasis on the scientific side. I have the feeling we may be leaning in that direction at this moment, and that perhaps we ought to divert more resources into the broader, comparative-historical approach. I would think a slight shift of the pendulum in that direction would probably be in order at this time.

Society: People, the Social Animals

The one fact about the human species that no one can refute (if for no other reason than that it has been asserted so many times) is that people are social animals. What the statement means, of course, is that people cannot live alone, but must converge in groups of one sort or another. Naturally, we can all think of exceptions: the antisocial hermit who allows no one in his mountain hideout; the elderly widow all alone in the world; the eccentric who guards his privacy with a shotgun. But these are exceptions, not the rule. All humans come into the world as creatures so little, so helpless, so weak, that they perish unless another human takes care of them. From that social beginning, the rest of human life is spent in one group or another: with family, with friends, as members of student organizations, interacting with coworkers, as officers of professional associations, and so on.

Because human life is a group way of life, people have had to devise ways of getting along, so that important group tasks may be completed efficiently and without unnecessary friction. Behavior patterns that have proven successful over generations are thus transmitted to each new individual in the process of growing up, sometimes so effectively that members of the group

Freeways are designed in such a way as to move the greatest number of cars in the fastest and safest manner. Similar, though invisible, patterns exist in our social lives, which are organized and structured to permit us ease and efficiency in daily living.

come to feel such behavior is natural, normal, and common to all. In turn, because behavior patterns are so entrenched, interaction between individuals and groups is relatively orderly and predictable, allowing daily life to continue as usual. Social life, contrary to general opinion, is not haphazard; it is a system with its own definite structure and organization.

The Social System: Structure and Organization

Sociologists, whose business it is to analyze social life, do so at two levels: the interpersonal or microsocial, and the group or macrosocial. On the *microsocial* level, the focus is on how individuals relate to one another; on the *macrosocial* level, relationships between and among groups are examined.

Among sociologists' most interesting findings on the microsocial level is the fact that relationships among individuals are based on the positions each holds in relation to others: husband to wife, father to daughter, teacher to student, employer to employee, and so on. On the macrosocial level, sociologists concern themselves with the largest group, a society, and the values and rules for behavior that emerge therein.

When we examine social life, then, we note that it takes place within a system. Sociologists speak of the **social system** as a model that illustrates how social relationships work in a society. Every group, whether it consists of two people or of many millions, is basically a social system. As is characteristic of systems, each part is connected to, and dependent on, every other part. It follows that the way each individual in a group behaves influences all other individuals in the group. This interconnectedness and interdependency eventually result in a shared pattern of behavior that members come to expect of one another. Knowing what is expected of oneself and what one can expect of others makes life easier and work more efficient.

The orderly and predictable patterns of interaction that emerge in social systems give those systems structure and organization. **Social structure** and **social organization** are terms that refer to the network of organized relationships among the component parts of a social system. They are the patterned, recurring ways in which individuals and groups interact. The structure of a social system consists of norms, institutions, statuses, roles, and groups. *Norms* are rules of behavior shared by a group; *institutions* are behavior patterns at a societal level that have developed around fundamental human needs; statuses, roles, and groups are discussed below.

However, we must not think of social organization as a fixed set of rules. It is rather a dynamic process in which stable and predictable patterns are continually redefined and altered to reflect situational changes. Let us look, for example, at a symphony orchestra. The members of a well-known orchestra meet every afternoon, Monday through Thursday, from 1:00 to 3:00 for the purpose of rehearsing a program to be performed Thursday through Saturday evenings. The musicians are there for a specific goal; to achieve it, they behave according to regular, predictable patterns. They come in carrying their instruments (except for the pianist!), take their assigned seats, tune their instruments, stop chatting when the conductor appears, and begin to play when the conductor gives the signal. Each member of this social system knows what to do; each expects the others to understand and act accordingly. As long as this happens, the orchestra–social system is a stable and enduring group. If, however, one or more members begin to show up consistently late for rehearsals, or fail to bring their instruments; if they continue to talk when they should be playing; if they question the conductor's right to assign their tempo; if they take out a sandwich and begin to eat it in the middle of a solo; or regularly engage in similarly disruptive actions, the organization of the system will be destroyed and the group will eventually have to disband. The social structure will have been ineffective because certain members failed to follow the norms, did not behave according to their statuses, or did not perform their expected roles.

Statuses and Roles: Elements of Social Structure

In its simplest definition, a **status** is a position in a social group—a mother in a family, a teacher in school, a plumber at work, a violinist in an orchestra. A **role** is the carrying out of the status, its dynamic aspect: what the mother, the teacher, the plumber, and the violinist do. Statuses are ranked: that is, value-rated according to prevailing standards of the group. Thus the teacher has a higher status than the plumber, and both have a lower status than the famous violinist Itzhak Perlman. A person who occupies a specific status is expected to behave in a way befitting that position. In other words, we do not expect the plumber to give us a lecture on English literature in the Middle Ages, nor do we expect the teacher to fix our leaking faucet.

Statuses and roles evolve out of the need of each group to perform its tasks efficiently. In any society, a great number of functions must be performed each day if the group is to operate smoothly. Food must be produced and made available for consumption; shelter must be built; the sick must be healed; children must be educated; and so on. The experience of early societies revealed that efficiency was much improved when tasks were allocated to particular individuals who specialized in their performance. Such allocation came to be known as the *division of labor,* the origin of most, though not all, statuses (some statuses being allocated on the basis of gender or age).

Statuses and the roles that accrue to them are not static. Change within particular groups and on a societal level constantly subjects them to redefinition, growth, and replacement.

Ascribed and Achieved Status

Some statuses and their satellite roles are ours at birth; we cannot avoid occupying them. A child is born either male or female; either white, black, Asian, or some mixture of these; its parents are either working-class, middle-class, upper-class, or fall somewhere along the class continuum; the family may claim allegiance to a given religion or ethnic group. These statuses are **ascribed** to the newborn child, rather than attained through individual effort or merit. Ascribed statuses are involuntary, based on gender, age, race, ethnic background, and on the social position and religious affiliation of one's family.

Most other statuses, however, are **achieved** through individual effort and choice. We become college graduates, wives, or bank managers because we decide on and work toward these goals.

In preindustrial societies, ascribed status is strongly prevalent. Feudal European society, for instance, was divided into estates—a kind of permanent and rigid social class—and mobility from one estate to another was almost impossible to achieve. In India too, until recent times, people were divided into castes based on occupation. In such societies, the scope of individual choice is small. Even with ability, talent, and hard work, one can rarely rise above his or her parents' occupation and social class.

In industrial societies, on the other hand, the commitment to individualism and personal achievement predominates. Freedom of choice is jealously defended and the accomplishments of the individual ardently applauded. As a result, achieved status is valued, although the ascribed status that comes from belonging to an "old-moneyed" family is also highly esteemed.

Sometimes a status may be considered either ascribed or achieved, depending on one's perspective. For example, the status of a high-school dropout may be considered ascribed if that individual lives in an environment where peers also become dropouts and there is no reward for continuing one's education; in different circumstances, the status of dropout may be achieved when a student *chooses* not to continue his or her education.

In most industrial societies, and especially in the United States, the past several decades have witnessed much upheaval as a result of dissatisfactions over ascribed statuses and the consequent roles certain groups have been forced to fulfill. Women and racial and ethnic minorities have fought against discriminatory treatment resulting from their ascribed statuses; although problematic aspects of their roles have not been totally eliminated, progress has been made in that direction.

The Multiplicity of Statuses and Roles

As is no doubt obvious by now, each of us occupies a large number of statuses and performs many roles in our lifetime. The president of Hot Dogs, Incorporated, is best known by his status of corporation executive, which becomes his *master status,* but he also holds statuses of son, husband, father, brother, lawyer, regent of the state university, country-club member, elder in the Presbyterian church, and fund-raiser for the Republican party. On an occasional basis, he occupies the statuses of patient (when he sees his doctor), client (when he visits his stockbroker), customer (when he goes shopping), and driver (when he drives his car).

Not all of these statuses carry equal social weight. The importance of a status is determined by the values of the group involved in ranking it. On a

The queen of England and the prime minister represent ascribed and achieved status. Elizabeth II (left) is heir to a title she acquired by virtue of having been the first born in a royal family. Margaret Thatcher (right) is the daughter of a small shopkeeper who achieved her position through her own effort: by acquiring an advanced education and becoming involved in politics.

societal level, the individual cited above would be ranked as holding a high status because of his position as a corporation president. But on a familial level, he may be ranked low by his wife and children, in whom he takes no interest. His status may be ranked equal with other elders in the church, though volunteers in the Republican party may consider him an upstart.

It goes without saying that a multiplicity of statuses will lead to an equal number of roles to perform. None of us performs all roles equally well. The corporation president must be successful in his master role or he would not remain very long in his position. But his performance as husband and father may leave much to be desired. Generally, people select the roles they consider most important and strive to perform these best. A relationship exists between a person's self-image and the role in which he or she chooses to excel. The above corporation president may see himself as a great American business leader and consequently fulfill his role of chief executive officer well; at the

This woman seems to fulfill her role of executive in a cool and professional manner. Behind the calm exterior, however, she may be torn by conflicting demands on her time by her family, and be anxious about her status as a black woman executive in a white male environment.

same time, he may feel that family pressures forced him to marry, and so perform his role of husband badly.

Roles: Real and Ideal   Frequently groups prepare their members to fill roles that never emerge. The young are often instructed in ideal patterns of behavior that in reality are seldom if ever followed. In Sunday school, for instance, children are taught to love their neighbors and "turn the other cheek." But their football coach tells them to "murder" the opposing team and take revenge for a previous loss. Such teachings do not necessarily constitute hypocrisy. Ideal patterns of behavior serve a necessary function, acting as a brake on real patterns that may decline to levels considered undesirably low.

Conflict, Strain, and Confusion in Roles   When real differs substantially from ideal, however, conflict ensues. Upon coming into contact with the "real" world, the young are frequently disillusioned and feel betrayed. Sometimes the disparity may have positive results, as when individuals resolve to bring the real more in line with the ideal and work to reach some social goal. But in other instances stress results from the discrepancy.

Stress also arises if a role has been improperly learned. In industrial societies, many tasks are performed outside the home; children therefore may grow up without knowing exactly what "work" their parents do. Rapid social change also contributes to a situation in which future life-styles are unpredictable and thus impossible to prepare for. Such conflicts, almost nonexistent in preindustrial societies, become in technological societies almost the norm.

Strain may be suffered when people are expected to simultaneously play several demanding roles. The corporation president's status demands that he spend an unusually large proportion of his time on business matters. To be a good husband and father, however, he must also spend time in family activities so that intimate interaction can take place. Which role should take precedence? An increasingly common role conflict faces women who are either forced or prefer to work outside the home but who still want to be responsible wives and mothers.

Role conflict may also exist within the limits of a single role. A person in a position of leadership must uphold discipline to ensure that the group reaches its goals. In the process, the leader may become disliked by subordinates. The alternative is to be a "buddy" and be well liked at the expense of successfully attaining group goals. A leader must thus constantly weigh his or her behavior in terms of the demands of the "leader" role.

Roles may create confusion, particularly when someone with a specific status must suddenly abandon one role and embrace a new one. An accountant pushed out of his job by mandatory retirement, for instance, may feel a loss of identity and refuse to accept the role of retiree, particularly if his interests revolve around his job and he cannot fill his new leisure hours. College-educated women, especially those on the threshold of promising careers, may experience confusion if an unplanned pregnancy pushes them into the role of mother and full-time housekeeper.

Faulty role performance causes not only temporary confusion and strain; such long-term effects as mental illness, maladjustment, or chronic frustration may ensue. For many reasons—sometimes simply by chance—men and women fail in the roles for which they have been prepared. In a highly competitive economic system, workers frequently fail in their businesses and professions. The high incidence of divorce shows that many adults fail in their marital roles. It should be noted, however, that a person who fails in one role may actually be succeeding in another. The woman who divorces her husband and leaves her children in pursuit of her career will be judged a failure on the family front but may turn out to be an excellent actress.

Social Groups

Statuses are held and roles carried out in all social systems, most of them constituted by one group or another. Groups, as components of social structure, and especially as places where most interaction takes place, are carefully examined by sociologists: they are frequently not what they seem to be.

What is commonly understood by the term **group** is a number of people congregated at the same time in the same place. But by the sociological definition, 15 students cramming for an exam in a student lounge do not necessarily constitute a group. Neither do twenty commuters on the morning train, nor eight salespersons eating lunch at the counter of Moe's Delicatessen. If we know nothing about these individuals other than that they are in the same place at the same time, we must call them **aggregates,** not groups.

There are also those who share certain characteristics: who have red hair, for instance, or who were born on the Fourth of July. These people do not make up a group, either; instead, they form a **category**.

Suppose, however, that 3 of the 15 students cramming in the lounge have been studying there since the beginning of the school year. And suppose, further, that they have an English class together, and that they all eat lunch at the same time. Because they are human and therefore social beings, these students, after the first exchange of greetings, begin to sit together in English class and in the cafeteria, and stop to chat when they pass each other in the hall. Out of an aggregate of 15, 3 have formed a group. By the same token, if all redheads in the United States who were born on the Fourth of July, 1945 decided to organize a club, if they corresponded regularly and met periodically, they too would have ceased to be a category and would have become a group.

Sociological Definition of Group

In sociological terms, in order for a number of people to constitute a group, the following conditions must be met:

1. There is **symbolic interaction** among the members. (Symbolic interaction refers to communication by means of speech, gestures, writing, or even music. Members are aware of one another, respond to one another, and behave in such a way as to influence one another.) Interaction is expected to continue indefinitely, but since many groups form and disperse within short periods of time, members may be aware of the finite nature of membership.

2. There is recognition by each member that he or she is part of the group, and by the group that each person is a member. Group membership gives those involved a sense of identity.

3. There is a certain amount of agreement or consensus among members about rules of behavior and shared values and goals.

4. Groups have structure; members are aware of their statuses, roles, rules of behavior, duties, and obligations, as well as the privileges that result from their membership.

To summarize, what constitutes a group in sociological terms is symbolic interaction, perceived membership, and a social structure. Symbolic interaction need not involve face-to-face communication; there must simply be some form of communication resulting in mutual adjustment of behavior, and awareness of common membership and its implications. In this sense, a nation's citizens united by common political processes and sharing similar loyalties, a common history, and the sense of a common future are considered a group.

Classifying Groups

Groups vary extraordinarily in number and diversity. In size, they may range from two, as in a couple, to several hundred million, as in a society. In fact, since each person is a member of more than one group at any one time, there

How many of the people in this photograph constitute a group in the sociological sense?

are more groups in a society than individuals. Consequently, for the sake of analysis, researchers must classify groups. Factors considered in classifying groups are size and specific characteristics.

Group Size   The smallest of groups consists of two members and is known as a **dyad.** German sociologist Georg Simmel (1858–1918) considered the dyad the most elementary social unit, and a fragile one at that: the unit ceases to exist as a group when one of the members withdraws.

The **triad,** consisting of three members, is a more stable social unit since one of the members may withdraw without destroying the group. Thus triads are considered more important to the structure of societies. In fact, contemporary sociologist Theodore Caplow (1968) maintains that triads are the building blocks underlying all social organizations and are particularly important in the formation of permanent or temporary coalitions entered into for the purpose of achieving specific goals. In a triad, according to Caplow, the two weaker members can form a coalition, thus preventing the high-ranking, powerful member from controlling the social group.

Size in general has a definite impact on group members. With each additional member, the number of possible relationships in the group increases, as does the probability of new coalitions forming. Rapid increases in membership may prove disruptive; in a group of more than ten or twelve, a leader becomes necessary to ensure that each member contributes equally. The addition of new members tends to be discouraged by insiders who feel comfortable with the status quo.

Small groups—families, close friends, a clique within a large organization, a committee formed to solve a problem—share common characteristics. Members generally hold similar values and relations among them tend to be face-to-face. Loyalty and a sense of identification on the part of its members make the small group quite durable. Small groups tend to have a profound impact on members' behavior and are more accepting than large groups of democratic leadership.

Large groups naturally display the opposite features. Above all, they tend to be highly organized. (Large groups are discussed under the heading of formal organizations and bureaucracies in Chapter 8.) The largest group to which people belong is society.

Primary and Secondary Groups As demonstrated in Table 2.1, primary and secondary groups represent an important classification. The term **primary group** was coined by Charles Horton Cooley, a pioneer American sociologist (see Chapter 1). Cooley designated as primary groups those whose members engage in intimate interaction and cooperation, the influence of which is basic to the development of an individual's personality. Additional characteristics distinguishing primary from other groups include (1) relatively small group size, (2) physical proximity of members, (3) intense interaction among mem-

Primary and Secondary Relationships

TABLE 2.1	Primary	Secondary
Groups	Family Playmates Clique Village	Nation Religious denomination Trade union Professional association
Dyadic relationships	Husband-wife Parent-child Teacher-pupil Friend-friend	Officer-subordinate Clerk-customer Performer-spectator Member of Congress-constituent
Social characteristics	Informal Feelings of freedom and spontaneity Inclusive knowledge of other person	Formal Feeling of external constraint Specialized and limited knowledge of other person
Physical conditions	Identity of ends Other-oriented Personal Small number Long duration Physical proximity	Disparity of ends Self-oriented Impersonal Large number Short duration Physical distance

Source: Adapted from Kingsley Davis, *Human Society,* 1949, p. 306. Reprinted by permission of Kingsley Davis.

bers, (4) group stability and relatively long duration, and (5) similarity of goals and preoccupation with the welfare of other members. The family is the foremost example of a primary group.

If primary groups were put on one end of an ideal continuum—a conceptual model representing a hypothetical ideal to which reality may be compared in analyzing phenomena—the opposite end would be occupied by **secondary groups.** Secondary groups tend to be large, and interaction within them formal, utilitarian, specialized, short, and temporary. The transaction between a salesperson and customer, no matter how friendly, is of a secondary nature. Secondary relationships may eventually develop into primary ones, as when acquaintances discover a common hobby of bird-watching and begin to meet on a regular basis. Occasionally, too, a primary relationship slides into a secondary one, as when friends quarrel and subsequently exchange only icy greetings on seeing each other.

Primary groups are universal and of tremendous importance to those involved. They may even be regarded as necessary to most people's well-being. The spirit of a person totally removed from primary relationships can be easily broken, severely affecting his or her mental health. This is why isolation as a method of brainwashing or torture is so effective. If primary relationships are lacking in what is generally considered a natural primary group—the family, for instance—humans will go out of their way to create such relationships in other groups. Even so, not all primary relationships are harmonious or satisfying. They may involve a high degree of conflict or the enforcement of conformity which stifle a member's individuality.

Urban industrial societies such as the United States are increasingly characterized by secondary relationships. Many functions once performed by primary groups are now carried out by secondary ones. In the past, for example, the sick were cared for by their families at home rather than by paid medical personnel in hospitals. Doctors and hospital staff members are much more efficient than family members and homegrown remedies and undoubtedly help cure many more people. But they cannot have the same emotional bond with their patients, nor their patients with them; hence the alienation and dehumanization experienced by many of those confined to hospitals and nursing homes.

Additional Classifications of Groups   In addition to their size and primary or secondary nature, groups are classified according to other features. **In-groups** and **out-groups** are based on the distinction between *us* and *them,* probably one of the oldest distinctions made and one with which we can all identify whether we belong to the Avondale Country Club or the Purple Sharks. **Reference groups** are those that provide the standards we use to evaluate our own status against that of others. They serve as points of comparison, often affecting our values, goals, attitudes, and behavior. **Membership groups** are formal or informal organizations to which individuals belong; for instance, the YMCA is a formal membership group, whereas one's friends from high school constitute an informal one. Finally, some groups are **voluntary** and some **involuntary**. A person's family (which cannot be chosen), or any branch of

This elderly woman would have been taken care of by her children and grandchildren (a primary group) in a traditional society. Today, in our urban, industrial societies, the elderly are increasingly cared for by strangers in nursing homes.

the armed services into which one is inducted are examples of involuntary groups. Conversely, there are thousands of groups, ranging from fraternities to political parties, fan clubs to bridge clubs, that individuals may join entirely of their free will, or for reasons of social and economic expediency. Such groups are voluntary.

Society

Society may be defined as the largest group of people inhabiting a specific territory and sharing a common way of life. Within this group, individuals interact on a regular, continuous basis using acquired patterns of behavior on which all more or less agree. Society differs from other large groups in the sense that its members live total, common lives. In short, unlike organizations limited to specific purposes (for example, the American Medical Association) society is a self-sufficient entity, its independence based on techniques developed for fulfilling the needs of its members.

From the sociological perspective, society is seen as the interrelated network of social relationships existing within the boundaries of the largest social system. In the past, the largest social system was a clan, a tribe, or simply a family. Today, the largest social system is the nation-state.

Societies, like many groups, assign certain representatives the power of making decisions and settling conflicts. Moreover, each society requires that its members feel greater loyalty to it than to any other group. This loyalty develops when members share a language and way of life uniquely their own, even though groups within the larger society may have traditions and languages that differ significantly from those of the majority.

Classification of Societies According to Subsistence Strategies

Throughout history societies have assumed a number of different forms. From an historical and archaeological perspective, it is clear that an evolutionary trend is at work in their technologies. Each society, in an effort to best adapt to its environment and exploit its food resources most advantageously, adopts a limited number of basic **subsistence strategies.** Through the process of evolution, societies that develop more productive strategies tend to prosper and increase, whereas those with more primitive strategies remain small and weak, or cease to exist altogether. Of course, such evolution is only a trend; not every society undergoes the process, nor do all societies experience it at the same rate or in the same way. Nonetheless, the fact that the process has been historically evident gives us another way of analyzing and classifying societies.

Sociologist Gerhard Lenski (1970) distinguishes 11 types of societies according to their chief mode of subsistence—the way they provide their members with food, shelter, and clothing. The most commonly occurring types include the following:

The *hunting and gathering* society. This is one of the earliest and least complex modes, characterized by a small, nomadic population, an uncomplicated technology, little division of labor or specialization, and particular stress on the importance of kinship ties. The family fulfills most of the functions needed for survival, and since there is little wealth to be acquired and food to satisfy immediate hunger can be easily found, people are not ranked according to their possessions. In this peaceful and leisurely society, members' values, beliefs, and expectations are very uniform. While a few such societies still exist in the modern world, unavoidable contact with modern societies dooms them to extinction or marked change.

The *pastoral* society has tended to develop in areas ill suited to the cultivation of land, but containing animals that can be domesticated and/or used as food sources. Such a subsistence strategy is more successful than hunting and gathering because the food supply is more secure and surpluses of animals are possible. A surplus raises the general standard of living, resulting in larger populations; it also leads to people being ranked according to their possessions. The wealthier individuals have more power which they transmit to their heirs, the seminal origin of social classes. Trade and religions depicting a deity interested in human activities make an appearance, as do also conflict and warfare. The social structure of pastoral societies, examples of which still exist in the Near and Middle East, is more complex than that of hunting and gathering societies.

The *horticultural* society appears when people discover how to cultivate grains, and the *agrarian* society follows with the invention of the plow around 3000 B.C. In these societies, even greater surpluses are produced and a settled life-style predominates. People become differentiated, principally into land-holders and landless peasants, and bureaucracies develop to oversee increasingly complex economies.

Lenski also lists the fishing, maritime, and herding societies in his classification. The most revolutionary change in the form of societies, however, comes with the emergence of the industrial society. Most societies in the world today are either industrial or trying to become so. Industrial societies are characterized by (1) urbanization, or growth of cities at the expense of rural areas; (2) massive mechanization and automation, or the substitution of machines for human labor and intelligence; (3) a complex bureaucracy, or organization into formal groups for greater efficiency; (4) separation of institutional forms, that is, the development of schools, hospitals, stores, and factories to perform functions formerly filled by the family; and (5) the substitution of impersonal, secondary relations for kinship ties. The transition from agrarian to industrial societies has frequently been accompanied by disorganization and disruption.

Classification of Societies According to Social Organization

Although modes of subsistence offer a significant basis of classification, societies are more often categorized according to basic patterns of social organization. German sociologist Ferdinand Tönnies (1855–1936) classified societies according to concepts similar to those of primary and secondary groups. He noted, for instance, that in small, homogeneous societies, members interacted with one another on an informal, personal, face-to-face basis, with behavior dictated by tradition. Tönnies called this kind of society a **Gemeinschaft,** roughly translated from German as a "communal, or traditional society." In large, heterogeneous societies, such as the modern industrial ones, relationships among members are impersonal, formal, functional, and specialized. Furthermore, they are often contractual, with dealings spelled out in legal contracts rather than by tradition or word of mouth. Tönnies called these societies **Gesellschaft,** or "associational societies."

The modern world has seen a marked and visible shift from Gemeinschaft to Gesellschaft societies. The growth of societies and the complexities of a technological economy require secondary groups, which are dedicated to efficiency rather than sentiment. Thus, in Gesellschaft societies, many of the tasks originally performed by primary groups, such as education and economic transactions, have passed to secondary ones. Although it is easy to romanticize the "good old days" of Gemeinschaft-type societies, when primary groups offered individuals moral and material support, we must keep in mind that the large-scale corporations characteristic of Gesellschaft societies have greatly improved our standard of living. In addition, secondary groups, representing a wide range of interests, counteract some of the narrow viewpoints found in small, tightly knit societies.

Social Interaction and
Social Processes

The various groups that exist in societies, and the societies themselves, are not static entities. They are in constant flux, undergoing changes and modifications. Interaction among members of a group and among groups is continually taking place.

Interaction, a sociological concept, refers to behavior or action that is symbolic, that is, uses words and gestures that have a shared meaning. It is behavior directed toward others, in the sense that each person can predict how others will respond; and reciprocal, in the sense that each is conscious of and responsive to the actions and reactions of others.

Although interaction is not governed by rigid rules, neither is it haphazard. Interactive behavior repeated sufficiently often creates a pattern capable of predicting future behavior when similar situations arise. Following behavioral patterns established by our predecessors is merely a way of simplifying our lives; constantly having to decide how to act in different situations would prove very difficult.

A number of key patterns of interaction are present and at work any time interaction takes place. They have been called the "microelements of the social bond, or the molecular cement of society" (Nisbet, 1970). These are the **social processes.**

Social Processes: Cooperation, Competition, and Conflict

A great many social processes take place during social interaction, whether on a primary or a secondary group level. Sociologists focus on three primary ones, since all other processes—accommodation, assimilation, coercion, exchange—are really combinations of, or derivations from, these primary sources.

Cooperation is a primary social process involving two or more persons or groups working in a common enterprise for a shared goal. It is often considered the most basic of the social processes because without it life would be difficult, if not impossible. Some social thinkers maintain that the human species, as well as other organisms, has survived only because individuals were able to cooperate, integrating their activities in such a way as to benefit the group. According to this view, evolution, or survival of the fittest, is actually survival of the most cooperative.

Although groups and individuals benefit from the social process of cooperation, each does not benefit to the same degree. Nonetheless, on both primary and secondary levels, without cooperation our lives would be immensely complicated.

Competition is a form of interaction occurring when two or more individuals try to take possession of the same scarce object, whether it be tangible, such as a precious gem, or intangible, such as someone's love. Competition is a basic process; most living organisms must compete for limited resources necessary to their survival. Plants, for instance, compete for sunlight, water, and nutrients. Animals, including humans, compete for food, shelter, and sexual gratification. But whereas plants and animals limit their competitiveness to objects necessary for survival, humans also compete for materials not strictly required for subsistence, but which they have learned to need. Young people, for example, are taught that they must perform well scholastically, obtain high-paying jobs, or win every tennis match, while in reality their lives would go on even if they accomplished none of these.

It is society that determines which things are desirable and worth competing for, and which are undesirable and need not be contested. Society also determines who can and cannot compete for specific items. Only a licensed physician can compete for patients. Regulation is needed so that conflict is contained and does not erupt into violence. Competition must also be tempered with cooperation or our lives would be impossible to bear.

Conflict is diametrically opposed to cooperation, a hostile struggle between two or more persons or groups for an object of value that each prizes. Conflict also refers to the process in which opposing parties attempt to injure, harm, or destroy one another in order to achieve specific goals.

Like cooperation and competition, conflict is present in most facets of life. At one time sociologists believed that conflict was a universal human trait, but the discovery of societies where conflict is kept to an absolute minimum largely disproved this belief. Conflict, although a very prevalent social process, is intermittent; that is, sooner or later one opposing party emerges victorious and conflict ceases, at least temporarily. Conflict need not involve violence; verbal abuse may destroy sensitive personalities, and gossip ruin reputations or careers. Conflict appears in all kinds of groups, from the most intimate to the most impersonal; it may revolve around a societal reward in short supply—either tangible, like money, or intangible, like power—or around ideological disagreements.

Finally, although it is simple to condemn all types of conflict, one should be aware that its effects are not always disruptive or negative. Conflict and competition both tend to divide people and groups, but in the face of a common antagonist, group unity is greatly enhanced. In addition, conflict often leads to social change, much of which is ultimately beneficial to society. Thus, as conflict theorists maintain (see Chapter 1), a certain degree of conflict actually serves as a creative, dynamic social force. (Of course conflict that results in continuous violence may do psychological harm to individuals and damage to a society.)

It should be clear that although these three foremost processes have been discussed separately, in reality they are not so distinct, often occurring in the same interactive situation. When two gas stations on opposite corners agree to charge the same price for gas, they are cooperating and competing at the same time. Two opposing teams compete for victory, but the members of each team cooperate with one another. Cooperation sometimes deteriorates into conflict, and history has shown many instances of conflict evolving into cooperation.

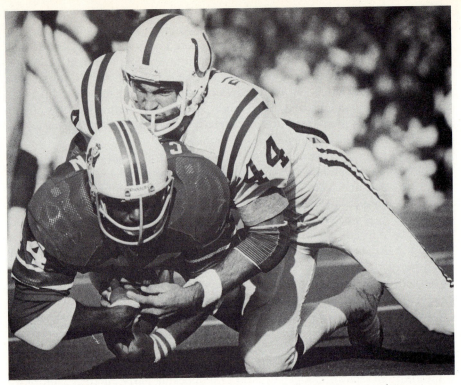

All three of the chief social processes are at work in a football game: team members cooperate among themselves but compete and engage in conflict with the other team for the duration
of the game.

The Chapter in Brief

Humans are social animals who spend the best part of their lives in **groups** of
one kind or another. Life in groups acquires a certain pattern through repetition; sociologists analyze these groups by viewing each as a **social system**
with a structure and organization. The **social structure** consists of shared and
repeated patterns of behavior that emerge from the interaction of group members. People interact by using a number of social processes and by relating to
others from the standpoint of their own position or **status** in the group while
carrying out the behavior or **role** befitting that position. Some statuses within
the group (gender, age, and racial or ethnic origin) are **ascribed,** that is,
members have no choice over them; others are **achieved** as the result of
personal efforts or merit. Because of the multiple statuses each person holds
in the various groups he or she participates in over a lifetime, role confusion,
conflict, strain, and failure are common. In general, people attempt to fill the
role attendant on their master status best.

Sociologists define a group very specifically: (1) it must display **symbolic
interaction** among the members; (2) members must be aware of their membership, and the group must recognize them as such; (3) members must be

aware of the roles, duties, obligations, and privileges resulting from group membership; and (4) members must agree on shared values.

Since groups are so numerous, they must be classified in order to be studied effectively. **Dyads** (consisting of two individuals) and **triads** (consisting of three) are the basic social units. Groups are also classified according to size, to whether they are **primary** or **secondary, in-groups** or **out-groups, reference groups,** formal or informal, **membership groups,** and **voluntary** or **involuntary** in nature. Of these classifications, the most important is the primary/secondary. Primary groups engage in intimate, intense, informal, spontaneous interaction on a personal and total basis; secondary groups tend to be large, temporary, formal, utilitarian, specialized, and short. While primary relationships are extremely satisfying and important to the individual, industrial societies are increasingly characterized by secondary groups.

The largest group to which humans belong is **society.** Societies are classed according to either their chief **subsistence strategies** (hunting and gathering, pastoral, horticultural, agrarian, fishing, maritime, herding, and industrial), or their basic patterns of **social organization** (traditional or communal—**Gemeinschaft;** modern industrial or associational—**Gesellschaft**). Gemeinschaft societies are relatively small, with homogeneous members whose behavior is dictated by tradition and who interact on an informal, face-to-face basis. Gesellschaft societies tend to be large and heterogeneous; relationships among members are impersonal, formal, functional, contractual, and specialized. The historical trend has been a transition from Gemeinschaft-type to Gesellschaft-type societies.

The reciprocal relationships that occur within and among groups are known as interaction. Interaction takes place through a number of **social processes,** the most basic of which are **cooperation, competition,** and **conflict.** These social processes give rise to accommodation, assimilation, coercion, and exchange. Whatever the type of relationship—primary or secondary—one or more of these social processes is at work.

Terms to Remember

Achieved status   A position attained through individual effort or merit.

Aggregate   A number of people who are in the same place at the same time, but who do not interact with one another.

Ascribed status   An inherited position—one that is not attained through individual effort or merit.

Category   (Referring to people): A number of people who have some characteristics in common but who do not interact with one another.

Competition   A social process (a form of interaction) that occurs when two or more individuals try to obtain possession of the same scarce object or intangible reward.

Conflict   A social process (interaction) consisting of a hostile struggle in which two or more persons engage for an object or value that each prizes.

Cooperation   A basic social process (interaction) involving two or more individuals or groups working jointly in a common enterprise for a shared goal.

Dyad   The smallest type of group, consisting of two members.

Gemeinschaft   A small, homogeneous, communal, traditional society. Relationships among members are personal, informal, and face-to-face and behavior is dictated by tradition.

Gesellschaft   A large heterogeneous society, typified by modern industrial societies. Relationships among members tend to be impersonal, formal, contractual, functional, and specialized. Also called an associational society.

Group   A number of people who engage in symbolic interaction. Members of a group are mutually aware of and influence one another; they recognize their membership in the group and are in turn recognized as members by it; they are aware of the roles, duties, obligations, and privileges that group membership involves; and they agree to a point about behavioral guidelines and shared values and goals.

In-group   A group to which an individual belongs and which confers on that person a social identity ("we" or "us").

Involuntary groups   Membership groups to which the individual cannot help but belong—such as one's family or the branch of the armed forces into which one is inducted.

Membership groups   Formal or informal organizations to which individuals belong.

Out-group   A group to which others belong, excluding the individual doing the defining ("they" or "them").

Primary group   A relatively small group of people who live in physical proximity to one another and who interact intensely. Primary groups tend to be stable and of relatively long duration. Interaction is informal and spontaneous; members deal with one another on an individual, personal, and total basis.

Reference group   A group providing individuals with standards against which to measure themselves.

Role   The carrying out of a status. A way of behaving that befits a status and is transmittable as well as fairly predictable.

Secondary group   A group that is in general larger and of shorter duration than a primary group. Interaction among members is formal, utilitarian, specialized, and temporary.

Social organization   The network of patterned human behavior that is the product of social interaction and that, at the same time, guides this interaction. Not a stable set of rules but a dynamic process in which stable and predictable patterns are continually being redefined and changed to fit the evolving conditions of the environment.

Social processes   Key patterns of interaction common to all human societies, the most important being cooperation, competition, and conflict.

Social structure   The content of the social system, consisting of statuses, roles, groups, norms, and institutions.

Social system   A conceptual model of social relationships in which each part is interdependent and interconnected to every other part. The elements of this system are the individual group members as they relate to one another, and groups relating to other groups.

Society   The largest social group analyzed by sociologists. Generally a large group of people who inhabit a specific territory and share a common way of life. An interrelated network of social relationships that exists within the boundaries of the largest social system.

Status   A ranked position in a social group. Statuses are rated according to their importance in a social group.

Subsistence strategies   A way of classifying societies according to the methods they have evolved in order to prosper and increase.

Symbolic interaction   Communication within a group through speech, gestures, writing, or even music. Members are mutually aware of one another and take into consideration how their behavior will influence others.

Triad   A group consisting of three individuals. A more stable social unit than a dyad.

Voluntary groups   Groups that individuals may join entirely of their own free will or for reasons of social and economic expediency.

Suggestions for Further Reading

Fukutake, Tadashi.   1982. *The Japanese Social Structure*. Tokyo: University of Tokyo Press. One of Japan's best-known sociologists examines the social structure of his society, which combines elements of high industrialization and traditionalism.

Lenski, Gerhard, and Jean Lenski.   1982. *Human Societies,* 4th ed. New York: McGraw-Hill. A textbook with a focus on the evolution of societies according to their survival strategies.

Simpson, Ida Harper, et al.   1979. *From Student to Nurse*. New York: Cambridge University Press. A step-by-step description of the process in which a novice internalizes the role of nurse.

Zurcher, Louis A.   1983. *Social Roles: Conformity, Conflict, and Creativity.* Beverly Hills, Calif.: Sage. An examination of the various ways in which individuals attempt to control their role performance. From a symbolic-interactionist perspective.

Top Women Executives Find Path to Power Is Strewn with Hurdles

HELEN ROGAN

The ascribed status of women has, for centuries and almost universally, carried with it roles of wifehood and motherhood, and by extension of cooks, maids, and chief bottle washers. What happens, then, when a social movement succeeds in making new statuses acceptable for women? How are their new roles judged by the men they work with? What conflicts are created for women in their personal lives? What strains are imposed on them? How do women reconcile the multiplicity of their roles? Which social processes do they engage in most? Some answers are provided in the following article commenting on the problems of newly minted female executives.

These women are the pioneers.

They have impressive titles. They earn comfortable salaries. Through persistence, adaptability, and hard work they have climbed to positions of influence in a corporate world dominated by men. And they like their jobs.

Yet they share a sense of frustration—and in some cases anger—toward the people and attitudes that have made their professional lives anything but easy. "You have to prove that you are not just a pretty face or a pushy broad," says a 50-year-old bank vice president. "The male attitude has made it very difficult. You live in a fishbowl when you're the only woman. You have to be more credible than a man would—every day." Adds a 35-year-old record company vice president, "I think being a woman has held me back. You have to work 10 times as hard to prove yourself."

The Wall Street Journal and the Gallup Organization surveyed 722 female executives to find out what their lives are like—how their careers have taken shape and how they feel about the business world and the rewards and sacrifices it involves.

All of the women surveyed have the title of vice president or higher in listed companies with annual sales of $100 million or more. Fifty-eight percent are under 45, younger than the typical male executive. The younger ones have educational backgrounds similar to their male counterparts. They also have higher incomes than female executives over the age of 45, who rarely had the same educational opportunities.

Exhilaration The women hold positions in a wide range of areas, including formerly male domains like operations and finance. At least half were the first women to reach management level in their companies, and they're exhilarated by their success. "You're just trying, and then, oh my God, all of a sudden you're there," says a 60-year-old bank vice president.

All know what it's like to be part of a small minority in a male corporate world.

Source: From the *Wall Street Journal,* October 25, 1984, p. 35. Reprinted by permission of the *Wall Street Journal,* © Dow Jones & Company, Inc. (1984). All Rights Reserved.

"At a conference, if there are 300 men and 6 women, people know what you've said," says a 37-year-old vice president in manufacturing. "You're always on display." At times, that minority status can be an advantage. "Everything I do stands out," says a 43-year-old insurance company vice president. "If I do a good job, everyone knows."

At the same time, these women are painfully aware of how unaccustomed most men are to dealing with women at their own professional level. Sixty-one percent say they've been mistaken for a secretary at a business meeting.

Many of the women have conflicting views toward men. On one hand, they depend on men for career advancement. Most are grateful to a particular man: 82% say the most helpful person in their career has been a man. And among those who have a preference, many more would rather work for a man (29%) than for a woman (4%).

Disadvantages Still, more than four out of five of the women interviewed say there are disadvantages to being female in the business world. More than 25% say that they have been thwarted on their way up the ladder by male attitudes toward women. Men, they say, don't take them seriously—they patronize them and undervalue their experience. The younger women in positions of authority complain that men resent them and resist taking orders from them. And a sizeable majority—70%—feel they are paid less than men of equal ability.

The women frequently describe the business world as a "male club" from which they are excluded. Almost half of them say men treat them differently than they treat other male executives; most say this treatment is negative. One woman in five, for example, complains of being shut out of male executives' social activities. "You're not invited to many functions," says one,

"not to the golf course or for the drink after work, where a lot of business gets transacted." A 40-year-old manufacturing company treasurer says, "I'm not one of the boys. I can't hook into the informal chain of communications." As a result, she says, "it's easy to be ignored."

As women slowly move up in the business world, their lives seem to become more like men's—up to a point. They work hard, from 50 to 60 hours a week; 63% admit to losing sleep over work problems. And, like men, they feel that they have made personal and family sacrifices for their careers.

Successful male executives have, of course, traditionally put their jobs before their personal lives. Female executives do that too—but it's often more difficult for them. A 41-year-old bank vice president says, "More time is required of me in my job because of a need to prove that a woman can do equal or better work. This translates into time away from my family."

Cooking Dinner The woman executive returning late from a business trip may find herself cooking dinner for her husband. A 36-year-old senior vice president in a bank points out that her male colleagues don't have to walk such a tightrope between job and family. "They have a spouse at home," she says.

Given the difficulty of the situation, it's not surprising that many female executives are unmarried, and that the married ones tend to have helpful husbands. A top executive with three children says she sees herself as having two full-time jobs. "But my husband helps with the children," she says, "and he's thrown in a load of laundry now and then."

Women executives are more likely to be single (26%) and divorced or separated (16%) than the national norms for women. The most senior women are the least likely to be married, and the divorce rate is highest among the age group with the highest status: one-fourth of the women age 40–44 are now divorced or separated. Less than half (48%) of female corporate executives have had children, and fewer than three in 10 now have a child at home.

These executives take feminist political positions. Seventy-two percent favor passage of the Equal Rights Amendment, compared with 61% of American women sampled by Gallup in 1982. On the issue of abortion, executives are much more likely than other American women to feel it should be legal under all circumstances (59%, compared with 22% of the women surveyed in a 1983 Gallup Poll).

Gender Gap   The survey also reflects the widely publicized gender gap. While 64% of the women interviewed say they would like to see Ronald Reagan reelected, their male counterparts are much more pro-Reagan. In a 1983 Wall Street Journal/Gallup poll of top male executives, Mr. Reagan's reelection was favored by 92% of those in large companies, 88% of those in medium-sized companies, and 80% of those in small companies.

Some of the senior women think that things are getting easier for young women, who have been able to take advantage of affirmative action legislation and changing attitudes. A bank vice president with 32 years of experience says that even a few years ago, as an assistant vice president, she found herself at meetings with 40 men and only one or two women. Now, she says, she sees younger men and women lunching together and thinks that for the first time women are being accepted.

The younger women tend to agree. But as they compete with men for prestige and power they find themselves making large sacrifices. "I have compromised spontaneity in my personal life," laments a vice president in a service industry. Another vice president in an electric company says, "My job has definitely stood in the way of marriage." This woman has a serious relationship with a man, but, she says, "I feel that if I were to marry him there'd be a new set of expectations and I would be unable to fulfill them at the same time as doing my job."

The female executives interviewed for this survey were selected by the Gallup Organization from a nationwide census of all women with the title of vice president or higher in listed companies with annual sales of $100 million or more.

Gallup found that more than 40% of the 2,037 women executives worked in banks or other financial institutions. Many of them, despite their titles, worked at relatively low levels. To obtain a more representative sample, Gallup removed the lower-level managers and limited to 30% the proportion of women in the survey from the financial industry. The 722 women who remained were interviewed by phone in April and May, by female interviewers.

Culture: The Blueprint for Life in Society

Though all human beings belong to the species *Homo sapiens,* and all are the product of the same evolutionary process, differences among human groups are nonetheless clearly apparent. The physical variations are slight: a lighter shade of skin or hair, more prominent cheekbones, a different shape to the eyes. Beyond these diversities all, however, are recognizably members of the human groups, as opposed to such animal groups as, for instance, dolphins or gorillas. Greater divergences among humans exist in the languages they speak, in the gods they worship, in the governments they support, in the traditions they follow. These differences are often dramatic, and their causes a source of curiosity, interest, and frequently conflict.

Basically, such differences arise from the scattering of the world's people throughout the planet into a multitude of different groups, the largest of which are societies (see Chapter 2). Within these societies, men and women choose mates much like themselves, until through the centuries specific biological traits become characteristic of the group—straight, blond hair and blue eyes, for instance, or dark, curly hair and brown eyes. Similarly, frequent interaction among societal members leads to shared values, beliefs, and patterns of behavior. This course of events, though simplistically explained here, lies at the bottom of differences in appearance, customs, languages, religions, and lifestyles in societies around the world. Even within the same society, individual groups are often differentiated by distinct characteristics.

In spite of such seemingly endless variety, humans share more profound similarities than differences. In part, these derive from our biological nature. We may travel far and wide, yet still we observe that all people eat, although what, when, and how may vary tremendously from place to place. All sleep, some in beds and others on mats or bare floors. All build shelters for themselves, some weaving their homes out of palm fronds and mud, others hewing them from ice. All classify themselves within some kind of kinship system, although in some places first cousins are considered the best marriage partners, while in others such alliances are taboo. All develop some kind of social system, with rules for behavior, values, attitudes, customs, and traditions. And the survival of all depends strongly on decisions made according to individual economic systems. In short, although humans are infinitely different, they are also infinitely alike. It is this common humanity that unites us, at the same time that our cultures set us apart.

Culture

The term **culture,** an important concept in the social sciences, represents the most easily observed and most distinctive product of our group way of life. A frequent source of division, it is also what makes us uniquely human.

As a term, culture is often misused or misunderstood. In everyday conversation people use it to refer to persons with good manners or to those who attend classical music concerts and art exhibits. In sociological terms, culture is the way of life of a people. Since whoever learns that way of life absorbs the culture of the group, every individual brought up in a social group is therefore cultured.

While culture is the product of a social group—usually a society—society and culture, being interrelated and interdependent, are in fact two aspects of the same phenomenon. Culture cannot exist apart from society—or at least a social group—and a society without a culture is also unthinkable. As noted in the previous chapter, an individual outside of a social group, unexposed to a group culture, can hardly be called human. Society, culture, and the individual, then, form a triangle within which human life is acted out from beginning to end.

In a social group held together by symbolic interaction, such interdependence is understandable; the behavioral patterns, values, beliefs, and rules of conduct resulting from this interaction become the substance of culture. Culture, then, is not only an outgrowth of but becomes itself a pattern for interaction.

The relationship of culture to society may be best understood in a theatrical context, where society is compared to a group of actors assigned roles befitting their characters or statuses. Culture represents the actors' script, though the creation of culture, of course, is a much less deliberate act than the creation of a play. As the playwright's script is the blueprint for the actors' performance,

55

CHAPTER 3

Culture: The Blueprint for Life in Society

Society is but the stage on which we, the actors, play our roles according to the script provided by our culture.

so a culture set down by earlier generations offers its descendents precepts to live by. Just as a playwright edits the script, so too each generation adds, deletes, changes, and modifies parts of its culture.

Definition of Culture

Because of its importance as a sociological concept, culture has been defined in a vast number of ways. In capsule form, it represents the totality of what humans learn, share, and transmit by means of their interaction within social groups. Additional characteristics include the following: Culture is considered uniquely human (though perhaps not exclusively so; recent studies of other primates indicate that they too are capable of some symbolic interaction and the use of simple tools); it includes all accumulated knowledge, ideas, values, goals, and material objects of a society; it is acquired through symbolic inter-action during the process of socialization; it provides the individual with methods of satisfying biological and emotional needs in a manner approved by society; each society develops a culture distinct from others, yet all cultures share similarities based on universal human needs; culture, just as society, is in a constant state of flux.

The most important element of culture is its capacity to be communicated symbolically. This symbolic nature, in fact, is its reason for being: One reason animals other than humans lack rich cultures is their inability to communicate symbolically.

Communication among these animals is based on a system of **signals** that are biologically determined, genetically transmitted responses to external stimuli. Animals yelp in response to pain, run in response to fear, kill in response to hunger. While animals can be taught to act in ways that are not instinctual—dogs can learn to sit on command, to stay in one place, to stand on their hind paws, to come close, and to fetch the paper—a dog so trained will not be able to pass on these skills to her newborn puppy.

Humans, on the other hand, transmit information to their offspring through endless chains of generations by means of communication based on **symbols.** Symbols are signs used in an abstract manner whose meanings are commun-ally agreed upon. All English-speaking people, for instance, agree that the word *bread* stands for a type of food made of flour, water, and several other ingredients. This word, which means nothing to a non-English-speaker, ac-quired symbolic value when a group of inhabitants of the British Isles, after generations of interacting together, began to refer to a particular food by a particular term. The word then became a symbol for the object.

Language: The Most Important Symbol

Language, the use of symbols to name things, individuals, and categories, is the most effective human system of symbols. Other symbolic communication systems include gestures, music, and the visual arts.

Language plays a particularly important role in the development and trans-mission of culture. It makes possible a wide range of communication, allowing people to engage in coordinated group activities that help them survive. Historically, language facilitated cooperation in hunting ventures. Successful hunting provided a relatively constant food supply, leading in turn to the establishment of permanent communities (cities and nations) and a more efficient division of labor.

In itself the most significant invention or product of culture, language serves as well as the foundation on which cultures are erected and transmitted. Human social life is dramatically affected by language. The range of knowledge is infinitely expanded when individuals no longer need experience events personally; countless experiences can be told to countless people countless times.

Human language goes far beyond the primitive biological warning systems. It permits the philosophical constructions of time and space, enabling events that occurred long ago (history, tradition) and far away (geography) to be related. With language, humans can even project their desires or anticipations into the future.

As a result of language, knowledge not only spreads but accumulates. This process is greatly expanded and accelerated when writing is added to the spoken word. Even in societies where writing has not been invented however, certain individuals are designated to preserve and pass on by oral means knowledge that is deemed necessary or desirable for the group's survival. Transmission of culture enables each new generation to build on the experiences of previous ones, rather than having to discover things anew. Cultures in fact frequently survive the societies in which they originate. Ancient Greece and Imperial Rome ceased to exist thousands of years ago, yet their cultures have left a profound mark upon Western civilization; the literature and art of the Greeks and Romans are still read and admired today.

Language, then, is a crucial social tool. It enables humans to coordinate their activities for the benefit of the social group and facilitates the sharing of individual thoughts, feelings, and information. Words may stand for, or symbolize, real objects, activities or events, or abstractions such as loyalty and love, intangible concepts which all humans experience. More curiously, language can be used to express concepts people have *not* experienced, such as God, as long as there is agreement that God *can* be experienced. Humans invent words to express all aspects of their culture, finding new terms to fit new cultural patterns as they emerge. The word "groupies" did not exist prior to the 1960s, nor did "Silicon Valley" before the late 1970s, nor "videos" before the 1980s.

The interrelationship of language and culture has led some social scientists to maintain that the very structure of language shapes one's reactions and attitudes toward reality. An example occurs in societies where the focus of time is an eternal present; in the language developed by these societies, no way exists of expressing the idea of past or future. The Sioux Indians, for instance, cannot verbalize the idea of being late or of waiting.. From their perspective of an eternal present, these ideas do not exist. In other languages, certain phenomena can be expressed with an infinite number of nuances. The Eskimos, for instance, use a multitude of terms to describe the snow that surrounds them a good portion of the year, while the English language possesses considerably fewer snowlike adjectives.

Linguistic experts Benjamin Whorf (1956) and Edward Sapir (1960) maintain, therefore, that language is a reflection of human thought, feelings, and actions that in turn shapes the way humans think, feel, and act (a theory known as the Whorf-Sapir hypothesis). In a way, if you can't say it, you can't think it. In fact, you can't *be* it either, since even the personalities we acquire depend on symbolic interaction in a social context.

Biological Predisposition to Culture

While biology is responsible for our ability to speak and symbolize—and thus, indirectly, for our ability to create culture—it is also very limiting. In many respects, human biological makeup has made it difficult for people to survive on earth. Since we cannot breathe underwater, vast parts of the earth are uninhabitable to us. Our thin layer of skin, lacking a hairy cover, requires protection from the elements. We are also rather small in size and, without the claws and fangs and poisons of many animals, must therefore develop other means of defending ourselves.

These human biological shortcomings are more than made up for, however, by qualities we *do* possess: (1) a grasping hand with a thumb that can be opposed to the other four fingers, enabling us to handle the most delicate of objects; (2) an upright posture, freeing our forelimbs for handling and carrying objects; (3) binocular (two-eyed) vision, enabling us to focus far or near; (4) a highly complicated vocal equipment, making it possible for us to speak; and (5) an extremely well-developed brain, part of a complex nervous system that coordinates the functioning of the whole human machine.

It is this biological equipment which has made possible the human creation of culture. In turn, culture has offered methods of adapting to the physical environment in those instances where human physical qualities were lacking. The use of language to communicate information has made this process that much easier and faster.

The Content of Culture

A society's culture is taken for granted by those within it, who believe their culture to be the only "right" one, and that all human actions are carried out, and have always been, as they are in their society. But a careful analysis of culture reveals a great number of possibly divergent elements.

Material Culture

A good portion of culture is visible and tangible, consisting of huge numbers of products conceived and manufactured by humans. All material objects, from the primitive stone ax of our ancient ancestors to a complex guided missile waiting in its silo, belong to the category of material culture.

Material objects are created to fill the shared needs of society. They come into being when one individual has an idea that is seized upon by others who may add to, modify, change, and put it to use.

The automobile, for instance, is the foremost symbol of contemporary industrial society. This object is the result of the interaction of countless generations: the prehistoric cave dwellers who first honed a stone into a circular shape; others who saw how rapidly round stones rolled down an incline; those who first thought of the possibility of inserting a stick through the center of such a stone and attaching a vine to the ends for the purpose of moving a heavy object, thus inventing the wheel as a method of transport. Generations later, after the domestication of animals, other ingenious (or merely lazy) individuals experimented with attaching four wheels to an oxen or a horse and allowing the animals to do the pulling! Much later, the steam and internal combustion engines were invented and wheels attached to them allowing people to ride comfortably and speedily in boats, railroad trains, and automobiles. The originators of the automobile industry simply applied the finishing touches to an idea born of the human brain and produced by human hands thousands of years ago. (See Chapter 9 for a discussion of how cultural inventions are borrowed and become diffused, thus serving as major contributors to social change.)

Nonmaterial Culture

The rest of culture consists of abstractions: knowledge, beliefs, values, and rules for behavior. This is the nonmaterial part of culture. Of course material and nonmaterial are not distinct entities: in the example of the automobile, both ideas about the necessity for rapid and comfortable transportation and the knowledge of how to make different parts of the vehicle work had to be present. Sociologists, as may be expected, are chiefly concerned with culture's nonmaterial aspects, since most human life is shaped by and carried out in the context of beliefs, values, and behavioral rules.

Components of Nonmaterial Culture: Cognitive and Normative

In addition to the manipulation of symbols, a primary source of the creation of culture, nonmaterial culture possesses two important components, the cognitive and the normative. The category *cognitive* includes definitions given to all that exists, or to all that people believe exists. More specifically, the cognitive component includes knowledge, beliefs, and technology. Knowledge refers to all information about the physical world that can be objectively substantiated. Information derived from the physical sciences yields this type of knowledge. Beliefs may be defined as ideas and speculations about physical, social, and supernatural reality not as easily supported by facts. Finally, technology is defined as the methods and techniques people apply to the physical and social world in order to better control them.

The *normative* component is, if possible, an even more important cultural feature, including as it does rules for behavior, without which human societies could not exist. The normative system deals with rules, or norms, that specify what ought or ought not to be. In sociological terms, norms "designate any standard or rule that states what human beings should or should not think, say, or do under given circumstances" (Blake and Davis, 1964, 456).

The Normative System

The normative component of culture holds the key to why societies function as they do. The elements of this component have been termed by sociologists the **normative system.** This system consists of values, norms (further divided into folkways, mores, and laws), institutions, and sanctions.

Values **Values** are abstract evaluations of certain kinds of behaviors, actions, or systems as good, right, moral, beautiful, or ethical—and therefore desirable. In American society, for instance, democracy is a value, as are peace, equality, freedom, and achievement.

Values are closely related to beliefs. If one believes that all persons are created equal, it follows that one values the democratic principles that guarantee political equality to all. In turn, values are concretely expressed by norms. If a society values education, it will provide laws requiring its members to attend school for a specific number of years. If it values human life, it will prohibit murder. If it values efficiency and punctuality, it will demand that its members follow schedules and come to work on time.

The values of a society can thus often be inferred from its norms. Sociologist Robin Williams (1970) has identified a number of basic value orientations in American society evident from the behavioral norms of a majority of Americans. He examines such themes as achievement, success, activity, work, morality, humanitarianism, efficiency, practicality, progress, material comfort, equality, freedom, external conformity, science, rationality, nationalism-patriotism, democracy, individualism, and group superiority. Williams' list is of course not definitive. Other sociologists have noted different or additional values in American society. Moreover, many of these values are evolving, and not all Americans accept them unquestioningly.

Norms **Norms,** defined as those rules or standards prescribing how one ought to act, think, or even feel on given occasions, cover a wide range of circumstances. They dictate conduct in formal and informal situations as well as in significant and less significant ones. They cover everything from when, how, and with whom to shake hands to when it is permissible and when it is forbidden to kill another human being.

Norms emerge in a group when, through experience, that group judges a particular act as either harmful or beneficial. A harmful act is given negative value and forbidden; a beneficial act is given positive value and encouraged. These beliefs about the relative value of actions eventually become the norms according to which group members regulate their lives, offering clues for behavior in specific circumstances. Individual members internalize these norms, incorporating them into their personalities and belief systems. So thoroughly are most norms internalized that they are obeyed not simply out of fear of punishment, but out of a belief that they represent the "right" or correct way to act; breaking such norms usually produces guilt feelings in a society's members. In short, the cultural norms that originate in a society are essentially a set of behavioral expectations, a system which informs members of that society how to act under a wide range of circumstances.

All cultural components are intimately interconnected. The normative system provides rules and standards of behavior, but these rules and standards derive from a culture's cognitive component. Thus beliefs, values, and norms may be differentiated in these terms: beliefs are what most people think is *true* about the world around them; values are what most people think is *good* and *right*; and norms are how most people think they and others should *behave*. Norms are reflections of values, which in turn are reflections of beliefs.

No components of culture are always in perfect agreement. Especially in heterogeneous societies (those made up of members of dissimilar backgrounds) people accept conflicting norms, values, and beliefs. Americans believe in the equality of all but also in the value of competition, which leads to the success of some and the failure of others and, as a consequence, to inequality of income and life-styles.

When its norms, values, beliefs, and other cultural elements are in agreement, a society is considered well integrated. Due to inevitable differences among people, no society is ever totally integrated, but social life can be orderly when at least a degree of cultural integration exists.

Categories of Norms: Folkways, Mores, Taboos, and Laws   Sociologists categorize norms according to their importance and function. One category of norms is **folkways,** a term coined by early American sociologist William Graham Sumner (1840–1910). Folkways are norms that specify behavior in everyday situations. How one greets a friend or a stranger, how one behaves in church or at a dance, how many times a day one eats—all these customary, habitual actions are guided by folkways.

Every culture develops a great number of folkways, and in complex societies they are especially numerous. Some become permanent features of a society, such as the celebration of holidays; others, such as fashions in clothes, furniture, or architectural styles, are transitory. Some are learned as part of socialization—to cut the meat on one's dish into bite-size pieces instead of filling one's mouth with a large chunk—while others are transmitted by media and a variety of other groups throughout a person's life.

Folkways are not easy to ignore. Violating them can cause great embarrassment to both violator and those connected in any way. Deliberate and repeated violation of specific folkways may result in lost jobs or reputations. Nevertheless, violation of folkways does not bring about such severe societal punishment as arrest or imprisonment since folkways do not dictate behavior in the truly significant areas of human life.

Mores   Norms that guide human behavior in areas of life considered extremely important are called **mores.** (Mores is a Latin word, the plural of *mos,* meaning custom.) Mores define the rightness or wrongness of a specific act, its morality or immorality. A person who consistently violates some folkway, by belching at the dinner table, for example, may be excluded from a hostess's dinner party; a person who violates mores, on the other hand, is punished in the name of society (that is, by legal action). The violation of mores is considered a crime against the whole society.

Mores are perceived by members of society in terms of absolute right or wrong. In reality, however, mores are relative to time and place. For instance, many societies formerly permitted ritual murder, infanticide, cannibalism, incest, and other practices that today are violations of mores. These societies did not perceive such behaviors as wrong, and in fact at the time the actions had justification, at least for those involved. As Sumner has maintained, mores can make any act either right or wrong. In our own society certain mores have changed considerably over a short span of time. Only a century ago, child labor and slavery were considered perfectly justifiable in the United States. Today no American, not even the most child-hating or racist would seriously propose putting eight-year-olds to work in factories or reinstating a system of slavery. On some mores there is more disagreement; the desirability of capital punishment, for instance, or the legalization of mind-altering drugs are still controversial subjects.

Taboos   Mores that are expressed in negative terms ("Thou shalt not") and that deal with acts considered extremely repellent to the social group are categorized as **taboos.** Incest and cannibalism are regarded as taboos by most societies.

Taboos are deeply etched on the conscience of most members of a society. While some people are physically incapable of performing such a strongly forbidden act, influences on the personality of others may weaken the hold of taboos and mores in general. To prevent this situation, or to clarify and strengthen the power of mores and taboos, societies pass laws which prohibit specific acts under penalty of imprisonment and even death.

Laws   **Laws** are formal codes of behavior that are binding on a whole society. They specify both deviant behavior and the appropriate punishment. Such punishment is meted out by official representatives of the society.

Laws are particularly necessary in a complex, heterogeneous society that is undergoing rapid social change, since many norms are often not clear enough for numerous different groups to understand or accept. In simpler societies with stronger kinship ties, fewer norms are needed to prevent deviation.

Unlike norms, laws do not become internalized as part of the individual's personality, but are learned and obeyed by a majority because they are based on rational reasons. The more closely laws reinforce universally accepted societal mores, the more successful they will be. This is why laws against the use of marijuana and other mind-altering drugs have been so difficult to enforce in the United States: a large number of people who use these substances do not believe they represent a danger, or that their use is wrong. Prohibition represents another good example of a law that failed to work because people refused to obey it. The injunction against the consumption and sale of alcohol was so difficult to enforce that it finally had to be repealed.

The advantage of laws over folkways and mores is that they can be repealed or modified if they do not work. Folkways and mores, on the other hand, tend to persist as habits and customs long after their usefulness to a society has passed. This is one reason laws are sometimes passed in a society with the hope that folkways and mores will eventually follow. Civil rights legislation enacted in the United States to make specific forms of discrimination illegal is such an example. This legislation did not eliminate racism, but defined and reinforced certain values; folkways and mores will, one hopes, eventually change to meet the conditions of the law.

The Basis of the Normative System: The Need for Social Control

Every group must ensure that its members conform to most of its expectations most of the time. If they do not, anarchy and disorder prevail, and the business of the group, the reason for which it was formed, cannot go on. This is especially true in a society, whose business concerns the health and welfare of a large number of people. Consider what would happen if we could not trust other drivers to stop at red lights. Rush-hour traffic, bad as it is when the rules of the road are obeyed, would be a total nightmare, leaving dead or maimed in its wake every day. Society, therefore, must have ways of exerting control over its members to make them obey at least those rules that are vital to the survival of the group.

There are numerous ways in which society exerts this power, termed **social control** by sociologists. The ultimate form is physical force, a method that lies at the core of political power and authority. A person representing such power and authority may use physical force against an individual who breaks the law. Thus a police officer may knock to the ground an alleged perpetrator of a crime who is trying to escape, may even shoot at him if he does not heed the request to halt. But a society depending on force alone for exerting social control is a harsh one indeed and contains much conflict.

More often, societies depend on more subtle methods of social control. Economic pressure is one such example: the need of getting and keeping a job keeps most workers toeing the line as far as company regulations are concerned. Occupational pressures also serve to keep individuals with specific statuses performing appropriate roles: a minister is not likely to be seen on Saturday night at the corner tavern, though some of his parishioners may spend their time this way.

Perhaps the most effective societal pressures stem from **sanctions.** These may be negative or positive, official or unofficial. Negative sanctions consist of punishments, while positive sanctions represent rewards. For instance, being named to the Supreme Court after a distinguished law career represents an official positive sanction, a reward offered in the name of the whole society.

Being told by an instructor that one's paper shows brilliant insights is an unofficial positive sanction, a reward received within a small group. A person who is jailed as a result of breaking a federal, state, or local law receives an official negative sanction by being punished in the name of society. The theater patron asked to leave because of noisy, rude behavior receives an unofficial negative sanction; he too is being punished, but more informally because his infraction is less severe.

It is unofficial sanctions, which appear on the surface to be less severe and important, that have the greatest impact on individuals, especially when received within primary groups such as family or friends. Families and friends are part and parcel of one's identity and self-image. Thus, when people are criticized—or encouraged—by family members or friends, their very self-concept is attacked or enhanced. Of course official sanctions, particularly negative ones, are very significant; they can lead to loss of freedom and even death.

In the final analysis, social control through the enforcement of norms relies on the human anxiety to be accepted by the group. Researchers have found that even in group discussions individuals tend to change their minds to conform to the consensus of opinions expressed by others. In a group of 20, if 15 argue one point and 5 argue the opposite, chances are good that in time the 5 opponents will come to agree with the majority. In society, too, people yearn for acceptance; many more are conformists than nonconformists.

Before closing this discussion of norms, a few more points must be made. First, although the norms of a culture may be firmly embedded in the personalities of most members, this is not true of each and every individual. There is always a minority in every society who ignore some norms; but no one who ignores or rejects all social norms can continue to live in the group. Second, in every society some norms emerge that are not officially accepted as proper behavior but are nevertheless widely practiced. It is possible therefore to speak of an *overt culture,* which describes the officially accepted patterns of behavior, and of a *covert* culture, according to which some people actually behave. For instance, a person who publicly subscribes to a highly moralistic system of sexual behavior may privately engage in promiscuous acts.

The fact is that we can recognize in each society an *ideal* culture, consisting of formal, approved folkways, mores, and laws, and a *real* culture, consisting of what people actually do, how they really behave. In sociology, it has become customary to refer to cultural norms when one means the ideal culture, and statistical norms when one describes how people really behave.

Traits, Complexes, and Institutions

The normative system of culture can be further divided, for purposes of analysis, into traits, complexes, and institutions. **Traits** are the smallest elements, or units, of culture. In material culture, each single object that society uses is a trait. In nonmaterial culture, each single idea, symbol, or belief existing in a society is a trait. A nail, a brick, and a house are traits of material culture, while saluting the flag (denoting patriotism), kissing (a symbol of

Can you name the culture traits and complexes surrounding this obvious American institution? Incidentally, the fact that you instantly recognized the institution illustrates the point that the essence of culture consists of shared meanings.

affection), voting (a belief in a particular political system), or praying (faith in a transcendent life), are traits of nonmaterial culture.

A number of related traits accumulating around an activity form a **culture complex.** Football is a culture complex consisting of material traits (the pigskin itself, uniforms, helmets, a field) and nonmaterial traits (the players' abilities, a set of rules, a belief in winning, team spirit). All areas of human life display numerous culture complexes.

When a number of culture complexes cluster around a central activity, an institution emerges. **Institutions** are formal systems of beliefs and behavior composed of interrelated norms and culture complexes. In the above example, sport is the institution of which football is the culture complex.

Primarily, institutions center on some fundamental human need which must be filled in order for the individual to survive and the society to prosper. The five basic or pivotal institutions, which arose from the five most fundamental human needs, are the family (the need to replenish society with new members, regulate sex, and care for the helpless newborn); the economy (the need to procure food, shelter, and clothing); government (the need to maintain peace and order); education (the need to transmit culture and train new generations); and religion (the need to pacify the fear of the unknown).

These five basic institutions are common to all societies. However, the forms they assume and the traits and complexes they display differ from society to society. In later chapters, each of the pivotal institutions in American society will be discussed in detail. For now, it is well to note that institutions are cultural instruments designed to show people how to behave in such a way as to benefit the society and themselves. For example, trial and error have shown that the presence of two parents in a household makes for an ideal environment in which to bring up children. Since children are the future of a society, it is to a society's advantage to provide its offspring with two parents. This is done by teaching societal members that each individual ought to marry and become a parent. Such instruction is so well entrenched that many men and women come to believe that marriage and parenthood are not only goals toward which to strive but the only alternatives open. Those who have failed to marry and have children have traditionally been ostracized and have frequently believed themselves failures in life.

As one sociologist has put it, institutions are to people what instincts are to animals: when a cat sees a mouse, instinct prods it to pursue, kill, and eat its quarry; when young persons meet appealing members of the opposite sex, internalized institutional learning prods them to pursue, fall in love with, and marry each other (Berger, 1963). Of course, institutions work like instincts only when functioning perfectly, which they seldom do. The family institution, for instance, has undergone dramatic transformations in recent decades, with the result that people no longer regard marriage and childbearing as necessities, but demand such alternate choices as living together, serial monogamy, childless marriages, and so on.

Differences and Uniformities of Cultures

Anyone who has visited a foreign country knows that societies differ in their customs, traditions, languages, and in some very commonplace details of daily life. These differences often lead to **ethnocentrism,** an attitude with which members of one society judge another according to their own standards. This approach is always unfair to the judged society, since humans tend to view their own societal customs as normal; hence, all customs differing from that norm are seen as somehow abnormal—strange at best, barbaric or uncivilized at worst.

All societies, and for that matter all groups, display a certain degree of ethnocentrism. In moderation, ethnocentrism has the positive effect of promoting unity and loyalty within a group. But in excess it leads to conflict between dissimilar groups or, in a situation where one group is more powerful than another, to oppression and sometimes even genocide.

To counter the negative effects of ethnocentrism, the concept of **cultural relativity** has been proposed. Proponents of this concept assert that cultures must be analyzed on their own terms in the context of their particular societal setting. According to cultural relativists, no society has the right to use its values and norms to judge the traits of another. In this view, there are no universal norms, no moral absolutes: under specific circumstances, any act can appear good or bad. Although this perspective seems to have much merit, it also reveals some troublesome implications: some societies may maintain (and have in fact done so) that nothing short of total annihilation of certain inhabitants will benefit the group. Does their contention make mass murder justifiable? Are there really no moral absolutes? Tolerance, respect, and understanding of the cultural values of others, rather than a mindless acceptance of them, seem to be more reasonable and attainable goals.

Cultural Differences and Universals

When early explorers, missionaries, and adventurers first came in contact with foreign societies, they naturally judged them according to their own ethnocentric standards. In some of the more exotic societies, such newcomers could not help experiencing what we now refer to as "culture shock." Their explanations of dissimilarities in foreign cultures centered on racial, geographical, even religious causes. But while these do influence the course of cultural development—geography, for instance, influences culture in the sense that no igloos will be built in the Amazonian jungle, nor palm huts become the customary dwellings of Alaskans—no one reason can explain perfectly what makes one culture different from another.

Whether similar or dissimilar, all cultures continually undergo change. Even the most static societies experience a constant state of flux in which new elements are added to those already present. But not all aspects of culture change at the same time, a condition that gives rise to *cultural lag.* Cultural lag occurs in many contemporary societies that have adopted certain Western customs but retain a value orientation geared to their own past. It is often responsible for social conflict and may be troublesome in the context of social change (see Chapter 9).

Only deeply entrenched characteristics tend to remain stable. As striking as their differences may appear, cultures share many more similarities. The pivotal institutions mentioned above are present in all societies. But many norms, values, and beliefs are also unexpectedly similar. All people enjoy adorning themselves, whether with rings through their nostrils or on pinky fingers; all people have some sort of food taboos, whether against eating cows, pigs, or grasshoppers. All people enjoy some form of music and dancing, and some form of art or handicraft.

Social anthropologist George P. Murdock compiled a long list of elements common to all known cultures (1945). This list includes such widely divergent elements as age-grading, hospitality, and weather control. Such common similarities among cultures are known as **cultural universals.** They offer general themes on which each culture develops its own variations. The existence of so many cultural universals leads to the conclusion that we truly share common bonds. No matter how strange our customs, how different our appearances, we are all human.

A family at dinner is a cultural universal that is repeated, with local variations, all around the world.

Subcultures and Countercultures

Variation and uniformity are characteristics not only of societies, but of groups within each society. This is especially true of contemporary, technologically advanced societies which tend to be heterogeneous, or dissimilar, because they attract and incorporate groups from all over the world.

Subcultures

In the United States, for instance, groups based on race, ethnicity, religion, and numerous other distinguishing features exist. Even in more homogeneous societies, groups form on the basis of region (Northerners or Southerners), occupation (musicians, circus acrobats), social class (Wasps or Yuppies), religion (Roman Catholics, Jews), even age (teenagers, golden-agers). Sociologists refer to these subdivisions, or groups within the larger society, as **subcultures.**

Subcultures have distinctive features that set them apart from the general culture of the society, while they yet retain the principal features of that culture. (The word subculture never implies inferiority to the larger culture—it refers only to a smaller subsection.) Membership in a subculture enriches one's life by providing additional alternatives—other actions or perspectives—with which to achieve one's desired goals.

Teenagers present a good example of a subculture. While they identify with the goals and values of the larger societal culture and are guided by its general behavioral patterns, many of their interests and some aspects of their behavior are peculiar to their age group: a special language, a distinctive manner of dress, a taste for certain music, a fondness for specific foods and forms of recreation.

Countercultures

In the late 1960s and 1970s, many observers and experts believed that teenagers and young people in general had formed a counterculture. A **counterculture** is a group within the society whose members adopt a value system and goals in direct opposition to those of the general culture. Some criminal groups, although not all, are countercultural; many criminals accept the goals of our society, rejecting only the means of attaining them. A gang of delinquent boys or girls is usually considered countercultural because its set of values and standards of behavior tend to run counter to those of the wider culture.

Almost every historical period has its counterculture, although in different eras some especially rigid and intolerant societies have suppressed any attempts at nonconformity. The countercultural movement of the 1960s had its origin in bohemianism, a phenomenon that appeared in France in the early nineteenth century. Young artists and intellectuals of this period declared their determination to lead lives free of restrictions imposed by middle-class values (which, they asserted, were dictated by the need of the capitalistic system for members who were sober, respectable, conforming, disciplined, rational, practical, and geared toward acquisitiveness).

The flower children, or hippies, of a generation ago emerged among American youth at a time when their age group was very large, during an expanding economy resulting from unprecedented technological advances. Young people in this group found that values held by the majority no longer seemed to fit the society in which they were living. For instance, while adults were still preaching the need for hard work and sacrifice, technological sophistication held the promise of continued affluence without the need for such efforts. Their confusion was further compounded by an isolation from other age groups due to long periods of schooling. The countercultural values that emerged tried to redefine what it meant to be human in the new societal context.

A lengthy period of economic recession, among other factors, put an end to all but a small residue of the countercultural life-style. Many countercultural ideas, however, have been absorbed into the popular culture, as have such outward symbols as long hair, colorful unisex attire, and rock and roll music. For instance, living with a "roommate" of the opposite sex, once considered a scandalous countercultural innovation, has become quite commonplace, almost respectable. Thus, it may be argued that the very success of the counterculture spelled its doom; since the mainstream culture accepted so much that was initially countercultural, there was no need for its continuing existence. However, the counterculture's primary goals, of a return to a preindustrial life-style and noninstitutional forms of sex, education, and religion, were never really achieved.

To recapitulate, countercultures reject the goals, values, and norms of the society at large. Their members defy conventional societal norms, remaining faithful to the norms of their particular group. Subcultures, for the most part, reinforce the cultural patterns of the wider society, allowing loyalty to the smaller group to coexist with loyalty to the larger.

The Chapter in Brief

The most important product of societal interaction is **culture.** Culture may be superficially defined as the way of life of a specific people, but it is much more than this. At the very least, it acts as a guide for further social interaction—a blueprint for living. The most basic element of culture is language, a system of **symbols** that allows members of a society to accumulate and transmit knowledge without relying on personal experience. Culture has both material content (tangible products and objects) and nonmaterial content (ideas, values, knowledge, beliefs, rules for behavior, and institutions). Much of a society's nonmaterial culture is made up of **norms,** rules of behavior learned and shared through the interaction of members. Norms include **folkways, mores, taboos,** and **laws.**

The structure of culture consists of **traits** (the smallest unit of culture),

culture complexes (a number of related traits), and **institutions.** Institutions are formal systems of beliefs and behavior, composed of interrelated norms and culture complexes. Institutions primarily center on and help fill universal human needs. Five basic institutions are common to all human societies: the family, the economy, government, education, and religion.

The culture of each society is both different than, and similar to, the culture of other societies. To members of a specific society, a foreign culture may appear irrational or barbaric, a biased impression based on **ethnocentrism,** or the tendency of one culture to judge other cultures by its own standards. A seemingly more just perspective is **cultural relativity,** where foreign cultures are analyzed in their own special context on the basis of how well each fills its members' needs.

Cultural differences among societies are the result of geographic and other little-known factors. Similar characteristics displayed by all cultures arise through the attempt to fulfill universal human needs, both biological and emotional. Characteristics common to all cultures are called **cultural universals.**

Because societies are made up of various groups, cultures also vary within societies. Groups within a society may be differentiated on the basis of geographic location, social class, occupation, race, ethnicity, religion, and so on. Such groups may produce a distinctive culture, including a separate language or jargon, customs, traditions, and rituals. If the principal values of such a group are the same as those of the general societal culture, the group is called a **subculture.** If the principal values are in direct opposition to those of the larger culture, the group is called a **counterculture.**

Terms to Remember

Counterculture   A group within a society that possesses a value system and goals in direct opposition to those of the larger society.

Cultural relativity   A perspective of judging each culture on its own terms and in the context of its own societal setting.

Cultural universals   Similarities common to all cultures (for example, the existence of pivotal institutions).

Culture   The way of life of people in a society. The totality of all that is learned and shared by members of a society through their interaction. The product of social interaction and a guide for further interaction. Culture includes material and nonmaterial aspects, the latter consisting of the important normative system, the combined accumulated knowledge of the society, and the society's belief system.

Culture complex   A number of related traits that gather around a specific human activity.

Ethnocentrism   The attitude in which one assumes that one's own culture is right and that cultural patterns different from it are wrong.

Folkways   Norms that direct behavior in everyday situations; customary and habitual ways of acting.

Institution   A number of culture complexes clustering around a central human activity.

Laws   Formal codes of behavior. Laws are binding on the whole society; they outline norm-deviating behavior and prescriptions for punishing it.

Mores   Norms that direct behavior considered either extremely harmful or extremely helpful to society. They define the rightness or wrongness of an act, its morality or immorality. Violation of mores is punished by society.

Normative system   A system of rules regulating human behavior.

Norms   Behavioral standards that dictate conduct in both informal and formal situations; a set of behavioral expectations.

Sanctions   Rewards (positive) or punishment (negative) directed at individuals or groups by either legal and formal organizations (official), or by the people with whom one interacts (unofficial) to encourage or discourage specific behaviors.

Signals   Biologically determined and genetically transmitted responses to external stimuli.

Social control   The process by which order is maintained within society through obedience to norms—folkways, mores, taboos, and laws.

Subculture   A group whose distinctive features set it apart from the culture of the larger society, but which still retains the general values of that society.

Symbols   Genetically independent responses to stimuli. Symbols are learned and can be changed, modified, combined, and recombined in an infinite number of ways. Language, music, and art are common symbolic systems.

Taboos   Mores stated in negative terms. They center on acts considered extremely repellent to the social group.

Trait   The smallest element or unit of culture. In material culture, any single object. In nonmaterial culture, any single idea, symbol, or belief.

Values   Abstract evaluations of certain kinds of behaviors, actions, or systems as good, right, moral, beautiful, or ethical—and therefore desirable.

Suggestions for Further Reading

Harris, Marvin.   1981. *America Now: The Anthropology of a Changing Culture*. New York: Simon and Schuster. An analysis, from an anthropological perspective, of current American culture, showing amazing relationships among social phenomena.

Kottak, Conrad Philip.   1982. *Researching American Culture*. Ann Arbor: University of Michigan Press. Another anthropological look at a variety of facets of American culture, this time including the views of college students.

Yankelovich, Daniel.   1981. *New Rules: Searching for Self-Fulfillment in a World Turned Upside Down*. New York: Random House. The well-known pollster turns to analyzing the statistics, noting the increasing trend toward self-fulfillment and self-indulgence visible in American culture.

Female Circumcision: Painful, Risky, and Little Girls Beg for It

BLAINE HARDEN

To Americans brought up during the sexual revolution, exhorted to "let it all hang out" and nurtured by the titillating images and lyrics of MTV, the notion that women demand to be circumcised knowing that it effectively prevents them from ever feeling any sexual pleasure must seem shocking beyond words. But then, Americans are looking at this cultural practice with American eyes: they are guilty of ethnocentrism. Viewed from the perspective of cultural relativity, such an example of cultural dissimilarity will still leave Americans bewildered. But they will be better able to place the custom in its societal context—it apparently fulfills the needs of extremely patriarchal societies—and to observe its universal aspect as a rite of passage much like a confirmation, first communion, or bat mitzvah ceremony.

Hodan Adan, who is 8 years old, feels cheated. Her girlfriends at school accuse her of not being a good Moslem. They call her a pagan. She says she has been unfairly singled out by her mother, a nurse-midwife, in a way that shames her in the eyes of her father, her grandmother, and all her friends.

Hodan Adan wants to be circumcised. She pleads with her mother nearly every day, "When is my time?"

A decade has passed since African women first dared speak publicly about female circumcision, which in Africa is both a ritual and a way to control female behavior. For all who practice it, female circumcision is a rite of womanhood; for most it is a religious obligation, and for many—both men and women—it is believed to be a shield for the virginity of unmarried girls and a means to extinguish the "impure" sexual appetites of married women.

African women now have written a handful of books describing and denouncing the practice, which affects millions of women in a belt of 20 countries that stretches from Mauritania on the Atlantic Ocean to Somalia on the Indian Ocean. The once-taboo subject is discussed in nationally controlled newspapers and on African radio. Official commissions have been appointed to study the issue, and several countries, including Sudan and Kenya, have laws prohibiting female circumcision.

Yet tradition-bound women, sober-minded men and the anxious little girls of this continent, like Hodan Adan, perpetuate the practice.

Hodan's grandmother, a 65-year-old woman who grew up as a nomad near the Juba River in southern Somalia, also nags at Hodan's mother nearly every day to consent to the procedure. The grandmother argues that Somali women, as Moslems,

Source: From the *Washington Post National Weekly Edition,* July 29, 1985, pp. 15–16. Reprinted by permission. © The Washington Post.

have no alternative. Besides, she says, the traditional Somali circumcision—called infibulation, an operation that surgically excises the clitoris, labia minora and inner walls of the labia majora and sutures up the two sides of the vulva—"takes away nothing that she needs. If she does not have this done, she will become a harlot."

Hodan's father, Ibrahim, 40, a college-educated businessman, is not so adamant. Still, he says society gives Hodan no choice. "Yes, I know it is bad for the health of girls. But I don't want my daughter to blame me later on because she could not find a husband."

Specialists on female circumcision in Africa say there has been little reduction in the 10 years in the percentage of African girls who are circumcised.

There is strong research evidence from Sudan and Somalia showing that, except in a few urban and highly educated families, the most severe form of female circumcision, infibulation, is just as common as ever, affecting more than 9 of 10 women. A survey this year in five regions of Ethiopia found that 87 percent of the women surveyed had undergone some form of genital mutilation. It remains common for expatriate African families living in Europe to fly their daughters to Somalia, Sudan, or Mali for the operation.

"I have never met a Somali woman who is not circumcised," says Raqiya Haji Dualeh, a vice minister in the Somali Ministry of Health and author of a book on female circumcision in Africa entitled "Sisters in Affliction."

Dualeh, with other women activists, who have taken up this issue, sees female circumcision as a symbol of male dominance on this continent where women bear more children than in other regions, do most of the farm work, and are considered male property, like camels and goats. Female circumcision, which many Africans believe curbs aggressive female sexuality, helps guarantee male property rights, Dualeh says.

Yet, as Dualeh readily admits, it is women who perform most circumcisions, and it is women who instill in their daughters attitudes that perpetuate the practice.

"Women have internalized this thing to the point where they cannot conceive of anything else," she says. "They laugh when I tell them that most of the world's women don't have to go through this."

"The belief is so deep that even mothers who can see the damage the practice causes them [chronic infections, painful menstruation, complicated childbirth, sexual fear and pain] are hesitant not to circumcise their daughters. The prestige of the family, the future of their daughter in the one most important duty in her life, marriage, depends on the tradition."

Faduma (she says she would be embarrassed to have her full name appear in a newspaper) is a 23-year-old nurse in Mogadishu who was married eight months ago. She says her marriage and her attitude toward sex have been altered forever by the operation she underwent when she was 7.

The operation was performed here in a hospital. It was unlike most of the female circumcisions performed in this desert country where per capita income is $250 a year. In rural Somalia, the operation usually is performed by an old woman, called a *gedda,* who uses an unsterilized knife or razor and sutures the wound with catgut or acacia thorns. The operation is painful (the girl is usually held down by six or seven women) and is often complicated by infection.

Faduma was given an anesthetic and remembers that her operation did not hurt. She had no infection. As part of the ritual before her circumcision, she remembers being lavished with attention and gifts of sweets and new clothes. Her relatives congratulated her on becoming a woman.

As a teenager, she found her period was often accompanied by extreme pain and nausea. A doctor told her he wanted to widen surgically her vaginal opening—which had been narrowed by her circumcision—to permit a freer flow of menstrual blood and relieve the pressure that caused her pain.

She refused. "I was afraid that my future husband might feel I was not a virgin," she says.

After her wedding, Faduma says it was two months before she and her husband succeeded in having sexual intercourse. Those two months, she says, were a time of pain and nightly bleeding.

"I was afraid more of the pain than anything else," she says.

"Whenever I go to bed with my husband, I am afraid of what will happen. There is no thought of pleasure."

The historical origins of female circumcision in Africa are murky. It is known that the practice predates Islam in Egypt, Arabia, and the Red Sea coasts. Some historians trace infibulation, which is common in Somalia, Sudan, and Mali, to ancient Egypt. Anthropologists believe female circumcision may be an ancient African puberty rite. It is practiced by Africans who are Catholics, Protestants, Copts, animists, and nonbelievers.

Although many women in black Moslem countries believe the operation is mandated by the teachings of Islam, Islamic theologians say there is no doctrinal basis for that belief. The custom is not observed in Saudi Arabia, the cradle of Islam.

What is clear, however, is that female circumcision, especially the severest form, is a major health problem for Africa. According to a report by the faculty of medicine at the University of Khartoum, complications arising from the operation include shock, infections, injuries to adjacent parts of the body, and urine retention. Later complications include chronic pelvic

and urinary infections, cyst formation, and infertility. A fertility survey in Sudan found that 30 percent of Sudanese women have complications related to circumcision.

During childbirth, infibulated women must be opened surgically, and afterward, according to tradition, they must be sewn up. Infibulated women often have especially painful labors. According to the University of Khartoum report, these difficulties can result in the death of the child or the mother.

A map of African countries that practice circumcision corresponds closely with a map of those countries having the world's highest rate of infant mortality. Somalia, which is believed to have the highest percentage of circumcised women in the world, has the world's fourth-highest infant mortality rate. A 1984 United Nations Children's Fund report says only half of Somali children live past the age of 5.

In Somalia, as in other Moslem countries where sexual matters are rarely discussed publicly, women campaigning against female circumcision say they can argue against the practice only on health grounds. It would ruin their credibility, they say, to mention sexual or psychological problems caused by mutilation.

"People in this country are not ready for the sexual aspect. I don't think we would get half as far if we spoke of orgasmic problems," says Edna Adan Ismail, a Somali midwife who, in 1976, was one of the first women in the country to discuss the issue publicly.

"Maybe in the distant future we can talk about sexual pleasure, but not now," says Dualeh. "Men are suspicious that the reason this issue has come up is that girls want to do something bad before marriage, that girls will have illegitimate children."

A major justification for circumcision in Somalia, as in Sudan and Mali, is to guarantee the virginity of a bride. Women in Somalia are less restricted in their movement and dress than women in many other Moslem countries. As nomads and pastoralists, they wear no veils and work with men constantly. Infibulation, Dualeh writes, was believed to be "the most effective means to keep the girls' virginity intact." Purity remains a priority in taking a wife, according to several men in Mogadishu.

"As far as Somali men are concerned, they want their girls to be virgins. That is a very important requirement," says Ibrahim Adan, father of Hodan Adan, the 8-year-old who wants to be circumcised. "Circumcision [infibulation] is the only way of knowing that your girlfriend has not slept with another man."

There has been very little research in Africa into how circumcision affects sexual desire in women. Most African women, researchers say, are too embarrassed to discuss the issue. Interviews with nurse-midwives in Somalia, all of whom were infibulated as children, indicate that sexual pleasure is, for most Somali women, a moot issue.

"When I was abroad in nursing school, all my friends talked of dreams for their husbands," says a 33-year-old nurse-midwife here. "But sexual desire I never felt. I missed my husband, but not for that reason. I have never looked forward to sex. It is the lack of sensation."

Europeans and Americans have been expressing shock and revulsion over African female circumcision for at least half a century. In Kenya in 1929, the Church of Scotland mission forbade children to attend its school unless their parents renounced the rite. Two years later, a conference in Geneva denounced the "barbarous" and "heathen" custom, demanding it be abolished at once by law.

But western attempts to force Africans to abandon the practice have been largely unsuccessful. African nationalists, such as Jomo Kenyatta in Kenya, took up the cause of female circumcision as a way of protesting colonial efforts to manipulate Africans.

African women who now are trying to abolish the practice say they, too, find criticism of it by westerners to be patronizing and counterproductive.

"It makes me very angry when I hear Europeans and Americans calling it a 'cruel' or 'barbarous' rite," says Edna Ismail, the Somali nurse-midwife. "I tell these people to be only as horrified by female circumcision as they are by measles or cholera. We need to deal with this as a medical problem, and, as a medical problem, western money can help us educate people.

"There is no quick fix for this. We are trying to change centuries-old attitudes of entire countries. It is a gradual process."

Hodan Adan will be circumcised. Her grandmother and father have agreed. As has her mother, Asli Adan, a nurse-midwife who has seen firsthand many of the medical problems caused by the procedure. Hodan, however, will not be infibulated.

Instead, her mother has persuaded her 8-year-old, her husband, and her grandmother to accept a ritualistic circumcision that will only nick the girl's clitoris with a razor, cause a little bleeding, but no lifelong mutilation.

"It pleases the family," says Asli Adan, "and Hodan will thank me someday."

Becoming Human: Socialization

*I*f one were to look into a hospital nursery most anywhere in the world, one would find a similar picture: rows of cribs or baskets containing infants of indeterminate gender, some squirming and crying, others sleeping peacefully. Careful scrutiny would reveal differences in appearance, but at first glance, the babies would look much alike. Should one meet these same babies twenty years later, variations among them would no doubt be dramatic: not only would these individuals look distinctive but, if engaged in conversation, would display a variety of attitudes, opinions, beliefs, and values, as well as differ in the manner in which they expressed them.

The infants of two decades earlier would have been subjected to two inexorable processes: maturation, or the physical development of the body, which proceeds at approximately the same rate for all; and socialization, or the process of becoming human, unique to the experience of each individual. We might well question at this point whether it is necessary to "become" human, whether in fact people are not born so. The answer, based on numerous instances of social isolation (cases where infants are left alone without human companionship, with only their minimal needs attended to) seems to be that one must indeed learn to become human from others. In this process of learning, we become unique individuals with distinctive personalities.

Personality

People are frequently described as having either pleasant personalities or none at all. But those are imprecise uses of the term; the complimentary description is partial and vague, and the uncomplimentary one impossible, for every person has a personality.

Personality may be defined as a complex, dynamic system that includes all of an individual's behavioral and emotional traits—actions, habits, attitudes, beliefs, values, goals, and so on. It is, of course, an abstract term referring to the fairly consistent characteristics of each individual. Its dynamic quality reflects its continually changing nature as one adjusts to significant events, or to one's perception of these events. Personality may also be viewed as circular; while the roles people fill in society affect their personalities, their personalities influence in turn the way roles are interpreted and accomplished. Finally, personalities are distinctive: each of us is born with a specific set of inherited traits and potentials to which we add experiences that are exclusively ours. Thus even identical twins, with the same biological heredity, may display personality differences based on different life experiences.

Personality: A Social Product on a Biological Basis

Personality is studied by a number of sciences—psychology, sociology, anthropology, and ethology (the study of animal behavior in natural surroundings). Most research confronts the issue of inherited traits versus learned behavior in personality makeup—are we predominantly biological or predominantly cultural creatures? Unfortunately, no easy answers are forthcoming; however, research seems to substantiate the opinion of anthropologist Clyde Kluckhohn (1953, 53) who states that:

> *Every man is in certain respects:*
> *Like all other men*
> *Like some other men*
> *Like no other man.*

In fact, personality development occurs as a consequence of the interplay of biological inheritance, physical environment, culture, group experience, and personal experience. In Kluckhohn's view, we resemble all other persons in that we all share a common humanity and biological makeup; we resemble some others in that we are members of the same society and of some of the same groups; and we resemble no others in that additionally we each claim a unique biological inheritance from a specific set of parents, as well as individually distinctive experiences.

The biological inheritance we all share in some respects predisposes us toward accepting the teaching of others, in the process of which we acquire personalities. Since we lack strong **instincts,** to a great extent we must *learn* how to act to our best advantage. Birds, for instance, know that they must build nests in which to hatch their young, and know instinctively how to build them. People, on the other hand, must learn, through trial and error or from others, that having some shelter is more comfortable than sitting out in the rain; and they must learn how to best build that shelter by using objects in their environment. Though lacking instincts, humans do possess biological drives such as hunger, thirst, and the need for sex. These are perceived as tensions or discomforts in the organism that must be relieved. Methods of relieving them are supplied by one's culture, which represents the accumulated learning of countless preceding generations.

Another biologically based requirement, one which humans share with a number of animals, is the need for social and physical contact that we interpret as a need for receiving and giving love. Repeated studies have shown how infants deprived of loving human contact—those institutionalized after being orphaned, those isolated due to illegitimacy or having mothers with mental illness, or those simply badly neglected—do not develop normally, either physically or mentally. Some fail to thrive and die in infancy; others grow up retarded or otherwise damaged (Spitz, 1964). Although the process is not clearly understood, it appears that an absence of body contact and stimulation in infancy inhibits the development of higher learning functions. In this respect, humans are not alone: our close biological cousins, members of the ape family, show a similar need for closeness and body contact. In a well-known experiment, researchers found that infant rhesus monkeys separated from their biological mothers preferred a soft and cuddly terry cloth "mother," even though she did not feed them, to a surrogate wire mother from whom they could receive food. The infants ran to the soft mother in times of stress and

If this child had no adults to relate to, he could not develop into a fully functioning human being. Socialization is the kind of relating that turns biological beings into societal members with unique and individual personalities.

preferred to spend most of their time near her (Harlow, 1966). In the wild, these animals engage in grooming behavior, thought to be an expression of bonding and of the need for shared activities, a form of social interaction.

The fact that human infants are born helpless and must depend on adults for sheer survival also predisposes their acceptance of learning and leads to the formation of strong human bonds. Finally, the biologically based potential for learning and using symbol systems makes possible and probable their acceptance of the culture into which they are born. In turn, the capacity for language makes the creation of culture possible.

Inheritance and Environment

In addition to the general effects of biology on humans as a species, biology also affects us as individuals, accounting for our uniqueness in both appearance and personality. Just as the inheritance of specific genes determines whether an individual is short or tall, has blue or brown eyes or straight or curly hair, so too heredity determines such characteristics of personality as intelligence, sociability, timidity, and basic temperament (Horn, 1976; Juel-Nielson, 1980; Herbert, 1982). Other traits, such as leadership abilities, control of impulses, attitudes, and interests, depend to a much greater extent on the environment in which one is raised. The effects of inheritance and environment on the personality are so interrelated that it is impossible to measure exactly the influence of either. All we can say with certainty is that the development of one's full potential depends on one's social experience and life environment.

Biological inheritance may determine personality in yet another way. Humans respond to certain physical traits in specific ways—favorably to some, negatively to others—and this reaction influences individual personality. A fat person may be considered beautiful in some societies and thus develop a positive self-image which in turn may result in a self-confident, pleasant, outgoing personality. A fat person in a society such as that of the United States, on the other hand, is not considered good-looking. As a consequence, such a person may have a low self-image and be withdrawn, shy, self-conscious, and unpleasant in interaction with others (an unpleasantness that may well be in self-defense). In short, it is not biological inheritance per se that necessarily influences personality, but the way in which a society and culture interpret such traits.

As to the physical environment, while the earlier belief that personality types correspond to climatic or geographic regions has been disproved, certain conditions in the physical environment may indeed influence dominant personality traits. An individual or population group born and raised in a location subject to continued famines is certainly less likely to have a sunny disposition or be exceedingly generous and unselfish than an individual or group living in a location where food is abundant and easily obtained. One recent example is that of the Ik, inhabitants of a region of Uganda, who, after losing their traditional hunting grounds through political partition, began to suffer profound deprivation to the point of starvation. A previously friendly and outgoing people, the Ik have become incredibly selfish and greedy, lacking compassion toward the old, whom they encourage to die, and snatching the last morsel from their own children in order that they themselves might survive (Turnbull, 1973).

Culture too has a definite impact on personality, in the sense that each society subjects its members to unique societal experiences. This commonality of social experiences causes most members of a specific society to share a particular configuration of personality traits. This so-called **modal personality** is thought to be representative of all members of that society: people speak of the Latin lover, the hard-drinking Irish, the keep-a-stiff-upper-lip British, the punctual German, the arrogant French. While such stereotypes do a disservice to their respective societies, each society, by virtue of its dominant values and beliefs, does develop certain personality types that reflect its culture. In a complex, heterogeneous society, moreover, there may be as many personality types as there are subcultures; witness the Southern belle and urban cowboy familiar to Americans.

Ultimately, however, even in extremely conformist societies, human personality retains a great degree of individuality. In no way do scientists suggest that each member of a society develops or displays all the traits associated with that society. At best, only some traits of the modal personality may be exhibited by a majority of its members.

Socialization: Becoming Human

The process of **socialization** benefits both society and the individual. Society profits as each new generation learns to behave as societal members ought (that is, to the advantage of the group), and the individual profits by acquiring a self and a unique personality in the bargain.

Goals and Functions of Socialization

From society's point of view, socialization has specific aims. First, it imparts the basics of societal life. Second, it transmits skills important to survival in that life. Third, it instills in new members a desire to work toward those goals considered important by the society at large. Fourth, it teaches members how to fulfill social roles, for only when a majority do so can the system continue to exist. Finally, socialization provides each individual with an identity, for we need to know who we are in order to act accordingly.

The process of socialization is not restricted to infants and children. Rather, it continues throughout one's lifetime, as new roles must always be learned and new circumstances adjusted to. But differences do exist at different life stages. Children must learn first of all how to regulate their biological drives in socially acceptable ways. They must acquire such values as will best serve their society's aims. They must develop self-images. Adults, on the other hand, primarily learn new roles on entering the labor force or changing their marital status. The personal experience of socialization thus differs in the two groups. Children become emotionally involved with their socializing mentors, making the process much more effective. While adults are usually socialized voluntarily, the involvement with their socializers, generally teachers or supervisors rather than mothers and fathers, is secondary in nature. Such socialization is less effective, easier to resist, and produces more superficial results.

Socialization occurs on both conscious and unconscious levels. Children are taught certain behaviors, attitudes, and values deliberately; but others they pick up unconsciously through overhearing adult conversations or observing their actions. These unconsciously acquired characteristics are usually much more difficult to shed.

Finally, socialization must take into consideration human feelings or emotions. Fundamental among these are love, anger, and anxiety. Love is needed to ensure normal development. Unloved children become unloving adults, who may display psychological disturbances. Parents who withhold love, respect, and self-esteem risk causing serious maladjustment and stunted development in their offspring.

Anger is the reaction to frustration and deprivation. A chief aim of socialization is to channel such anger in nonaggressive ways. Parents unable to so direct their children's anger most often put up with temper tantrums—the child's own destructive and disruptive attempt at control—and possibly antisocial behavior when the child reaches adolescence.

Anxiety, unlike anger, is neither definite, nor sharply defined. Rather, it represents a diffuse state of mind in which the individual feels uneasy but does not know exactly why. In this respect it differs from fear, a response to a definite threat. Anxiety has been viewed as the hallmark of modern Western societies; some of our values, in fact, are very anxiety-producing.

If socialization is to be successful, these emotions must be handled in such a way that their potential destructiveness to individuals and society is defused.

Theories of Socialization

From the individual's perspective, socialization serves to define the self, a primary step in building personality. The **self** represents the human perception of being an individual to whom others react. Initial realization of this concept attends the recognition by each individual of being a separate, distinct, and different creature. The self—the awareness of one's distinctiveness—emerges as a result of interaction with others.

Exactly how this process occurs is the subject of numerous sociological and psychological theories. The most widely accepted, those further supported by research, are analyzed as follows:

Sociological Theories

Charles Horton Cooley and George Herbert Mead, two pioneering American sociologists, formulated interactionist theories based on the finding that the self is the result of a learning process that occurs when individuals interact with those around them.

Cooley and the Looking-Glass Self   Charles Horton Cooley (1864–1929) speculated that the development of a socially defined self begins in the early stages of life. Through interaction with immediate family members and later with peer groups, maturing individuals learn that they are distinct from others and that their needs are satisfied because they are loved. Essentially they learn how they stand in particular relationships and how other individuals feel about them.

The young human being senses others' opinions from their reactions. If a toddler's parents smile and encourage her to take her first faltering steps, perhaps kissing her and picking her up when she attempts to walk, she realizes that they are pleased with her and her activity. She will continue to try to walk because she now perceives herself as they see her—cute and courageous, willing to take chances. On this basis she determines that her self must be "good" and will continue to behave in such a way as to elicit this parental response. Cooley felt that this process, which he called the **looking-glass self,** consisted of three steps:

1. We imagine how our behavior appears to others.

2. We imagine how others judge that behavior.

3. We feel either pride or shame about others' judgment of us (1964, p. 152).

In short, people continually peer into an imaginary mirror. The mirror reflects back their image as others see it. If the image is good, they are satisfied with themselves. If the image is bad, they feel ashamed and dissatisfied. To emerge and develop, the human self needs this reflecting mirror; that is, it needs other humans who react toward it, although others need not always be physically present—the individual soon learns to generalize others as "they" and to perceive their reactions and judgments in their absence.

Summarizing Cooley's ideas, then, we may say that individuals are born without a self-image or consciousness of self. The self-image we gradually acquire is not static, but continually reshaped into new forms. Finally, because others are needed to reflect our self-image, by changing the people with whom we associate, we can change our self-image as well.

Mead: Mind, Self, and Symbolic Interactionism   The notion of social, particularly symbolic, interaction as the basis of the emergence of self and personality was further developed by George Herbert Mead (1863–1931). Mead is considered the founder of a school of social psychology known as **symbolic interactionism** (Mead, 1934), although the term itself was coined by Herbert Blumer. Many complex ideas are embodied in symbolic interactionism, but all center on the interrelationship of **mind** (the abstract whole of a person's ideas), self (a person's self-concept or self-awareness), and society.

Symbolic interaction, according to Mead, is the first prerequisite for personality formation. Such interaction is initially nonverbal—the infant cries and the parents respond. This sets the stage for more meaningful communication through language. Once language is acquired, mind and self can emerge and actions be replaced by ideas. Mind and self are social products: through language, individuals internalize, or make their own, the attitudes of those around them. Thus, as they think about others, individuals become capable of thinking objectively about themselves. They begin to realize that there are distinctions among I, me, and you. They begin to treat themselves as they treat others; that is, in addition to thinking about themselves, they hate themselves, love themselves, relate to themselves. This enables them to control their own behavior and direct it into meaningful channels. For instance, they become self-critical when others are critical of them. In this manner society acquires control of its individuals.

This uniquely human ability to get outside oneself, to view oneself as others do, relies on the capacity to take on various roles. Role-playing is learned by children in the course of play. When they pretend to be mothers or fathers, police officers or mail carriers, they speak to and answer themselves both in their own roles and in those of the character they are pretending to be. Mead thought that this preparation for adult roles occurred in three stages. In early childhood, or the *preparatory stage,* children imitate the behavior of those around them without really understanding that behavior. In the *play stage* (ages three to four), they gain more understanding of these roles but do not consistently carry them out. During the last stage (ages four to five and on), role-playing assumes consistency and purpose as children discover the roles of other players and their mutual relationships. When playing baseball, each player knows not only what he or she must do, but also the duties of every other team player. This *game stage* is important to a child's development because in a sense all human groups are game groups: each individual has a role in the group and must understand how the roles of others fit into the social system.

In early childhood, individuals take on the roles of family members and of their peer group, those Mead called **significant others.** During the game stage, they learn to take on the role of society as a whole; in Mead's terms, they adopt the **generalized other.** This evolution becomes complete when the child, considering some action, no longer thinks, "Mommy says I must not do it," but rather, "It's not right to do it." At this point the child has internalized—made a part of himself—the folkways, mores, values, and other norms of his society, thereby acquiring a conscience.

Although the self that emerges from the internalized attitudes of others is principally of a social nature, it possesses a more creative, spontaneous element. Mead called this element the *I,* positing that it emerged before the social element, which he called the *me.* The I is the subjective, acting, natural, uninhibited part of the self. The me, in contrast, is the objective representative of the cultural and societal expectations that individuals incorporate into their personalities. The I is unique to each individual; the me is conventional in that it is shared with others.

The importance of understanding how the self emerges, especially how the I interacts with the me, lies in the connection of the self to human behavior. Mead theorized an ongoing conversation between the I and me, a conversation called **minding.** Minding, a kind of reflective thinking, influences action. For example, suppose a student is taking an exam for which she is not prepared, and another student's paper is easily visible. The I portion of the lazy student's personality will suggest that it would be smart to copy the well-prepared student's paper. The me—mindful of the social value that cheating is wrong and of the norm that forbids it—will argue against this course. In the end, either the I will win out and the student will cheat, or the me will triumph and societal values will be upheld. In either case, the result of the conversation, the expression of the self, will have determined the student's behavior.

Freud and a Conflict Theory of Socialization

The best-known name among personality theorists is that of Sigmund Freud (1856–1939). Freud attempted to explain the structure of personality in light of human biological drives. The psychodynamic theories that he and some of his followers espoused rely on a sophisticated definition of the word instinct and assume that culture and society have a definite impact on human behavior.

Freud's **psychoanalytic theory** presupposes the existence of unconscious as well as conscious processes. Unconscious processes result from the repression of painful experiences and reveal themselves in dreams or psychoanalysis. Freud also speculated about the existence of the **libido,** an instinctual drive toward pleasure whose embodiment within the personality is the **id.** Social learning, according to Freud, results in the development of the **ego,** that part of the personality which functions to restrain the primitive, irrational actions of the id. Finally, the **superego** emerges from the internalization of the values and norms of one's culture. The superego operates subconsciously, while the ego functions on a conscious level.

In addition, Freud insisted that personality develops according to a fixed number of **psychosexual stages** during the period from infancy to adolescence. Each stage represents the attempt to gratify the libido at different periods of physical maturation. The stages are (1) *oral,* in the first year of life; (2) *anal,* in the second and third years; (3) *phallic,* or *Oedipal,* in the third through fifth year; (4) *latency,* from age five to the beginning of adolescence; and (5) *genital,* during puberty and into adulthood. The success of the ego and superego in channeling the energy of the id into socially approved activities depends upon how well an individual has resolved the conflicts at each stage.

Freud's influence has extended far beyond the field of psychology, and his theories have given us valuable insights into the human personality. Today, however, psychoanalytic theory is accepted with reservations by most behavioral scientists. A key criticism involves the importance Freud assigned to the early years of life. Contemporary theorists believe that personality, rather than ceasing to develop past puberty, is a never-ending process, changing in response to changing demands.

Freudian thought has spawned numerous theories enlarging and modifying its basic assumptions. Among the works of neo-Freudians, Erik Erikson's contention that human personality development takes place in eight psychosocial stages closely parallels Freud's psychosexual stages. Erikson's phases however, as illustrated in Table 4.1, encompass the entire life of the individual and as such are more compatible with contemporary thought (Erikson, 1968).

Learning Theories

Some theorists maintain that becoming socialized and acquiring a self are basically learning processes. While all animals have some capacity for learning, humans have more than most since they cannot count on instincts to direct their behavior. Questions about exactly *how* humans learn have been answered by behaviorist and developmental theories.

Behaviorism   The theory of **behaviorism** proposes that scientific research can concern itself only with overt behavior, or behavior that can be observed objectively. Behaviorists are thus not concerned with perception, motivation, or unconscious processes. Scientific experiments on animals and humans have

TABLE 4.1

Stage	Approximate age	Psychological crisis
Infancy	0–3	Trust/mistrust
Early childhood	3–5	Autonomy/shame and doubt
Play stage	4–5	Initiative/guilt
School age	6–12	Industry/inferiority
Adolescence	12–20	Identity/confusion
Young adulthood	20–40	Intimacy/isolation
Middle adulthood	40–60	Generativity/stagnation
Old age	60–death	Integrity/despair

Source: From Erik Erikson, *Childhood and Society* (New York: W. W. Norton, 1963).

led to the behaviorist belief that the process governing action is essentially one of stimulus and response. A stimulus—say, hunger—requires a response—eating. How to obtain the food necessary for eating is a task that must be learned by both animals and people. Such learning takes place through conditioning. Conditioning is based on **reinforcement:** reward and punishment. Responses that are rewarded are repeated, becoming a central part of an individual's behavior. Responses that are punished or ignored are discontinued. Of the two kinds of reinforcement, reward is the most effective. Through experimentation, behavioral scientists may, for example, attempt to teach laboratory rats to find their way out of a maze. A rat that heads in the correct direction gets a piece of cheese. A rat that heads in the wrong direction gets an electric shock. Soon, the smart rat associates food with the correct turn and no longer takes the wrong one. According to behaviorists, humans learn in similar fashion; with the right conditioning, they can be made to do almost anything.

Behaviorism holds a great deal of fascination for people. The work of the eminent American behaviorist, B. F. Skinner, *Beyond Freedom and Dignity* (1971) was, in fact, greeted with a mixture of criticism and acclaim. Skinner's basic argument is that society ought to use conditioning to cause people to behave in a moral and ethical manner, and not be so concerned with the freedom and dignity of individuals. The problem with this argument is, of course, that in a heterogeneous society there is no total agreement on what is moral or ethical behavior. Were Skinner's suggestion implemented as law, it would give a small group of people control over the behavior of many.

Sociologists have incorporated aspects of behaviorism into the so-called **social learning theory.** George C. Homans, for example, introduced the concept of *symbolic* reward and punishment. In effect, we influence one another's behavior by symbolic reinforcers. Dissenting sociologists point out that certain learning occurs in the absence of rewards. We learn from our physical environment and by imitating other human models even though rewards are not forthcoming. Some critics question the ethics of conditioning individuals, since such a procedure can easily lend itself to abuse at the wrong hands. In addition, the concept ignores the important human role of free will. Finally, some argue that this view of human nature appears greatly oversimplified.

Developmental Theories: Piaget The **developmental theory** of personality formation originated in modern psychology. Its chief proponent was Swiss psychologist Jean Piaget (1896–1980).

Developmentalists reject the notion that learning occurs only through conditioning or is so strongly affected by such external factors as punishment and reward. On the contrary, developmental theorists stress the importance of individual interpretation of situations according to moral values and intellectual skills rather than according to automatic conditioned response.

Intellectual and moral development, however, can only proceed in stages. In turn, these stages depend on an individual's degree of physical maturation. Piaget insists, for instance, that a child of three cannot understand the concept of speed, regardless of any amount of conditioning. On seeing two cars traveling at unequal speeds, the child will invariably say that the first car is traveling faster.

Piaget designates the stages of cognitive development as (1) the sensorimotor stage, from birth to age two, in which the child cannot understand societal rules; (2) the preoperational stage, from ages two to seven, in which rules are learned but not questioned, although they may be disobeyed; (3) the concrete-operational stage, from ages seven to eleven, in the course of which such concepts as numbers, weight, cause and effect, and other necessary cognitive skills are mastered; and (4) the formal-operational stage, from ages eleven to sixteen, during which the capacity for rational and abstract thinking is fully developed and education becomes the best vehicle for exploring the mind. Table 4.2 outlines these stages.

Developmentalists assert additionally that humans are essentially active organisms, capable of judging, interpreting, defining, and creating their own behavior provided they have reached a certain stage of physical maturation. Thus, while a child of five cannot be forced to reason abstractly, an adolescent of fourteen or fifteen can do so to the same extent as an older adult.

The developmental approach is increasingly favored by social scientists who appreciate its stress on the elements of free will and individual choice.

Although no socialization theory offers a completely comprehensive explanation of personality development, all make significant contributions to our

Piaget's Stages of Cognitive Development

TABLE 4.2		
Stage	Approximate age	Intellectual activity
Sensorimotor experience	0–2	Senses interact with environment.
Intuitive operational thought	2–7	Mental images are understood and remembered; language is grasped and used.
Concrete-operational thinking	7–11	Concepts of numbers, weight, cause and effect are understood.
Formal-operational thinking	11–16	Capacity for rational and abstract thinking is developed.

Source: Jean Piaget and Barbel Inhelder, *The Psychology of the Child* (New York: Basic Books, 1969).

understanding of the process. All stress the importance of the early years in the development of personality: Cooley by focusing on how self-concept evolves from the judgment of others; Mead by insisting that a knowledge of the functioning of roles is necessary; Freud by emphasizing the conflict between individual and society; the behaviorists by pointing out the plastic nature of the individual; and Piaget and the developmentalists by zeroing in on the child's cognitive abilities.

Agents of Socialization

Certain people, groups, and organizations are chiefly responsible for transforming a raw bundle of tissues and nerves into a functioning human being, knowledgeable in the ways of society, competent in enough skills to survive, sometimes to thrive and excel, with features and traits familiar to others yet still recognizably unique.

The Family

Foremost among socializers are those who raise the newborn. Barring unusual circumstances, these are in most societies the infant's parents. Thus most early socialization occurs within the family.

This role of the family in socialization is crucial. First, the family influences the child in its earliest stage of development, when it is most receptive. It satisfies all the child's needs, both physical and emotional. Its influence is constant, most people maintaining their family relationships from infancy through adulthood. The family is also a primary group, with the personal and emotional ties conducive to effective socialization. Finally, the family provides the infant's initial identity, bringing it as a family member into a particular racial group, religion, and social class.

Although parents try to teach, guide, influence, and control their offspring, children are not mere clay in parental hands. Socialization, in fact, is reciprocal. The way infants look and act has a bearing on how parents feel and act toward them. Even the most helpless infant can initiate interaction simply by crying. The infant who obtains a positive response—who is picked up, cuddled and comforted—receives a different view of the world and his position in it than the infant whose crying is ignored.

The School

Second to the family, the school acts as a powerful agent of socialization. As the first formal agency charged with the task of socializing children, the school represents the first link to the wider society: In school, for the first time, the child experiences secondary relationships over extended periods of time. Schoolchildren are no longer surrounded by family members whom they have learned to trust and who offer love and protection; here they must obey strangers who evaluate and compare them to other children more or less

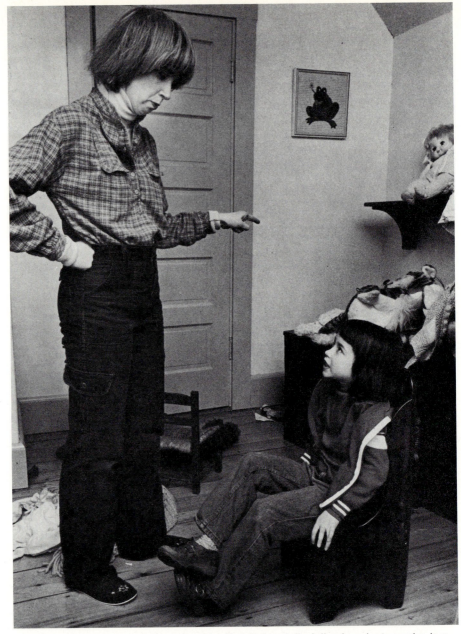

All children must learn a certain degree of self-control and discipline in order to survive in a group setting. Those in charge of socialization, however, differ in the way they teach this lesson: some favor a repressive pattern, others a participatory one.

impartially, not because they are loved and cherished as unique. In addition, schoolchildren must learn not only basic societal skills but the hidden curriculum of how to cope successfully in a competitive environment where they must sit quietly, wait their turn, obey those in authority, cooperate with others, and compete in regimented activities. Excessive regimentation and competitiveness have periodically evoked strong criticism. American schools continue to be hotbeds of controversy (school prayer and the decline in standards being the most recent topics of debate) probably because they are recognized as such important socializing agents.

Many children today are exposed to school situations at a much younger age than in the past. Day-care centers have become a necessity as increasing numbers of women join the work force. Such centers are by no means sufficiently numerous to meet the demand, nor are their effects free from controversy. Many Americans disapprove of them on the basis that the biological mother represents to them the child's best socializing agent. This notion itself is in some dispute: many women seem, in fact, better mothers when their lives are not focused on purely domestic matters. Research too has shown that when children from stable families attend high quality day-care centers (with ratios of 3 to 1 for infants and no higher than 6 to 1 for toddlers), their intellectual development is neither helped nor hindered to any extent, although their ability to interact with others is increased (Belsky and Steinberg, 1978).

The Peer Group

The peer group has become increasingly important in American society, where school-age children often spend more time with friends than with their parents. Socialization within the peer group takes place informally, unintentionally, and extremely effectively. Activities within peer groups tend to be strictly pleasurable, unlike those in school and in the family, which involve work as well as fun. Membership is voluntary, again unlike family or school, and members treat each other as equals without having to answer to those of a higher authority. All these factors explain the attraction of the peer group and its great influence upon the individual. Whether that influence is to a person's benefit or detriment depends, of course, on the particular group.

However, any peer group contributes to the individual's breaking away from the authority of school and family and to the formation of a distinct identity and roles not always approved by school and family. In a classic sociological treatise, David Riesman suggests that socialization in which the peer group is more influential than the family results in a personality type he terms *other-directed* (1961). The other-directed person, unlike his *inner-directed* counterpart in more traditional societies, does not act primarily according to well-defined and internalized standards and values. Rather, he behaves in ways that will make others like and approve of him. The danger inherent in such socialization, Riesman points out, is the creation of opportunistic individuals.

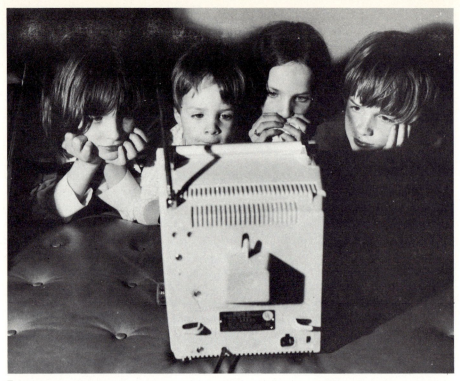

Television has become the most powerful agent of socialization, equaling the peer group and stronger than the family or school in influence. What kinds of individuals is socialization via the tube likely to create?

The Mass Media

A supremely powerful agent of socialization, the influence of mass media easily equals that of the peer group and in many instances overcomes that of school and family. Newspapers, magazines, radio, and above all television have infiltrated every American home to the point where characters from numberless TV shows are more familiar to people, especially children, than any other heroes or villains, past or present. Although the amount of time an individual spends watching television and the quality of the entertainment presented (centering on sex and violence) have been faulted for inciting criminal and delinquent behavior, as well as for decreasing the level of taste and general knowledge of the population, no simple cause-and-effect relationships have been unfailingly established. However, definite factors point to the negative influence of television as a socializing agent.

Television does not reproduce reality as most of us experience it, selecting instead specific areas, themes, topics, and interpretation for presentation. Children may thus easily derive a false idea of what the world, and our life in it, is all about. TV also popularizes norms prevalent among only a small minority of people, again giving the young and unsophisticated a skewed impression of how the majority lives. Even incidental learning—what the audience unintentionally learns as a side effect of entertainment—may lead to distortions and stereotyping.

Television, however, has proven a very effective teaching tool; in fact, its very effectiveness frightens many thinking persons.

Occupational Groups

The role of occupational groups or organizations as socializing agents cannot be ignored. The experience provided by such groups is termed *specialized* or *occupational socialization,* and consists basically of training to fit a particular occupational role: that of clergyman, or labor-union public-relations official, or corporate executive. The successfully socialized individual will eventually display personality traits that reflect the needs of the occupational role: conformity, cooperation, team-orientation, and so on. The importance of occupational socialization makes us realize that the process of socialization occurs throughout our lifetimes.

Socialization as a Lifelong Process: Resocialization

Socialization, in other words, is more than a simple matter of infants learning the ways of their society and acquiring a personality in the process. Since life is a succession of changes in which men and women continually assume new statuses, they must go on learning new roles; socialization thus continues throughout human life. Some changes are so profound as to require almost total resocialization, a radical alteration of formerly held values and behavior. Changes in values and modes of behavior in turn bring with them the need to adjust and accommodate. Certain periods of the life cycle—adolescence and old age, for instance—and crises such as divorce, death of spouse, loss of job, or becoming handicapped also force individuals to submit to resocialization in order to reintegrate themselves into the social system and continue to live a productive life. So complex are the various aspects of socialization that classification into a typology is necessary for easier analysis.

Primary Socialization   Primary socialization represents the basic process occurring in the early years and centering on the acquisition of language, the mastery of fundamental knowledge and skills, the internalization of norms and values, the development of emotional relationships, and the learning of roles. By adulthood primary socialization is complete, and the individual possesses a clear self-image as well as a degree of commitment to the values, rules, and expectations of society.

Anticipatory Socialization   Anticipatory socialization involves preparation for future roles. Playing house, studying accounting, or taking a course in computer programming, as preparation for the roles of parents, accountants, and computer programmers are all examples of anticipatory socialization.

Developmental Socialization   Developmental socialization refers to the expansion of learning occurring in primary socialization. New learning is added to and integrated with existing knowledge and skills, resulting in continuous personality development.

Reverse Socialization   In urban, industrial societies the younger generation often transmits knowledge and skills to the older, a turnabout from the course of events in older, traditional, agricultural societies. In the United States, for instance, American-born children of immigrant families often better understand and feel more at ease in American culture and thus find themselves explaining cultural processes to their parents and grandparents. During rapid social change the same phenomenon can occur with the native-born: young children may understand more about new math or computers or the effects of mind-expanding drugs, for instance, than their middle-aged parents do.

Resocialization

The process of role transition—shedding old roles in favor of new—is sometimes so radical as to require total resocialization. **Resocialization** refers to the acquisition of an entirely new set of norms and values—and the abandonment of old ones—that is necessary when an individual is suddenly thrust into a foreign culture or subculture, is isolated from a former primary group, becomes handicapped through accident or illness, or embraces a new religion or political ideology. Some situations requiring resocialization are entered voluntarily; most are not. In either case, a radical redefinition of one's self-concept and a rethinking of values and beliefs are in order.

The most dramatic instances of resocialization occur when an individual is forced, either by an organization or societal representatives, to alter his former identity. An instance of this is the brainwashing of prisoners of war by foreign powers in order to convince them of the superiority of the alien political system. Resocialization also occurs when society, to protect itself, isolates certain individuals and denies them freedom of movement by containing them in prisons or mental hospitals.

Total Institutions   Prisons and long-term hospitals, as well as branches of the military service, convents and monasteries, prisoner-of-war or refugee camps, and similar places are **total institutions.** In such institutions, individuals live in groups cut off from the rest of society for a period of time, residing and working in a controlled and rigidly structured environment. Total institutions attempt to instill in their inmates through resocialization totally new identities and behavior patterns: former criminals are expected to become productive citizens, drug addicts to become drug-free, and converts to a cult to develop

These people are undergoing occupational socialization, preparing to enter a specialized field. They may be entering a total institution, such as the military, in which case they will undergo a great deal of resocialization.

blind loyalty for their new religion. Toward this end, a definite set of procedures is followed.

First, the individual's current identity is destroyed through the required performance of a series of menial and meaningless tasks meant to degrade, mortify, and humiliate. Individuals are also required to surrender their personal possessions and adopt a standardized uniform; they may even have to give up their name and be called by a number. Next they are taught to adhere to the privilege system by being punished for breaking any norms that govern the group and rewarded for compliance with the inmate system and obedience to the authority of its staff (Goffman, 1961).

Through such procedures, and in extreme cases through additional brainwashing techniques, individuals can be made to deny former personalities and take on those assigned by the total institution. However, evidence shows that even under conditions of extreme stress some individuals cling stubbornly to their old identities, refusing to take on the new. We must conclude, then, that some aspects of personality are susceptible to alteration in some individuals, but other aspects, or other individuals, are resistant to change.

Socialization: Successes and Failures

Socialization is a crucial process that enables humans to develop into functioning members of a social system. Nevertheless, the procedure is not always accomplished successfully. Perhaps this is as it should be, for otherwise we would be carbon copies of each other, accepting unquestioningly values and beliefs of preceding generations which are often subsequently proved wrong.

As may be readily observed, a totally harmonious adjustment of individual to society does not exist. Some people are outrightly hostile to societal values and norms, defying them frequently. Most others are only partially in conflict, occasionally differing on or disobeying societal norms. One criticism sociologists make of the socialization process is the unreasonable emphasis placed on successful integration of the individual and society. According to sociologist Dennis Wrong, (1) socialization cannot be perfect since many people feel coerced by society into doing things they would rather not do; (2) socialization can never totally eradicate certain inherited traits, nor can our basic drives always be easily channeled into socially acceptable behavior; (3) experiences of past socialization are not simply totaled up but are integrated differently within each individual's personality; (4) socialization is often contradictory, and the roles we are called on to play conflicting; the individual must therefore still face decisions and choose courses of action; and (5) in spite of socialization, we all violate some norms at some time, and many of us feel impelled to march to a different drummer, sometimes with positive, even spectacular results (Wrong, 1961). In short, the human animal should never be underestimated.

The Chapter in Brief

Personality is an abstract term denoting a dynamic system that includes all of an individual's behavioral and emotional traits—attitudes, values, beliefs, habits, goals, actions, etc. Personality develops on the basis of (1) a unique genetic heredity; (2) a unique physical environment; (3) socialization into a shared culture; (4) common, or group, experiences; and (5) unique, or individual experiences.

Biology plays an important role in personality formation. Each individual is born with specific inherited physical and temperamental traits to which others in the society react. More importantly, all humans are born with certain biological drives and needs which they must learn to satisfy in socially approved ways. **Socialization** is the process by which they learn to do so. In the bargain, the individual develops a **self** and personality.

Sharing a unique physical environment, being socialized into a shared culture, and sharing common experiences leads to the creation of a **modal personality,** representative of a particular society, even though in some aspects the modal personality is a stereotype.

Humans are predisposed by biology toward accepting socialization. They lack **instincts** and must learn how to behave to their best advantage. They need to be physically touched and loved by others. As infants, they are totally helpless requiring the ministrations of others for sheer survival.

Socialization involves learning how to act as humans and members of a society. It is a process advantageous both to the individual and to society. The individual acquires a self and learns how to satisfy innate biological drives. Society teaches individuals to play roles that will allow the perpetuation of that society.

Cooley sees socialization as a process involving a **looking-glass self** supplied to the individual by others and used accordingly in judging one's self. Mead insists on the need for symbolic interaction with others and on the necessity of learning a variety of roles and determining their complementary nature. Freud's **psychoanalytic theory** stresses the importance of **psychosexual stages** of development from infancy to adolescence and the resolution of the struggle between **id, ego,** and **superego. Behaviorism** views socialization as a conditioning learning experience using **reinforcement,** in which rewarded experiences are repeated and punished behavior abandoned. And Piaget's **developmental theory** speculates that intellectual and moral development proceeds in stages according to the individual's physical maturation.

The principal agents of socialization include the family, the school, the peer group, and increasingly the mass media. In traditional societies, the family is the most important socializing agent. In technologically advanced societies, the peer group usurps this function, particularly during adolescence, leading to the potentially socially damaging creation of opportunistic individuals. The danger of the mass media as a socializing agent lies in its presentation of an unrealistic and selective view of the world.

Socialization is a continuing process as individuals learn to fulfill new roles befitting new statuses acquired throughout the life cycle. In some cases, new roles require that old patterns of behavior and old identities be completely abandoned. This process is called **resocialization** and is used most frequently when the individual enters a **total institution** such as the military service, a prison, or a mental hospital. Resocialization occurs in two stages, the first being one in which the individual is humiliated and degraded, and the second in which he is punished or rewarded according to whether he obeys or disobeys the rules and the authority of the institutional staff.

Socialization is never perfect, and perhaps should not be. While a society needs fairly disciplined members to ensure its continuation and avoid chaos and disorganization, it must allow sufficient personal freedom to avoid creating totally conforming robots.

Terms to Remember

Behaviorism   Theories of personality formation based on the speculation that behavior is the result of a type of learning called conditioning, a process involving rewards and punishment.

Developmental theories   A school of thought in modern psychology whose chief exponent was Jean Piaget. Developmentalists hold that personality development proceeds in stages dependent on physical maturation (sensorimotor, preoperational, and concrete- and formal-operational).

Ego   (Freud) That part of the personality functioning on a conscious level. The ego attempts to force the id to satisfy its instinctual needs in socially acceptable ways.

Generalized other   (Mead) The individual's perception or awareness of social norms; learning to take into consideration the role of others with whom one interacts, or society as a whole.

Id   (Freud) The representative of the libido in the personality, existing on an unconscious level as the primitive, irrational part of the personality.

Instincts   Genetically transmitted, universal, complex patterns of behavior.

Libido   (Freud) The instinctual drive toward pleasure which is the motivating energy behind human behavior.

Looking-glass self   (Cooley) The process of personality formation in which an individual's self-image emerges as the result of perceiving the observed attitudes of others.

Mind   (Mead) The abstract whole of a person's ideas.

Minding, or reflective thinking   (Mead) The conversation between the I and the me, components of the self; ultimately, minding influences behavior.

Modal personality   A personality type representative of all members of a society resulting from common social experiences.

Personality   A complex and dynamic system that includes all of an individual's behavioral and emotional traits, attitudes, values, beliefs, habits, goals, and so on.

Psychoanalytic theory   A theory of personality developed by Sigmund Freud. It assumes the existence of unconscious as well as conscious processes within each individual.

Psychosexual stages   (Freud) The manner in which individuals attempt to gratify the force of the libido at different periods of physical maturation. The phases are oral, anal, phallic (or Oedipal), latent, and genital.

Reinforcement   The use of rewards and punishments to achieve a desired behavior.

Resocialization   A process in which the individual's existing self-concept and identity are erased in favor of a new personality more in keeping with the requirements of a total institution.

Self   (Mead) The individual's self-conception, or self-awareness.

Significant others   (Mead) Important people in an individual's life whose roles are initially imitated.

Socialization   The learning process by which a biological organism becomes a human being, acquires a personality with self and identity, and absorbs the culture of its society.

Social learning theory A sociological approach to personality formation, introduced by George C. Homans, incorporating aspects of behaviorism as well as the concept of symbolic rewards and punishments.

Superego (Freud) A final element of personality existing largely on an unconscious level and functioning to impose inhibition and morality on the id.

Symbolic interactionism A school of thought founded by George Herbert Mead whose theories center on the interrelationship of mind, self, and society and include the belief that society and the individual influence each other through symbolic interaction.

Total institution An organization or place of residence where inmates live isolated from others and freedom is restricted. The staff of total institutions attempts to resocialize the individual through degradation and the privilege system.

Suggestions for Further Reading

Elkin, Frederick and Gerald Handel. 1984. *The Child and Society,* 4th ed. New York: Random House. The latest information from the fields of psychology, sociology, and sociobiology on early childhood socialization, presented in a readable style.

Lewontin, R. C., Steven Rose, and Leon J. Kamin. 1984. *Not In Our Genes: Biology, Ideology, and Human Nature.* New York: Pantheon. Proponents of the "nurture" factor in the "nature versus nurture" controversy present a critical examination of sociobiology, concluding that it is at best speculative.

Wilson, Edward O. 1984. *Biophilia: The Human Bond to Other Species.* Cambridge, Mass.: Harvard University Press. The leading sociobiologist of our era presents the "nature" point of view of the nature–nurture controversy.

What Shapes the Child?

Sharon Begley

The exact process that turns infants into either upstanding citizens or mass killers has never been completely understood; nonetheless, it remains a source of fascination for behavioral scientists, since the payoff for such discovery would be tremendous: if we could learn how to produce perfect human specimens, we could create a utopian world society where people would easily recognize their brotherhood. Unfortunately, the more we delve into personality development, the more we realize how impossible the task of controlling the innumerable variables would be. Still, the search for knowledge goes on. Jerome Kagan's psychological approach yields interesting

Source: From *Newsweek,* October 1, 1984, p. 95. Copyright © 1984 by Newsweek, Inc. All Rights Reserved. Reprinted by permission.

notions regarding child development: it stresses the importance of physical maturation, and posits that morality originates in emotions.

When Genie was 13 1/2, she was rescued from a home where she had been isolated from other people and subjected to more than a dozen years of repeated beatings. She was malnourished, apparently unable to speak or understand words and could not even stand erect. But four years later she had learned social skills, was taking a bus to school and scored close to average on some IQ tests. While not a typical California 18-year-old, Genie is slowly shaking off the effects of the abuse she suffered in childhood.

That Genie was not necessarily condemned to a life of bitterness and failure by her early experiences confounds some of the most cherished ideas of human development. Ever since Swiss psychologist Jean Piaget chronicled the smooth progression of the young mind from one stage to another, "connectedness" has been the paradigm of development. Parents have been bombarded with warnings that while a happy, successful future awaits the energetic and smiling four-month-old, there is trouble ahead for the cranky or unloved infant. But now, in a provocative assault on this and other dogmas of development, Harvard University psychologist Jerome Kagan argues that the past is not necessarily a prelude. In "The Nature of the Child," he takes issue with the idea that parents, by the right combination of love and firmness, of mobiles and music, forever set the course of their child's life. Instead, he claims, an equally important factor is biology. "In the first years of life," says Kagan "most of the major changes" from the blossoming of emotions to the emergence of a principled morality "depend on the maturation of the brain."

Scowling Because the organization of the brain grows steadily more complex for some months after birth, the traits of the infant are being constantly reshaped. Kagan notes that in one survey of children in Boston, for instance, psychologists measured how attentive, irritable, active, and likely to smile, four-month-olds were, and found that these behaviors changed through the first three years of life—a scowling baby did not always become a scowling toddler. Nor did such qualities as attentiveness, which supposedly foreshadows intelligence, predict how smart or good at reading the children would be at 10. One reason is that the child "is remarkably plastic," Kagan writes. A behavior persists only if parents and playmates encourage it and if the environment that bred it stays the same—which is why—abused children moved to loving homes may become healthy, happy adults.

One trait, however, shows exceptional persistence: shyness. Kagan's own studies have shown that 10 percent of children seem to be born with a biological tendency toward sociability, while an equally small percentage seem naturally introverted. These characteristics show themselves early: infants who stop playing when a stranger enters the room frequently remain restrained and watchful as adolescents. These children are also more vulnerable to stress: strange sights or sounds make their hearts beat faster. Kagan speculates that these traits are rooted in the involuntary nervous system, which controls stress, and could be determined either by genetics or by the influence of maternal hormones on the fetus. As a result, some children have a lower threshold for arousal and so try to avoid anxiety. They therefore seem shy and tend to avoid pressure-cooker occupations like air-traffic controller or trial lawyer.

Other traits, too, rest more on biology than on experience. As the prefrontal cortex develops through the first year of life, for instance, babies' memories improve. Only then can infants feel "separation anxiety," crying when their mothers go away, because memory allows the child to compare the mother's absence with her former presence. Unable to reconcile the two, the child becomes confused and cries. Similarly, young toddlers cannot feel guilty over unruly behavior because they are as yet unable to think in the abstract and imagine behaving differently; by four, they have that ability. Since infants in settings as different as American nuclear families and Israeli kibbutzim all develop these emotions at roughly the same age, they seem to depend more on biology common to all children than on specific social environments.

Kagan analyzes emotions so carefully because he believes that they are the basis of morality. The evidence, while hardly conclusive, is quite suggestive. For one thing, little children seem to know right from wrong long before they are able to make rational arguments, but at about the same time that important emotions first show up. They know it is wrong to hit their playmates by their second year, when they are able to show empathy for the distress of others. They try to conform to adult standards because they feel troubled when they don't: one three-year-old who bullied other children and knew that their parents disapproved of this used to pinch himself violently, explaining, "I don't like myself." Since children in many cultures feel anxious or ashamed when they fail to live up to standards, Kagan believes that these emotions underlie the sense of morality.

Furthermore, the emotions emerge at about the same stage of development. "We can count on . . . an appreciation of right and wrong in all children before the third birthday," Kagan writes.

Variety By arguing that biology shapes the child, Kagan does not mean to ignore the influence of parents. "The least impeachable principle" in development, he writes, is that exposing a child to a rich variety of sight and sound and experience promotes the fullest development of thought and intelligence. But other do's and don't's in the canon of child-rearing are more ambiguous. For one thing, the way a child interprets a parental action is more important than the action itself: yelling at children will produce hurt or not depending on whether they realize it is for their own good (which they can do by three). "Rarely will there be a fixed consequence of any single event . . . or special set of family conditions," Kagan writes. "The Nature of the Child" thus carries a reassuring message, arguing as it does that a "mistake" in rearing the infant will not necessarily doom the child. Obviously Kagan hasn't written the last word in the controversial arena of child development. But it is hard to argue with his conclusion: although parents exert a subtle and complex influence, a child's destiny can be equally shaped by experience outside the home and inside the unfolding mind.

Deviance and Deviants

*M*ost urban Americans are familiar with the daily ritual of returning home from work in rush-hour traffic. The scenario is similar in every city of a certain size. A seemingly endless procession of cars winds its way slowly down the road. Drivers creep forward a few feet, then step on their brakes as cars in front of them come to a halt. At an agonizingly slow pace, a traffic light changes color, allowing a limited number of cars to proceed across an intersection or turn off onto a secondary road.

This familiar activity, boring and irritating and dreaded by most, illustrates two important aspects of societal life: (1) people in a society share common norms; and (2) people (at least most) obey those norms and trust others to obey them.

In this instance, the common norm is the command (transmitted by the symbol of the traffic light) to stop on red and proceed on green. This norm is so well ingrained that most drivers will stop on red even in the wee hours of the morning, unobserved by any other living soul. And trust is exhibited by motorists who proceed with the green, as well as pedestrians crossing the street, sure in their belief that those who have the red light will unfailingly stop. Should this trust be betrayed and the motorist fail to stop, catastrophe would result. Cars would collide and pedestrians face injury or death. The orderly flow of vehicles and people would have been disrupted, substituted by temporary chaos.

Social Control

Most of the time, individuals can be trusted to follow social rules and avoid chaotic situations. However, no society could exist for long if it left the maintenance of order to the goodwill of its members alone. A much stronger force is required to make each individual *want* to act to the advantage of the whole society, and not just his or her own benefit. As was pointed out in Chapters 2 and 3, human life thrives only in societies able to provide a certain degree of order. In turn, order in society is promoted by adherence to norms and fulfillment of roles learned in the process of socialization.

As has also been noted, however, socialization is never entirely successful; a society must always attempt to condition its members to want to act in ways that will allow the society to prosper (Fromm, 1944).

Most individuals do sufficiently internalize the norms and values of their cultural and subcultural groups, incorporating them into their self-concept and self-identity, and thus ensuring they do not grow up to be murderers, thiefs, and rapists. Indeed most members of a society will resist murdering, stealing, and raping not out of fear of punishment but because they believe these actions to be wrong.

But societies cannot depend on the process of socialization alone to accomplish this internalization. As discussed in Chapter 3, social control is supported by a system of sanctions: informal and formal, positive and negative, exercised by members of both primary and secondary groups. Positive sanctions are represented by the praise, smiles, and compliments we receive from members of our primary group, or promotions, medals, and commendations received from secondary ones. Negative sanctions are the frowns, sneers, and disappointed or embarrassed looks of family and friends, or the loss of jobs, expulsion from school, or arrest meted out by secondary group members.

Internalized norms and the network of informal sanctions keep most societal members in line most of the time. For a minority in every society, however, neither internalized norms in the form of self-control nor informal sanctions suffice to induce conformity. Even formal negative sanctions, including the ultimate one of force, may be insufficient to prevent certain individuals from breaking certain norms. (By the same token, norms unpopular with the majority, even when formally enforced, must eventually be repealed. This was the case with Prohibition, and may be the fate of the 55-mile-per-hour speed limit.)

Those who break rules, particularly important social norms, are termed deviant. Sociologists try to determine why some individuals remain generally conformist while others become deviant in various ways.

Deviance

The term **deviance** has immediately negative connotations; when we hear *deviant,* we think *bad.* This is a common erroneous perception, for the term simply denotes a departure from social norms, or behavior that does not conform to these norms. By this definition, Joan of Arc was certainly deviant, for it was against the social norms of the time for women to lead armies into battle. Yet, she has been viewed by history not as a villain but as a heroine and a saint.

Nonetheless, "departure from social norms" is too broad a definition of deviance. There are many gradations of norms; while violation of a folkway may be informally sanctioned, it would make little sense to call the violator deviant (wearing a slinky dress to church will occasion condemning looks, perhaps even an invitation to leave, but it does not constitute deviance).

To make matters more confusing, we must note that even in instances of universally held mores, deviance is relative. Killing is a universal taboo, prohibited by both society and religions. Yet exceptions exist to the proscription: in time of war, as self-defense, or in defense of one's family, killing is not only permitted but encouraged, sometimes even rewarded.

Certain other departures from social norms cannot be termed deviant. Some individuals are able to do calculus at six and graduate from college at fourteen.

Mozart was composing splendid music before he was out of his teens. Such people are statistical rarities whom we admire; they are not deviants. On the other hand, individuals who are statistical rarities due to defects or handicaps—those afflicted with dwarfism or born with obvious malformations or abnormalities—tend to be viewed as deviant. Thus it is the departure from social norms that is perceived negatively by a majority of people that is considered deviant.

The perception of a single act as deviant or not may depend upon who performs it. A small child who finds a gun and discharges it fatally into a passerby would hardly be considered a murderer. And a white-collar crime like embezzling, committed by a respectable banker, is condemned but punished more lightly and considered less deviant than the same act committed by an unemployed drifter who uses violent means.

Distinctions must also be made between nonconforming behavior prompted by ideological convictions and aberrant behavior engaged in out of greed or for personal gain. A person arrested for obstructing access to a nuclear power plant cannot be placed in the same category of deviance as someone arrested for hitting an elderly man on the head and stealing his social-security check.

The Relative Nature of Deviance

As demonstrated, deviance can be neither easily defined nor pointed out with assurance. In the past—and in some cases even today—people tended to endorse more absolutist views, believing that social norms were clear-cut and

In a heterogeneous society such as that of the United States, there exist numerous subcultural and countercultural groups deviant in a variety of ways—like these punk rock fans.

The life-style of this homeless person conflicts with the norms and expectations of a majority of Americans.

certain types of behavior obviously deviant. Moralists among the American population still cling to the notion that deviants are immoral, antisocial sinners. The medical view which speculates that societies, like individuals, are healthy and deviance evidence of disease is also still widely held.

Social scientists and those who approach human behavior scientifically admit the ambiguity of the term and stress its relativity. Deviance varies according to the circumstances, time, place, age, and mental health of the individual, even to the social status of both deviant and the defining observer. The relative nature of deviance is particularly apparent in extremely heterogeneous societies, such as that of the United States, comprising large numbers of subcultural and occasional countercultural groups.

Definition   Once the relative nature of deviance is acknowledged, its definition may be expanded. From the perspective of relativity, no person or act is deviant in and of itself. A person or behavior becomes deviant when defined so by an external majority. Deviance, then, may be redefined as traits or behavior that conflict with significant social norms and expectations and are thus judged negatively by most members of a society.

Functions of Deviance

It seems odd to attribute functions to deviance and deviants, yet neither it nor they are altogether disruptive to society. It has been said in fact that if deviants did not exist, societies would have to invent them.

Reinforcement of Group Norms

Deviants become examples of how not to be and their behavior a model of how not to act. Thus, deviants help to define the boundaries of permissible behavior. They are clearly differentiated and pitted against conforming members of society, who can then feel self-righteous and united in their contempt. In other words, the example of deviants and the punishment meted out to them reaffirms the existing norms of the group, serving as warnings not to stray too far from the straight and narrow. Group cohesion is enhanced as members reassert common values and are reassured in the conviction that they are worth preserving. The example of deviance makes conformance to norms seem more desirable, especially if the deviant act is punished. Paradoxically, deviance may thus add to the stability of society: "Deviance cannot be dismissed simply as behavior which disrupts stability in society, but may itself be, in controlled quantities, an important condition for preserving stability" (Erikson, 1964, 15).

Adaptation to Social Change

Deviance serves another important function as a contributor to social change. Social change is a constant of life in societies, especially in those that are technologically advanced. Thus the acquisition of new norms and the abandonment of old ones becomes imperative. Some of these new norms may actually emerge from the deviant activities of a minority.

The first individual who challenges the status quo or attempts an unprecedented action is usually considered deviant. For example, the women who first picketed the White House and staged demonstrations in their attempt to win suffrage were no doubt considered deviant: they showed an interest in matters outside their sphere (they were out on the streets instead of at home caring for their husbands and children), creating disturbances, slowing traffic, and generally making nuisances of themselves. And yet, had they not acted in this deviant manner, women of today would still be unable to vote. These "deviant" women, then, contributed to social change and in the process helped make universal suffrage a common value of our society.

Attempts to Explain Deviance

Good and evil have often been proclaimed two sides of the same coin, existing in equal measure in all human beings. Because good is understood by most as that which ultimately benefits the individual and the group, acting in conformity with group norms is not generally questioned. What *is* questioned is why certain individuals break the rules.

Explanations of deviance have existed from earliest times, couched in the idiom and philosophy of different eras. Most religions approach deviance as sin: in Judeo-Christian terms, the breaking of God's commandments. These days, psychologists search within the individual for causes of deviance, while sociologists seek explanations in the interaction of groups. Sociological theories run the gamut from stress on the deviant person to social and cultural factors that may themselves provoke deviant behavior.

Biological Explanations

The instinctive fear inspired by threatening individuals is explored in the theories of Cesare Lombroso, an Italian criminologist who believed that deviance was linked to inborn, genetically transmitted traits (1911). Convinced that his ideas could be supported by scientific research, Lombroso described and measured traits he attributed to a "criminal" type: a jutting jaw, red hair, a sparse beard, and insensitivity to pain. Despite the initial popularity of these theories, it later became apparent that such traits appeared as frequently among the noncriminal population as among the criminal.

In the United States, psychologist William Sheldon revived a version of the theory by claiming that body structure was related to personality. Sheldon classified people into **endomorphs,** with soft, round bodies and social, easygoing, self-indulgent personalities; **mesomorphs,** with muscular, agile bodies and restless, energetic, insensitive personalities; and **ectomorphs,** with thin, delicate bodies, and introspective, sensitive, nervous, artistic personalities (1940). In a later study, Sheldon revealed a disproportionate representation of mesomorphs among a sample of delinquent boys (1949), a finding subsequently expanded by behavioral scientists Eleanor and Sheldon Glueck (1956). The latter, however, were careful to add that body type *in addition* to other traits and experiences probably predisposed certain people to deviance.

This was a very important qualification. In fact, body type per se is less likely to predispose one to specific behavior as how others react to this type, and how that reaction reflects on one's self-image. A small individual, called Shorty by others in a ridiculing, denigrating way, may well acquire a poor self-image and choose to strike back at his tormentors in ways that may be termed deviant. On the other hand, a thin, fragile youth is unlikely to be invited to join a juvenile gang, or an overweight one to become a cat burglar. Thus, body type is likely to be only indirectly linked to behavior.

Another biological explanation of deviance focuses on the genetics of sex chromosomes. In a normal male, these consist of an X and a Y; in a normal female the sex genes carry two X chromosomes. Certain individuals, however, are born with more than their share of chromosomes: *XXY, XYY,* and so on. A study of male patients with an *XYY* chromosome configuration revealed that they were taller than average, tended to be severely psychopathic, and appeared more often in criminal than in noncriminal groups (Owen, 1972). Here, too, however, it is possible that the deviance is caused more by the warped self-image of an extremely tall, ungainly looking male than by any specific effects of the extra chromosome.

Psychological Explanations

Psychological explanations of deviance have become popular in this century as a result of the work of Sigmund Freud (see Chapter 4). Freud assumed that humans were born with impulses toward sexuality and aggression, potentially destructive drives that must be inhibited through the development of the ego (which directs people to solve physical needs in socially approved ways) and the superego (a kind of conscience prohibiting behavior the individual has learned to consider wrong).

In the Freudian scheme, deviant behavior occurs when the superego remains too undeveloped to impose its will on the uncivilized and primitive id. Deviance may also result from an overdeveloped superego, which causes people to act in deviant ways in order to bring punishment upon themselves for experiencing drives they consider impermissible, even if inhibited successfully.

Psychological theories resemble biological theories and follow a medical model in their assumption that deviance results from mental defects, abnormality, or illness. This relationship is difficult to unravel: There is little doubt that mental illness may cause behavior perceived as deviant. Once diagnosed, however, mental illness can be used as the rationalization for deviant behavior. Thus alcoholism, drug addiction, child abuse, and crimes committed for reasons other than greed or financial gain are attributed to mental illness. The popularity of these theories is evidenced by the fact that they are used in the judicial system to exonerate certain criminals from punishment.

Yet not all deviants are mentally ill, nor all mentally ill persons deviant. The psychological theories and their variants—that deviance is caused by aggression triggered by constant and profound frustration, or that it originates in unconscious processes having to do with improperly developed superegos or consciences—are very difficult to verify empirically. Moreover, they fail to take into account the relative nature of deviance and the role played by its social interpretations. They focus too exclusively on the act (deviance) and the actor (the deviant), and not enough on the stage (society) on which the latter performs.

Sociological Explanations of Deviance

It may be safely stated that human behavior cannot be explained by any single factor. Sociologists, nonetheless, feel that all human behavior, including deviant, is a product of the social organization in which people live, of the social structures they erect, and of the social processes in which they take part. The focus in sociology is not just on the act and the actor, then, but also on the set, the scenery, the script, and the audience.

Anomie Theory

Émile Durkheim, an important nineteenth-century sociologist and philosopher, introduced the concept of **anomie** in his attempt to explain deviance. His classic study, *Suicide* (1897), maintains that at least one type of suicide (considered deviant behavior in Western thought) is attributable to what he called anomie. Anomie may be defined as a condition of normlessness occurring in individuals when the established rules of behavior are weak, conflicting, or no longer valid. Such conditions develop in times of crisis or during rapid social change, when norms that formerly gave structure to people's lives no longer produce this effect, resulting in general confusion. In short, when norms are strong, people know what to expect and what is expected of them. On the other hand, when norms are weak or nonexistent, people no longer know how to behave, or what to expect from the behavior of others. At this point, anomie sets in.

A society with a high degree of anomie is in danger of disintegration because the cement that holds it together has lost its ability to bond people. When people no longer share goals and values or agree on what constitutes right and wrong, social disorganization ensues, one expression of which is suicide.

The concept has been further explored by Robert Merton who applies anomie theory to a variety of forms of deviant behavior (1938, 1968). Merton, a structural-functionalist, sees deviant behavior as the consequence of imbalance in the social system, or a gap between the goals a society sets up for its members and the means it puts at their disposal for reaching them.

An obvious example may be found in American society, which sets up success, usually translated in economic terms as making lots of money, as one of its most important goals. Socially accepted ways of satisfying this goal are either to be born into a wealthy family or to obtain the type of education which will guarantee employment in a profitable enterprise where one can, by dint of hard work and innovative thinking (or just plain good luck), rise to the top.

Obviously, the first way relies strictly on chance; only a small percentage of families in American society belong to a high social class. The second method also has its drawbacks. Higher education is expensive and requires intellectual ability that is not universal, and even the best education does not guarantee success. Consequently, a substantial segment of the population is denied access to success through acceptable ways. Such individuals may experience anomie, and in frustration may turn to various forms of deviance—socially unacceptable means—in order to achieve the societal goals they have internalized.

Merton classifies various forms of deviance according to whether deviants accept or reject cultural goals or the means of achieving them.

Conformity: The individual accepts both cultural goals and socially acceptable methods of reaching them. Conformity is the only nondeviant response.

Innovation: The individual accepts the cultural goals, but rejects the approved methods of reaching them. A student who wants a good grade cheats instead of studying. A political candidate who wants to be elected blackmails his opponent instead of running on his own record. An accountant who wants to live better than his salary permits embezzles money from his company instead of saving. A teenager who wants a car steals it instead of working to buy it.

Is this drug user retreating from the goals of society and the methods of achieving them? Was he once labeled a drug user and is merely living up to the label? Or did he learn to "do drugs" from his associates?

Ritualism: The individual has forgotten or ignores the goals but out of force of habit or compulsion toward conformity pursues the institutional means of achieving them. This is the mildest form of deviance, exemplified by petty bureaucrats who follow the most insignificant rules without regard for their intent.

Retreatism: The individual rejects both the goals and the methods of achieving them that society offers. Retreatists simply give up, living marginal existences as drug addicts, vagrants, bag ladies, street people, winos, and so on.

Rebellion: The individual rejects both cultural goals and socially approved means of achieving them, but instead of retreating, substitutes disapproved goals and means. Rebels, for example, may create new ideologies in which wealth is no longer a cultural goal. Rather, social equality may be their aim, to be achieved by such socially censured means as revolution.

Merton's theory, although quite general, has been very influential, spawning a number of more specific theoretical explanations of deviance. Albert Cohen asserts that gangs are usually made up of lower-class youth to whom middle-class methods of achieving success are unavailable (1955). Gang members achieve success among their peers by deviating from society's norms to follow the norms of the band. Criminologists Cloward and Ohlin use anomie theory to suggest that gangs supply members with a respectable status they cannot obtain through socially approved means (1960). These researchers classify juvenile gangs into three subcultural groups: the criminal, interested in material benefits; the conflict, involved in territorial squabbles; and the realist, which uses alcohol and drugs to bind its members together. In all three types, members feel they are achieving success in spite of how others in society regard them.

The anomie theory, however, fails to explain all forms of deviance. It does not cover, for instance, behavior such as homosexuality or transvestism. It focuses on society as the source of deviance rather than on the individual. True to its functionalist perspective, it assumes an agreement on values in the society which does not in reality exist to the extent that Merton implies.

Sociologists Simon and Gagnon have also observed (1976) that Merton's conception of anomie originated in a society where scarcity was a predominant characteristic and the sheer difficulty of survival experienced by a large majority. Today, many succumb to anomie even though surrounded by unprecedented affluence. Simon and Gagnon propose a new typology to more effectively explain the sources of deviance at higher socioeconomic levels.

Cultural Transmission (Differential Association) Theory

The **cultural transmission** or **differential association** theory is based on the proposition that deviance, much as other human behavior, is learned through symbolic interaction. As is true of learning in general, the acquisition of deviance occurs most effectively in small, intimate, primary groups such as the family, the peer group, and the neighborhood. Thus the individual in close interaction with deviants learns deviant techniques and rationalizations for deviant acts, as well as developing conceptions of law, property, and human rights from a deviant perspective.

According to Edwin Sutherland, factors that influence an individual's becoming deviant include (1) the intensity of association with others—whether they are friends and relatives or merely acquaintances; (2) the age at which interaction takes place—children and adolescents are more impressionable than older individuals; (3) the frequency of association—the more one associates with deviants, the more one is influenced by them; (4) the duration of contact—the longer the association with deviants, the better the chance of acquiring deviant tendencies; and (5) the number of contacts—the more deviants an individual knows, the greater his chance of becoming deviant in turn (1949, 1961).

Interaction and association with others transmits both norm-conforming and deviant behaviors since both types of behavior answer the same needs and are responses to the same values. Thus, persons involved in business, industry, and politics, as well as those involved in organized crime, create organizations for attaining money and power and learn their behavior through symbolic interaction. Becoming deviant, however, is not simply a matter of having bad companions, but rather a question of choices made in response to particular needs.

One implication of this theory is that a heterogeneous society with a number of subcultures will experience a higher rate of deviance since its members do not share universal values, norms, and goals. Members of the subcultures may feel greater loyalty to their own group than to the majority group or dominant culture, while members of the dominant culture may perceive certain subcultural values and norms as deviant.

The cultural transmission theory has been applied to the study of juvenile delinquent gangs by sociologist Walter Miller, who points out that youths with lower-class norms and values can easily run afoul of the law because of the focal concerns of lower-class culture (1958). These include toughness, or a stress on physical strength; smartness, or being streetwise; excitement, or the need to relieve the boredom of a life limited in its horizons; autonomy, or the desire not to submit to authority; and belief in the power of fate, luck, or fortune. Young people who have internalized these norms rather than those of the wider society feel more at ease in gangs, where they derive support, security, and stability from one another.

The focus of the cultural transmission theory, that deviance is learned, is important. It overlooks the possibility, however, that deviance may be learned from ideas rather than people. An individual may join the American Nazi Party after reading works which espouse Nazi ideology. On the other hand, those who have frequent dealings with deviants, such as lawyers and social workers, seldom learn deviant behavior from their clients, or at least seldom act on it. Finally, knowledge gained from associating with nondeviants can be used in deviant ways. A pharmacist who traffics in drugs for his own gain is engaging in deviant behavior not learned from deviants. The theory thus explains only partially why some learn deviance and others do not; nor does it touch on the reasons specific behaviors are regarded as deviant.

Labeling Theory

A different conception of deviant behavior and how deviants are thus defined is represented by the **labeling** theory, which uses interactionism as its point of departure. This approach emphasizes the process by which individuals are labeled as deviant (rather than specific deviant behavior) and societal treatment of the individual as a consequence of having been thus labeled. Questions posed by labeling theorists include: How does the majority group come to define a specific individual as deviant? How do members of this group modify their reactions and interactions with an individual so defined? What are the consequences of behavioral changes on the deviant individual?

Howard Becker, a sociologist instrumental in developing the labeling theory, maintains that we are all guilty of deviant behavior at one time or another (1963). This *primary deviance* is temporary, unimportant, prompted by curiosity, and easily concealed. Examples of primary deviance include the junior executive who slightly pads his expense account; the exasperated mother who taps her child on the bottom; or the boy who engages in one homosexual experience or tries a single illegal drug. Such behavior is usually not discovered by others, and the perpetrators do not think of themselves as deviant.

Under some circumstances, however, the act *is* discovered, perhaps by parents, friends, employers or employees, school administrators, teachers, or the police. In such cases the perpetrators are on their way to being labeled as deviants. They are accused, sermonized, and often punished in what Becker calls a "degradation ceremony." They are made to feel morally inferior to their accusers and called by such unflattering labels as nuts, weirdos, or queers. Others, in response to these labels, react to the accused persons as if the labels represented a reality. Eventually, the marked individuals come to accept their labels, altering their self-concepts to fit the reactions of others, and begin to act out the roles befitting their new status. Now their behavior is *secondary deviance* and becomes habitual.

After thus being labeled as deviants and accepting the label, the offenders' lives take a new turn. They are stigmatized (pointed out, isolated, and avoided) by nondeviants and forced to seek the company of other deviants who reinforce their aberrant behavior. Being deviant becomes their master status and, lacking a way out, they are well on their way to a deviant career. This effect of labeling applies to past experiences as well: nondeviants are allowed moments of irrationality but not so those who are known to be former mental patients. The latter's momentary loss of control is interpreted as a sign of continuing mental instability.

The Symbolic-Interactionist Perspective in Labeling Theory   In other words, once someone is labeled as deviant, even on the basis of a single antisocial or even criminal act, society's attitudes toward and expectations for that individual are totally altered. It is believed and expected that such a person will continue to commit deviant acts. The tragedy is that such assumptions are seldom false. The labeled individual's life becomes a self-fulfilling prophecy. This is in keeping with the symbolic-interactionist view of socialization as a process in which the self emerges and is characterized by the reflected reactions of others.

The Conflict Perspective in Labeling Theory   Labeling theory also draws on the conflict perspective to explain why certain transgressors and not others may be labeled deviant. The conflict perspective assumes a societal interaction based on a lack of harmony, particularly on the tensions between the powerful and powerless. Thus Becker and other labeling theorists insist that those who possess political and economic power in society are able to enforce rules that work to their advantage. Traditionally, therefore, men have dictated to women, whites to minorities, and the middle and upper classes to the lower. Others who are able to force behavior include the so-called moral entrepreneurs who launch crusades on behalf of some strongly held belief, creating new norms if their campaigns succeed. Prohibition was such a movement that later became a law. Eventually the law was repealed, but while it was in effect, a minority was able to force a majority into conforming at least superficially to the norm of abstaining from drinking alcohol.

Another version of labeling theory from the conflict perspective is even more forcefully stated by Richard Quinney, who maintains that crime in a politically organized society is defined by authorized agents who label any behavior that conflicts with their own interests as deviant (1970). These definitions are amplified by the media and imposed on society at large. Many laws, especially those dealing with theft, embezzlement, and other economic crimes are in reality designed, according to Quinney, to help capitalists protect their property.

In the same vein is Edwin Schur's assertion that those in positions of power or with sufficient resources are better able to resist being labeled as deviant (1965). They are arrested, prosecuted, and imprisoned less frequently than those who lack power and wealth; indeed they are often themselves in a position to impose the norms that define behavior for others.

Others have pointed out that a chief of state who leads a country to war is seldom called criminal, nor is the executive whose company pollutes the environment, yet their actions often effect more widespread damage than many less significant acts for which "deviants" are arrested and punished.

The labeling theory is helpful to students of deviance in demonstrating how only certain people or actions are labeled as deviant by society. But the theory has its shortcomings. Labeling is not always involved in deviance. Many persons who escape discovery nevertheless continue to act in deviant fashion: Are they less deviant because others are not aware of their actions?

Labeling theory also overlooks the possibility that some deviants may be so jolted by the labeling process that they are consequently moved to change their behavior to conform to societal norms (Liazos, 1972). The theory, finally, obscures the fact that even though those in power may in fact define and enforce certain norms that support their self-interested belief and value systems, jails and mental hospitals in this country contain not only victims of labeling, but countless men and women who have committed horrible or gruesome acts against others and themselves.

New Trends in Criminology

A more radical approach to deviance occurs in the work of a number of criminologists who criticize biological, psychological, and sociological theories alike. Neither do they spare the labeling theory, maintaining that it gives the impression that without labels there would be no deviance (Taylor et al., 1973, 145, 269).

New theories emerging from this research focus on the nature of society in light of its attempts to segregate members considered in need of control. From the criminologist's perspective, it is society and not the individual that must be reformed. In keeping with the conflict perspective, these researchers maintain that the capitalist ideology uses mental hospitals, prisons, and juvenile institutions as holding places for those it deems undesirables.

One criticism of these theories is that they are essentially ethnocentric, being based on American, or at best on Western European history. They rely on the experiences of capitalist societies, with no effort made to compare these experiences to those of socialist societies. The capitalist system is consequently blamed for many patterns of criminality that comparison with socialist societies would reveal to similarly exist in opposing economic systems. It seems that it is not so much the economic context that creates such patterns but rather the process of modernization, which has been occurring for the past 200 years in all contemporary societies (Shelley, 1981, 15).

Because its incidence has been constantly rising, crime, the most visible and destructive form of deviance, has lately been a focus of interest for social scientists and the media alike. But any behavior that violates norms can be solely attributed neither to capitalism, nor to modernization, nor to labeling or anomie. Whether referred to as evil, sin, the work of the devil, or deviance, behavior perceived as other than good has been part of human life in societies since the beginning of history. In spite of the scientific method, in spite of all we know about human behavior, no theory has yet been offered which would explain all facets of deviance, nor even the basic question: Why do some individuals become deviant, when others, in apparently identical circumstances, continue to conform to prevailing norms?

Crime: Deviance that Hurts

Although most people equate deviance with crime, the two are not the same. We are all at one time or another deviant to some extent, but not every one of us is a criminal. Criminals, in fact, represent only a small minority in society; it is the damaging nature of their actions that keeps crime and criminals very much on the public's mind.

In most contemporary societies informal social control cannot sufficiently contain such deviance. Formal social controls must therefore be instituted. One type of such control is the enactment of statutes, or laws, that define the actions prohibited as being too destructive to society. Such prohibited actions are termed crimes and are punished by the society through its judicial system.

Crime, then, is any action that violates the law. Laws in turn are passed at a number of governmental levels: local, state, and federal. Laws differ from unwritten societal norms in that (1) they are put into effect by political authority; (2) they represent specific rules rather than informal understandings; (3) they are uniformly applied; (4) they carry specific punitive sanctions; and (5) they are administered through official agencies of a society.

Even though crimes and punishment are thus specifically defined, they too are relative, varying in kind and extent. A distinction is made between criminal behavior on the part of adults as opposed to that perpetrated by juveniles under 18. This distinction is based on the belief that minors are not yet fully socialized (unless they commit an especially serious crime, when they may be treated as adults under the criminal justice system). Another distinction exists between so-called index crimes and those actions defined as criminal by legal codes but not by a majority of people. **Index crimes** include murder (including homicide, voluntary, and involuntary manslaughter), rape, robbery, aggravated assault, burglary, larceny, arson, and auto theft. Crimes that most people ignore range from the prohibition to serve alcohol by the glass to the 55-mile-per-hour speed limit on the nation's highways which American drivers seem to observe only when a police car is in sight.

Classification of Crimes

Criminal behavior covers a wide spectrum. Most crimes, however, fit into one of the following classifications.

Juvenile Delinquency   Crimes committed by minors are on the increase, while the age of delinquents is on the decrease. Almost half of all serious crimes are committed by those under 18.

Social Order Crimes   Criminal acts such as gambling, prostitution, illegal drug use, vagrancy, and public drunkenness do not impose physical suffering on others, but do offend the moral sensibilities of the majority. (There are exceptions: Drunken drivers can become killers, drug addicts can rob, burglarize, and kill, and so on.)

White-collar Crime   White-collar crime refers to criminal acts committed by respectable persons, often of high status, in the performance of their occupational roles. Such crimes include false advertising, copyright infringement, swindling, stock manipulation, price-fixing, tax evasion, embezzlement, forgery, and fraud. These crimes are tolerated more than others since they seldom involve violence and tend not to be committed by seasoned criminals. In sheer numbers of dollars, however, white-collar crime costs society three times more per year than the four other major categories of property crimes (robbery, burglary, larceny, theft) combined.

Organized Crime   The criminal activity of groups organized to maximize efficiency and minimize the danger of apprehension and punishment is collectively referred to as organized crime. Organized crime serves the business of satisfying human desires prohibited by a society's ideal norms and legal codes: Members provide houses of prostitution and call-girl services, direct gambling establishments, supply illicit drugs, manufacture and distribute pornographic materials, and make loans to high-risk borrowers at exorbitant rates of interest.

Crimes Against Person and Property   These crimes, also referred to as the index crimes and almost always involving violence, are consequently the most feared by society's members. In the United States, one homicide occurs every 28 minutes, one forcible rape every 6 minutes, one robbery every 63 seconds, one aggravated assault every 44 seconds, one motor-vehicle theft every 29 seconds, one burglary every 10 seconds, and one larceny-theft every 5 seconds (U.S. Department of Justice, *Uniform Crime Reports,* 1986, 6). The country's homicide rate is among the highest in the industrial world. Murder committed by strangers in the act of robbing or burglarizing is on the increase, although most rapes and murders are still perpetrated by persons known to the victim.

Crime Statistics

Crime statistics are compiled annually by the FBI and published as the *Uniform Crime Reports (UCR)*. However, crimes reported by the FBI, such as those illustrated in Figure 5.1, are limited to 29 categories and focus only on the index crimes. It is believed that since many crimes are never detected and less serious ones may go unreported, the actual crime rate is two to three times higher than reported. Surveys of citizens asked whether they were victims of or committed crimes show a much higher incidence than do official reports.

One can easily determine the sex, age, and race of those who commit the majority of crimes in the United States by noting the figures in the *UCR* and examining officially prepared graphs like that shown in Figure 5.2. According to such statistics, black males under the age of 21 living in urban areas commit more crimes than any other group. These figures, however, are based on arrests for a variety of crimes. Since many crimes go unsolved, undetected, and even unreported, those arrested represent only the unsuccessful criminals.

The Criminal Justice System

While it may be said that deviance performs a useful function in society—by showing the boundaries of permissible behavior, it unifies nondeviants and

Figure 5.1 Although the crime rates shown here seem high enough, it is believed that the actual crime rate is two to three times higher. Many crimes are never detected, and the less serious ones go unreported. *Source:* From chart prepared by U. S. Bureau of the Census (*Statistical Abstracts* 1986, p. 162).

Selected Crime Rates: 1972 to 1984

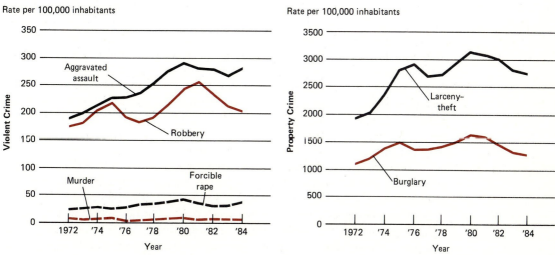

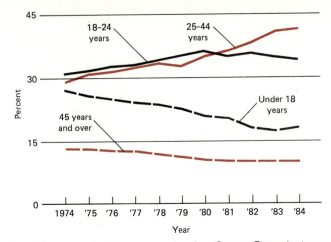

Persons Arrested—Percent by Age: 1974 to 1984

Figure 5.2 Most of those arrested are young and male. *Source:* From chart prepared by U. S. Bureau of the Census (*Statistical Abstracts* 1986, p.162).

strengthens their resolve not to break the rules—deviance in the form of crime cannot go ignored. Humans have always felt the need for justice, generally regarded as the need to punish those who have committed deviant acts. Unfortunately judicial systems—the institutions constructed to deal with the dispensation of justice—are anything but ideal. In the United States, as in most societies, the police, courts, and prisons are fraught with problems, and only seldom is the cause of justice served.

The dilemma that faces a democratic society is how to protect the innocent, punish the guilty, yet still respect each individual's freedom. It would not be difficult to prevent the commission of crimes or their swift punishment if law enforcers could restrict people's movements, tap their phones, and search their homes any time they wanted to. But in the process, the freedom and privacy of many innocent individuals would be violated. To prevent such abuses, the writers of the U.S. Constitution provided a number of safeguards, such as allowing citizens the rights to be presumed innocent until proven guilty and not to incriminate themselves, among others. Law enforcers are thus restricted in their ability to search homes and question suspects. While such procedures protect the citizen, they enfeeble the criminal justice system, which cannot act as decisively as it could in a repressive or totalitarian political system.

As a result of its perceived ineffectiveness, the criminal justice system is criticized by both the political left and right: the latter maintains that it coddles criminals, and the former that the police treat suspects brutally, that the courts convict unjustly, and that the prisons are hellish places.

Are these criticisms justified? Yes and no. On the one hand, it is true that a large percentage of serious offenders are never apprehended, that large numbers of white-collar criminals are never punished, and that of those ar-

These two boys are engaging in primary deviance. If the police officer catches them, will they be on the road to delinquency?

rested, better than half manage to get off free because busy court dockets force many judges and prosecutors to drop charges. The vast majority of those who are convicted receive a reduced penalty as a result of plea bargaining, a procedure in which defendants agree to plead guilty to lesser charges. The result is that only about 5 percent of all perpetrators of serious crimes ever serve time, and of those, nearly 80 percent are released early on parole.

On the other hand, among democratic nations, the United States has a high imprisonment rate. Our prisons are bulging because we apparently jail more people for lesser crimes than do other Western industrial nations. Compare the American rate of 244 people in prison for every 100,000 citizens to that of 32 imprisoned in Sweden and 28 in the Netherlands (Doleschal, 1979). The length of incarceration is also high compared to these nations: murder in the United States is punished by life imprisonment or execution, while in Sweden the punishment is 24 months in prison.

Neither the certainty nor the length of imprisonment seem to deter crime. In fact, prisons are termed "crime schools" where inmates learn how to be better criminals. Rates of recidivism—the repetition of criminal offenses—show that approximately 74 percent of those released from prisons will be arrested again within three years (Coleman and Cressey, 1984). In addition, between 61 and 64 percent of inmates are serving sentences for the second or third time (U. S. Department of Justice, 1985).

Imprisonment, of course, is contemporary society's form of punishment. Punishment is thought to fulfill a number of functions in society. It is done for retribution, in which an offender suffers comparably to the suffering he has caused. It is done for the sake of deterrence, with the goal of instilling fear of punishment in the offender. It is done for rehabilitation, with the hope that offenders will learn skills and develop attitudes with which to lead crimeless lives. Finally, it is done for social protection, meaning that if an offender is incarcerated, he is for the time unable to commit further crimes.

The issue of punishment is one that every society has wrestled with, but one that has not been resolved even with the insights of the social sciences. Although punishment of a criminal makes the noncriminals in the society feel better—in the Durkheimian sense of reaffirming norms—imprisonment has worked as neither a deterrent nor a form of rehabilitation (and even the social protection function it serves is temporary). Societies will have to continue to search for causes and solutions in their political and economic systems, whose inequalities and competitiveness may impel some individuals to crime; and individuals will have to search within themselves for the dark side of the personality that allows them to do harm to their fellows.

The Chapter in Brief

Life in society requires a sufficient degree of order to allow the peaceful coexistence of its members. By performing the roles assigned to their statuses and obeying most of their society's norms, individuals ensure that the social system works.

Norms and roles are learned through socialization but the latter is never perfect, nor are informal controls adequate in large societies to maintain social order. Therefore, sanctions—positive or negative, formal or informal—must be exerted. Of these, positive, informal sanctions are most effective.

Even sanctions, however, are insufficient to prevent deviance. **Deviance** refers to behavior or traits that conflict with significant social norms and expectations and are judged negatively by a large majority. Deviance is relative to time and place, to the perpetrator of the deviant act, and even to the defining agent. Moreover, there are kinds and degrees of deviance.

Deviance performs some useful functions in society: It strengthens nondeviants' faith in the value of conforming to social norms; by unifying nondeviants, it contributes to social stability; and it often heralds positive social change. Large-scale deviance, on the other hand, is damaging to the social order and when allowed to go unpunished tends to demoralize those who conform to social norms.

Explanations about why some conform and others deviate from social norms have been offered by theorists from the perspectives of biology, psychology, and sociology. Biological theories attribute deviance to certain physical traits, or body types; psychological theories attribute it to mental illness or an imperfect development of the superego.

Sociologists offer a number of theories: According to the **anomie** theory, weak or ill-established values and a lack of balance in the social system will trigger the individual to respond with some sort of deviance. Thus if a society sets up certain goals but does not offer the means of achieving them, individuals may respond with such deviance as innovation, ritualism, retreatism, or rebellion. According to the **differential association,** or **cultural transmission** theory, all behavior, including the deviant's is learned through personal interaction in small, intimate primary groups. Juvenile delinquents are socialized into lower-class norms which contribute to deviant behavior. **Labeling** theory examines the process by which individuals are labeled as deviant and their subsequent treatment as a result of that label. Since all people are guilty of primary deviance, but only those who are found out and punished are singled out as inferior and labeled as deviant (secondary deviance), labeling theory (in conflict-perspective terms) sees deviants as victims as well as perpetrators. Contemporary criminologists focus on the nature of society and its segregation of certain members it considers in need of control.

None of these theories can be accepted uncritically; all contribute to the explanation of deviance but fail to explain its existence in absolute terms.

One form of deviance extremely damaging to individuals and society is crime. Crimes are actions defined by law as wrong because of their destructive nature. As such, they are prohibited to members of society, and those who disregard these injunctions are punished. Chief categories of crime include juvenile delinquency, social-order (victimless) crime, white-collar crime, organized crime, and crime against person and property, the most threatening and frightening category. Statistics on crime, compiled annually by the FBI and published as the *Uniform Crime Reports,* stress the eight **index crimes**: murder, rape, robbery, aggravated assault, burglary, larceny, arson, and auto theft. These statistics reveal that the majority of those who commit such crimes are under 21, male, urban residents, and black. Since only unsuccessful criminals are arrested and most crimes go unsolved, undetected, or unreported, these statistics cannot be considered totally valid.

The job of punishing offenders belongs to the criminal justice system consisting of the police, the courts, and the prisons. The functions of the system are hampered by the dilemma facing democratic societies: how to reconcile the need of punishing the guilty without infringing on the rights of the innocent. While some of the criticisms of the criminal justice system are justified, the facts are that that U. S. has the highest rate of arrests and longest prison terms. Punishment, however, whether meted out for retribution, for deterrence, for rehabilitation, or for social protection, has not worked in ridding society of crime.

Terms to Remember

Anomie   Émile Durkheim's term for a condition of normlessness. Robert Merton uses anomie to explain deviance, which he maintains occurs when cultural goals cannot be achieved through legal institutional means.

Cultural transmission (or differential association)   Theories of deviance (Sutherland, Miller) based on the proposition that all human behavior, including deviant, is learned through symbolic interaction, especially in primary groups.

Deviance   Norm-violating behavior beyond the society's limits of tolerance.

Differential association   See **cultural transmission** theory.

Ectomorph   In Sheldon's typology (biological theory of deviance), a thin and delicate body type whose personality tends to be introspective, sensitive, nervous, and artistic.

Endomorph   In Sheldon's typology, a round and soft body type whose personality is social, easygoing, and self-indulgent.

Index crimes   The eight crimes whose rates are reported annually by the FBI: murder, rape, robbery, aggravated assault, burglary, larceny, arson, and auto theft.

Labeling   A sociological theory of deviance that explains deviant behavior as a self-fulfilling reaction to a group's expectations about a member who has been decreed as deviant.

Mesomorph   In Sheldon's typology, a muscular and agile body type whose personality is restless, energetic, and insensitive.

Suggestions for Further Reading

Currie, Elliott.   1985. *Confronting Crime: An American Challenge*. New York, Pantheon. A cross-cultural perspective adds a special dimension to this analysis of the high crime rates of the United States.

Orlansky, Michael D. and William L. Heward.   1981. *Voices: Interviews with Handicapped People*. Columbus, OH: Merrill. A collection of the life stories of a number of physically disabled persons whose disability made them susceptible to the label of deviants.

Schur, Edwin M.   1984. *Labeling Women Deviant: Gender, Stigma, and Social Control*. New York: Random House. A text focusing on the various ways in which women are labeled as deviant in a sexist society.

Schwendinger, Julia R. and Herman Schwendinger.   1983. *Rape and Inequality*. Beverly Hills, CA: Sage Publications. A violent crime against women is analyzed in its various facets of myth and reality.

Simon, David R. and D. Stanley Eitzen.   1986. *Elite Deviance*, 2nd ed. Boston: Allyn and Bacon. A thorough exploration of white-collar crime, or how the rich and powerful carry on deviant activities with relative impunity.

Stalking the Criminal Mind

DAVID KELLEY

Burning at the stake, drawing and quartering, pouring boiling water or oil, stoning: these and many others have been the methods by which the "moral majority" of a society has seen fit to punish its deviants through the ages. Such punishment was predicated on the assumption that the deviants knew their actions were wrong and could control them. The advent of scientific thinking has brought with it a reversal of the way in which deviants are perceived. Increasingly, they are seen as the victims of circumstances beyond their control. As such, it is felt that they ought not be subject to punishment. The conflict between these two viewpoints is explored in the following essay.

Crime is a social problem; in a sense it is *the* social problem, because it breaks the bond of trust that makes society possible. But that's about as far as the consensus on the subject goes. On March 3, for example, the Justice Department released a study showing that 40 percent of the people who entered state prisons in 1979 were on probation or parole for previous crimes—and thus would not have been free to commit new crimes had they served full terms for their earlier ones. The following day, the Eisenhower Foundation issued a report denying the efficacy of punishing criminals and urging that public policy address the "real" causes of crimes, such as high unemployment among minority youth.

These two reports neatly illustrate the philosophical dispute that runs through the debate about crime. If our actions are a product of causes outside our control, then it is unfair—and ineffective—to blame criminals for what is really the fault of society, or their parents, or their genes. We must try to alter those causes, and use punishment solely as a means of rehabilitation. If our actions are freely chosen, however, then society can hold us responsible for them and refuse to indulge the kinds of excuses that determinism offers. Punishing wrongdoers is then a form of retribution, and a way of removing them from our midst.

For more than a decade, the public has been moving steadily into the free will camp. Outrage over the trial of John Hinckley led Congress to tighten the insanity defense. Earlier, in the 1960s, the sight of social theorists fiddling with determinism while the cities burned helped elect Richard Nixon on a law-and-order platform. The crime rate, despite a recent dip, is well above the level of two decades ago and remains high on the list of public anxieties. Politicians across the spectrum have long since learned the electoral advantages of being (or seeming to be) tough on crime, and on criminals.

Determinism is more difficult to resist in criminology, however, where the goal is to *explain* criminal behavior. The most powerful models of explanation we have are drawn from the physical sciences. The social sciences have not abandoned the hope of finding laws that govern human action in the way that the law of gravity governs the motion of a stone, and journalists who set out to explain particular crimes, to get behind the "story," are drawn ineluctably into the search for causes. But the search always runs into problems, problems that arise from the very assumption that criminal behavior is solely a product of causes beyond the criminal's control. Thus to solve the social problem of crime, we must first confront a philosophical one. We need to acknowledge the inadequacy of determinism.

It has commonly been assumed that science is the natural ally of determinism. Science, after all, trades in causal explanations. Immanuel Kant, two centuries ago, argued that the scientific perspective leads inevitably to determinism, that freedom could be defended only by opposing the authority of science. In *Walden Two,* B. F. Skinner claimed that the increasing success of a science of behavior would make determinism more and more plausible. But the progress of science has not borne out Skinner's prediction. The problem is not that scientists haven't discovered any causal influences on human behavior. The problem is that they have found too many.

No category of human action has been studied in as much depth, or from as many angles, as crime. Here is some of what we have learned from that inquiry:

Young males are disproportionately responsible for crimes of violence and property crimes. The Baby Boom partly explains the massive rise in crime from the early 1960s to the early 1970s. But only partly. In some areas of the country, the murder rate in those years went up ten times faster than demographic changes alone would have led one to predict.

Psychologists have found that criminals tend to fall outside the normal range on a number of personality traits. These include some we might expect, such as disrespect for authority and diminished capacity for empathy. But among them are also such unexpected traits as hy-

peractivity and slower response to aversive stimuli.

There is a link between poverty and crime, but it is a complex one. Crime rates are higher in poor areas than in wealthy ones (for violent crimes, at least), and poor people are more likely to be arrested and convicted. But the rates are higher in urban slums than in rural areas of equal poverty, and they vary widely among ethnic groups of the same economic status; poverty per se may not be the crucial variable. There is also some evidence that crime rates fluctuate in accordance with the business cycle, suggesting a correlation, if a weak one, between crime and unemployment.

Delinquents are much more likely to have been abused as children than nondelinquents.

The incidence of alcoholism—and, especially since the 1960s, of drug use— is much greater among criminals than among the population at large. There is also some evidence that about a third of all serious crimes are committed by people under the influence.

When a criminal has a twin, that twin is at least twice as likely to be a criminal himself if he is an identical rather than a fraternal twin. And among adopted children who commit crimes, the biological parents are more likely to be criminals than the adoptive parents.

This criminological sampler, brief as it is, shows that no single factor is sufficient to explain criminal behavior. This should not come as a surprise: no social scientist expects to find a single explanation for any human action. It is precisely the job of theory to explain how various causal influences interact. But this raises another, deeper problem. The factors mentioned above are of diverse types: economic, cultural, psychological, physiological, genetic. It is far from clear how one should go about explaining the interaction of causes at such different levels.

The conflict between free will and determinism first arose in philosophy, and most of the philosophical arguments for human freedom have been variations on a common theme. Because we are capable of self-consciousness, it is claimed, we can focus attention on an impulse or feeling and examine it from a kind of inner distance that can weaken its aura or grip. Because we are capable of conceptual thought, we can evaluate these impulses and feelings—their consequences, their effects on others, their compatibility with our principles—and choose whether to act on them. We are free agents because those capacities give us veto power over the forces that move us.

Determinists have always found this argument naive: science, they say, will show that behavior is governed by causes beyond the reach of conceptual thought and self-awareness. But in the case of crime, at any rate, the trail of scientific inquiry keeps circling back to those very capacities. It would be too much to say that science can establish human freedom. That will always be a philosophical issue. But the old assumption that science is a witness against free will is not true, either—it will not survive a close look at what scientists have actually discovered. Human beings have turned out to be far more complicated than the sciences of man anticipated. We may just turn out to be as complicated as we always thought.

Patterns of
Social Life

PART

Two

Social Differentiation: Ranking and Stratification

overnments proclaim their citizens
to be equal before the law. Religions stress that we are all "God's children."
Scientists assert that all humankind is descended from common stock. Humanitarians lobby for legislation to equalize the life-styles of all members of society, while communist and socialist governments proclaim their achievement of such equality. Philanthropists donate money for the same purpose—or to lessen their guilt for having more than others. In short, the idea that all humans are equal is a common theme, at least in Western cultures. Yet perhaps this very insistence reflects the reality that people are anything but equal.

Even a casual observer on any city street corner can vouch for the existence of inequality. Passersby are unequal in appearance: some male, others female; some young, others old; some tall, others short; some thin, others fat; some light complexioned, others dark; some well dressed, others shabby, and so on. Should the observer manage to engage various pedestrians in conversation, it would soon become clear that some were more intelligent than others, some better educated, and some more pleasant. Our observer would rapidly reach the conclusion that there is no end to variation among people.

The differences a casual observer might notice, particularly physical ones, are characteristic of all life forms. In human societies the way in which these differences are interpreted—the social meanings people give to chance biological facts or cultural traits—is immensely important. Particularly significant is the ranking of differences, and the inequality that results from it. In other words, since certain traits are valued more highly than others, those who lack such traits are unequal to those who possess them. By the same token, since many resources in society are scarce and hard to obtain, those who possess fewer of these resources are ranked as inferior to those who possess more.

Social Differentiation, Ranking, and Stratification

The world is full of examples of inequality: even twins may be born at different weights, giving the heavier twin an advantage in survival. Sociologists do not concern themselves with this type of imbalance. In addition, some inequality is justified: if one student spends several evenings studying and as a result obtains a perfect score on a test, while another spends the evenings at a local bar and receives a barely passing grade, the two are obviously unequal in their commitment to learning and thus logically can expect their grades to reflect this inequality. This type of differentiation also matters little to the sociologist.

Ranking and Stratification

What concerns sociologists is the fact that all societies practice social differentiation; that is, that society members are assigned different tasks on the basis of their different characteristics. As a result, people come to occupy different statuses closely interrelated with the tasks (roles) they perform. Moreover, these statuses are evaluated or ranked, and consequently rewarded in varying degrees. In short, humans are categorized according to some trait— sex, age, race, ethnic background, religion. The trait is then ranked in value, and society's scarce resources—wealth, power, prestige—distributed accordingly. Eventually ranking results in stratification, a condition in which not only individuals but whole categories of people are evaluated on the basis of the traits they possess and rewarded with differing amounts of scarce resources.

All groups, animal as well as human, eventually develop a social hierarchy, or dominance order. The purpose of such hierarchy is to provide orderly access to the distribution of resources, thereby preventing continuous fighting over scarce—and thus especially desired—commodities.

In simple societies, social differentiation occurs on the basis of sex and age. Sometimes, as a reward for special talents, differentiation is also expressed in varying allotments of prestige, influence, and wealth. The Siriono of Bolivia, a nomadic hunting and gathering group, have very few possessions, consisting largely of bows and arrows, primitive knives, and a few utensils made of shells, animal skins, or animal organs. When a hunt is successful, all members of the tribe are given a fair share of the kill, and all gorge themselves. When no kill is made, everyone goes hungry. Hoarding, especially of meat, is impossible without methods of preserving it. As a result, no individual or family can accumulate more food than another. From an economic point of view, the Siriono are all equal, although they are differentiated according to sex and age: men and women, young and old, have different statuses and perform different roles. The most talented hunters, those who exhibit special magical skills, and the elderly whose experience affords them greater knowledge, all hold higher positions in the band. They are accorded more respect and honor; their words and decisions carry more weight then those of the lesser endowed. Thus, even in the simple societies inequality exists: Rewards are not equally divided. This inequality, however, is limited to individuals. It is not attributed to whole categories of people, as is true in more complex societies.

Stratification The more complex societies are, the more unequal their distribution system. Unequal distribution of scarce resources is termed **social stratification,** meaning that the society is divided into a number of strata, or layers.

In stratified societies, ranking occurs on the basis of (1) *wealth,* or the degree of ownership of societal resources; (2) *prestige,* or the degree of honor one's position evokes; and (3) *power,* or the degree to which one can direct others as a result of the preceding factors. Wealth, which includes income and property, is an element of social class, whereas prestige is an element of status. In turn, class, status, and power are the so-called dimensions of stratification. Stratification systems are analyzed by examining each of these phenomena.

Stratification occurs in every society that produces a surplus. A society that produces no surplus gives little opportunity to acquire wealth or prestige, and the power based on them. Stratification is thus intimately related to economics since the layering of people into social levels boils down to attempts to answer the questions "Who gets what, and why?", or "How shall scarce resources in the society be distributed?" Different societies answer this question differently. Consequently, their stratification systems vary accordingly. (The Siriono, for example, distribute wealth equally, but prestige unequally; since prestige usually gives the bearer more say in decision making, power is therefore distributed unequally as well.)

Theories of Inequality

The fact that inequality is so visible—because stratification systems separate people, basically, into haves and have-nots—has prompted many scientists to seek its cause. Most have concluded that some degree of social inequality is inevitable.

The dominant sociological theories derive from two opposing philosophical traditions, conservative and liberal. From the *classical conservative* position, inequality is considered part of the law of nature, the product of humankind's gross selfishness and greed. Inequality is the price societies must pay to ensure their smooth functioning, for greed and selfishness must be curbed by social institutions that promote differentiation. Darwin's biological theory of the survival of the fittest has been applied in this philosophical tradition. Social Darwinists propose that because the resources of society are scarce and people must compete for them, only the strongest, most intelligent, or most willing to work acquire them. This situation results in inequality but at the same time ensures that only the "best" in society rise to positions of power and privilege. Ultimately, this benefits society, for such people provide enlightened leadership.

In the *classical liberal* view, humans are considered basically good, rather than selfish and greedy. Society and its institutions are blamed for corrupting them by making each individual or group struggle for a share of scarce goods and services. The struggle becomes divisive, ending with the dominance of one group over the rest. The dominant group is able to exploit, and once in a position of power impose its will on, the remainder of society. Inequality and stratification are thus unavoidable.

Structural-Functional Theory

Sociological explanations of inequality have echoed classical conservative and liberal views. Intellectual descendants of the conservative viewpoint are represented by sociologists of the structural-functionalist school of thought (see Chapter 1). The **functionalist theory of stratification** stresses the needs of society rather than those of the individual, reasoning that members' needs can only be satisfied within the larger group. The existence of every society depends on the regular performance of specific tasks requiring special intelligence, talent, and training. Societies must therefore institute systems of rewards to lure the most talented, most intelligent, and best-trained individuals to perform these tasks. Positions most essential to the welfare of society, and for which there are few qualified personnel, must be highly rewarded (Davis and Moore, 1945). One may argue that garbage collection is as vital to the health of a society as practicing medicine, since uncollected garbage is a threat to public health. But the task requires little training or talent, and there are therefore many capable of performing it. Practicing medicine, on the other hand, involves long periods of study and training. Not all are capable of undergoing such discipline. There are therefore fewer potential doctors than garbage collectors, and consequently doctors must be better rewarded.

In addition to function, these theorists stress the need for order, stability, and balance in society. A system of stratification, even though it produces social inequality, has a stabilizing influence on society by preventing conflicts among those competing for scarce resources from erupting and disrupting its orderly functioning. (Structural functionalism is also referred to as the equilibrium theory because of its emphasis on harmony and balance.) Finally, functionalists conclude that inequality is built into the social system, since not all types of work are equally necessary for and thus valued by society.

Criticism of structural functionalism centers on the facts that (1) essentialness is subject to interpretation (Is a professional football player essential? Is an entertainer?); and (2) stratification systems prevent certain talented individuals from developing their talents, while other untalented ones receive rewards in spite of their limitations.

Conflict Theory

The intellectual descendants of the classical liberal view are today's conflict theorists. Adherents of the **conflict theory of stratification** argue that inequality is a product of the conflicts and dissensions that originate in people's desire for power. The possession of scarce resources gives the possessor power. Groups struggle with one another to obtain this power, and the group that emerges victorious attempts to impose a stratification system on the rest by enrolling some institutions—religion, education, the political system—to legitimize it. From this viewpoint, stratification systems are seen as mechanisms of coercion.

The best-known conflict theorist was Karl Marx. Marx stated that all history is a record of class struggle caused by unequal distribution of rewards. All societies are stratified, according to Marx, because in every society one group attempts to protect its economic interests at the expense of others. Further, private ownership of the means of production leads to the modern division of societies into social classes. These classes conflict with one another because the owners (the bourgeoisie) have, and want to keep, a monopoly of power over the nonowners (the proletariat). They obtain and maintain power both by force and by instilling a value system and ideology in the masses that legitimizes their power. Once control is established and a system of stratification put into effect, the system is perpetuated through various institutions.

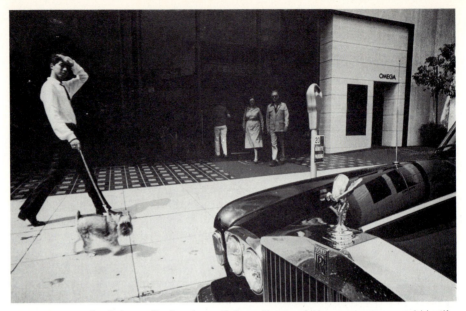

If this were your dog being walked and your Rolls waiting to whisk you away, you could justify these perks by seeing them as rewards for your talent, intelligence, and hard work, as the functionalist theory proposes. But the conflict theorists would point to you as a member of an oppressive and powerful social class.

The family transmits to succeeding generations either wealth, opportunity for education, and prestige or poverty and lack of opportunity. Schools, too, prepare some individuals for leadership roles, others for menial occupations. Religion helps its followers accept values that justify the status quo, encouraging the poor to seek their reward in an afterlife.

According to Marx, even though stratification provides a technique for oppression of one social class by another, it may also serve as a mechanism for developing a classless society. Such a society will emerge when the proletariat develops class consciousness, recognizing its own self-interest and rebelling against its oppressors. In a classless society, Marx theorized, there would be an end to political power and class distinctions and antagonisms.

Marx has had a profound influence on contemporary conflict theorists. His theories on class conflict, inequality as a result of the struggle for power among various groups, and the role of certain institutions in maintaining that inequality are echoed by contemporary conflict sociologists C. Wright Mills (1956, 1959) and Ralf Dahrendorf (1959), who maintain that stratification systems are not necessary for the smooth functioning of society, but simply convenient and advantageous devices for those in power.

Criticism of conflict theory, Marxism in particular, centers on its neglect of two important issues: first, that people are naturally unequal in talent, intelligence, and the work they are willing to expend; and second, that to a great extent inequality acts as a motivating force. The awareness that members of a higher social class enjoy many more privileges and rewards will tend to spur individuals to work hard and develop their talents and potential in order that they too might achieve a more exalted status in society.

An Attempt at a Synthesis

Neither functionalist nor conflict theories of stratification are mutually exclusive. There is evidence that societies exhibit both stability and consensus, conflict and dissension. The two approaches provide different viewpoints of societal stratification, but do not offer definitive causal theories or possible methods for eliminating inequality.

A partial synthesis of these perspectives exists in the evolutionary theory of Gerhard Lenski, who maintains that inequality is unavoidable since humans inevitably differ in capability and intelligence (1966). However, inequality can serve positive functions: in preagricultural societies, for example, inequality was necessary to free an elite of scholars and priests from productive work. But this elite produced technological innovations which ultimately increased the society's productivity and welfare. Increased productivity led to more people being freed from the necessity of direct labor, thus lessening the degree of inequality overall.

Lenski suggests that a society's level of inequality is directly related to its level of productivity: the more productive a group is, the lower its level of inequality. In societies with high levels of productivity, the need for inequality does not exist, at least in terms of consumption. But because it is human nature to try to maximize and perpetuate one's advantages, inequality is unlikely to diminish unless government is willing to restrict the ability of those in power to accumulate wealth. Lenski concludes that wealth, division of labor, and stratification increase in proportion to a society's complexity. (See Chapter 2 for Lenski's classification of societies according to the method of subsistence and degree of complexity.)

Dimensions of Stratification: Class, Status, and Power

All systems of stratification, in any society, share the following characteristics:

1. *Differentiation:* People are divided into and identify with a number of social groups.

2. *Ranking:* People are ranked in hierarchical order according to the amount of wealth, privilege, and power they possess.

3. *Institutionalization:* People accept the stratification system as right and proper.

4. *Influence on individual personality:* People's personalities reflect their position in the system.

At the basis of all such systems, of course, is the ranking of people according to their possession of commodities that are scarce and therefore highly prized. These scarce resources are popularly categorized as wealth, prestige, and power. In sociological terms, as mentioned above, these categories or dimensions of the stratification system are class, status, and power. It is according to these dimensions that individuals are assigned a rank in society and relegated to a stratum with others similarly ranked.

Class

Although discussions of **social class** figure prominently in the media and everyday conversation, most people would have difficulty accurately defining the term. Americans have an especially mistaken conception of social class: most will readily volunteer that they belong to the middle class while appearing only slightly aware of vast differences in life-styles between separate groups. Table 6.1 illustrates how social scientists categorize Americans into social classes based on income, occupation, and education.

Model of the American Class Structure: Classes by Typical Situations

TABLE 6.1

Proportion of Households	Class	Education	Occupation	Family Income 1983
1%	Capitalist	Prestige university	Investors, heirs, executives	Over $500,000 mostly from assets
14%	Upper middle	College, often with post-graduate study	Upper managers and professionals; medium business-men	$50,000 or more
60%	Middle	At least high school; often some college or apprenticeship	Lower managers; semiprofessionals; sales, nonretail; craftspeople; foremen	About $30,000
	Working	High school	Operatives; low-paid craftspeople; clerical workers; retail sales workers	About $20,000
25%	Working poor	Some high school	Service workers; laborers; low-paid operatives and clericals	Below $15,000
	Underclass	Primary school	Unemployed or part-time; welfare recipients	Below $10,000

Source: Dennis Gilbert and Joseph A. Kahl, 1987. *The American Class Structure,* 3rd ed. (Chicago: Dorsey), p. 332. Reprinted by permission.

Definitions of Class: Marx and Weber

As noted earlier, Marx viewed the division of society into classes as stemming from the unequal distribution of scarce resources. Specifically, he maintained that class is determined by the relationship of a group in society to the means of production. Groups owning a large proportion of a society's wealth—particularly the tools and capital necessary to produce it—exert control over groups owning little of either. Groups lacking capital must market their labor in order to survive. Thus Marx's concept of class and approach to stratification are essentially economic. Classes, in his view, are composed of the haves who want to maintain their positions of privilege, and the have-nots who eventually revolt against the exploitation and oppression imposed on them.

Arguing that the Marxist view was too simplistic and that class was only one dimension of stratification, renowned sociologist Max Weber (1864–1920) proposed a threefold approach to the phenomenon, adding the concept of life chances to his definition of class (Gerth and Mills, 1946). Weber defined class objectively as consisting of groups with similar life-styles dictated by their economic position in society—that is, by the goods they possess and opportunities available for increasing their income. Modern social scientists refer to money, goods, and services as *property*.

But property is not the only determinant of class, according the Weber: equally important are a person's life chances. He defines **life chances** as the opportunities given to individuals to fulfill their potential in life. Life chances are determined by one's position within the stratification system. The higher that position, the more access to scarce resources; thus, the more positive the individual's life chances. The lower the position, the less access to scarce resources, and the more negative the individual's chances.

The Weberian concept of class has predominated among sociologists. Gerhard Lenski defines social class as "an aggregation of persons in a society who stand in a similar position with respect to some form of power, privilege, or prestige" (1966, 74–75). In other words, certain people with similar occupations, income, education, and life-styles set themselves apart from the rest of society. In time, they become sufficiently differentiated from others and unified—sometimes unknowingly—among themselves to constitute a separate social level or stratum: a social class.

Status

Social status is the degree of social esteem an individual or group enjoys in society. In the Weberian sense, status refers to prestige rather than simply position within the social system. The most important element of status is its ranked position—as high, middle, low—determined by the value of the corresponding role. For instance, the role of physician, particularly a specialist in a difficult field, is highly valued in our society; that position therefore holds a high status in the United States.

Frequently an overlap exists between class and status, but not always, or

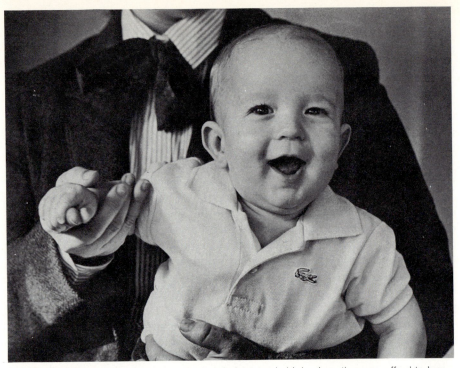

This baby's parents are telling the world that their status is high, since they can afford to buy their baby a shirt with an alligator on it.

necessarily. Some may earn high incomes and lack high status; conversely, some may enjoy high status and lack substantial incomes.

Status is highly important to most individuals; the desire to attain high status is learned as part of socialization. Lenski comments that this concern "influences almost every kind of decision, from the choice of a car to the choice of a spouse. Fear of the loss of status, or honor, is one of the few motives that can make men lay down their lives on the field of battle" (1966, 37–38).

Most people are quite adept at judging the status of others. In the United States, status tends to depend primarily on occupation (achieved status occurring more commonly than ascribed status). Occupations serve as accurate indicators of income and particularly education. In surveys where respondents are asked to rank a variety of occupations, occupations requiring graduate-school training are invariably ranked highest (see Table 6.2).

Although high-ranking occupations generally produce high incomes, such is not always the case: The association holds true for specialized physicians, some attorneys, and many corporate executives, but not for college professors and research scientists.

Additional determinants of status include being born into a highly respected family, living in the "right" kind of neighborhood, attending private prepara-

How Occupations Are Ranked by Americans

TABLE 6.2

Occupation	Score	Occupation	Score	Occupation	Score
Physician	82	Statistician	55	Barber	38
College professor	78	Social worker	52	Jeweler	37
Judge	76	Funeral director	52	Watchmaker	37
Lawyer	76	Computer specialist	51	Bricklayer	36
Physicist	74	Stock broker	51	Airline stewardess	36
Dentist	74	Reporter	51	Meter reader	36
Banker	72	Office manager	50	Mechanic	35
Aeronautical		Bank teller	50	Baker	34
engineer	71	Electrician	49	Shoe repairman	33
Architect	71	Machinist	48	Bulldozer operator	33
Psychologist	71	Police officer	48	Bus driver	32
Airline pilot	70	Insurance agent	47	Truck driver	32
Chemist	69	Musician	46	Cashier	31
Minister	69	Secretary	46	Sales clerk	29
Civil engineer	68	Foreman	45	Meat cutter	28
Biologist	68	Real estate agent	44	Housekeeper	25
Geologist	67	Fireman	44	Longshoreman	24
Sociologist	66	Postal clerk	43	Gas station	
Political scientist	66	Advertising agent	42	attendant	22
Mathematician	65	Mail carrier	42	Cab driver	22
Secondary school		Railroad conductor	41	Elevator operator	21
teacher	63	Typist	41	Bartender	20
Registered nurse	62	Plumber	41	Waiter	20
Pharmacist	61	Farmer	41	Farm laborer	18
Veterinarian	60	Telephone operator	40	Maid/servant	18
Elementary school		Carpenter	40	Garbage collector	17
teacher	60	Welder	40	Janitor	17
Accountant	57	Dancer	38	Shoe shiner	9
Librarian	55				

Source: General Social Surveys, 1972–1983: Cumulative Codebook (Chicago: National Opinion Research Center, 1983), pp. 338–349. Reprinted by permission.

tory schools and Ivy League universities, belonging to exclusive country clubs, and being members of the right church denominations.

Factors that influence social status, then, include occupation and source of income, race, education, sex, age, religion, and ethnic origin. A composite of a high-status American would appear something as follows: a white male in his late thirties with a graduate degree from Harvard, holding the position of chief executive officer in a nationally known corporation. His income is in the six digits; in addition, he receives substantial annual bonuses. He belongs to the most prestigious country club in his city, is an elder in the Episcopal church, and is active in civic groups as well as in the Republican party. His mother and wife are members of the Daughters of the American Revolution and his children are enrolled in preparatory schools.

Status Inconsistency

One would be justified in assuming that characteristics directly opposed to those associated with high social status would indicate a low status. However, in studying industrial societies, sociologists have encountered a phenomenon they refer to as *status inconsistency.* An individual may amass immense wealth, but if this is derived from organized crime and the owner lacks education or other traits associated with high status, that individual's status is judged inconsistently. Conversely, one may, having gambled away a family fortune, lack visible means of support but retain a high status due to past glory attached to the family name.

These findings have given origin to theories speculating that such individuals will tend to suffer greater frustration and dissatisfaction than those whose status is consistent (Lenski, 1966). Those ranked higher on one status variable than another—women doctors, for instance, or Puerto Rican baseball stars—tend to stress the high-ranked variable and deemphasize the low. Unfortunately, others continue to judge them by their master status, that which society considers the most important. The woman doctor will be seen first as a woman, and may even be mistaken for a nurse. The successful baseball star will be seen as a dark-skinned, uneducated man who speaks broken English and wears too many gold chains. People who suffer from status inconsistency, particularly those who are denied high status, often take out their frustration by rejecting upper-status groups, at least in terms of political action or philosophy (Cohn, 1958; G. Marx, 1967).

Power

The third important dimension of stratification, which some consider the foremost dimension, is **power,** defined as the ability to carry out one's wishes despite resistance. Power represents the ability to make others do what one wants them to do, with or without their consent. Stratification based on power is in Weber's view essentially political rather than economic. In fact, Weber used the term political class or party to mean an elite, a group more powerful than other groups in society. Power is exercised in all social systems, from the simplest to the most complex.

As applied to stratification, power can be separated into personal power and social power. Personal power is the freedom of individuals to direct their own lives as they choose without much interference. Such freedom often accompanies great wealth. Social power is the capacity to make decisions that affect entire communities or even the whole society. Social power may be exercised legitimately, with the consent of members of society, in which case it is known as authority. Parents, teachers, and the government all represent different levels of authority. Social power may be also exercised illegitimately, without the official approval of society. Organized crime represents one instance of such power.

Because it affects the manner in which goods and services are distributed, power is probably the most important dimension of stratification. It is deeply interwoven with the other dimensions of class and status. Upper-class people with high status have little trouble attaining positions of power, either in government, the professions, or corporate and banking circles. In turn, those in such positions control decision-making processes to generate events favorable to their needs. In traditional, nonindustrial societies power is often held by a small elite, while the majority are relatively powerless. In industrial societies, however, power is spread among many largely as a result of universal suffrage and the generally better living standard of the majority.

Systems of Stratification

Historically, societies have exhibited a variety of stratification systems. (A **stratification system** is the manner in which societal members are ranked into classes, status groups, and hierarchies of power.) To distinguish among them, social scientists use models, abstract conceptions placed on an ideal continuum. At one extreme of the continuum is the closed stratification system. The middle is represented by the estate system. At the other extreme is the open, or class, system. The stratification system of each society fits somewhere along this ideal continuum.

The Closed Society: Caste

What determines whether a society's stratification system is open or closed is the way in which its members obtain wealth, prestige, and privilege (the Weberian class, status, and power). In a **closed, or caste, stratification system,** class, status, and power are ascribed, determined strictly on the basis of family inheritance rather than on individual effort or merit. The individual is born into a specific social stratum, called caste, with no opportunity of moving in or out of it.

Classical India offers a good example of a closed society. The caste system that flourished in India for many centuries divided members of society into a number of rigid groups, representing areas of service to society and ranked in order of their importance to it. Some ranking was also determined by struggles for power or conquest by other groups. Religion and tradition forbade members of different castes to intermarry or interact in any way. Each caste was restricted in occupation and the status of each individual was ascribed, so that he or she inherited a specific social position that could not be altered through effort or achievement. (Only a limited number, particularly those exhibiting extraordinary military prowess, were able to attain a higher caste, although disobeying certain norms could plunge someone into a lower one.) The caste system has been legally abolished in modern India, which has been deeply influenced by Western democratic thought; many Indians, however, particularly those living in rural areas, still follow the structure that religion and traditional mores have justified for so long.

The Estate System

The **estate system of stratification** formed the economic and social structure of feudal Europe and, in different forms, a number of nations in Asia. As in

Class membership and status are much more apparent in societies without an open class system. In India, where vestiges of the caste system remain, it is obvious who ranks higher in the stratification system.

the caste system, the estate system ranked social positions according to their functions; however, in theory at least, all estates were considered of equal importance. The three main estates were the nobility, the church, and the peasants, and within each existed a stratified hierarchy of positions.

Supported by religion and tradition, the estate system permitted more mobility among social strata than did the caste system. Because only eldest sons could inherit a noble family's title and possessions, the remaining ones were forced to enter either the military or the clergy. Occasionally, serfs who had distinguished themselves were freed and given their own land, and some peasants were allowed to enter the lower ranks of the priesthood.

The remnants of the estate system are still visible in some modern societies that retain a landed gentry and inherited titles of nobility. Some elements of this system may be recognized as well in the nineteenth-century plantations of the American South, although slavery falls closer to the caste spectrum on the continuum.

The Open Society: Class System

Modern industrial societies such as the United States most nearly approximate the model of an **open, or class society.** Open societies share these characteristics: (1) classes exist but are not institutionalized as in the caste and estate systems; (2) class lines are unclear enough that individuals cannot display excessive class consciousness, but inequality stemming from class divisions is readily apparent; (3) although status is usually achieved, evidence indicates that it tends to be ascribed to the lowest and highest social classes; (4) social mobility is possible and frequently occurs.

Open, or class, systems work best in industrial societies with market economies; they offer more opportunities for achieving status and wealth than do societies with centralized economies. In government-controlled economies, people may have little opportunity to choose their jobs and maximize their advantages.

Social mobility—essentially, changing class membership—is possible and encouraged in open systems; however, such choices are rarely evenly distributed. Limitations based on racial, ethnic, regional, educational, even religious factors restrict mobility. Nevertheless, the individual is permitted far more leeway for social as well as physical movement than in closed systems.

Class systems in all societies have certain characteristics in common. The rise of social classes is almost always accompanied by the development of central political institutions, foremost among which is the state. Even so-called classless societies espousing communist or socialist ideologies—all of which support strong states—exhibit class systems. In addition, the more surplus a society produces, the more stratified it tends to be, and the more

A cruel side effect of an open class system is that people can move down, as well as up, through the stratification system.

complex its class system. Even though in technologically advanced societies a large surplus filters down to all social classes, virtually eliminating starvation-level poverty, class inequalities remain flagrant. Finally, power and wealth wield the greatest influence, prestige playing a less important role.

In contemporary industrial societies, both capitalist and socialist, power and wealth are closely interconnected. In capitalist economies, the wealthy are likely to achieve power, and in socialist, the powerful are likely to accumulate wealth. But the stratification systems of both are strikingly similar.

Determining Social Class

Sociologists disagree not only about the overall number of social classes in existence, but about standards determining their makeup. Categories used by researchers to slot people into social-class pigeonholes are arbitrary and artificial.

In general, social class is determined by one of the following approaches:

1. *Life-styles approach:* The researcher observes and questions individuals about their life-styles, noting with whom they interact, what material objects they possess, what recreational activities they engage in, what organizations they belong to, what speech mannerisms they employ, and so on.

2. *Reputational approach:* The researcher asks individuals to act as judges in ranking others. This method is most effectively used in small communities whose inhabitants know each other well. The approach presents problems since it is difficult for one to know all members of a community, and one's biases may influence the way a person is ranked.

3. *Subjective approach:* The researcher asks his subjects to rank themselves. This approach is unreliable chiefly because the average individual often suffers gross misconceptions both about society's stratification system and his or her place in it.

4. *Objective approach:* The researcher develops categories based on income, education, occupation, and position of authority without relying on the feelings, evaluations, or perceptions of either the individuals being examined or a panel of judges. Objective methods permit significantly more exact measurements than do subjective and reputational approaches. However, they fail to accurately describe reality in all cases.

5. *Occupational-prestige approach:* The researcher asks his subjects which occupations and sources of income are most prestigious. This approach is sometimes considered part of the reputational method but depends on a much larger sample, usually on a national scale. The practicality of the occupational-prestige approach makes it the best index of social class in the United States. Occupation determines the amount of money earned,

which in many cases determines the degree of power wielded and prestige accorded. But money alone does not determine social class. Some occupations with relatively low monetary rewards are rated high, and vice versa.

The Sociologist's View of Social Classes

One of the earliest attempts to categorize the American population according to social class was made by Robert and Helen Lynd (1929, 1937). As noted in Chapter 1, these researchers found that a representative midwestern town (Muncie, Indiana) consisted of two classes: the business class and the working class. They concluded that social class was the most significant single culture factor influencing one's daily activities throughout a lifetime.

Another classic set of studies by Warner and Lunt (1941), the Yankee City Series, examined the stratification system of a New England seaside town. Here, the population was categorized according to six class divisions: upper upper, lower upper, upper middle, lower middle, upper lower, and lower lower. These divisions, as well as those of white-collar, blue-collar, and professional middle class, are still frequently used in literature dealing with stratification.

Socioeconomic Status The methodology of contemporary researchers generally relies on some index combining a number of dimensions relevant to stratification. One such index measures socioeconomic status (SES), demonstrating at a glance the position of individuals in the social and economic pecking order. Despite instances of status inconsistency, sociologists are able to develop such indexes because of the relative nature of dimensions of stratification in American society.

Social Class and Its Consequences

The concept of life chances, particularly their variation according to social class, has already been noted in our discussion of Weber above. Not only do life chances differ, however; life-styles as well exhibit marked variations, encompassing such elements as family life, child rearing, education, personal values, consumption, leisure activities, political outlook, religion, and health. Different positions in the stratification system thus engender much inequality. Table 6.3 shows that people in the lowest social class live shorter and less healthy lives, that they are more frequently the victims of violent crime, that their marital lives are unstable, that fewer of their children attain college educations, and finally, that they are in general less happy about their lives.

Family Life

With regard to marital stability, fewer divorces occur among the upper classes. The higher divorce rate among the lower classes may be due to the frustration

Life Chances by Income Class

TABLE 6.3			
	Lower Class	Middle Class	Upper-Middle and Upper Class
Mortality ratio: White males 45–54 (mean, all classes = 1)	2.12	1.01	.074
Victims of heart disease: Prevalence per 1,000 persons	114	40	35
Obesity in native-born women	52%	43%	9%
Marital instability: White males, 25–34, ever divorced	23%	10%	6%
Victims of violent crime: Per 1,000 population	52	30	27
Children who attend college	26%	37%	58%
Describe selves as "very happy"	29	38	56
Favor liberal economic policies	48%	38%	28%

Source: Dennis Gilbert and Joseph A. Kahl, 1987. *The American Class Structure,* 3rd ed. (Chicago: Dorsey), p. 111. Reprinted by permission.

and anxiety economic problems and unemployment create. Additionally, the upper classes have an interest in maintaining marriage alliances since families are the chief medium of transmission of property. In lower-class families, marriages tend to be more patriarchal, with women interacting to a greater extent with female relatives and men with their male friends than in the upper classes. The lower class, finally, has a higher percentage of families headed by women, particularly among blacks.

Child Rearing

Child rearing practices in the middle and upper classes stress independence of action and behavior according to principles of right and wrong. Parents tend to use temporary withdrawal of love rather than physical punishment for social control. As a result, although children in these classes may be prone to guilt feelings, they are likely to become more independent, self-directed, and achievement oriented than children in the lower classes. Parents in the latter tend to emphasize obedience to rules and staying out of trouble, punishing infringements more harshly.

Education

Different socialization experiences lead children of the upper and middle classes to be more successful academically, a pattern reinforced by values which stress academic achievement. This advantage tends to further their upward social mobility, whereas children from the lower classes, lacking models and valuing education less, are hampered in upward mobility as a result. In terms of income alone, differences between those with only eight years of education and those with five or more years of college are staggering.

Religion

The upper and upper middle classes are overwhelmingly Protestant, and a close correlation exists between various Protestant denominations and social class. Higher social classes identify more closely with the subdued rituals of the Episcopalian, Congregationalist, Presbyterian and Methodist churches. Lower social classes appear more comfortable with denominations offering colorful rites such as the Baptist and certain fundamentalist and revivalist sects.

149

CHAPTER 6

*Social
Differentiation:
Ranking and
Stratification*

Politics

Being a registered voter, voting regularly, and taking an interest in civil and political affairs are activities engaged in more frequently by the higher social classes. Party affiliation is similarly correlated: the higher one's social class, the more likely one is to vote Republican; those lower in the social-class hierarchy are more likely to be Democrats. Tolerance on civil liberty issues tends to be greater among higher social classes, whereas working class members are liberal on economic issues and conservative on other matters that do not favorably affect them.

Health

Because health care in this country is neither free nor as cheap as in many other industrial societies, Americans with higher incomes can afford more health and medical care than those with lower incomes. Studies have shown that for this very reason the incidence of disease among higher social classes is less than among the lower. The expense involved prohibits a substantial segment of the population from being covered by any form of health insurance, yet it is only such insurance that allows middle-income people to obtain adequate care. Life expectancy itself is therefore greater at higher social levels.

Mental Health

Both the incidence and treatment of mental illness are much higher in the lower-class population. In particular, lower-class patients are more likely to undergo electroshock therapy, be prescribed tranquilizing drugs, or be hospitalized in state institutions for long periods. Upper-class patients tend to be treated by private analysts with various types of psychotherapy and spend only brief periods in private mental clinics. Studies have also indicated a high degree of mental impairment among persons in the poorest social classes.

Arrest and Conviction

The rates for arrest and conviction are higher for lower-class individuals than for members of the upper and middle classes. Harsher treatment by the criminal justice system is partially due to the types of crimes committed by lower-class persons—robbery, burglary, larceny, and auto theft—as opposed to those committed by middle- and upper-class persons—forgery, tax evasion, fraud, and embezzlement. The latter crimes are not considered as heinous as the former since violence is seldom involved. Finally, persons of higher social-class status can generally afford a better line of defense.

Values

Research has shown that in general, members of the middle and upper classes have feelings of mastery over their lives whereas lower-class individuals tend to be fatalistic, believing that luck and forces beyond their control govern their lives. The higher social classes engage in long-range planning and postpone present pleasures for future goals (deferred gratification) to a greater extent than members of the lower social classes, probably because the futures of the latter hold much less promise. Higher social classes also display more liberated attitudes toward sexual behavior and religious beliefs. The working class, in particular, is intolerant of nonconformist behavior. However, the values and attitudes of the higher classes tend to set the standard for the society.

Social Mobility

A principal difference between open and closed societies is the degree of social mobility offered: substantial in open societies, little or none in closed societies. **Social mobility** refers to an individual's ability to alter social-class membership, status, life chances, and life-styles by moving up (or down) the ladder represented by the stratification system of a society.

Sociologists also distinguish between vertical mobility, which occurs in an upward or downward direction, and horizontal mobility, which occurs through a change of status without consequent change of class. For instance, a high-school teacher promoted to principal is upwardly mobile, while the principal who proves ineffective as an administrator and is demoted back into the classroom is downwardly mobile. But a school superintendent who changes jobs to become an executive of an insurance company, at approximately the same salary and with neither loss nor increase of prestige, is horizontally mobile. A certain amount of horizontal mobility is generally necessary to maximize one's chances for vertical mobility.

The Upwardly Mobile: Who Are They? A variety of factors are responsible for vertical mobility, some dependent on personality traits, others on social circumstance. From studies of this phenomenon, a profile of the upwardly mobile individual has emerged. He or she tends to be (1) an urban resident; (2) an only child, or one of two children; (3) influenced by ambitious parents, particularly a mother; (4) likely to acquire more education than his or her parents; (5) one who marries late and chooses a partner of higher status; and (6) one who waits to establish a family, limiting the number of children to no more than two.

The reasons such an individual is successful are obvious. More and better-paying jobs exist in urban centers; an only child, or one in a small family, is generally offered greater educational opportunities and more of the parents' time and attention; ambitious parents, through socialization, instill values of upward mobility and direct their children toward higher education, a first important step in acquiring this goal. Marrying late enables people to delay the assumption of economic responsibilities, leaving them free to continue their educations or further their careers. Finally, waiting to have children ensures that parents are capable of caring for them, and limiting family size repeats the cycle, leading to upward mobility for the children.

Individuals who are upwardly mobile in comparison to their parents or the preceding generation display intergenerational mobility. If they also do better than their peers of the same generation, they are exhibiting intragenerational mobility.

Social Mobility in the United States

The United States has long been known as the land of opportunity, embodying the persistent myth that anyone, regardless of origin, can rise to become a leader of the country, or at least to acquire wealth and prestige. This is, in fact, the "American dream," the source of such terms as "from rags to riches," and "Horatio Alger stories." The notion that hard work, thrift, ambition, and willpower are sufficient to ensure one's rise through the stratification system have been part of the American ethic from the nation's inception.

How much truth is there in this notion? How does mobility in the United States compare with mobility in other industrial nations?

On gathering opinion-poll studies from a number of industrial nations, Lipset and Bendix (1959) discovered much social mobility in all industrialized democracies, refuting the idea that the United States was unique in the openness of its stratification system. The researchers concluded, firstly, that much mobility was due to the high value placed on efficiency in technological societies. Inefficient offspring of even upper-class parents are replaced by more talented persons from lower classes. Secondly, mobility is caused by industrialization itself, which results in the creation of more high-status occupations to replace the largely blue-collar occupations of an agrarian system. This type of mobility is termed **structural mobility**. Lipset and Bendix found that while the United States did not claim an unusual degree of mobility, it did display more of the kind in which people may rise, but also fall, through merit or lack of it.

A later study measuring long distance mobility, that is, the rise of individuals in one generation from the very bottom to the very top of the stratification system, found that Americans do exhibit a high rate of this phenomenon. Blau and Duncan (1967) discovered that 1 out of 10 sons of manual laborers in the United States reached an elite managerial occupational status. This is a substantially higher proportion than is true of Italy (1 in 300), Denmark (1 in 100), or even Sweden (1 in 30). Only Japan approaches the American pattern, with 1 son in 14 rising from bottom to top.

Blau and Duncan also found that although 37 percent of white-collar workers had fathers with blue-collar jobs, an individual's own level of education was more responsible for upward social mobility than the father's occupation. Thus the well-educated son of a working-class father has the same chance of being upwardly mobile as the poorly educated son of a middle-class father. The researchers concluded (pp. 152–161) that an individual's chances of occupational upward mobility were most greatly influenced by educational level, the nature of the first job, and father's occupation.

According to Blau and Duncan, upward mobility in the twentieth century is due to (1) the expansion of the American economy, which brought in its wake an increase in white-collar occupations, allowing some working-class members to fill the newly created jobs; (2) upper-class families having lower birthrates than the working class, resulting in some necessary upward movement to fill a proportion of high-status jobs; and (3) the immigration of unskilled workers from abroad and from rural regions into urban ones, causing existing skilled urban workers to be pushed upward into higher-status occupations. This kind of **structural mobility** represents a wholesale movement in the stratification system rather than simply a movement of individuals.

The existence of long distance mobility as characteristic of American society has been substantiated by a study of the American business elite. Lipset (1976) found that only 1 in 10 top executives came from wealthy homes and more than one-third had humble origins.

A particularly telling finding regarding mobility, and the subject of inequality in general, indicates that almost as much economic inequality exists among brothers raised in the same homes as among the population in general (Jencks, 1972). It seems inequality is newly created within each generation, even among those who begin life in similar circumstances.

To summarize, we may say that on the whole more upward than downward mobility occurs in the United States (Hauser and Featherman, 1977). In spite of changes in the occupational structure of society—in which farm jobs are substituted by urban factory positions, and blue-collar jobs by service occupations—the total amount of social mobility has hardly altered in the past decades. Cross-cultural surveys, moreover, show that despite the greater degree of mobility implied by democratic ideology, upward mobility in the United States is no greater than that in other industrial nations.

With regard to factors leading to upward mobility, in addition to structural occupational changes, government intervention, in the form of antidiscrimination, affirmative action legislation, training programs, and other projects, plays an important role. Over and above the impact of life chances, individual characteristics play a part in mobility: capability, work habits, the ability to defer gratification, and finally, sheer luck.

Poverty

The existence of inequality as a constant feature of human societies would be more acceptable if it did not produce a tragic result: poverty. Poverty exists in some societies because they lack sufficient resources, because there are too many people for the available resources, and because the societies are not sufficiently industrialized. And even within affluent societies, poverty exists among a segment of the population which, for a variety of reasons, fails to prosper. Around the world, deficient diets as well as unsafe water supplies are the destiny of hundreds of millions of people.

In the United States, considered to be the most affluent of the societies of the world, poverty has a different face. The United States government defines poverty as the level of income at which a person is incapable of providing such basics as food, clothing, and shelter. In 1964, the Social Security Administration developed a poverty index that established a range of income levels according to factors such as family size, sex and age of the family head, number of children under 18, and urban or farm residence. Every year revisions of price levels are based on changes in the consumer price index. For example, in 1984, an urban family of four that averaged $10,609 in income was considered to be at the poverty level. The average family income for that year was $26,430.

Obviously, then, poverty in this society means a condition of having less income than the average. Thus, we are not dealing with *absolute deprivation* which would be not having enough income to provide the barest necessities for survival. We are instead dealing with *relative deprivation,* a condition in which people are deprived when compared to others in their own society at a particular time and place.

Poverty occurs more frequently among some groups than among others. It is chronic, for instance, in families with a female head of household in which no husband is present. In 1983, for instance, 60.4 percent of households with children were headed by women (*Statistical Abstract,* 1985, 46). More than half of these female-headed families were in poverty, as compared with 13 percent of male-headed families. In addition, poverty is widespread among children. Whereas children make up only 27 percent of the nation's population they make up 40 percent of the people in poverty.

Even though in numerical terms more whites are below the poverty level than are any minority groups, in proportion to their percentage of the total population more blacks and persons of Spanish origin are in that category. In 1983, for instance, of the 15.2 percent of persons of all races who were below the poverty level, 12.1 percent were white, 35.7 percent were black, and 28.4 percent were of Spanish origin (*Statistical Abstract,* 1985, 454).

The elderly, meaning people over 65, are another group that has a large percentage of individuals who are below the poverty level. In 1982, 14.6 percent were found to be living in poverty (which is considerably lower than the 35.2 percent who did so in 1959) (*Statistical Abstract,* 1985, 456)

Finally, the poor are concentrated in nonmetropolitan, rural regions where employment is difficult to obtain, and in central areas of cities, in the least desirable neighborhoods.

Causes and Effects of Poverty

For most of human history, poverty has been considered an inevitable side effect of the human condition. Even Jesus Christ, whose ideas on human society were quite revolutionary for his times, said that the poor "will always be with us." Many modern thinkers attribute the presence of poverty to the unequal ways in which resources are distributed in a society, and to the social systems that maintain and enforce such inequalities.

The distribution of resources in society is the function of the institution of the economy. The functioning of the economy will be discussed in a later chapter. It is clear, however, that the causes of poverty must be sought in interdependent factors of an economic, political, and cultural nature, and not in any one institution alone.

In general terms, poverty occurs when people are unable to work. When the predominant type of work in a society changes, many people are displaced, causing many social problems, including poverty. For instance, technological progress displaced a large number of agricultural workers, or farmers, taking them from the land and pushing them into industrial work during the so-called Industrial Revolution. At first, the new industrial jobs meant upward mobility for industrial workers who received higher wages than they had doing farm work. But with continued technological progress, low-skilled workers were again displaced by automation. The higher-paying positions require ever greater amounts of education and greater skills. The latter are easier acquired if a person belongs to a higher social class. Thus, those with marginal skills must be content with "dead end" low-paying jobs that offer little security or future.

The fact that minority groups, women, children, and the elderly are disproportionately represented among the poor also points to degrees of prejudice against and discrimination toward these groups. Clearly, then, the causes of poverty are multi-faceted and cannot be simplistically pinpointed or blamed on any one factor.

The Chapter in Brief

Social stratification is a phenomenon present in all societies that produce a surplus. Stratification is the process by which members of a society rank themselves and one another in hierarchies (from low to high) with respect to the proportion of desirable goods they possess and the prestige and power they enjoy.

All systems of ranking are based on differences. Differences of age and sex are present in all human groups; in more complex societies, members are differentiated in categories and ranked on the basis of social as well as biological characteristics.

Ranking leads to the existence of inequality, which has been explained by a number of theories. Functionalists maintain that inequality works to the advantage of societies: Rewarding the performance of certain tasks more than others ensures that difficult jobs get done. Conflict theorists assert that inequality results from conflict among societal groups struggling for power, where victors impose their values upon the rest. In a synthesis of these two, Lenski states that while inequality is inevitable, it tends to lessen as a society becomes more productive. However, government intervention is needed to reduce the advantage of some groups over others.

All stratification systems involve differentiation, ranking, and institutionalization. The most important dimensions of such systems are **social class, social status,** and **power.** A social class is a group of societal members who hold similar positions with respect to power, privilege, or prestige. Status is the ranked position of an individual in relation to others in the social system. Power is the ability of a person or group to control the actions of others with or without the latter's consent.

Stratification systems may be measured on an ideal continuum. At one extreme, the **closed system** displays social inequalities that are institutionalized and rigid. In the middle lies the **estate system,** less rigid and allowing for some mobility. At the other end, the **open system,** typical of modern industrial societies, allows for **social mobility** among a number of classes, although not to the same extent for all. Mobility is restricted by life chances—the opportunity to become a complete human being and reap the satisfactions of society—which differ according to social class.

Upward mobility in industrial societies is aided by urban residence, a small family background, ambitious parents, higher education, late marriage (preferably to a mate from a higher social class), and having no more than two children.

Much mobility in the United States is **structural mobility,** caused by the upgrading of jobs through industrial and technological change. More horizontal mobility (across the job continuum) than vertical mobility (up or down the job continuum) takes place, although talent, education, work habits, and luck sometimes lead to spectacular success.

Poverty is a tragic side effect of inequality. In the affluent societies, poverty is understood in terms of relative deprivation, of having less than one's peers. Women, children, minorities, and the elderly tend to be poor in greater proportions than other segments of the population.

155

CHAPTER 6

*Social
Differentiation:
Ranking and
Stratification*

Terms to Remember

Closed, or caste, stratification system   A system in which class, status, and power are ascribed, mobility is highly restricted, and the social system is rigid.

Conflict theory of stratification   A theory of stratification based on a view of the natural condition of society as involving continual change and conflict resulting from class struggles. Inequality is the product of such conflict, as the victorious group asserts itself over the rest of society.

Estate system of stratification   The prevailing system of feudal Europe, consisting of three estates of functional importance to society: the nobility, the church, and the peasants. These were hierarchically arranged and permitted a limited amount of social mobility.

Evolutionary theory of stratification   Proposed by Gerhard Lenski, this theory maintains that inequality is unavoidable, but that it sometimes serves positive functions. In addition, the theory holds that a society's level of inequality is directly related to its level of productivity: the more productive a society is, the lower its level of inequality.

Functionalist theory of stratification   A view of social inequality as inevitable since society must use rewards to ensure that essential tasks are performed. Natural conditions of society are thought to be order and stability (equilibrium).

Life chances   The opportunity of each individual to fulfill his or her potential as a human being. Life chances differ according to social class.

Open or class society   A society in which the stratification system allows for social mobility and in which one's status is achieved rather than ascribed at birth. Open systems are characteristic of industrial societies.

Power   A dimension of stratification consisting of the ability of one person or group to control the actions of others with or without the latter's consent.

Social class   A dimension of stratification consisting of an aggregate of persons in a society who stand in a similar position with regard to some form of power, privilege, or prestige.

Social mobility   An individual's ability to change his or her social class by moving up (or down) the stratification system. Upward or downward mobility is vertical, whereas mobility that results in a change of status without consequent change of class is horizontal.

Social status   A dimension of stratification consisting of an individual's ranked position within the social system, rank being determined mainly by occupational role.

Social stratification (ranking)   A process occurring in all but the simplest societies whereby members rank themselves and one another hierarchically with respect to the proportion of desirables (wealth, prestige, power) they possess.

Stratification system   The manner in which members of society are ranked according to classes, status groups, and hierarchies of power. Analyzed on a continuum from closed to open.

Structural mobility   Upward mobility caused by industrial and technological change that pushes skilled workers into higher status occupations.

Suggestions for Further Reading

Fussell, Paul.   1983. *Class: A Guide Through the American Status System.* New York: Summit. An amused and amusing look at the foibles of the various social classes in the United States.

Gilbert, Dennis and Joseph A. Kahl.   1987. *The American Class Structure: A New Synthesis.* Chicago: Dorsey. A concise and insightful overview of the American class structure.

Domhoff, G. William.   1983. *Who Rules America Now? A View for the Eighties.* Englewood Cliffs, N. J.: Prentice-Hall. A sociologist who probed the upper class in the 1950s does so again thirty years later.

Harrington, Michael. 1984. *The New American Poverty.* New York: Penguin. A portrait of America's poor of the 1980s, from the unemployed and unemployable, to women raising children alone.

Harrison, Paul. 1984. *Inside the Third World: The Anatomy of Poverty.* New York: Pelican. Poverty as Americans have never seen it.

Scott, Hilda. 1984. *Working Your Way to the Bottom: The Feminization of Poverty.* Boston: Routledge & Kegan Paul/Pandora Press. The correlation of being poor and female in the United States.

Dead-End America: Who Gets Ahead?

WALT HARRINGTON

Every society has its "anointed," destined to enjoy the best life has to offer. It also has its "Skunk Hollowers" with their faded clothes and dead-eyed stares. Why? Is this basic injustice fated to be forever part of human life? The author of this article evokes his own journey from Skunk Hollow and comments on the similar progress of his society. He ends on a hopeful note.

We moved to town as I entered the sixth grade, and on my first day in class I found myself among children whose faded clothes and dead-eyed stares reminded me of so many poor children I had gone to school with in the country, where rich and poor, smart and dumb were lumped in a single classroom.

We were assembled in Sixth Grade, Section D—the bottom of four classes sorted by ability. My father, a milkman, was told that this was the only classroom with space for an extra child.

In a few days a teacher from my old school had heard of my assignment and raised such a stink that I was bumped—in what still must rank as the grandest promotion of my life—from the slow learner to the accelerated classroom.

That teacher, I believe to this day, changed my life.

In my new class were the elementary-school elite, the children of lawyers and business executives, doctors and dentists, brokers of stock and real estate.

They won the student-council elections. They led in mimicking high-school fashions, white socks and white Levis being the first in my memory. They turned out in force for lessons in ballroom dancing and held Friday-night parties where parents disappeared and boys and girls paired off for clumsy necking sessions. They did hours of homework every night. They talked of college. They played golf.

My new, more sophisticated friends also

Source: From *The Washington Post,* September 22, 1984, pp. 34–36. © The Washington Post. Reprinted by permission.

had a name for the countryside where I had grown up: They called it Skunk Hollow.

They were the anointed in our small, midwestern suburban town. Even then, I knew that in some mysterious way everything from personal popularity to "ability" was shaped by how our fathers earned a living.

It shaped the way we looked and dressed, the way we talked, the way we were treated by our teachers. It shaped our friendships, our aspirations and our chances. It also would shape us as adults.

More than two decades later my friends were sorted in adulthood in much the way they were sorted in sixth grade, though a handful of smart and affluent children have fallen despite it all.

Who gets ahead? Well, rich is better. That has always been true, and it is true today. But much has changed in a generation.

America is today a land of less opportunity. Predicting our children's futures will be more difficult. Just getting ahead will be more difficult—for those anointed and those in Section D.

"The ethos in our society that everyone gets better, moves upward and onward, is in for bad times," says Alan C. Kerchkhoff, a Duke University sociologist.

"That experience has been mostly due to changes in our labor force, and our labor force is not going to change that much in the next 20 to 50 years. If the image is, 'I've got to outdo the old man,' then there are going to be a lot of disappointed people."

In 1962, the year I moved to town, about half the sons of American fathers with prestigious jobs held prestigious jobs themselves as adults, according to a massive U.S. Census Bureau study.

Affluent boys clearly had an edge in life, but not a blank check. After all, half of them had moved down, while nearly half the sons of laborers had moved up. If this wasn't equal opportunity, it was at least evidence that merit mattered. For blacks, merit didn't matter.

The sons of a black lawyer in 1962 had about the same chance of making it to the top in America as did the son of a black ditch digger. Only about a tenth of black sons—regardless of dad's job—held prestigious jobs that year.

It was a revealing measure of black and white inequality: affluent blacks, unlike affluent whites, could not expect their children to have a much better chance at a good job than the children of poor blacks. Blacks were equal in their inequality. They could not build from one generation to the next.

Yet, for white men the economy boomed in '62. Everyone seemed to go to college. Educated professionals were in demand. In a way, children were forced to move up, as farm and, later, heavy manufacturing jobs disappeared. Even educated white wives with children were sucked into the expanding work place.

The ride was about to end, however. The demand for managers dropped, and professions such as law and medicine became glutted. The value of a college degree sagged. The baby-boom generation moved through the work place like a frog through a snake. They took good jobs from the next generation.

Women flexed their aspirations, taking good jobs, too. Well-to-do blacks became a new class. For the first time, black sons maintained their parents' advantage.

The rules of who gets ahead had shifted subtly and dramatically by 1973.

The percentage of sons of prestigious fathers who themselves held prestigious jobs dropped by about 2%—while the number of sons of laborers and farm workers entering high-status jobs increased by about the same percentage, a Census study showed.

About twice the percentage of sons of,

say, office managers still entered prestigious jobs compared with the children of truck drivers, but the subtle shift was toward greater opportunity for those at the bottom, and less security for those at the top.

What happened to blacks was anything but subtle. By 1973, a third of the sons of prestigious black workers held high-status jobs themselves—more than three times the percentage of only a decade before. Though still moving up at about half the rate of white sons, black sons from all backgrounds were getting ahead at about twice the rate of 1962.

The Census hasn't done a mobility study in the 1980s, but there are clear hints—and considerable fear and loathing—about what has occurred:

The value of a college degree declined. The percentage of recent college graduates in prestigious jobs dropped, and the gap between the expected lifetime earnings of high-school and college graduates narrowed, as the number of young workers with college degrees jumped from 9 million in 1976 to 13 million in 1982.

"The chances that you will end up a plumber with a college degree are greater today than they were 20 years ago," says Paul Siegel, chief of the Census Bureau's education section.

Women began the climb. About 8 of 10 women are expected to work by 1995, compared with about a third in 1960. In 1982 about 15% of lawyers were women, compared with 4% a decade earlier. In 1974 about a fifth of Harvard University's graduating class was women; this year it was 40%. As of 1979, more women were in college than men.

The baby boomers took over. The bulge of baby-boom workers devoured good jobs. Today's squeeze on young workers is not about women and blacks moving into prestige jobs, says Siegel: "It's about the baby boom."

The new black "haves" emerged. About a third of American blacks now have incomes about equal to the average white—and incomes far beyond other blacks, says William Julius Wilson, a University of Chicago sociologist and author of "The Declining Significance of Race."

"There is a gap emerging between the black haves and the have-nots," says Wilson. Since about 1970 the number of blacks working as professionals or managers and the number of homes owned by blacks has risen by about 50%. That compares with about a one-third rise for whites, Wilson says.

The number of blacks in college doubled from 1970 to 1980, and young black men with college degrees today start at salaries virtually the same as white college graduates. Young black women with college degrees actually start earning slightly more than white female graduates.

Despite these gains, Wilson says, the bottom third of American blacks has lost economic ground, and the middle third has barely held its own.

The new jobs aren't good jobs. Job growth in the future will be in lower-paying service jobs, not professional and managerial jobs, says Christopher Jencks, a Northwestern University sociologist and co-author of "Who Gets Ahead," a summary of what determines who moves up or down in America.

"As the market tightens, particularly at the top," says Jencks, "you would expect more downward mobility."

Tough times are ahead even for the children of doctors and lawyers in business on their own. About half of these children traditionally became professionals themselves. But that once "risk-free" path is closed, says Srully Blotnick, a psychologist whose new book, "The Corporate Steeplechase," follows the careers of 5,000 men and women over 25 years. "The professions as 'Easy Street' are clogged up," Blotnick says.

In some ways that is more fair, more equal, because it means a breakdown in the inheritance of the nation's highest-paying jobs from one generation to the next.

In some ways the drop in the value of a college degree also is more fair, more equal, because it means a high-school degree is worth more—and that the "paycheck gap" between the educated and less educated has narrowed.

But as always, if times are tight for those at the top, they will be tighter for those below, especially since women and newly affluent blacks are competing in full force.

The fallout of fewer jobs at the top will be a scramble for jobs in the middle, where blue-collar and poor children have traditionally taken their first steps up.

This competition gets to the heart of why one person gets ahead of another—and to the heart of whether America will remain a land of opportunity without an expanding economy to accommodate its ideology.

Rich is better. It has always been true, and it is true today. Children of the well-off often become well-off.

Conservatives say they get ahead because they value achievement, grow up in stimulating homes, get better educations, and are intelligent. Liberals say they too often get ahead because of social and financial advantages unavailable to poorer children. Pick a viewpoint.

If there is a fact that emerges from "Who Gets Ahead" by Jencks and 11 colleagues, it is that all the advantages a parent can buy mean little without college.

Jencks and his colleagues concluded, after reviewing all the available studies of social mobility, that two men—black or white—with the same years of college will earn about the same income and hold similar-status jobs—despite earlier differences in aptitude test scores, social background, and personality.

No way around it: College is the ticket for rich and poor in America. And despite student-aid cutbacks, the percentage of college students with various family incomes has changed little in recent years, says Siegel.

Whether we like it or not, college will remain the most powerful force in determining who gets ahead in America—even if the jobs graduates fight for aren't as good as those their parents sought.

"It's just going to be worse for everybody," says Jencks.

"How important mobility is depends on what stakes are," says University of Wisconsin sociologist Erik Olin Wright, author of several books on social class in America. "The stakes are very high in the meritocratic game in the United States."

That is unlikely to change. Our adult self-esteem will still be shaped by the jobs we hold, and the gap between the richest and the poorest will remain wide.

Not only will our children strive to "outdo the old man," as sociologist Kerckhoff says, but parents will also continue to measure their success or failure in how well their children do. Childhood may be painful with parents whose notion of success was shaped in the boom times of a bygone era.

My childhood friends were of that bygone era, and they got ahead pretty much as expected.

The affluent children have done well. The son of an executive works in his father's business. The daughter of a lawyer is a lawyer. Several sons of dentists are dentists. The daughter of a stockbroker is an accountant. Two boys are bankers.

Those born of Skunk Hollows urban and rural have done all right, too. They are cosmetologists and auto-body repairmen. They sell home products door-to-door. Several own their own businesses and probably earn more money than a banker or an accountant.

A boy who was as close to me as any in my childhood became a heroin dealer. One boy became a policeman in a small town. Another boy sweeps the hallways of the country school I attended before moving to town.

Too few surprises here. Perhaps we'll find more among our children.

Social Differentiation: Majority and Minorities

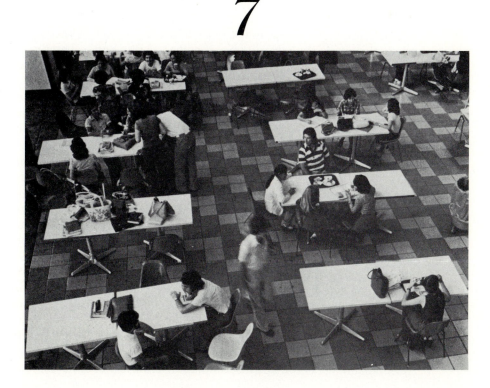

*T*he human species is rich in its diversity. For a variety of biological and cultural reasons, we differ in the way we look and speak, the gods we worship, the types of governments to which we owe allegiance, the customs and traditions we cherish.

Such divergence among groups would cause little difficulty if each remained permanently isolated in its own territory or if a genuine spirit of tolerance predominated. Neither situation, however, prevails. On the contrary, the world is growing smaller as the economies of most nations become global and rapid transportation and mass media make products and information instantly and universally available. Such interaction has led to cultural diffusion (see Chapter 9) where even the most preindustrial society has been exposed to the products of the most technologically advanced. Another result of this interaction is interbreeding on a large scale, leaving no "pure" stock in the world (with the possible exception of small groups perhaps still existing in inaccessible locations).

Because humans tend to stress their differences rather than similarities, their history has been primarily a record of struggles and conflicts, of conquests and oppression, even genocide, with one group of people pitted against another. This conflict and suspicion among humans has not measurably decreased despite constant and continued interaction.

As previously noted, all societies differentiate among their members on such bases as sex, age, handicaps, and social status. But conflict among groups that differ in either appearance or culture—or both—has been particularly bitter in societies where such groups must live side by side. With the creation of the nation-state, this situation has become the rule rather than the exception, as immigration, colonization, or conquest lead to the formation within nations of plural societies. In plural societies, groups differing in ethnicity, race, or religion—the so-called minorities—occasionally coexist in peace. More often, their coexistence is marred by conflicts characterized by discrimination and prejudice, sometimes by oppression, and occasionally by a cruelly bloody conflagration—one need only mention Northern Ireland or Lebanon.

Intergroup conflict should come as no surprise. The fear of strangers is a very strong human emotion. It is speculated that this fear goes as far back as prehistoric times. Strangers represent danger: their intentions are not clear, their interpretations of reality differ, their languages fail to communicate. Distrust and dislike of the stranger, then, are part and parcel of human society, as is the ancient belief that members of different nationalities cannot live side by side, "that when fate has cast two peoples upon the same territory, one must inevitably be 'the hammer and the other the anvil'" (Janowsky, 1945, 30–31). Hospitality and cooperation are of course also part of the human experience, but these represent a reasoned, civilized attitude acquired only when suspicion and hostility have been overcome.

A change evident in recent decades, particularly in the United States but also in other nations, is the increased visibility of minorities and their growing rejection of oppression and discrimination. A variety of social movements has helped to effect this shift. These have succeeded in bringing the minority status of various groups to public awareness, if not in overturning that status. Raising a society's conscience in this manner is an important first step in remedying injustices and inequalities that result from minority status. Minority status, in fact, has always been intimately bound with the stratification system of a society in a way that is easily understood: Minorities occupy the lower rungs of the stratification ladder.

Majority and Minorities: Definitions of Terms

Whenever two or more groups are brought into contact with one another and one of those groups gains dominance, the dominant group is considered the majority and the nondominant groups are called minorities. The terms majority and minorities do not imply any numerical value; that is, a majority is not necessarily larger in number than a minority. On the contrary, in many instances (although not in the United States) one or more minorities are superior in number to the dominant majority (South Africa is a glaring example).

As noted, the origin of minorities is attributable to the development of the nation-state. "Both the spread of dominance over formerly separate groups and the common desire to create a homogeneous nation (leading to attempts to repress cultural variation) have created the minority-majority situation" (Simpson and Yinger, 1972, 16). Even today, people view the world from a tribal perspective, expecting members of the society to which they belong to mirror their own physical and cultural type (Wagley and Harris, 1958, 241–2).

Minority status is conferred on those categories of people who, on the basis of race, ethnicity, and religion (and to an extent gender, age, and handicaps) lack the kinds of power held by the majority group, or "possess imperfect access to positions of equal power and to the corollary categories of prestige and privilege in the society" (Yetman and Steele, 1971, 4).

Racially based minority status is ascribed to groups which differ biologically from the majority. Ethnically based minority status is ascribed to those who differ culturally from the majority, due to their own foreign origins or those of their parents or grandparents. Similarly, minority status can be based on religious beliefs different from the majority's. Finally, some groups are treated like minorities on the basis of sex, age, and handicaps. In the United States, for instance, women and the elderly hold less status than men and young adults.

By contrast, the **majority or dominant group,** although it may be numerically smaller, controls the important sectors of social life, influencing the society's culture in such vital areas as language, ideology, even standards of beauty and worth. In the United States, white Anglo-Saxon Protestants—the so-called Wasps—constitute the majority. Those other than white, Northern

European, or Protestant have traditionally been set apart for different—meaning unequal—treatment.

Not all societies exhibit a majority-minorities configuration. Some are almost totally homogeneous, their members belonging to the same racial stock, the same cultural and ethnic background, and the same religious organizations. But most contemporary, technologically advanced societies are heterogenous, with members of varying appearances, cultures, and religions.

Defining Minority Status

People considered as belonging to a **minority group** share certain common features. First, they are recognizable, possessing visible traits: appearance, accent, surname. Second, because they possess these traits, they are subject to differential treatment. Third, their self-image and identity center on their membership in the minority group. Finally, they are aware of their common identity with others in the group. Wagley and Harris (1958, 10) suggest these additional characteristics of minorities: (1) they are subordinate segments of complex state societies; (2) they exhibit physical or cultural traits held in low esteem by the majority; (3) they are held together by the traits they share; (4) their status is inherited, even in the absence of readily apparent physical or cultural traits; and (5) either by choice or necessity, they tend to marry within the group.

As a consequence of the above, minorities constitute subcultures (see Chapter 3) within the larger society. Subcultural membership provides individuals with in-group identity, enabling them to define themselves (to know who they are). Membership also permits individuals to interpret mainstream society through the eyes of the group, making sense of it from a perspective not always available to a single member. But membership in a minority subculture can also, on occasion, stand in the way of absorption into mainstream society, if that is the individual's goal.

Ethnicity, Religion, Race

As stated earlier, ethnicity, religion, and race are the three principal factors on which minority status is based (gender, age, and handicaps will be discussed in the next chapter). **Ethnicity** refers to a group's distinctiveness on social and cultural grounds that differ from those of the majority due to national background. Most immigrants who share a common language, culture, traditions, history, and ancestry, and are recognized as such by the rest of society, are ethnics. Among those who have been part of a society for several generations, some may retain and some give up the language, customs, and surnames of their country of origin. However, as long as they share bonds of solidarity with others originating from the same background, they are considered members of an ethnic group.

Religion refers to a set of beliefs and rituals dealing with the sacred. Members

167

CHAPTER 7

*Social
Differentiation:
Majority and
Minorities*

of a particular religion share these beliefs and rituals and derive a sense of identity from their membership. In the United States Catholics and Jews, differing in religion from the Protestant majority, were subject until a few decades ago to differential treatment. The importance of minority status based on religion has lessened since.

The most difficult factor to define is race. **Race** is a concept used by scientists to describe biological differences in the human species. Unfortunately, even scientists cannot come up with an exact definition. People are classified into racial categories according to visible differences in appearance. Those who share a certain skin color, eye shape, hair texture, or thickness of lips are said to belong to a specific race. However, most physical traits overlap. Skin color, for instance, spans a spectrum from light to dark in each group. It is impossible to determine the cutoff point where one race ends and another begins because all people share more physical traits than they differ on.

The reason we are more similar than dissimilar, in spite of the physical variations among us, is that we are all descended from common stock, the species *Homo sapiens*. This species is classified into a number of groups representing variations within it (or races). Variations are caused by inbreeding (breeding within a restricted group), a process that tends to crystallize and perpetuate traits that may have appeared randomly in our ancestors. Scientific racial classifications are also formulated on the basis of the relative frequency with which certain genes occur among populations. Genes transmit hereditary traits. Thus, genes determine what physical traits are concentrated in a particular population.

In addition to inbreeding, interbreeding (breeding among different populations) has been occurring for thousands of years. Consequently, there are no "pure" human groupings left, with the possible exception of small tribes living in areas so isolated they have not yet been discovered.

It may be concluded that the classification of humans by race is artificial and does not correspond to clear and definite distinctions. Neither does it correspond to national, religious, linguistic, cultural, and geographic boundaries, although in the past isolation may have contributed to different gene pools (the combined sum of all genes present in all individuals in a given population). No social trait or behavior of population groups has any connection with inherited racial traits. Finally, there is no scientific support for the idea that differences in personality, temperament, character, or intelligence are based on race (the controversial findings of some researchers who claim that intelligence is genetically transmitted and cannot be socially changed are not universally considered valid; additionally, even these researchers link lower IQs to lower class levels and not to race).

Differentiation According to Social Class

The interest of sociologists in social differentiation lies in the causes behind it. The preceding chapter noted that people are differentiated, and consequently ranked, on the basis of their wealth, prestige, and power. In modern industrial societies, social class is generally an achieved position. Minority status, on the other hand, is ascribed: an individual is born into a particular racial or ethnic group and into a family that practices a specific religion.

In the case of religion and ethnicity, this ascription need not be permanent. One may change one's religion, and ethnic background can be hidden or made less obvious by a change of name. Race, however, remains an unchangeable status.

By definition, access to positions of wealth, prestige, and power is controlled by the majority. Such access evades minorities the more they differ in looks and customs from the majority, and the fewer skills, talents, and years of education at their disposal. Mobility within the stratification system, therefore, varies accordingly for different minorities.

E Pluribus Unum: *"Out of Many, One"*

This inscription, familiar to all Americans because of its strategic location, is an expression of an ideal, rather than real, situation. In fact, one of the fundamental problems facing the United States has been how to create a functioning social unit, a society, out of the many disparate groups that periodically come to its shores in search of better futures for themselves and their children. Although imperfect, a solution has been achieved, and a majority of Americans do share sufficient common values and norms to maintain social stability. The following sections will analyze this solution.

Anglo-Conformity

At different times in American history different ideologies regarding the treatment of minorities have prevailed. The first, **Anglo-conformity**, represented an attempt to superimpose Wasp values on immigrants. Thus it was expected that the language, institutions, and cultural patterns of the United States (in turn based on the English model) would be learned and absorbed by all newcomers.

The Melting Pot

During the nineteenth century, the idea took hold that immigrants could make important contributions to American society. As a result, it was hoped that United States society could fuse, both biologically and culturally, the various stocks within it, ultimately resulting in a type to be known as the "New American," a concept known as the **melting-pot theory.**

While educational systems and the mass media have succeeded in molding second- and third-generation immigrants into Americans who accept most of the values and institutions of the society (they tend to be, in fact, the most ardent patriots), in other ways ethnic minorities have remained resistant to melting. It was true by the middle of the twentieth century that the children and grandchildren of immigrants had entered the mainstream of American society, moving from ethnic neighborhoods into the suburbs, sometimes anglicizing their names, and beginning the climb through the stratification system by acquiring college educations and entering professions. But while their ethnic background no longer served as a focus of identity, their religion still did. Sociologists found that marriage among descendants of immigrants followed religious lines: British, German, and Scandinavian Protestants intermarried, creating a Protestant pool; Irish, Italian, and Polish Catholics intermarried, creating a Catholic pool; and Jews married other Jews of varying national origins, creating a Jewish pool (Kennedy, 1944; Archdeacon, 1983). Although a melting down of ethnicity had occurred, America was becoming a triple melting-pot nation. This realization paved the way for the ideology of cultural pluralism. As for the racial minorities, they hardly melted down at all.

Cultural Pluralism

The ideology of **cultural pluralism,** the most widely accepted today, stresses the desirability of each ethnic group retaining its cultural distinctiveness but still functioning within the wider American culture. In other words, every citizen's first commitment should be to the welfare of the United States; but beyond that, in matters of food, family, religious rituals, community associations, and so on, individuals should retain, if they so desire, their ethnic ties.

The United States aspires to achieve cultural pluralism, a condition in which a variety of ethnic, racial, and religious groups coexist, retaining some cultural distinctiveness within the wider American culture.

In this manner, according to current thought, members can contribute much more to society, somewhat in the fashion of a great dish whose taste transcends the variety of separate ingredients incorporated within it.

The decade of the 1960s saw a revival of ethnic feelings as it became apparent that success and upward mobility were extremely difficult for some ethnic and most racial groups to achieve. Blacks, Hispanics, and Native Americans became active in protest movements to end their unequal access to opportunities; in the process many seemed to rediscover their ancestry, using it as a springboard for political action. Activity in political organizations generated previously absent feelings of solidarity within many ethnic groups.

Majority and Minorities: Processes of Coexistence

The ideologies described above do not always reflect the reality of how a dominant majority treats the minorities in its midst, nor how the minorities react to their condition. Actual processes by which societies attempt to deal with minorities range from segregation to amalgamation.

Segregation is the attempt to isolate a minority from the majority. South Africa offers one such example. There, the dominant group has forced minorities that are numerically superior into a condition of inferiority, restricting their freedom of movement and isolating them on rural reservations where it is difficult for them to survive, or in urban ghettoes. Prior to a number of Supreme Court decisions making the segregation of public facilities illegal, the practice was also rampant in the American South.

Accommodation refers to a situation in which a minority is conscious of, accepts, and adapts to the norms and values of the majority, but chooses also to retain its own norms and values. Thus it rejects full participation in the host culture, remaining culturally, sometimes linguistically, distinct. The Cuban community in Miami is a good example of a minority that has chosen accommodation.

Acculturation, or cultural assimilation, occurs when a minority group accepts and adopts the norms and values of the host culture, often surrendering a native language and traditions. In spite of their sacrifice, such groups are often still refused the status of equals by the majority.

Assimilation refers to the process by which minorities completely absorb the culture of the majority and enter into its mainstream. In the United States, minorities that most resemble the majority in looks and culture are generally assimilated most rapidly. The most distinct fail to be assimilated, and some no longer want to be.

Amalgamation takes place when all distinctions between majority and minorities are erased. In amalgamation, members of different ethnic and racial groups intermarry so that their offspring eventually form a new and distinct ethnic, cultural, and racial group. Brazil is an example of an amalgamated society, although its effects have not reached the entire spectrum of the population. In the United States, amalgamation has not taken place.

Of course, majorities in different societies deal differently with the minorities in their midst. Some welcome assimilation, others force it under penalty of expulsion. Most preach pluralism, but few attain it. Some rid themselves of undesirable minorities by wholesale population transfers or expulsion. In Uganda, for instance, the entire Asian population, constituting a substantial merchant middle class, was given a specific deadline within which to leave the country.

171

CHAPTER 7

*Social
Differentiation:
Majority and
Minorities*

Other societies economically exploit minorities, keeping them in a state of ignorance and submission. This was true in the American South when slavery was legal, and is still true in South Africa today. In some—fortunately rare—instances, recourse is made to genocide, or the slaughter of entire groups of unwanted minorities. In our own century, this method was employed by Nazi Germany in its attempt to exterminate the Jews, and genocide on a smaller scale has occurred in Armenia and Bangladesh.

A list of policies developed by dominant groups for dealing with minorities is suggested by Simpson and Yinger (1972, 17): (1) assimilation, either forced or permitted; (2) pluralism; (3) legal protection of minorities; (4) population transfer, peaceful or forced; (5) continued subjugation; and (6) extermination. The authors conclude: "These six policies of dominant groups are not, of course, mutually exclusive; many may be practiced simultaneously. Some are conscious long-run plans; some are *ad hoc* adjustments to specific situations; some are the by-products (perhaps unintended) of other policies. In some instances they are the official actions of majority-group leaders; in others they are the day-by-day responses of individual members of the dominant group" (1972, 23–24).

In the Way: Obstacles to Full Integration

Not all relations between groups coexisting in a society involve conflict. But on any given day we may read or hear about group conflicts in disparate corners of the world: between Moslems and Christians or Shiites and Palestinians in Lebanon, between Sikhs and Hindus in India, between Catholics and Protestants in Northern Ireland. Certain theorists have suggested that recurring conflicts of an ethnic and racial nature in the United States have prevented conflicts of a political or economic nature from erupting.

Majorities employ a variety of mechanisms to prevent minorities from achieving equal integration into the social system. Most of these methods are no longer legal in contemporary societies, nor are they even necessarily conscious. Among them the most destructive are racism, prejudice, and discrimination.

Racism

Although **racism** is generally interpreted as the hatred of members of certain racial groups, in sociological terms it refers to the incorrect belief that physical traits and behavior are inherited. Related to this belief is the judgment that physical and behavioral traits of specific racial groups are inferior or undesirable.

The function of racism has been to provide a rationale for a social order based on race; that is, "to use beliefs in genetic superiority-inferiority as a means of justifying domination and exploitation of one racial group by another" (Yetman, 1985, 14). Thus, the definition of racism contains a behavioral component and implies that the dominant majority racial group exerts power over the minority racial group. In particular, it prevents the minority from securing access to prestige, power, and privilege.

As an ideology, racism originated in Darwin's theory of evolution, particularly its concept of survival of the fittest. This theory was applied to human groups (social Darwinism) and used to rationalize why some Northern Europeans maintained positions of superiority in the societies they colonized. The conclusion of the Darwinists was that these groups represented the most highly evolved and civilized humans, a fact evidenced by their development of self-rule and representative government.

Today, racism as an ideology is in worldwide decline and few Americans admit to racist beliefs. The ideology, however, has been replaced by a form of institutional racism, the discimination against racial minorities which is built into a society's institutions. Institutional racism is one aspect of institutional discrimination (discussed below), a form of discrimination inherent in the norms and values, and particularly the behavior, of members of a society, and reinforced by the society's agents of social control.

Prejudice

Prejudice derives from a Latin word meaning to prejudge. Prejudgment implies that one makes up one's mind previous to acquiring any real knowledge about a subject. Prejudgment is often a useful tool, even though based on stereotypes and hearsay; it is sometimes necessary to depend on another's word or to act on superficial impressions. But prejudice goes beyond prejudgment in the sense that not only do prejudiced individuals make judgments before having all the facts, they refuse to change those judgments even when confronted by unassailable evidence to the contrary.

Prejudice, as well as racism, leans heavily on stereotyping. In *stereotyping,* common, uniform characteristics are assigned to an entire group without allowance for individual difference. Such characteristics may portray the group as inferior or superior: blacks, for instance, are stereotyped as being intellectually inferior but athletically and musically superior to whites. Stereotypes develop when the traits or behavior of certain individuals are considered typical of a whole group, or if a superficial aspect of a group's behavior is interpreted as representing the group's total behavior, without any attempt at explaining its cause.

Scapegoating, another mechanism that fuels prejudice, is derived from the biblical practice of offering a goat as sacrifice in exchange for divine forgiveness of one's sins. In sociology, the term refers to the tendency of frustrated individuals to respond with aggression and, if the source of frustration cannot be directly attacked, to project this aggression onto a third party. Thus a society undergoing troubled times—high unemployment, high crime rates, inflation—can always find some group to take the blame.

Causes of Prejudice   Prejudice, being an obvious cause of intergroup hostilities, has been the subject of much research. Early studies seemed to indicate that prejudice resulted from the isolation of groups from one another. But the example of the American South, where whites and blacks lived in close proximity and often on intimate terms (though always in master-servant relationships) did not support this belief. In *The Nature of Prejudice* (1954), social psychologist Gordon Allport proposed a theory of contact. According to Allport, when two groups of equal status come into contact, prejudice decreases; however, if status inequality exists and one group is dominant, prejudice remains level or actually increases. In fact, in the South today, a decrease of prejudice has occurred at the same time as southern blacks have risen in the stratification system; with the elimination of "separate but equal" public facilities, blacks and whites of the same social class are brought closer together.

Allport, however, had to qualify his findings: it seems that even between groups whose status is equal, if competition exists, prejudice intensifies. Conversely, if groups cooperate to achieve common goals, prejudice declines.

Another influential theory, focusing on prejudice as a personality trait, was based on a now-classic study by T. W. Adorno (1950) in which researchers discovered a high correlation between development of prejudice and a personality type they termed *authoritarian*. People with authoritarian personalities, according to the proponents of this theory, are socialized so well that they accept only their own group's norms and values. When confronted with different norms and values they become extremely anxious and convince themselves that those who differ from them are somehow inferior, subhuman, or sinful.

Other characteristics of an authoritarian personality include submission to authority, admiration of power and toughness, conventionality, condescension toward inferiors, insensitivity in relationships with others, and a deep-rooted, partly subconscious sense of insecurity. In such persons, prejudice is merely part of a total outlook in which situations and problems are perceived in terms of absolutes—good or bad, right or wrong—and in which people are either heroes or villains.

Discrimination

Whereas prejudice is an attitude or a feeling, **discrimination** consists of actions taken as a result of prejudicial leanings; for instance, the belief that all blacks are violent is a prejudice, but the organization of a committee to prevent them moving into a neighborhood represents discrimination.

Prejudice and discrimination usually go hand in hand. But they can also occur independently of each other. A person may, for example, continue to believe that blacks are violent. If, nonetheless, that person, being a law-abiding citizen, allows black families to move into the neighborhood without any harassment or interference, he or she is exhibiting prejudice without discrimination. On the other hand, a person may not believe blacks are violent at all, but if, in order to retain the friendship of neighbors, he or she signs a petition to keep a black family from buying property on their street, that person is discriminating without being prejudiced.

In general, however, prejudice and discrimination are mutually reinforcing. If in a society strong prejudices exist against a minority group, these will be acted upon and will result in discrimination. In addition, prejudice tends to lead through a vicious circle to discrimination. If prejudice exists regarding a certain group's lack of intelligence and education is denied them (discrimination), the prejudice becomes a self-fulfilling prophecy.

Discrimination is against United States law. However, being so closely interrelated with prejudice, certain kinds of discrimination still prevail. Such discrimination can be divided into two types: individual and institutional. **Individual discrimination** refers to behavior prompted by the personal prejudice of a majority member. If a landlord refuses to rent to minorities because he does not like or trust them, he is displaying individual discrimination. **Institutional discrimination** refers to the system of inequalities existing within a society apart from the prejudices of individuals. Due to institutional discrimination, few minority group members can rent apartments in pleasant, middle-class neighborhoods, even with the most unprejudiced of landlords. The obvious reason for their inability to afford such apartments is that they are unemployed. But the roots of their lack of employment are institutional: They may have grown up in decaying sections of the city and failed to acquire educationally oriented values; their schools may have failed to motivate them to acquire those skills necessary for high-paying jobs; they may be apathetic, feeling that the political system in power does not represent them; the justice system may have worked against them, furthering their difficulties in obtaining jobs; and they may never have acquired the habits of punctuality, deferring gratification, and good grooming that lead to upward mobility in the job market.

Institutional discrimination, in turn, takes structural and cultural forms. Structural discrimination refers to discrimination built into such social structures as the political and economic institutions. Historically, the source of social inequality is rooted in the castelike system that has ensured the majority its dominance. Although caste distinctions are diminishing, their effects continue to persist. Structural discrimination is the most pervasive in our society; due to the way our economic structures work, for instance, we no longer need a large force of unskilled laborers. Consequently, a large reservoir of persons remain unemployed. In turn, most of these consist overwhelmingly of minorities who were denied the opportunity to acquire higher skills. These workers are fated to remain locked in a condition of subemployment, and thus of poverty, until the economic institution is somehow changed.

Cultural discrimination results from the interplay between majority and minorities in a multicultural society. In such a society, a number of groups, due to ethnocentric feelings, regard their own values, norms, attitudes, and interpretations of reality as the only valid ones. **Ethnocentrism** (see Chapter 3), normal in all groups, becomes discriminatory when a majority holds the power to define its own values, norms, attitudes, and interpretation of reality as the standards for the entire society.

Prejudice and Discrimination: A Question of Economics

Although to a certain degree, ethnocentrism and distrust of strangers generate prejudice and discrimination, sociologists now feel that both, as Allport proposed, depend more upon inequality of status, a factor which has its roots in economics. It seems whenever two groups with cultural or physical distinctions come into contact—as is unavoidable in multigroup societies—each tends to magnify the differences of, and attribute negative traits to, the other. This initial reaction does not necessarily continue. If the groups are of equal status, and it is to their advantage to cooperate rather than compete, relations between them generally improve rapidly. If, on the other hand, they hold unequal statuses, economic competition seems unavoidable and in its wake, prejudice and discrimination appear.

Comparing previous conflicts between Catholics and Protestants in America and current ones in Northern Ireland, sociologists are able to support this conclusion (Lieberson, 1980). The arrival of large numbers of Irish, Polish, and Italian Catholics in the latter decades of the nineteenth century provoked the Protestant majority to complain bitterly about the intellectual inferiority, loutish behavior, even physical deficiencies of the new immigrants. Nonetheless, the newly arrived groups were willing to work for much smaller wages than were members of the majority, and therein lay the true problem. Such economic competition represented a threat to the majority, who feared losing their jobs and thus pressured the government to pass the exclusionary immigration laws of the early 1920s. Not until Catholics gained enough economic power to equal Protestants in occupational status did conflicts between them cease to exist (so rapidly and thoroughly, in fact, that few current youth are aware of the country's history of ethnic and religious strife).

Time after time, groups at the bottom of the stratification system have encountered virulent prejudice coupled with gloomy predictions that their inferiority precluded their ever rising from their low status. Yet time after time, on improving their occupational position and achieving economic status comparable to the majority's, they discover that prejudice against them quickly diminishes. Mechanisms of such upward mobility, Stark suggests (1985), include geographic concentration, internal economic development and specialization, and development of a middle class.

Geographic Concentration   Although concentration of minority groups in ethnic enclaves segregated from the majority (Chinatown, little Italy) is usually attributed to discrimination, it also benefits the minorities, sparing them the negative aspects of intergroup conflict and allowing them to continue their traditions, including the use of their native language. Most importantly, congregating in a specific area gives a subordinate group a numerical majority (or

Concentrating in an ethnic enclave has benefited some minorities, allowing them to retain language and cultural traditions. Such enclaves are also in a good position to exert pressure on local governments to pass legislation advantageous to the group.

at least a substantial minority), enabling it to exert pressure on local governments to its advantage. An excellent example is the case of the Irish who maintained control of several city governments and played an important role in the Democratic party in the last years of the nineteenth century and first few decades of the twentieth.

Economic Development Concentration in specific neighborhoods also allows subordinate groups to achieve a small measure of economic independence through supplying services to other members of the group. Because minorities prefer to patronize stores and banks where they can speak their own language, such businesses usually prosper, bringing their owners economic self-sufficiency and sometimes developing into large concerns. Most minority groups, moreover, take advantage of whatever occupational opportunities are available upon their arrival and so develop a kind of occupational specialization (witness the Irish overrepresentation among civil service positions [police and firemen], the Italian among barbers, the Greek among restaurant operators, the Jewish among tailors, and so on).

177

CHAPTER 7

*Social
Differentiation:
Majority and
Minorities*

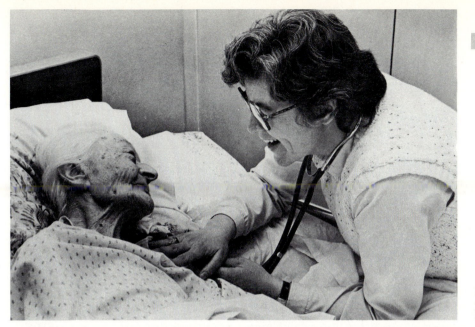

In order for a minority group to achieve parity in a society, it must work to establish a substantial middle class of educated professionals.

Middle Class Finally, in order to prosper, subordinate groups need a substantial middle class to provide members with leadership and expertise. Some groups—the Cubans, and earlier the Jews—arrived with a contingent of middle-class members, or with skills (or values directed toward attaining them) that ensured prompt entry into the middle class. Others stressed the value of higher education to their children as a means to achieve upper-salaried occupations. This method is used by the Jews, who now have the highest average family income of any racial, religious, or ethnic group (Greeley, 1974), and by the Japanese. Upward mobility is slowed for groups that lack a substantial middle class; until such time as one develops, prejudice and discrimination tend to persist. Figure 7.1 illustrates comparative class divisions among ethnic groups from the perspective of the respondents themselves. It is clear that the groups with the largest middle classes are also the most upwardly mobile and feel the least discriminated against.

Racial Minorities

The three visible racial minority groups in the United States are the Native Americans, blacks, and Asian Americans. With the exception of Asian Americans, the history of racial minorities differs from that of more recently arrived ethnic minorities.

Social Class

Question: If you were asked to use one of four names for your social class, which would you say you belong in: the lower class, the working class, the middle class, or the upper class?

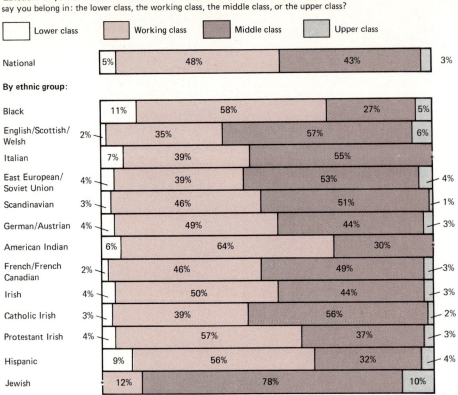

| | Lower class | Working class | Middle class | Upper class |

National — 5% | 48% | 43% | 3%

By ethnic group:

Black	11%	58%	27%	5%
English/Scottish/Welsh	2%	35%	57%	6%
Italian	7%	39%	55%	*
East European/Soviet Union	4%	39%	53%	4%
Scandinavian	3%	46%	51%	1%
German/Austrian	4%	49%	44%	3%
American Indian	6%	64%	30%	*
French/French Canadian	2%	46%	49%	3%
Irish	4%	50%	44%	3%
Catholic Irish	3%	39%	56%	2%
Protestant Irish	4%	57%	37%	3%
Hispanic	9%	56%	32%	4%
Jewish	* 12%	78%		10%

Figure 7.1 A substantial middle class is a prerequisite in order for a minority group to prosper. *Source:* From surveys by National Opinion Research Center, General Social Surveys (*Public Opinion*, October/November 1984, p. 21). Reprinted with permission from *Public Opinion*.

Native Americans

The original inhabitants of the North American continent had occupied the land for over twenty thousand years when they were displaced by European settlers more technologically advanced than themselves, who took advantage of the natives' lack of unity and tribal loyalties. The Native American population was greatly decimated through diseases imported by the white settlers as well as the constant warfare waged against them.

Because the settlers believed their culture to be superior to that of the so-called Indians, they rationalized their seizure of land and felt free to ignore any treaties or agreements between themselves and the natives. After the United States became an independent nation, its government forcibly removed the Indians from desirable land, pushing them onto infertile reservations, where they remained isolated from mainstream society. This reservation land is managed in trust by the Bureau of Indian Affairs, an agency historically more interested in conservation than economic development. Hence, reservations have been characterized by economic backwardness, inadequate education, substandard housing, and inferior health care.

As of 1980, about 1.4 million Native Americans inhabited the United States, most in the western states of California, Oklahoma, Arizona, and New Mexico. Many have left the reservations and live in urban areas. They remain, however, the most disadvantaged of minority groups, with almost one-third living below the poverty level and suffering high rates of unemployment. High mortality rates with alcohol-related causes as well as high rates of suicide also indicate the substandard conditions in which many Native Americans are still forced to live.

The problems of Native Americans are complicated by tribalism—many think of themselves as primarily Navahos or Cherokee, since no overall Native American culture or language exists to unite them. (Approximately 500 tribal groups exist, and around 50 original languages are still spoken.) Only lately has a new militancy arisen, evidenced by the increase in political activity of the American Indian Movement. As a result restitution of certain lands and the development of a degree of economic self-sufficiency has occurred.

Asian Americans

The two largest Asian minorities in the United States are the Chinese and the Japanese. Although culturally, religiously, and linguistically different from each other as well as from the dominant majority, they are generally classified together in the public mind.

Chinese immigration began in the midnineteenth century, following the news of a California gold rush. Chinese men also came as miners and were imported as cheap labor for building the transcontinental railroad. Initially unable to bring their wives, they formed an almost exclusively male society; many took advantage of this situation to establish such small businesses as laundries and restaurants. The Chinese soon became the object of virulent prejudice and discrimination: it was felt that by accepting low wages they were competing unfairly with white laborers; their success as small business-men was also resented. Following several incidents of lynchings and other violence directed against them, the government passed legislation in 1882 to restrict their immigration. These restrictions were not lifted until 1952 and 1965.

Today there are approximately 800,000 Americans of Chinese descent, most living in California and Hawaii. As a group they have been upwardly mobile and are characterized by rising professionalization, being highly represented in the fields of medicine, engineering, and scientific research. Due to their high socioeconomic status it has been easier for the Chinese to amalgamate if they choose, as evidenced by their relatively high rates of intermarriage.

Japanese   The Japanese began arriving during the early part of this century and, like the Chinese before them, were subject to similar discriminatory practices, being considered part of the "yellow peril" that threatened to engulf white culture. Their troubles, however, peaked during World War II when they were labeled security risks and potential traitors and interned in detention camps, with their property subsequently confiscated or sold.

At present, approximately 700,000 Japanese Americans live in the United

States. The generation born here, known as the Nisei, were socialized to value education and conformity to the norms of the dominant majority. As a result, third-generation Japanese Americans rank highest among nonwhite groups in education and income. They have experienced high rates of upward mobility, and with this, a shift from jobs in small ethnic businesses to executive positions in the corporate hierarchy. This trend has also resulted in much amalgamation (40 percent have non-Japanese spouses) particularly among the best educated and most economically successful. Paradoxically, as a result, they are now less cohesive as an ethnic group and run the risk of losing their cultural identity.

Other Asians   According to the 1980 census, an additional 1.5 million persons of Asian background live in the United States: Filipinos, Asian Indians, Koreans, and Vietnamese. Although resentment against these groups has been sharp, particularly in areas where they are highly concentrated, many are economically upwardly mobile and appear to be entering the mainstream with greater ease than their predecessors.

Black Americans

American blacks represent almost 12 percent of the total population and have been here longer than any other nonwhite group: By 1776, the year of American independence, nearly all blacks were native born. However, blacks have failed to attain the proportion of the economic success that many other groups have achieved in two or three generations. This is is partially due to certain special problems, but more especially to economic causes.

Special Problems   The foremost difference between blacks and other minorities is their history of arriving in this country not voluntarily, in search of a better future, but as groups forced into slavery by greedy merchants. Originating from numerous African societies, and totally cut off from any native culture on their arrival, they found themselves in a particularly vulnerable position, forced to live in an alien culture without any possibility of integration. In creating their own black American culture, they could not help but incorporate into it some of the negative perceptions toward themselves exhibited by the dominant majority. Finally, while most other immigrants were free to return to their homeland if life did not work out in the new, no such alternative was open to blacks.

As a result, according to certain social researchers and thinkers, blacks became heirs to a "tangle of pathology," a phrase coined by social scientist Daniel Patrick Moynihan, who later became a politician in the state of New York. Moynihan maintained that the black family had been weakened or destroyed suffering a disproportionate number of female-headed households, and that rampant crime and drug abuse in black neighborhoods was caused by difficulties in adapting to northern urban environments. This report was criticized as an example of "blaming the victim." Female-headed households, it was pointed out, were a characteristic of poor, rather than only black, families.

Other commentators disagreed. Two economic historians, Robert William Fogel and Stanley L. Engerman, challenged the common view of slavery as a debilitating institution and denied that it was at fault in splitting families or breeding slaves for market (1974). They proclaimed slavery both profitable and efficient, a measure of black achievement. As to the black family, the norm was seen as a stable nuclear unit with a Victorian morality. Social historian Herbert Gutman also demonstrates that black family life was vital and enduring during slavery, pointing out that the single-parent black household is primarily a phenomenon of recent decades and not a holdover from slavery times (1976). Although slavery was oppressive, Gutman maintains, blacks were able to adapt to and subtly resist their oppression, particularly through the strength of family ties.

The especially deep prejudice and discrimination against blacks, for many years supported by law and embedded in the society's entire institutional system, has required a longer period of time to wane than has been the case for other immigrant groups. Additionally, as mentioned earlier, while other groups could more easily "get lost" among the majority, such an option was not available to blacks who are, of course, highly visible.

Other theories have suggested that the very size of the black population may work to their detriment: As by far the largest minority group, they represent the greatest threat to whites in competing for jobs. This was especially true in the past, when restrictions on immigration left blacks as the only source of cheap labor and pitted them against a large pool of unskilled white workers. Size is a powerful political tool: after barriers to their voting were removed, blacks took advantage of their numbers and elected increasing numbers into offices around the country.

Economic Causes Until World War II, the great majority of blacks inhabited the rural South, a region until recently characterized by backwardness and poverty. With the demise of the plantations, southern agriculture took place on subsistence farms on which sharecroppers eked out a miserable living. Although conditions for blacks were even worse than for whites due to their segregated (inferior) facilities, both groups suffered from substandard education, housing, and health care, since the southern states were unable to tax their citizens sufficiently to support such services.

The advent of World War II brought a need for workers in defense industries, located chiefly in the urban North. Poor blacks began leaving the South by the trainload in search of the better pay that industrial work entailed. However, these subsistence farmers and farm laborers lacked education and technical skills and were not acquainted with the nature of urban life. According to Stark, such traits made them comparable to immigrants from foreign cultures (1985). White southerners with agricultural backgrounds who came north experienced similar disadvantages, indicating that not so much race as lack of skills and urban ways has stood in the way of upward mobility for both blacks and whites of southern origins.

When viewed as immigrants, blacks can be said to have arrived in mass only about forty years ago, some even more recently. From this perspective, their progress compares favorably with that of other ethnic and racial minorities who improved their economic situation and began their entry into mainstream society in two or three generations.

Blacks have made rapid gains in education and income in recent decades. In 1960, the average American black had not completed eighth grade and was three years behind his white counterpart in the level of education attained. By 1984, the average American black aged 25 and over had 12.2 years of schooling compared with 12.6 for whites. In addition, by 1978, black college graduates earned more than white college graduates: $15,217 for those aged 25 to 29, compared with $14,013 for comparable whites (U.S. Bureau of the Census 1980b, 224–225). At the same time, whereas in 1984 the proportion of United States residents aged 25 and older who had attained four years of college rose to 19.1 percent, only 10.4 percent of blacks had this amount of education. This statistic reveals that college attendance for blacks means a two-year community college rather than a four-year university.

In income, black families before World War II earned only one-third the income of whites. This proportion had grown to 78 percent by 1979, but declined to 58 percent by 1981, owing to a weak economy. In 1984, the median family income of black Americans was $12,429, as opposed to $20,885 for the entire United States. In younger northern families (headed by those under 35) where both spouses work, the gap is considerably smaller. In sum, while equality in education and income remains to be attained, and the barriers to progress for the black minority are difficult to ignore, differences between whites and blacks are growing smaller.

The Underclass   The pace of black progress has been much slowed by the continued existence of the so-called **underclass.** This social class consists of members of racial minorities and whites who, due to lack of skills or health problems, are forced to live a subsistence life-style supported by government help. Strong feeling exists among the black underclass that it has been passed over, and its frustration against the majority, but also against the black middle class and other more fortunate minority groups, occasionally spills over in violent riots. Much urban crime may also result from frustration.

The two major problems faced by the black underclass are a high rate of unemployment and the single-parent family. Unemployment has resulted partly from the exodus of unskilled and semiskilled jobs from the central cities to the suburbs, and partly from the disappearance of such jobs altogether in favor of those requiring more education and technological know-how. The American economy is currently undergoing a shift from an industrial to a service and information society. This shift creates displacements for older unskilled workers, and allows no entry for young workers who lack training. Thus a disproportionate number of blacks aged 16 to 19 are unemployed. The longer they remain so, the more difficulty they will experience finding jobs, particularly if they also lack work habits, having had to survive in the past by hustling. In this way, the vicious circle of the underclass goes on.

By 1984, 41.3 percent of all black families were headed by females compared with 12.6 percent of white families (U.S. Bureau of the Census, 1985). This represents a dramatic increase from 1950, when only a tenth of black families with children under 18 were female headed. Since families headed by women, black or white, tend to have lower incomes, a greater proportion of black families are poor. When traditional black families, in which both parents worked, were compared to female-headed black families in 1981, the former averaged $19,368 in income while the latter averaged $7,921 (U.S. Bureau of the Census, 1983, 23). It is chiefly as a result of this increase in female-headed households that any expansion in individual earnings for blacks is canceled out. The stubbornness with which the underclass endures and even increases has convinced experts of the existence of two black societies: one progressing and vigorous, the other poor and stagnant.

183

CHAPTER 7

*Social
Differentiation:
Majority and
Minorities*

In fact, about 40 percent of the black population can now be considered middle class, as compared with 5 percent in 1940. This middle class consists of well-educated blacks who, thanks to policies such as affirmative action, are able to obtain high-paying positions. But the lack of education keeps poor, ghetto blacks in the same condition as before. Black sociologist Wilson (1984, 99) maintains, that:

> The existence of a black underclass, as I have suggested, is due far more to historic discrimination and to broad demographic and economic trends than it is to racial discrimination in the present day. For that reason, the underclass has not benefited significantly from "race specific" antidiscrimination policies, such as affirmative action, that have aided so many trained and educated blacks. If inner-city blacks are to be helped, they will be helped not by policies addressed primarily to inner-city minorities, but by policies designed to benefit all of the nation's poor.

Ethnic Minorities

With a monument such as the Statue of Liberty as its national symbol, it is not surprising that the United States has come to be called a nation of immigrants, who form the society's **ethnic minorities.** Looking back a generation or two, a majority of American families will find an ancestor who was born "over there," or "in the old country." The ethnic experience thus lies in the background of a great number of Americans.

Hispanic Americans

The better than 15 million Hispanic Americans do not constitute a unified community, nor do they possess a common culture. This fragmentation results from their arrival at different times and from different places of origin. However, they are bound by a common language, by Spanish surnames, and by the Catholic religion. Three major Hispanic subdivisions are the Mexican Americans or Chicanos (approximately 60 percent), the Puerto Ricans (14 percent), and the Cubans (6 percent). Other Spanish-speaking groups include natives of South American countries.

Many Mexican Americans are actually native to the United States, having occupied the Southwest before the American colonization and annexation of Mexican land occurred. Others continue to trickle across the Mexican border in search of better jobs. Although opportunities may be better for them in the United States than in their home country, Chicanos have been the least upwardly mobile of the Spanish-speaking groups, exchanging the farm labor their parents performed for urban, unskilled work at no significant increase in pay. Illegal aliens who pour in on a daily basis are generally employed in low-wage services or manufacturing jobs whose employers are attempting to keep labor costs down and unions out.

Some of the reasons for the lack of upward mobility among Chicanos may be attributed to (1) the traditional Mexican family, which is extended and large, providing much support to its members but also restricting their mobility; (2) life in the "barrio," the neighborhood where most tend to live, which protects members from prejudice and discrimination but also works to isolate them from the mainstream; (3) the closeness to Mexico, to which members often return for visits or to retire; this proximity helps them retain their native language and homeland ties, but hinders their progress in the United States; (4) the clash of cultures which children encounter between home and school, resulting in a high rate of school dropouts; (5) the subsequent lack of training and education which traps younger generations into the same low-income jobs.

As their numbers increase—they are fast becoming the second-largest minority in the United States—Chicanos are acquiring more political clout. As a result, more of their younger members are becoming involved in political processes and elective offices.

Puerto Ricans   Although Puerto Rico has the status of an "associated free state" and Puerto Ricans have been considered American citizens since Spain ceded the territory to the United States in 1898, immigration from the island did not begin in large numbers until the 1950s (Puerto Rico became a Commonwealth in 1952). Today about two million Puerto Ricans live in the United States, concentrated mainly in the cities of the Eastern Seaboard, particularly New York, and in the large cities of the Midwest.

As a group, Puerto Ricans are culturally and racially distinct from Chicanos, being a blend of predominantly black and Spanish culture, as opposed to Spanish and native Indian cultures. Some upward mobility exists for a number of Puerto Ricans who are entering the professions and moving into suburban areas. But many are hampered by a language deficiency which makes them perform poorly on standardized tests and contributes to their high dropout rate. Another obstacle lies in the fact that 44 percent of Puerto Rican families are headed by women. Attempts are under way to channel the energy of the new generation into political activism and thereby improve the group's welfare in this country.

Cubans   Most Cubans came to the United States following Fidel Castro's rise to power. They differ substantially from other Spanish-speaking groups, being generally much older and better educated. The first wave to enter this country, professionals fleeing the communist regime, were able to utilize their skills, experience, and expertise in the economy almost immediately upon their arrival. Their success is reflected in their income, higher than that of other Spanish-speaking groups. A second wave of immigrants who arrived in 1980 do not appear equally skilled, and it is doubtful this group will attain the success of its predecessors.

Religious Minorities

Of the three factors affecting minority status, the religious has been the least destructive in this society. The United States, founded by English and Dutch settlers, remained a relatively homogeneous Protestant society until the arrival of the first waves of European immigrants around 1820. Even then, since most were also Protestant, these immigrants were generally easily absorbed into the Wasp majority. Between 1860 and 1920, however, immigrants hailing from central, eastern, and southern Europe arrived differing not only in language but in religion.

The descendants of these immigrants (Poles, Italians, Slavs) have, since the 1970s, been dubbed **white ethnics.** White ethnics, who prize both their American citizenship and their ethnic origins, include the largest religious minorities, Catholics and Jews.

Catholics

Catholics represent about 25 percent of the American population. Until a few decades ago, the Protestant majority viewed Catholics with great suspicion, attributing their loyalty to the Pope as a form of betrayal of the democratic ideology. Nonetheless, individual Catholics and Catholic families have fared well, culminating in the 1960 election of Catholic president John F. Kennedy.

A stratification hierarchy is visible among Catholics, with Irish and other Northern Europeans at the top, Eastern Europeans in the middle, and Hispanic groups at the bottom. These internal divisions, however, have subsided as anti-Catholic feelings in the society at large have disappeared. Similarly, differences between Catholics and Protestants in family size, income, education, and occupation are also vanishing (Greeley, 1977; Archdeacon, 1983).

At one time, white ethnics tended to congregate in cultural enclaves (such as "little Italy") where it was easier to retain native tongues and customs. Later generations became dispersed in the suburbs, and with dispersion came a loss of ethnic traditions. Adherence to a particular religion, however, frequently endures. As a result, Catholicism serves as a means of retaining identity and forming primary group relationships.

Jews

Jewish Americans, some six million strong, are ethnics in the sense that they share cultural traits to a greater extent than physical similarities or religious beliefs. In fact, although they may be affiliated with either Orthodox, Conservative, or Reform branches of Judaism, most adult Jews are not overly active in religious affairs. Still, they think of themselves as Jews.

The Jewish people represent a classic example of a minority persecuted throughout the world. In the United States, prejudice and discrimination against Jews were rampant in the form of denied access to neighborhoods, schools, jobs, and social clubs. Anti-Semitism in America, however, never acquired the proportions it did in other countries. It exists today in a subtle form only occasionally marred by incidents of vandalism against Jewish property.

In general, Jews have been highly successful in educational and economic spheres, being widely represented among college graduates and attaining positions with substantial earnings. Figure 7.2 shows the extraordinarily high percentage of Jewish respondents who are college graduates. They are, none-

Figure 7.2 The Jewish minority has chosen the road of higher education to attain upward mobility. *Note:* 1982, 1983, 1984 combined. *Source:* From surveys by National Opinion Research Center, General Social Surveys (*Public Opinion,* October/November 1984, p. 21). Reprinted with permission of *Public Opinion.*

Education

Question: What is the highest grade in elementary school or high school that you finished or got credit for?

	Less than high school graduate	High-school graduate	Some college	College graduate/ postgraduate
National	30%	34%	20%	17%

By ethnic group:

	Less than high school graduate	High-school graduate	Some college	College graduate/ postgraduate
Black	41%	30%	19%	10%
English/Scottish/Welsh	18%	32%	23%	28%
Italian	28%	35%	25%	13%
East European/Soviet Union	24%	32%	25%	19%
Scandinavian	25%	40%	21%	14%
German/Austrian	24%	41%	18%	18%
American Indian	38%	38%	20%	4%
French/French Canadian	19%	41%	22%	18%
Irish	26%	32%	24%	19%
Catholic Irish	13%	33%	28%	27%
Prostestant Irish	34%	32%	21%	13%
Hispanic	45%	30%	17%	8%
Jewish	8%	18%	29%	45%

theless, still not proportionately represented among the corporate elite. Inter-marriage rates for Jews are high, a fact that worries many Jewish leaders inasmuch as it portends the end of ethnic solidarity. A recent rash of anti-Semitism, perhaps fueled by conflicts in the Middle East, may act as a unifying force to bring Jews back together.

The Chapter in Brief

Conflict appears to be an integral part of group life, especially when a number of groups of dissimilar culture or appearance must share the same territory. In such a situation, a majority-minorities relationship develops, in which minorities are denied equal access to societal rewards. The status of **minority** is usually applied to groups that differ from the dominant one in appearance and/or culture, and sometimes also in religion, gender, age, and through being afflicted with handicaps.

The United States contains minorities based on all these factors in its midst. **Racial minorities** have been the victims of racist ideology as well as prejudice and discrimination. **Racism** is based on a faulty conception of the term **race**, whereby cultural traits and behavior in a group are considered genetically inherited. Scientists actually use the word race to make broad distinctions among populations that have inbred and interbred. Inbreeding causes a group to share similar physical attributes, setting them visibly apart from other groups. Interbreeding disperses such traits throughout a vast spectrum, so that a "pure" race no longer exists.

In contrast to race, **ethnicity** refers to a group's distinctive social features: language, religion, values, beliefs, food habits. Ethnic groups form subcultures within the larger society. Such groups are maintained by common national origin or history, by strong in-group feelings, and by belief in a shared destiny.

All minorities are subject to **prejudice** and **discrimination.** Prejudice is the holding of unproved beliefs about a group and the retention of these in the face of facts disproving their truth. Discrimination is action based on such beliefs in the form of denying a minority equal access to a society's sources of wealth, power, and prestige. Of the various types of discrimination, the **institutional,** in its structural and cultural forms, is the most difficult to eliminate. However, as a minority's socioeconomic status approaches that of the dominant group, prejudice and discrimination against it tend to disappear. Conflict between groups is exacerbated only when the minority competes for scarce jobs; equality of status tends to engender cooperation among groups.

Dominant groups deal with minorities in a variety of ways. The ideologies of **Anglo-conformity**—taking on the language, values, and beliefs of the original English Protestant settlers—and of the **melting pot**—becoming **amalgamated** into a new breed of American—have given way to the ideal of **cultural pluralism.** In a truly pluralistic society, various racial, religious, and ethnic groups retain their culture but coexist in harmony with the majority and enjoy equal access to societal rewards.

The United States, long a haven for foreign immigrants, is aspiring to become a fully pluralistic society. In the meantime, while some minorities have been absorbed into the mainstream, others remain distinct and subject to prejudice and discrimination. Among the latter are blacks, Hispanics, and Native Americans. The racially distinct Asian Americans (Chinese and Japanese) have achieved upward social mobility through education and professionalization.

The group described as **white ethnics** includes descendants of Poles, Irish, Italians, Greeks, and Slavs. These groups were sufficiently different from the Wasps of the dominant group to suffer considerable discrimination as a result. Today, many no longer live in ethnic enclaves and their younger, college-educated generation has entered the mainstream. The older generation is represented in large numbers in the lower and working classes.

Among religious minorities, Catholics and Jews were subject to prejudice and discrimination at the turn of this century and throughout the first several decades. Feelings of hostility may have been directed toward their ethnic origin—Eastern and Southern European—as much as toward their religions. In any event, both groups have done well socioeconomically, being represented among high earners and in the professional ranks.

Terms to Remember

Accommodation   A situation in which a minority is conscious of, accepts, and adapts to the norms and values of the majority, but still chooses to retain its own norms and values.

Acculturation   The process of adopting the culture, including the language and customs, of the host country.

Amalgamation   The product of intermarriage between distinct racial, ethnic, and cultural groups, resulting in the erasure of differences between majority and minorities.

Anglo-conformity   The attitude, once held by the majority group, that the institutions, language, and cultural patterns of England should be maintained.

Assimilation   A process through which a minority group is absorbed into, or becomes part of, the dominant group in a society.

Cultural pluralism   An ideal condition in which the cultural distinctiveness of each ethnic, racial, and religious minority group within a society is retained, while individual members maintain allegiance to the larger society.

Discrimination   Actions taken as a result of prejudicial feelings.

Ethnicity   A group's distinctive social, rather than biological, traits.

Ethnic minority   A group that differs culturally from the dominant group.

Ethnocentrism   Belief in the superiority of one's own group.

Individual discrimination   Negative behavior against a particular group—or individual members of that group—prompted by personal prejudice.

Institutional discrimination   Negative behavior toward minority groups prompted by the knowledge that such prejudice exists on a societal level; that it is, in effect, a norm of the society. Institutional discrimination takes structural forms—in the demands and characteristics of such structures as government and the economy—and cultural ones—in which the majority defines its own values, norms, attitudes, and interpretations of reality as the standards for the entire society.

Majority or dominant group   Group in society that may be numerically smaller than the minorities, but that controls the important sectors of social life—language, ideology, and values.

Melting-pot theory   The belief that it is possible and desirable to fuse both culturally and biologically the various racial and ethnic groups in society.

Minority group   Any group in society kept from attaining societal rewards on the basis of culture, race, religion, sex, or age. A category of people who possess imperfect access to positions of power and to the corollary dimensions of prestige and privilege in the society.

Prejudice   Prejudgment of an individual or group based on stereotypes and hearsay rather than on fact or evidence, and the inability or unwillingness to change such judgment even when confronted with evidence to the contrary.

Race   An arbitrary subdivision of the species *Homo sapiens* based on differences in the frequency with which certain genes occur among populations.

Racial minority   A group within a society that differs biologically from the dominant group in such characteristics as skin color, hair texture, eye slant, and head shape and dimensions.

Racism   The belief that racial groups display not only physical but also behavioral differences, and that both are inherited and inferior or undesirable.

Segregation   The attempt to isolate a minority from the majority.

Underclass   A social class consisting of members of racial minorities and whites who, due to lack of skills or health problems, live a subsistence lifestyle supported by government help.

White ethnics   Non-Wasp descendants of immigrants from eastern and southern Europe.

Suggestions for Further Reading

Kitano, Harry H. L.   1985. *Race relations.* 3d ed. Englewood Cliffs, N.J.: Prentice-Hall. This text provides a thorough survey of race relations in the United States.

Lieberson, Stanley.   1981. *A piece of the pie: Blacks and white immigrants since 1880.* Berkeley: University of California Press. The author speculates on the reason for the greater economic success of immigrants from southern and eastern Europe as opposed to blacks.

Lukas, J. Anthony.   1985. *Common ground: A turbulent decade in the lives of three American families.* New York: Knopf. A Pulitzer-winning book relating the social conflict produced by the order to desegregate the school system of Boston.

Rose, Peter I.   1983. *Mainstream and margins: Jews, blacks, and other Americans.* New Brunswick, N.J.: Transaction. An authority on ethnic and race relations selects an array of sociological articles dealing with the subject.

Moore, Joan and Harry Pacon.   1985. *Hispanics in the United States.* Englewood Cliffs, N.J.: Prentice-Hall. The social problems encountered by recent immigrants to the United States as well as their everyday lives are explored in this paperback.

Wilson, William Julius.   1980. *The declining significance of race: Blacks and changing American institutions.* 2d ed. Chicago: University of Chicago Press. Although the past decades have seen an improvement in the conditions of blacks, the pursuit of economic equality with whites is being won by the middle and upper middle segments of the black minority. Conditions for the underclass, on the other hand, are deteriorating.

A New American Dilemma

GLENN C. LOURY

Forty years after Gunnar Myrdal declared that America was facing a dramatic dilemma with its black minority—having failed to either assimilate it or give it parity—it is facing a similar dilemma with a segment of that minority. While a substantial black middle class has risen in the stratification system, those left in the ghetto are sinking further into crime, poverty, and despair, while black leaders are becoming politically more isolated. It is a time for reexamining their ideas, according to this black social scientist.

Forty years ago the Swedish economist Gunnar Myrdal argued in *An American Dilemma* that the problem of race in the United States cut to the very core of our definition as a people. Myrdal described America as a nation which, although founded on the ideals of individual liberty and personal dignity, could not bring itself—through either law or social practice—to treat the descendants of slaves as the equals of whites. The dilemma for white leaders in particular was that these racial practices were so deeply ingrained that even if they wanted to get rid of them, it seemed politically impossible to do so. In 1944 Myrdal hardly could have foreseen the extent to which the United States would confront and begin to resolve this great dilemma. As recently as twenty years ago many conservatives denied as a matter of principle that the government should interfere in private decisions in order to assure equal opportunity for black people. (Ronald Reagan, for example, opposed the 1964 Civil Rights Act.) Two decades later that position has been completely discredited, both legally and morally.

The old racism is not gone, but the disparity between American ideals and racial practice has narrowed dramatically. Today the civil rights debate is dominated by the

Source: From *The New Republic* (December 31, 1984), pp. 14–16. Reprinted by permission of THE NEW REPUBLIC, © 1984, The New Republic, Inc.

issue of affirmative action, in which the question is whether the history of racism warrants special—not simply equal—treatment for blacks. Whereas blacks were once excluded from politics by subterfuge and the threat of violence, they now constitute a potent political bloc with often decisive influence on local and national elections. Martin Luther King Jr., whose passionate, relentless, and compelling articulation of black aspirations made him the nemesis of Presidents, governors, and F.B.I. officials alike, is now honored as a national hero. The moral victory of the civil rights movement is virtually complete.

And yet racial divisions remain. Today we are faced with a new American dilemma, one that is especially difficult for black leaders and members of the black middle class. The bottom stratum of the black community has compelling problems which can no longer be blamed solely on white racism, and which force us to confront fundamental failures in black society. The social disorganization among poor blacks, the lagging academic performance of black students, the disturbingly high rate of black-on-black crime, and the alarming increase in early unwed pregnancies among blacks now loom as the primary obstacles to progress. To admit these failures is likely to be personally costly for black leaders, and may also play into the hands of lingering racist sentiments. Not to admit them, however, is to forestall their resolution and to allow the racial polarization of the country to worsen. If the new American dilemma is not dealt with soon, we may face the possibility of a permanent split in our political system along racial lines.

It is deeply ironic that this dilemma has arisen in the wake of the enormous success of the civil rights movement. In little more than a generation, the United States has changed from a country callously indifferent to the plight of its black citizens into one for which that plight is a central feature of our political life. A new middle class of well-educated and well-placed blacks has emerged, whose members can be found in technical, managerial, and professional positions throughout the leading institutions of the nation. Differences in earnings between young, well-educated black and white workers have diminished dramatically; and something approximating parity in economic status has been achieved for young, intact black families.

Yet, in general, even this class of blacks does not view itself as being in the American mainstream. There is a keen appreciation among blacks of all social classes that at least one-third of their fellow blacks belong to the underclass. There is no way to downplay the social pathologies that afflict this part of the black community. In the big-city ghettos, the youth unemployment rate often exceeds 40 percent. It is not uncommon for young men to leave school at age 16 and reach their mid-20s without ever having held a steady job. In these communities, more than half of all black babies are born out of wedlock. (In Central Harlem the most recently reported figure is 79.9 percent.) Black girls between the ages of 15 and 19 constitute the most fertile population of that age group in the industrialized world; and their birth rate is twice as high as any other group of women in the West.

The undeniable progress of the black middle class has been accompanied by the undeniable spread of these problems. Today nearly three of every five black children do not live with both their parents. The level of dependency on public assistance for basic economic survival in the black population has essentially doubled since 1964. About one-half of all black children are supported in part by transfers from the state and federal governments. Over half of black children in public primary and secondary schools are concentrated in the nation's twelve largest central city school districts, where the quality of education is notoriously poor, and where whites constitute only about a quarter of total enrollment. Only about one black student in seven scores above the 50th percentile on the standardized college admissions tests. Blacks, though little more than one-tenth of the population, constitute approximately one-half of the imprisoned felons in the nation.

Among those great many blacks who have entered the middle class in the past twenty years there is, understandably, a deeply felt sense of outrage at the injustice of conditions endured by the black poor. Somewhat less understandable is their reluctance to consider their own success as evidence of the profound change that has taken place in American attitudes, institutions, and practices. The position of poor blacks is perceived as being inherently linked to the racist past of the nation, as proving that the historic injustice of which Myrdal spoke still flourishes.

Moreover, middle-class blacks do not generally look to their own lives as examples of what has become possible for those blacks still left behind. Talented black professionals, who in decades past would have had scant opportunity for advancement, now, in the interest of fairness and racial balance, are avidly sought in corporate board rooms or on elite university faculties. Nonetheless they find it possible, indeed necessary, to think of themselves as members of an oppressed caste.

The great majority of Americans do not see the situation of blacks in this way. Whereas black politicians and intellectuals consider the ghetto and all that occurs there to be simple proof that the struggle for civil rights has yet to achieve its goals, others are repelled by the nature of social life in poor black communities. Though most are too polite to say so, they see the poverty of these communities as

substantially due to the behavior of the people living there. They are unconvinced by the tortured rationalizations offered by black and (some) liberal white spokesmen. They do not think of themselves or their country as responsible for these dreadful conditions. Most nonblack Americans know something of hardship. Most were not born wealthy; many have parents or grandparents who came here with next to nothing, and who worked hard so that their children might have a better life. Most aren't hostile or even indifferent to the aspirations of blacks. In fact they point with pride to the advancement that blacks have made, to the elaborate legal apparatus erected since 1964 to assure racial fairness, and to the private efforts undertaken by a great number of individuals and institutions to increase black participation in their activities.

A recent Gallup poll conducted for the Joint Center for Political Studies, a black think tank in Washington, revealed the dimensions of the gulf between black and white perceptions. More than two out of three whites said they believe that "all in all, compared with five years ago, the situation of black people in this country has improved," compared to only about one in three blacks. Nearly one-half of the whites polled were "satisfied with the way things are going at this time," but only one-seventh of blacks were. One-half of blacks felt that "blacks should receive preference in getting jobs," compared to one in eleven whites. Some 72 percent of blacks but only 31 percent of whites thought of Ronald Reagan as "prejudiced."

The 1984 Presidential election made distressingly clear why this gap is not likely to be bridged. Two-thirds of all whites voted for Reagan, while nine-tenths of all blacks voted against him. And black leaders went beyond merely opposing the President. Roger Wilkins lambasted the Administration for engaging in a "concerted effort to constrict the democratic rights" of blacks, an effort which Coretta King said was aimed at "turning back the clock" on black progress. Benjamin Hooks declared that the Administration had to be "eliminated from the face of the earth."

It strains credulity to attribute Reagan's broadly based landslide to a resurgent racism among whites. Much broader forces are evidently at work—just as there are forces broader than racism sustaining and encouraging the social pathology of the ghetto. But black leaders, like their constituents, cannot seem to bring themselves to admit this. They prefer to portray the problems of the ghetto as stemming from white racism, and to foster racial politics as the primary means of fighting it. Within the Democratic Party, racial splits such as the one created by Jesse Jackson's Presidential candidacy or the civil war between Chicago Mayor Harold Washington and his white opponents may be a sign of things to come. By casting their political battles in starkly racial terms, black leaders help to promote a racial schism in American political life, without necessarily addressing the most fundamental problems of their constituents.

Unfortunately, neither Democratic leaders nor Republican leaders nor black leaders have much incentive to prevent this political fracas from exacerbating the general racial division of American society. The Democrats, having just finished a campaign in which a quarter of the votes for Walter Mondale were cast by blacks, appear to have a big stake in the perpetuation of racial schism. Far from viewing the "color gap" with alarm, Democratic strategists have come to depend on it. Yet under electoral pressure the Democrats have had to keep their distance from the black leadership. The Democrats' chief problem is how to maintain the enthusiasm of black supporters without alienating white supporters. Witness one of the cen-

tral dilemmas of the Mondale candidacy: how to keep Jesse Jackson close enough to win blacks but far enough away to placate whites.

The Republicans cannot, in the short run, expect to win much support from blacks, no matter what they do. Some right-wing Republican candidates are not above exploiting the vestiges of racism. (Jesse Helms, for example, managed to mention Jesse Jackson's name twenty-four times in a fund-raising solicitation during his recent reelection campaign.) Thus, from the Republicans' point of view, the benefits of rapprochement will seem slight, and the costs as potentially great. Representative Jack Kemp's speech at the Urban League convention—in which he made an overt appeal for black support, pledging to include the black poor in his "new opportunity society"—was a hopeful exception to the Republicans' indifference.

But of all the actors in this drama, black leaders play the most important role, and the most problematic. The prevailing ideological cast of many prominent black leaders and intellectuals is considerably to the left of the national mainstream, and often of the black community itself. Because of the long history of racist exclusion, many blacks place group solidarity above mere philosophical differences when deciding whom to support. A black ideologue of the left (or, for that matter, of the right—Louis Farrakhan, for example) is almost immune from challenge by another black, since it is precisely in ideological terms that whites most often oppose him. By posing the challenge, the black critic seems to ride with whites against his own race. The black challenger may thus forfeit black political support if he expands his appeal to white voters by criticizing incumbent black leadership. The opposition of whites to the black incumbent is taken by other blacks as proof that he is "sticking it to the man," and thus deserves support.

The black challenger winds up appearing, in the eyes of his own people, to be an agent of forces inimical to their interests.

As a result, many black leaders act in ways which exacerbate their isolation from the American political mainstream without fear of reproach by more centrist blacks. The way in which the Voting Rights Act has come to be enforced compounds the problem. To avoid redistricting battles in courts, legislatures routinely create overwhelmingly black, electorally "safe" districts for black incumbents. As a result, most nationally prominent black politicians do not require white support to retain their prominence. Those blacks who do require white support—Los Angeles Mayor Tom Bradley, for example—are discernibly closer to the center of the Democratic Party.

The results can be bizarre. Jesse Jackson actually campaigned in the Deep South urging local politicians to join his Rainbow Coalition so that, working together, they might enact the Equal Rights Amendment, eliminate state right-to-work laws, and secure a nuclear freeze. Most candidates running in the South on such a platform have short political careers. Lasting alliances between poor southern blacks and whites, if they are to emerge at all, will not emerge with this as the substance of the black politician's appeal. Yet southern whites who are repulsed by such "progressive" candidates are written off as racists. And the incentive for the emergence of a centrist black leadership which might someday achieve significant white support is diminished even further.

Social Differentiation: Sex, Age, and Handicaps

Gender and age—as well as a variety of physical handicaps and distinct sexual preferences—have always been factors in the treatment of certain members of society: Males have been treated differently from females; the young differently from the old; those with physical abnormalities or who prefer same-sex partners differently from their more orthodox counterparts. Although social differentiation is part and parcel of all societies—and inequality of every society that produces a surplus—only in the past several decades have socially differentiated groups been viewed in the contexts of stratification and minorities.

The concept of stratification accurately reflects the conditions of women, the aged, the handicapped, and the homosexual, since these categories of people occupy a lower status in society as a result of biological causes not of their own choosing. The concept of minority is relevant in its description of groups denied equal access to society's rewards on the basis of ascribed traits (those with which they are born and cannot change), or of achieved status (that of homosexuals, for instance) that a majority in the society consider deviant or at least undesirable.

The Making of Men and Women

One is born either male or female; maleness and femaleness are therefore *biological* terms, descriptive of biological facts. Masculine and feminine, on the other hand, are adjectives reflecting *social* constructs, descriptive of how males and females act in a given society. The first is a *sex status*, ascribed and not subject to change except in extraordinary circumstances; the second is a *gender role*, achieved and subject to change according to time and place.

As noted in Chapter 4, members of every society must be socialized to fill the roles that correspond to their statuses. Sex roles are no exception: They, too, must be acquired. But before we discuss societal roles assigned to men and women, we must first specify the biological differences between the sexes.

Biological Differences: Nature

Biological differences between men and women may be roughly divided into those of an anatomical, genetic, or hormonal nature. Anatomical differences are the most obvious, consisting of physical structure and bodily appearance. Variations here include height, weight, distribution of body fat and hair, and musculature. These differences are referred to as **secondary sex characteristics** and may be measured on a continuum: that is, not every woman is shorter, lighter, more rounded, less hairy, and less muscular than every man, just as not every man is taller, heavier, more angular, hairier, and more muscular than every woman. In fact, the most important anatomical difference lies in the distinct male and female reproductive systems. The reproductive system of women allows them to become pregnant, give birth, and nurse the young of the species. The reproductive system of men allows them to impregnate women.

Pregnancy and nursing periodically incapacitate women from performing certain economic and social functions, whereas the man's role in reproduction ends with impregnation. These facts have profound social consequences.

Genetic differences become apparent when analyzing sex chromosomes, receptacles of the genes which determine heredity in all living creatures. Humans inherit two sex chromosomes, one each from the mother and father. Females inherit two X chromosomes, while males inherit one X and one Y. A male is born when an ovum bearing the X chromosome is fertilized by a sperm bearing a Y. A female is born when the ovum is fertilized by a sperm bearing an X. Females produce ova, all of which contain X chromosomes; males produce sperms, half of which contain X chromosomes (inherited from the mother), and the other half Y chromosomes (inherited from the father).

Whether chromosomal differences influence personality, ability, and behavior in males and females has not been scientifically established. We do know, however, that many more male than female babies are stillborn or malformed; that male babies suffer over 30 hereditary disorders; that more male than female babies die, so that even though more males are born, the ratio evens out or females actually outnumber males by the middle twenties. Even beyond infancy and early adulthood, males are more likely to be killed in violent crimes and auto accidents, and older men suffer from heart disease and occupational hazards to a greater extent than older women do. In short, in spite of being stereotyped as the weaker sex, women appear more resistant to disease and more adept at survival, which may be nature's way of insuring a sufficient supply of them to keep the species going.

Hormonal differences begin to appear about three months after fertilization and are responsible for the differentiation into two genders. (Up to this time, the fetus is sexually undifferentiated: it may become either male or female.) **Hormones** are chemicals secreted into the bloodstream by specific glands. Their function is to stimulate or inhibit chemical processes. Hormones involved in the development of sex characteristics include estrogen and progesterone produced by the ovaries in females, and testosterone and androgen produced by the testes in males. Both males and females produce male and female sex hormones, in proportions which vary by gender. The fetus with an XY chromosomal formation begins to secrete testosterone, which functions to inhibit development of female characteristics; hence, the fetus will be born a male. At puberty, sex hormones determine the development of secondary sex characteristics, inducing the growth of beards in males and breasts in females.

Hormones, then, influence physical development. They also affect behavior. Animal experiments have shown that an increase of testosterone, even in females, produces an increase in aggressive behavior and sex drive.

If behavior of the two sexes differed on the basis of biology alone, men and women in all societies and in all instances would behave distinctly in the same ways. But they do not. A few examples will illustrate this fact.

Researchers Money and Erhardt (1972) studied a pair of identical male twins, one of whom, in a tragic accident, had lost his entire penis during the surgical procedure of circumcision. The parents were subsequently convinced to raise the twin who had suffered the accident as a female. Other than surgically constructing a vagina, nothing was done to the twin until puberty except that the parents treated "her" as a girl: they let her hair grow long, adorned her with hair ribbons and jewelry, and dressed her in frilly "feminine" clothes. Soon the child was behaving as little girls are expected to in our society: she was neater than her brother, more willing to help with housework, and requested dolls and a dollhouse as Christmas presents. Even though biologically male, she acted as females do in American society.

Cross-cultural evidence also indicates that nurture can affect behavior to a greater extent than nature. A classic study by anthropologist Margaret Mead (1935), who based her findings on an analysis of three preliterate tribes in New Guinea, revealed that men can act as women are expected to do, and vice versa. For instance, in one society Mead studied, both men and women were gentle, emotionally responsive, uncompetitive, and lacking in aggression. Additionally, both were responsible for the care of children. In another tribe, however, both possessed personality types that could be characterized as masculine; that is, aggressive and violent. Women disliked anything connected with motherhood (such as pregnancy, nursing, and caring for their children) and were especially obnoxious to their daughters. Finally, in a third tribe, Mead found profound differences in the behavior of men and women. But contrary to expectations, each sex behaved in a manner Americans would consider the opposite of how they "ought" to: Women were domineering and aggressive, and the economic providers in the household. Men were passive, took care of the children, engaged in gossip, and liked to adorn themselves. Mead concluded from her analysis that sex roles had little to do with biological sex; that is, a person born either male or female does not necessarily and always act in ways determined by his or her biological makeup.

Such a conclusion is not without challenge. One cross-cultural comparison of six societies showed that in each boys were more aggressive and violent than girls, and girls more nurturing and emotionally responsive, especially to children (Whiting, 1963). Findings such as this substantiate long-held conclusions that fighting and leadership are predominantly associated with males, and that males are more prone to sexual attack, promiscuity, homosexuality, voyeurism, and other forms of aggressive sexual activity (Ford and Beach, 1951; Murdock, 1957). Contemporary medical studies also suggest that male and female brains function differently, in particular that the two hemispheres of women's brains are better integrated than those of men (Durden-Smith and deSimone, 1953).

What is to be done with these conflicting facts? Do men and women behave

199

CHAPTER 8

*Social
Differentiation:
Sex, Age, and
Handicaps*

In spite of important biological differences between the sexes, women can learn to do carpentry and men to bake pies.

differently due to biological differences? Or are they merely socialized to accept different roles? In short, what makes men and women? Nature or nurture? As usual, the issue cannot be resolved in simplistic terms. In the social sciences, it is not sufficient to focus simply on biological differences. These indeed exist, in some areas to a notable extent. The question to be pursued, however, concerns the social significance that such differences acquire in human societies.

Sex Roles: Whys and Wherefores

Traditional thought would have us believe that biology is responsible for the different **sex roles** men and women have been called upon to perform in societies around the world. But as has been amply demonstrated, socialization can subvert biology to a certain degree. The fact that women give birth does not necessarily make them tender and nurturing mothers: In certain historical periods, mothers had no scruples about exposing their infants to ice and snow to see if they would survive, or sending them to live with strangers, or even throwing them on trash heaps to die. What, then, determines the roles men and women fill?

The question should be rephrased in the past tense, for the sex roles we fill to this day derive their original logic from the dawn of human history when the species survived by hunting and gathering. Early bands of hunters and gatherers had to pool their resources in order to survive: Each individual had to contribute his or her best effort. Hence tasks that had to be performed were divided according to who could best accomplish each. Men were taller and stronger than women, children, and the old; they were thus assigned the more dangerous chore of hunting. Women, often incapacitated by pregnancy and possessing the only means of feeding the young, found it easier to remain close to the home base, gathering fruits and grains, sheltered from the hazards of the open road. Women were also regarded as the more precious of the two sexes, the continuation of the species depending upon their ability to give birth and raise their offspring to maturity. They therefore (along with their children who were small and weak) had to be protected. This basic division of labor is characteristic of preliterate societies throughout history.

Different tasks, it was also soon discovered, required different skills, and certain kinds of personalities were deemed best suited to specific activities. If one had to fight off an enemy band, it was better to be aggressive; if one had to spear a young deer for the family supper, it was better to be somewhat callous. On the other hand, if one wanted the species to continue, one had to raise children; and parents who wanted their children to cherish or at least care for them in old age understood it was better to act lovingly toward them and have their welfare at heart when they were young.

Distinct personalities needed to fit these tasks were produced by socializing those destined to perform them in different ways. By treating sons one way and daughters another, parents could mold them to behave distinctly, in the best interests of the group.

Unfortunately, this very sensible solution to the problems facing early hunting and gathering groups had two consequences which still affect contemporary societies today. First males, who were most familiar with issues of hunting and fighting, began making decisions on behalf of the group about when to move to better hunting grounds and whether to take on enemy tribes or flee to safer territory. Decision making on these critical matters soon led to decision making on most other major issues and hence to power and dominance over the rest of the group (women, children, and the elderly). Second, roles which had evolved out of an original division of labor became so rigidly crystallized that people began to think of them as being inborn, as inherently characteristic of men and women, instead of simply the effects of socialization. Thus the result of different socialization became further justification for the perpetuation of the process.

Gender-Role Socialization

Socialization into **gender** roles begins early. Though infants require the same care, there are differences in the way parents treat their infant boys and girls. Baby girls get touched more often and handled more gently than baby boys (Sears, Maccoby, and Levin, 1957; Weitzman, 1975). On the other hand, assertive and aggressive behavior on the part of little boys is not only tolerated but expected and encouraged. The messages that come across to most children are clear: Girls must be clean, neat, pretty, docile, passive, and noncompetitive. Boys should engage in rough-and-tumble activities, be competitive, aggressive, strong, clever, and value independence. So clearly are messages about what constitutes masculine and feminine behavior given and received that by age three almost all children know their sex and, shortly thereafter, how each sex is expected to behave. Some individuals, however, apparently fail to understand these clues, or understanding them, fail to accept them. This failure may partly explain the existence of homosexuality, which some behavioral scientists attribute precisely to a mistaken perception of appropriate sex roles for specific genders.

Sex Typing The process of socialization into sex roles takes place through *conditioning,* where rewards are given for correct behavior and punishment or at least discouragement for incorrect behavior; through *imitation* or identification, in which older children and adults perceived most like the self are imitated; and through *self-definition,* or putting oneself in a category—male or female—according to norms learned through interaction with others about what constitutes maleness and femaleness.

The above are merely refinements of the basic socialization process, particularly of symbolic interaction. Through symbolic interaction, individuals begin early on to label people and behavior: male and female, masculine and feminine. Operant conditioning may also figure in sex-role socialization: children at first engage in all kinds of behavior but as they are rewarded for sex-appropriate actions and punished or ignored for inappropriate ones, they learn

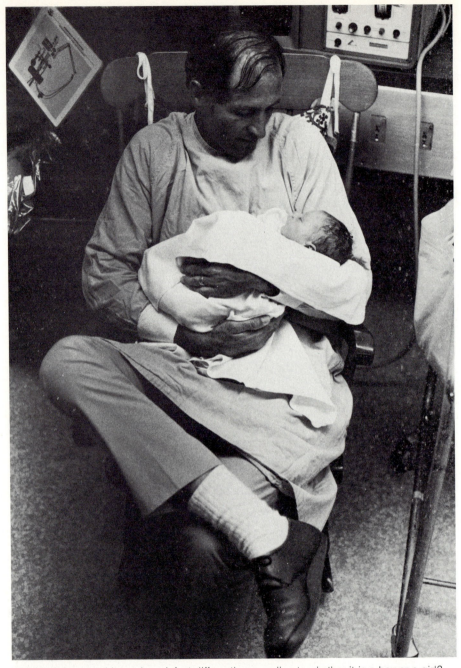

Will this father treat his newborn infant differently, according to whether it is a boy or a girl? He definitely will, for sex typing and socialization into sex roles begin almost from the moment of birth.

203

CHAPTER 8

*Social
Differentiation:
Sex, Age, and
Handicaps*

How would the little boy's parents respond if he chose a doll to play with?

to behave in ways consonant with their gender. Identification, or modeling, provides yet another method of sex-role socialization. Jerome Kagan points out that from their very birth, parents respond to children in sex-typed ways (1964). In response, children learn to perform in ways adults believe are appropriate for their gender. Essentially, Kagan concludes, it is the desire not to be socially rejected that prompts a child to engage in sex-appropriate behavior, even more than the desire to win a parent's love (1964, 137–167).

Kagan also demonstrated in an experiment that by age six children of both sexes were able to give good descriptions of sex roles appropriate to males and females (1961, 625–636). Those who are able to understand sex roles and live with a role model will identify with the same-sex parent, especially when this behavior is conditioned through positive and negative reinforcement.

The cognitive-developmental model, also proposed as explanatory of sex-role socialization, is based on the assumption that individuals are capable of active self-definition and not simply subject to passive conditioning (Kohlberg, 1966). Children perceive their environment, eventually make sense of it, and proceed to find their place in it, categorizing themselves as belonging to one sex or the other. They then acquire behaviors appropriate to that sex.

Behavioral scientists conclude that socialization into sex roles is a complex process, in which negative and positive reinforcements play an important role; in which imitation and identification are elements; in which biological predispositions may be active in prompting specific behaviors; in which cues are interpreted from the environment and pressures are felt; and in which, finally, one imposes on oneself a specific gender identification.

Agents of Sex-Role Socialization

As may well be imagined, the same agents responsible for socialization in general are also responsible for socialization into sex roles. The family serves as the most crucial agent of socialization into sex roles, though it is certainly far from being the only one. Peers, teachers, and the media reinforce messages first learned within the family. Children's books, from picture books given to the smallest toddler to textbooks used in school have, until very recent times, presented wholly stereotyped images of male and female roles. One team of researchers found the ratio of male to female representations in children's books running heavily in favor of males; a majority of the illustrations dealt entirely with boys (Weitzman and Eifler, 1972). In these books girls were shown engaged in domestic chores, playing with dolls, helping their mothers, or being subservient to the male heroes. Little boys were depicted as specialists or professionals, busy with such dramatic adventures as saving little girls' lives or rescuing animals from certain death. Most showed complete and intact families, where fathers were handed pipes and slippers when they came home, and mothers were shown in aprons, puttering about the kitchen. Working mothers and divorced parents were almost totally absent, an obvious distortion of truth in a society where nine out of ten married women work outside the home at some time during their lifetime, and where one out of three marriages ends in divorce. In recent years, an attempt has been made by publishers and textbook authors to eradicate the most flagrant stereotypes.

In addition to sex stereotypes found in books, children are exposed to traditional sex roles in school, where boys and girls are segregated in a number of activities. In sports, extracurricular activities, and even academic subjects, students of different sexes are steered onto different paths. Again, awareness of this situation has prompted remedial steps; by the time a child reaches school age, however, such traits as competitiveness, independence, self-reliance, and emotional expressiveness are already largely established. Thus even if girls are allowed to play football and take shop, they will most likely fail to benefit from an unbiased approach to sex roles.

The mass media, especially television and women's magazines, are perhaps most responsible for reinforcing traditional stereotypes. Not only the content of articles and programs, but especially the advertising that precedes, follows, and constantly interrupts them, present women as housecleaners, child-carers, and husband pamperers. In addition, their conversation is depicted as revolving around rings on their husbands' shirt collars, mud on their sons' pants, and the difficulty of maintaining shiny kitchen floors. Women are also used as sex objects in advertising directed at men: Young, beautiful females are shown seductively caressing automobiles, being thrilled by the aroma of an after-shave lotion, or succumbing to the man who drinks a particular brand of whiskey.

To summarize, to the best of our knowledge, gender identity is developed through socialization and does not appear automatically at a certain point in physical maturation. Socialization experiences begin with the awareness of physical differences, continue with the consciousness of sex-related differences in activities, skills, and behavior, and develop into conscious or unconscious acceptance or rejection of roles associated with one's sex. It should also be emphasized that *gender assignment* (psychological traits connected with maleness or femaleness) does not necessarily correspond to *sex* (one's biological status) or *sexuality* (the direction of one's sexual response). That is, a biological female may feel herself to be masculine and respond sexually to women, and a biological male may feel feminine and respond to men. Or either may respond to both sexes.

Inequality and the Ideology of Sexism

The results of traditional assignment of sex roles are easy to ascertain: in all parts of the world, the status of women has consistently been inferior to that of men. All the world's religions stress the superiority of men over women. The Bible maintains that woman was created as an afterthought to keep man company. Christians state that men are the "image and glory of God: But the woman is the glory of man." Pious male Jews say a daily prayer of thanksgiving for not having been born a woman. Moslems, too, learn that men possess virtues that make them preeminent.

Historically, few women are remembered as great artists, great political leaders, great financial tycoons, or great thinkers. Some choose to believe that this void is explained by women's inferiority; that their "natural" role in life is to give birth and nurture children, and little more. Increasingly, however, it is becoming apparent that the void exists not because of women's inherent inadequacies but because social factors have not allowed them to fill any but the most limited of roles. Since the twentieth century awareness has grown of the existence of a sexist ideology.

Sexism is a system of beliefs justifying the inequality that governs the treatment of sexes in society. This outlook is so pervasive many women embrace it as fervently as do men. Until recently, for example, the notion that women belonged at home with their children was strongly argued by both sexes. Figures 8.1 and 8.2 illustrate the widespread conviction that women's role should be primarily that of mother (especially when her children are young) and homemaker. The recent preference for a job outside the home may even be on the decline among some women (see Figure 8.2).

The most pernicious aspect of the sexist ideology is not simply the belief that different, sex-linked natures result in different kinds of behavior. Rather, it is that "different" has acquired the value superior/inferior, specifically that men are superior and women inferior. Although men are undoubtedly superior

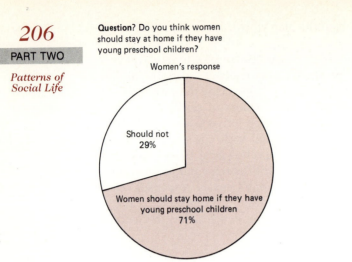

Question? Do you think women should stay at home if they have young preschool children?

Women's response

Should not
29%

Women should stay home if they have young preschool children
71%

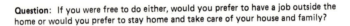

Question: If you were free to do either, would you prefer to have a job outside the home or would you prefer to stay home and take care of your house and family?

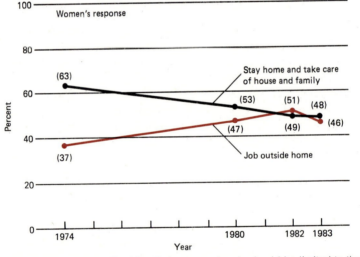

Figures 8.1 and 8.2 The idea that a woman's role should be limited to that of wife and mother is so ingrained that women espouse it as fervently as men. *Notes: (Figure 8.1)* Sample = 1,000 women. Of those 18–24 years old, 62% felt women with young preschool children should stay at home. Of those women 55 or older, 81% felt that way; part time—71%; those not employed—80%; *(Figure 8.2)* Sample size for 1983 = 1,309. *Sources: (Figure 8.1)* Survey by Mark Clements Research, Inc. for *Glamour Magazine*, September 7–16, 1982 (*Public Opinion*, August/September 1984, p. 36); *(Figure 8.2)* Surveys by the Roper Organization for Virginia Slims, 1974 and 1980, CBS News 1982, and *New York Times*, November 11–20, 1983 (*Public Opinion*, August/September 1984, p. 36). Reprinted with permission of *Public Opinion*. Copyright © 1983 by The New York Times Company. Reprinted by permission.

in certain activities and women in others, the sexist ideology has twisted these truths. Inasmuch as women have systematically been denied access to status and power; in that they are treated unequally by men who outrank them at all levels of the stratification system; and in that they have been the targets of prejudice and discrimination, many consider themselves a minority group. Social scientists, who perceived similarities in the condition of women and minorities some time ago, point out that as well as suffering inequality in treatment, women are physically distinct and vulnerable. However, women are not residentially segregated, and their social distance from men is less great (in fact, women control much of the wealth of the nation, although most have inherited it from husbands or fathers).

In what ways are women unequal? Without even considering historical inequalities, we may quote some statistics gathered for a worldwide report on women. This report, sponsored by the Carnegie and Rockefeller Foundations and compiled by economist Ruth Leger Sivard, revealed the following facts:

Ten of the 11 oldest democracies in the world did not give women the right to vote until well into the twentieth century.

Women hold no more than 10 percent of the seats in national legislatures.

In the 25 countries reporting, women's earnings ranged from 90 percent of men's in Sweden to 43 percent in Japan.

The average number of children per woman ranges from 2 in developed nations to 7.9 in less developed countries.

Women are disproportionately represented among the poor, the illiterate, the unemployed, and the underemployed.

Even though the greatest strides have been made in education, in developing countries two-thirds of women over 25 have never been to school, compared with half the men.

The study concludes that women have not reached broad parity with men in wages and salaries in any country in the world. Women are concentrated in women's work and only a small elite has entered law, medicine, and other traditionally masculine professions. Finally, poverty among women is spreading due to unemployment, low pay, and lack of skills, and most importantly because women are left with children to support, particularly in nations where divorce has become endemic.

The United States has recently seen a dramatic change in the proportion of women who work outside the home. The percentage of women in the labor force, as illustrated in Figure 8.3, rose from 34 in 1950 to 53.4 in 1984. Much of this increase may be due to the feminist movement, heralded by the publication of Betty Friedan's *The Feminine Mystique* in 1963, a book which charged American society with denying women the possibility of reaching their human potential by constricting them in the roles of housewives and mothers. But the increase of women in the labor force also has economic roots: Growing inflation in the 1960s and 1970s required most young families to bring in two paychecks. And the growing number of divorces forced many mothers to work for their own and their children's support. Thus, both males and females appear to work out of economic necessity as is made clear by Figure 8.4.

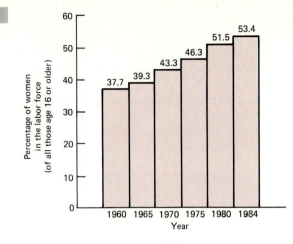

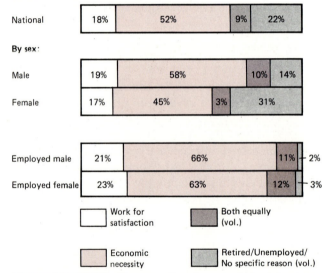

Figures 8.3 and 8.4 The proportion of women in the labor force has been steadily climbing in the past two decades, but both men and women work out of economic necessity and not specifically for the satisfaction a job ought to provide. *Note: (Figure 8.4)* Sample size = 1,003. *Sources: (Figure 8.3)* From *U.S. News & World Report,* October 29, 1984, p. 76 (Basic data: U.S. Department of Labor). Copyright, 1984, U.S. News & World Report. *(Figure 8.4)* Survey by Mark Clements Research, Inc. for *Parade* magazine, November 21–December 12, 1983 (*Public Opinion,* August/September 1984, p. 36). Reprinted with permission of *Public Opinion.*

Although half of American women are employed, however, they consistently earn lower salaries than men. In 1984 the median full-time income for men 15· and over was $24,004, for women, $15,422 (U.S. Bureau of the Census, 1985). The average earnings of employed women represent, in short, only 64.2 percent of those of men, and this gap has grown larger rather than smaller over the last 25 years.

209

CHAPTER 8

*Social
Differentiation:
Sex, Age, and
Handicaps*

Such a switch of roles as shown here is not common in our society: the increase of women in the labor force is much more related to the necessity of having two paychecks in a family.

One reason for this is that women are relegated to lower-paying job categories. "Women's work," which includes that of secretaries, child-care workers, bank tellers, telephone operators, and registered nurses, is notoriously low in pay, as well as in prestige and the opportunity for career mobility. As demonstrated in Table 8.1, even with the same educational credentials and years of experience, women earn less and hold less authority (Treiman and Terrell, 1975; U.S. Bureau of the Census, 1982, 146). In turn, much job discrimination originates in the widespread cultural belief that women will interrupt their careers to have and bring up children (which in fact they do, especially in the decade between ages 25 and 35, years in which men consolidate their careers) and that, consequently, they will not invest sufficient effort in their chosen field. Women who reenter the job market when their children are raised, or after a divorce or the death of a husband, generally lack the necessary skills or are too old for high-paying jobs so that they too end up on the low-paid, low-prestige end of the job continuum.

Earnings of Full-time Workers 15 Years of Age and Over, 1984

TABLE 8.1

Selected Occupational Categories	Median Income (dollars)		Women's Income as a Percentage of Men's
	Men	Women	
Executives, administrators, and managers	32,510	18,860	58.0
Professional specialties	31,534	20,899	66.3
Technical workers	26,336	17,566	66.7
Sales	24,053	11,997	49.9
Precision production, craft and repair workers	22,580	13,777	61.0
Clerical and other administrative support workers	22,140	14,417	65.1
Transportation workers	20,382	12,194	59.8
Machine operators, assemblers, and inspectors	19,217	11,817	61.5
Service workers	15,537	9,506	61.2
Farming, forestry, and fishing	9,564	5,089	53.2
All occupations	24,004	15,422	64.2

Source: *Current Population Reports: Consumer Income.* Series P-60. No. 149. Washington, D.C.: U.S. Government Printing Office, 1985, pp. 13–14.

In spite of the vice-presidential candidacy of Geraldine Ferraro in 1984, women are also minimally represented in government and politics. In 1960, 2 women held positions in the United States Senate and 18 in the House of Representatives. As of 1985, there were still only 2 women senators, and 2 governors, although the number of representatives had risen to 22. Only 14 percent of state legislators were women in 1985. Sandra Day O'Connor is the first and only woman to have been named to the Supreme Court, and only 10 have ever served in the cabinet. In short, although they constitute 51.4 percent of the population, women hold only 12 percent of all government offices (U.S. Bureau of the Census, 1982, 489).

The Women's Movement

Women, particularly college-age and college-educated, took an active part in the civil-rights movement of the early sixties protesting discrimination against blacks. In addition, many were attracted to the ideology of the radical left which emerged in the wake of Vietnam and promised, above all else, opportunity to all. Soured by the discovery that prejudice and discrimination against women were rampant even among committed radical males, these women began joining women's organizations, chief among which was the National Organization for Women (NOW) formed by Betty Friedan in 1966. The aims of NOW included the ratification of the Equal Rights Amendment (ERA) to the Constitution, the repeal of the law against abortion, the creation of day-care centers for children, and equal pay for equal work.

The effects of the women's movement are difficult to assess. Although NOW has survived for almost two decades, its goals have only partially been achieved, and its membership has remained small. Critics have stressed that activists in the women's movement have been disproportionately young, white, educated, middle or upper middle class, unaffiliated to any religion, and radical in their political beliefs and sexual norms. The implication of this criticism is that the great majority of American women—the older, less-educated, working-class, minority, and religiously active women—accept the status quo and remain uninterested in change.

Partly as a direct result of the movement, and partly because the time was ripe for change, women's roles have undergone alterations in the last two decades, reflected in certain changes in legislation. Although the ERA has still failed to be ratified (opposed by conservative groups who feel its passage would deprive women of such benefits as alimony and exemption from military service), other laws have been enacted to prevent women from being legally discriminated against in hiring, pay, and eligibility for bank loans or credit. Federal funds can be denied to organizations that discriminate in the hiring, pay, and promotion of women. And although the issue is still controversial the Supreme Court has legalized abortion.

On a social level, women face far less pressure now to marry and have children. Many in fact opt for a single life-style or a childless one. Occupational choices have expanded and no occupation is categorically off-limits (male and female listings in help-wanted ads are in fact now prohibited). Increasingly, women are acquiring training and skills formerly the exclusive prerogatives of men. At Columbia University's School of Business, 38 percent of the 1983 graduating class was female, as compared with 5 percent in 1972. Of the female graduates, 26 percent are entering investment banking as a career, compared with 3.8 percent in 1972. According to experts in the industry, one-third of entry-level investment banking jobs, with salaries in the $50,000 range, are now filled by women (Gross, 1985, 18).

In spite of such obvious progress in the treatment of women in the United States, certain problems remain. First, traces of discrimination still exist, although at a subtler level. Women's salaries remain approximately two-thirds those of men in comparable jobs. Sexist stereotypes still abound in spite of attempts by publishers and educators to "desex" the language. Instances of sexual harassment, often with the veiled threat of job loss, are frequently reported. And social problems like rape and sexual abuse, while perhaps no more frequent in recent years, are a source of increasing anger and frustration to women, who are beginning to demand solutions.

In addition to the problems above, the issue of sexual equality poses new dilemmas. In the past, men and women were encouraged and socialized to acquire separate roles: men were expected to be independent, ambitious, assertive, aggressive, and career oriented. Women were to be dependent, nurturing, passive, emotional, and home oriented. In the hunting and gathering societies where these roles emerged, they functioned to the benefit of society. In modern-day post-industrial society, such divergent roles make far less sense. Instead, some have suggested the preferability of androgynous roles. (**Androgyny** refers to the possession in one personality of both male and female sex-typed traits and abilities.)

Such elimination of sexism in favor of equality has been attempted in several societies but never achieved. Communist societies, acting on Marx's contention that sex discrimination represents a form of class exploitation characteristic of capitalism, have in theory instituted total sexual equality. Studies show, however, that salaries in the Soviet Union are highest for those occupations which employ few women. When more women enter an occupation, the wages come down. Soviet women average 65 percent of male wages, and in addition carry the entire burden of housekeeping, for Soviet husbands refuse to share in shopping and housework of any sort (Swafford, 1978, 657–73; Gordon and Klopov, 1975). An ironic twist to this disparity is that Soviet men have lately been faring very poorly in comparison to women. Due to high rates of alcoholism, the male mortality rate is mounting at a much faster pace than the female; the difference in life expectancy between the two was 12 years in 1980 (Schlapentokh, 1984, 13). Increasingly men are failing to compete with women in education, or humanitarian and artistic endeavors; they are less law abiding, and take the lead in absenteeism and employment change. An increasing number of Soviet women are remaining unmarried, preferring loneliness to ties with men whom, in the words of a Soviet sociologist "they cannot help despising" (Schlapentokh, 13).

Even results on the Israeli kibbutzim have proved disheartening. These organizations have held strong commitments to the socialist ideology, stressing total economic and sexual equality. Although economic equality has been achieved, over the years sex-role differences have begun to reassert themselves (Tiger and Shepher, 1975).

The danger of erring in the opposite extreme exists as well. In Sweden the socialist government, intent on achieving its version of sexual equality, pressures its female citizens to enter the job market en masse and entrust their children to child-care centers. Opinion polls indicate that most Swedish women would prefer to stay at home with their children but cannot, since the Swedish economic and tax system, geared to leveling individual wealth, does not permit families to survive on one income. Almost 89 percent of working-age Swedish women are employed; in less than 20 years families with one breadwinner have almost disappeared. While this may be considered a positive trend, it does not take into account the desires of those women who would prefer to fill more traditional roles (Sweden discourages full-time housewifery, 1985, 25P).

Obviously, mere reversal of sex roles is not the answer. Nothing will be gained by more aggressive women and more passive men. Perhaps a rapprochement between the two extremes is preferable, allowing men and women to participate equally in production of income, housework, and child care. The viability of such a solution is indicated by studies which reveal that individuals nearer the midpoint on the continuum from masculine to feminine personality types feel more contentment than those at either extreme. Additionally, research shows that the mental health levels of women have improved in the decades between 1954 and 1976, whereas the mental health levels of men have remained constant. Ultimately, equality between the sexes should offer each individual the opportunity to follow his or her inclinations with regard to family and career.

Age

All societies differentiate among members according to age. Each age group is assigned different duties, responsibilities, privileges, and roles. United States residents cannot drive before age 16, vote before 18, or run for Senate until at least 30. These age restrictions are set by law. On a more informal basis, a person in his seventies would hardly be expected to work in construction. In other words, to a certain degree, age stratification is based on common sense, on what works best for individuals and society.

Problems arise when a society is unwilling or unable to provide its members with satisfactory roles at certain ages. Many of the difficulties parents in contemporary societies are experiencing with their adolescent children may be attributed to the vague roles children and young adults are assigned in industrial societies. While they are universally expected to prepare for future careers not all are able or willing to do so. At the same time, while many are biologically capable of functioning as adults, this option is denied them. Their frustrations often erupt in rebelliousness and truancy, or worse, delinquency and criminality.

In the United States and other industrial and post-industrial nations an even more dramatic example of age-related discrimination is provided in the devaluation of the role of the elderly. By contrast, agrarian and other preindustrial societies assign these members honorable and prestigious roles.

An examination of American society reveals an obvious permeation by an ideology, **ageism,** which rationalizes discrimination against groups on the basis of age. Specifically, this discrimination is directed against the very young and those in their sunset years.

Discrimination against young societal members is difficult to assess and based on a degree of common sense: The young do lack the wisdom, experience, and knowledge to behave as adults. There is thus some justification in limiting their rights. However, as increasing information about sexual and physical abuse of children surfaces, it becomes obvious that certain adults do wield an abusive power toward junior members of society. Such social problems have already given rise to a number of organizations designed to combat them.

In wake of the vague nature of ageism as it concerns the young, the ideology is most often considered to affect the elderly. In this context the problem is perceived as more pressing—especially by the elderly themselves—perhaps because their number is increasing in the United States and will continue to do so for the foreseeable future (see Figure 8.5). The existence of such an ideology and its prejudice and discrimination makes the elderly prime candidates for minority group membership.

The Graying of America

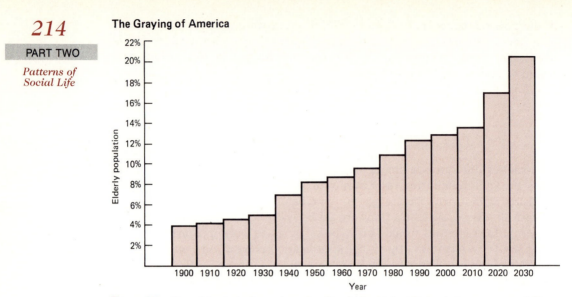

Figure 8.5 One of the fastest growing minorities in the United States is the group aged 65 years old and over. As a proportion of the population, this group has risen from 4 percent at the turn of the century, to 11 percent in the 1980s, and will rise to an estimated 21 percent in the year 2020. *Source:* Cynthia M. Taeuber, "America in transition: An aging society," U.S. Bureau of the Census, Current Population Reports Series no. 128, p. 23 (Washington, D.C.: U.S. Government Printing Office, 1983).

Ageism

The elderly—a term used to refer to those aged sixty-five and older—comprise 11 percent of the American population, about 26.5 million in number. Their proportion will increase (they will constitute 20 percent of the population in the decade of the 1980s) in the United States and in other industrial nations well into the next century. Their problems will then become everyone's problems.

The ideology of ageism asserts, basically, that the young are superior to the old. It provides justification for discrimination against the elderly in economic, political, and social areas. The elderly may be considered a minority group for many reasons. Like most minorities, they are highly visible: They are wrinkled, their hair is white or they are bald, and many walk in a stooped manner. As is the case with most minorities, negative characteristics are attributed to them: They are stereotyped as physically deteriorated, passive, inefficient, dependent, and senile (a condition which includes loss of memory or even intelligence). Finally, the lower status of the elderly is rationalized on the basis that they actually prefer to be released from their former roles in order to enjoy their leisure time and their grandchildren.

Age Discrimination

The most obvious area of discrimination against the elderly occurs in their lack of access to employment. To an extent, it is understandable that em-

215

CHAPTER 8

*Social
Differentiation:
Sex, Age, and
Handicaps*

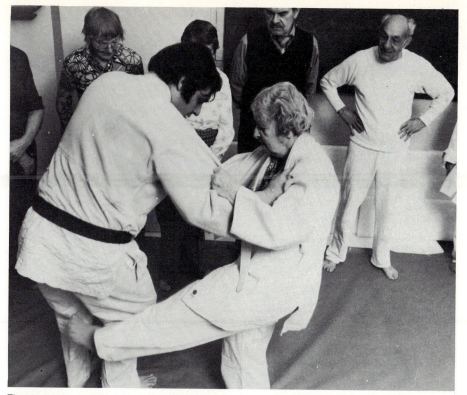

The stereotypes of the elderly as physically deteriorated, inefficient, dependent, and senile are often given the lie by vigorous retirees who do not allow their age to put an end to pleasurable or useful activities.

ployers prefer to hire young workers. After recruiting and training them, they hope their new employees will remain with them for some time. Older employees also expect higher salaries while their fringe benefits, such as health and life insurance, are costlier. Finally, older employees may have formed certain work habits and attitudes that are difficult to break.

Due to the factors above, and particularly because it is often cheaper to hire a young worker, those who find themselves over 40 and out of a job have serious difficulties in obtaining new employment. The Age Discrimination Act of 1967 protects such workers to a certain extent. This act was amended in 1978 to include the prohibition of enforced retirement before age 70.

Early retirement has two disadvantages: one for the individual, the other for society. People are not all alike in their readiness or inclination to retire. For some, the period may indeed be a welcome one; for others, it may bring feelings of uselessness and of being dispensable, leading to depression and in acute cases a wish for early death. On a societal level, if the trend to early retirement continues with the increasing age of the population, the danger of bankrupting pension plans, including Social Security benefits, may become critical. Already there is talk of increasing the minimum age at which benefits can be paid out. It appears likely that in light of these contingencies the trend toward early retirement will be reversed.

Disengagement

The elderly, it has been suggested, willingly withdraw from many of their previous interactions, social obligations, and occupational roles so that those who are younger may assume these functions. This process, known as **disengagement,** should ideally occur by mutual consent and be reciprocally satisfying to all (Cumming and Henry, 1961). Disengagement was thought to be functional for both the elderly and society because it served to protect society from the disruptions of career interruptions and prepare the elderly to face death with indifference. Unfortunately, the concept of disengagement has been found to be oversimplified. It is not always voluntary and mutual, and where this is the case, life satisfaction is much reduced. More current thinking supports the view that an individual who continues to participate in group activities is likely to perceive his or her old age with a much greater degree of satisfaction than one who is forced to disengage from such activities.

Problematic Areas

In addition to outright discrimination in the area of employment, many societies hold negative attitudes toward senescence, or the process of growing old (despite its being one we are all fated to undergo if we live long enough). Senescence, a gradual process, affects individuals at different rates of speed and involves a decline in both physical strength and mental functioning.

Because mental and physical decline can alter behavior to the point where everyday living arrangements are disrupted, institutionalization often becomes necessary. Institutionalization can be problematic since those who run retirement and nursing homes are basically strangers doing a job, rather than family members caring for one of their own. The atmosphere in such places tends to be sterile and businesslike, and before stringent federal regulations were enforced, fraud and exploitation were rampant. Institutionalization is equally problematic for the families of the elderly, involving as it does considerable expense and many guilt feelings. Although only about 5 percent of the elderly are permanently in institutions, a high proportion spend at least part of their time in hospitals and other medical facilities, since they tend to be saddled with acute or chronic illnesses.

Another source of negative feelings toward the elderly is the poverty suffered by a large segment of them. Workers at menial jobs are usually unable to accumulate savings and must later exist on low federal benefits. Low incomes in turn force the aged to live in substandard housing, often in dilapidated inner-city hotels where they become prey to criminal elements. Even those who remain in their homes often feel like prisoners, afraid to venture outside. In addition, in most American cities, inhabitants rely on automobiles for their transportation needs, and public transportation is inefficient or unavailable. This creates difficulties for those who because of failing eyesight or health or lack of funds can no longer drive.

Widowhood and Loneliness

217

CHAPTER 8

*Social
Differentiation:
Sex, Age, and
Handicaps*

In addition to problems of failing health and economic straits, many old people encounter loneliness, frequently resulting from the death of a spouse and the gradual dying off of one's relatives and friends. Because of the prevalent nuclear life-style—a couple and their children living independently in one household—when one spouse dies, the remaining one is left alone. About one-fourth of the elderly live by themselves, most of them women, who tend to live longer than men.

The death of a spouse often brings economic hardships—to women who no longer receive their husbands' support, and to men who must pay for services previously supplied by their wives (or perform them themselves, which many are unwilling or unable to do). Survivors must also deal with bereavement, a condition that improves only if the bereaved is allowed to work through the process of grief. Most recover from their loss, but some are paralyzed by deep depression. Suicide rates, as well as incidences of mental distress and depression, are significantly higher among the widowed than among their married contemporaries.

Because the elderly differ in terms of income, education, and occupation, they do not tend to form cohesive groups that could exert political pressure on their behalf. As the aged segment of society increases, however, they are likely to take more advantage of their numbers to demonstrate their influence as consumers and voters.

Minority Status Based on Handicaps, Appearance, and Sexual Preference

Large segments of the population are accorded differential treatment on the basis of physical handicaps, unattractiveness, shortness, obesity, homosexuality, and singleness. Of these, the most substantial group are the physically and mentally handicapped, of whom at least 40 million (Statistical Abstracts, 1982–1983, 53,515) and perhaps as many as 60 million live in the United States.

Differential treatment of the handicapped stems from their high visibility. Some handicaps evoke horror and disgust on the part of the public, others merely pity, but all lead to stereotypes and misperceptions. For instance, people tend to speak loudly to the blind, assuming they are also deaf, or suppose that all those confined to wheelchairs are unable to have sex, or categorize a physically handicapped person as also being mentally retarded.

Discrimination against the handicapped runs the gamut from attitudes to architecture, from education and occupation to transportation. Most nonhandicapped feel uneasy in the presence of handicapped persons and thus try to avoid coming into contact with them. Similarly, provisions are seldom made for those who cannot avail themselves of stairs or standard bathroom facilities. Of course, removing all barriers for all handicapped persons would entail enormous expense. Some progress in the direction of ameliorating their lot, however, has been made, beginning with the Rehabilitation Act of 1973, which prohibits any federally funded agency from excluding them from any programs or facilities on the basis of their condition alone. Greater acceptance of the handicapped, as well as willingness to employ them, would make sense not only in ethical terms but because studies have shown that with proper training this group can equal and even exceed normal workers in terms of productivity and dependability.

The Unattractive Good looks, which have nothing to do with intelligence, industriousness, reliability, responsibility, and other positive attributes, and which are totally beyond an individual's control, have been shown to determine to a large degree a person's success in life. Pretty children are treated better than ugly ones; attractive students get better grades than unattractive ones; handsome men and beautiful women get the best jobs, have the most dates, and achieve the most in their careers. Attractive people are even judged more morally upright, are less likely to become mentally ill, and recover more rapidly than unattractive ones (*New York Times,* 1980, 16; Farnia, 1977, 510–17).

The injustice represented by such differentiation is not likely to be remedied soon, nor can it be affected by legislation of any sort. Apparently all societies engage in this behavior, although their definition of what constitutes attractiveness or the lack of it varies immensely.

Obesity in men and women, and shortness in men or extreme tallness in women are also traits that evoke discriminatory behavior, particularly in the areas of employment and mating. Obese persons tend to be employed in low visibility jobs and do not achieve their career goals as successfully as their less corpulent colleagues. Tall men, on the other hand, do much better than short ones: In one study, business graduates over six feet two inches were offered starting salaries 12 percent higher than those offered their shorter classmates (Deck, 1971, 102). In love, too, the tall man is favored over the short one, whereas the opposite is true for women, creating a pool of short men and tall women who do not generally find mates.

Homosexuals In puritanical societies, such as the United States was until a few decades ago, homosexuality was viewed as shockingly deviant behavior and homosexuals literally subjected to persecution: They were imprisoned, socially ostracized, and their careers ruined if they were caught in a homosexual act. As a result, most hid their sexual preferences, often leading hypocritical double lives. The situation today is quite different, and most homosexuals feel free to admit their sexual orientation. Still, discrimination and misconceptions—for instance, that homosexuals are child molesters—are common, and instances of dismissal from jobs or the military services regularly occur. The Gay Liberation Movement has been quite successful in dispelling the negative self-image of homosexuals, but less so in ending legal and social discrimination against them or in making homosexuality acceptable as a valid alternative life-style. It has been speculated that the homosexual life-style will be greatly curtailed by the increasing incidence of Acquired Immune Deficiency Syndrome (AIDS), a disease transmitted through the exchange of bodily fluids whose principal victims appear to be homosexuals.

The list of those in society who at one time or another are victims of prejudice and discrimination is endless. It is probable that some forms of discrimination will inevitably persist, since no society is perfectly homogeneous and integrated, nor can all individuals fit the ideal cultural model.

But perhaps sociocultural change, ever present in societies, can diminish the negative results of differentiation. By undermining the established social system, change creates a degree of social disorganization; especially in a heterogeneous society, people ultimately subscribe to a variety of conflicting values. And although legislation can reduce discrimination in employment and pay scales, only a change of values can reduce many forms of social discrimination. There is always the risk that those working to change the status quo may themselves be viewed as deviants, although all new norms are initially considered deviations from established ones. Thus, changes in sex roles were at first frowned upon but are today fairly well accepted. In short, all modern societies display at least some evidence of social disorganization, of value conflicts, and of personal deviation. The tendency, particularly in American society, has been toward more tolerance and subsequently less harmful differentiation.

The Chapter in Brief

People in societies have been socially differentiated—treated unequally, subjected to prejudice and discrimination—not only on the basis of race, ethnicity, and religion, but also of gender, age, handicaps, physical appearance, and sexual preference. Women, for instance, although not numerically a minority, may be viewed as one in the sociological sense. In most societies, women have suffered from an unequal access to societal rewards. Men and women are socialized from birth into different **sex roles** which originated in the division of labor functional in early societies. To justify these differences, and the false notion of feminine sex roles as inferior, an ideology, **sexism,** has evolved that contains a number of stereotypes. It has also engendered the belief that sex roles are biologically determined and thus unchangeable. The sexist ideology has been responsible for unequal treatment of women, especially with regard to their access to jobs at the same level of achievement and pay as men's. Although biological differences do of course exist between the sexes, in societies where brawn is less important than brain these differences do not justify inequalities in employment and pay.

The women's movement has helped female members of society to obtain legal protection and redefine their self-images. The displacement of marriage and family that often follows their entrance into the work force, however, has left many women puzzled and confused; many still find it difficult to reconcile their aspirations for personal achievement with their desire for a traditional family life.

The elderly in the United States suffer a loss of status, income, and prestige, even though they form an ever-increasing proportion of the population. The speed of technology in modern industrial societies results in a young population that is better informed and possesses more skills than the old, at least in certain areas. As a result, the elderly are devalued. Additionally, they may suffer declining health and vigor, and so deviate from the ideal societal norms extolling youth, beauty, and fitness. Many of the elderly experience financial difficulties along with health problems because of inadequate pension plans.

Discrimination against the elderly is obvious in the area of employment where the cards are stacked against anyone over age 40. In addition, many employers implement a mandatory retirement age of 65 or 70 which forces certain employees to disengage before they are ready. **Disengagement** is ideally a mutual process whereby the elderly voluntarily surrender social and occupational roles in order that these may be filled by younger persons. Disengagement is apparently more often forced on the elderly and thus violently opposed.

The elderly also must face widowhood and its consequent loneliness and, when their physical and mental health wanes, possible institutionalization. None of these are pleasant conclusions to life; a growing proportion of the elderly are becoming active in movements to forestall and reverse some of the negative experiences common today.

The physically and mentally disabled, as well as those who physically deviate from the norm through extreme obesity, shortness (if men), and tallness (if women) constitute other groups of minority status subject to unequal treatment. In particular, such groups are discriminated against in terms of marriage, employment, housing and transportation, and in the achievement of their career goals.

In heterogeneous societies, some form of discrimination against particular groups will undoubtedly continue. Certain factors, however, may help ameliorate this situation. First, in such societies change is rapid, and changing norms require accommodations in attitudes. Second, values differ among large varieties of groups. Finally, a degree of personal deviance is necessary for all social change to occur.

Terms to Remember

Ageism An ideology asserting the superiority of the young over the old. Used to justify discrimination against the elderly in political, economic, and social areas.

Androgyny The possession in one personality of both male and female sex-typed traits and abilities.

Disengagement A process in which the elderly withdraw from their former social and occupational roles so that these may be filled by the young. Ideally occurs by mutual consent.

Gender Psychological characteristics that develop when an individual is assigned either a male or female sex. Expressed in terms of the adjectives "masculine" or "feminine" as opposed to genetically determined sex, which is expressed in terms of "male" or "female."

Hormones   Chemical substances which, when secreted by the glands of the fetus, determine sex by stimulating or inhibiting certain chemical processes.

Secondary sex characteristics   Anatomical differences between men and women that develop when specific hormones are introduced into an organism.

Sexism   An ideology stressing that real or alleged differences between men and women point to the superiority of men. Used to justify inferior conditions of and discriminatory practices against women in most societies.

Sex roles   The socially determined norms into which males and females are socialized and according to which they subsequently feel and behave.

221

CHAPTER 8

*Social
Differentiation:
Sex, Age, and
Handicaps*

Suggestions for Further Reading

Atchley, Robert C.   1985. *Social forces and aging.* 4th ed. Belmont, Calif.: Wadsworth. One of the most comprehensive texts on gerontology, or the sociological study of aging.

Ehrenreich, Barbara.   1983. *The hearts of men: American dreams and the flight from commitment.* Garden City, N.Y.: Anchor-Doubleday. The focus in this book is on masculinity, particularly in the time frame of 1950 to the present.

French, Marilyn.   1985. *Beyond power: On women, men, and morals.* New York: Summit. The author relates the history of patriarchy, and explores the meaning of gender and the impact of feminism.

Levin, Jack and William C. Levin.   1980. *Ageism: Prejudice and discrimination against the elderly.* Belmont, Ca.: Wadsworth. A discussion of the aged as a minority group and the implications of this status on the society.

Lipman-Blumen, Jean.   1984. *Gender-Roles and power.* Englewood Cliffs, N.J.: Prentice–Hall. The relationship of gender to the functioning of the major social institutions is explored in this revealing paperback.

Following a Wife's Move

GORDON MOTT

*The 1980s have witnessed the first gener-
ation of husbands, and men in general, to
have to contend with a changed view of
the role of wives, and women in general.
It has not been easy. Habits that have
been honed by thousands of years do not
yield easily to change. But intelligence
and thoughtfulness, not to mention compassion and love, help men to accept
women as equal partners in the voyage
of life.*

My wife's announcement was not dramatic.
She walked into the house after work and
said, "They want me for the Paris job." The
offer was not unexpected nor unattractive.
The bank my wife works for was giving her
a promotion and transferring her to its Paris
office. I reacted with excitement. I imagined all the wonderful aspects of a life in
Paris: springtime, restaurants, the Louvre
and weekend jaunts to quaint country inns.

The announcement did not violate the
set of rules established by our two-career
couplehood. Seven years ago, I ambushed
her outside a New York City squash court
with the declaration that I'd been transferred to Mexico. She made the move and
began work in her company's Mexico City
office. Ever since, I have been reminded
that living in the third world had been my
idea and that the next move, in our two-
career couple jargon, was "hers."

But within days of letting "Sure, sure,
sounds great" slip out, I succumbed to
second guessing, reluctance and terror.
This wasn't for play. We were moving. My
rationalizations about the career flexibility
of freelance journalists crumbled. I was
forced to face the reality that I would be
throwing away a network of contacts in
Central America that I had built up over
the years; I was also abandoning work as
a stringer for the New York Times after
months of struggling to get my freelance
writing off the ground. I envisioned weeks
of inactivity, huddled with my dog, Nica, in
a Paris apartment, waiting for my wife to
return from her job.

Then it struck me where my fears came
from. The man in the family—me—was putting his career at the mercy of his wife's.
In the starkest psychological terms, I was
following her and abdicating my traditional
male role.

I can't deny that special factors, some
sounding exotic and glamorous, distinguish a move between Mexico City and
Paris from, let's say, a move between New
York and Boston. However, the same emotions, career concerns and the reactions of
colleagues are probably common to most
professional men confronted with making
career choices dictated by their wife's job.

My psychological reactions are the
toughest to understand and verbalize. My
generation—men and women in the 30's
and 40's—had the rules switched. I grew
up believing that I would be the breadwinner and those little girls across the school-
house aisle would be housewives and
mothers, not professional competition or
providers. Although I have embraced the
notion of career women for the last 10
years, the move opened mental cubby-
holes in which the idea of a working
woman just didn't seem right. Even though
I cringe at the admission, I've had strong

emotional responses that I'm less a man for not putting my foot down and saying, "Stop this career stuff, woman, and get into the kitchen." That reaction is probably unavoidable because of my background and expectations. But the anxiety also undermined my resolve and led to arguments with my wife about whether we would leave at the same time, about where we'd live in Paris.

Professional colleagues and acquaintances betrayed their own prejudices and unease. Innocent queries such as, "Well, isn't that nice, but what are you going to do?" rang with not-so-subtle implications. The questioners' tone suggested that I was giving up the rest of my professional life and denying my own personal desires for my wife's career. The offhand, joking remarks about "How does it feel to be a kept man?" or "What will you do in your spare time?" revealed inflexible attitudes about the best way to pursue a career and an unwillingness to accept women as equal partners.

On the other hand, not many men have the opportunity to explore alternative career options or take a break from the career-ladder syndrome. My wife's move gave me that chance. Even though I know I will now be forced to devote long and difficult hours to establishing a new network of people and publications, the freelancer's lifeblood, there also will be time for improving my French, visiting and writing about the eight countries in which my wife will be traveling for business, immersing myself in European politics and finishing a novel.

I'm also glad that I've opted for what is perceived as the uncommon choice. I've heard complaints from many single women that they can't trust any man's willingness to promote their careers. At least I know I'm not in that category. My worries about losing my self-worth or masculinity are offset by feeling courageous.

Another benefit has been the strengthening of my marriage. I think my declaration that being with my wife is more important than anything else is an absolute expression of love. I think she understands my commitment more clearly because of my willingness to take a chance with my own career. In addition, our ability to work out the problems caused by the stress of moving has deepened the bond between us.

A subtle shift has occurred, too, in our perceptions of each other. I've always been the one to initiate change. This time, it was her turn, and I'm the one enjoying the results of our belief that it's good to be adventuresome in our lives, jobs and relationships. That has enhanced my trust and respect for my wife.

Finally, I've experienced something broader. Like the characters in the movie *The Big Chill,* I've been dismayed as many ideals espoused by me and my friends in the early 1970's slipped quietly out of vogue. One thing that didn't change was my relentless support for women's rights. But until now my advocacy existed in the abstract. It was never tested, even as I enjoyed the benefits of a two-salary family and a dynamic, involved partner.

The issue of women's rights is real for me now, although it's still not easy for me. I know my fears are not going to disappear magically, nor is this move the last time we'll have to juggle our careers. But I'm actively challenging my assumptions about traditional male roles and forcing myself to live the beliefs about women that I've held for the last 10 years. That seems right.

Social Change: Processes and Results

PART

Three

The Making of Contemporary Society

*H*umans have a tendency to romanticize the past, as in the oft-heard phrase, "the good old days." The reason for this may well be that the present is so transitory that in the blink of an eye it *becomes* the past. The passage of time, then, is a constant in human experience and brings with it another inevitable constant: change.

While we need not belabor the old saw that there is nothing permanent except change, the increase in the *rate* of change over the past few centuries is a significant occurrence. For most of human history, those born in one generation lived very much as their parents had done and could count on their children to do the same. Whatever change occurred was so slow as to be almost imperceptible.

Today, such vast changes take place between one generation and the next that people separated by 20 or 30 years may be said to inhabit altogether different societies and be strangers to one another. Futurologist Alvin Toffler has termed this concept future shock, a condition akin to the culture shock that a person confronting a totally alien culture for the first time would experience. At the same time as dramatic changes take place, a thread of stability, represented by institutions, values, and traditions, is also apparent in societies, a factor which holds members together and binds each generation to the next.

The subject of change fascinates social scientists, as it has other social thinkers and philosophers before them. All realize that change, although never still, must be analyzed as if it were frozen in time and space. In other words, social phenomena must be observed from the perspective of statics, as they exist at one given moment in history. For a more accurate picture, however, they must also be viewed from the perspective of dynamics, the study of the sources of change. *Statics* and *dynamics* are coexisting entities, two dimensions of the same phenomenon. All processes take place within a structure, and it is impossible to understand the structure unless its underlying dynamics are also laid bare.

Sociologists have focused on the balance between stability and change, the causes of change, and particularly its effects on the interrelationships of people in societies. Certain theories and theoretic models have been developed in the attempt to explain change and the way it operates. Many revolutionary changes that have profoundly transformed human societies in the past several hundred years have also been analyzed.

Change: Cause and Effect

Revolutionary changes that have ushered in modern times originate in the technological progress that transformed hunting and gathering societies into agrarian ones and much later into industrial ones. Higher standards of living that followed each transformation as well as improved hygiene and advances in medicine have resulted in a worldwide population explosion. Population growth, and later industrialization, forced more advanced societies to become predominantly urban rather than rural. Urban societies with industrial and postindustrial economies tend to develop into mass societies requiring efficient organization. Efficiency, in turn, is achieved through the implementation of formal organizations with bureaucratic structures. Mass societies are also prone to experience collective behavior, most visible in the phenomenon of mass movements.

Modernization

The social changes described above are usually referred to as **modernization,** an all-encompassing process involving primarily the change from preindustrial to industrial modes of production and affecting all areas of human life. Modernization has already been accomplished in those technologically advanced nations of the world said to be entering a postindustrial era. It is eagerly sought by less-developed nations who view it as the road to a better standard of living for their inhabitants.

In all societies the process of modernization is fraught with difficulties. In the past, totally new systems of production have been superimposed on relatively isolated societies whose members previously lived at subsistence levels (by hunting and gathering, horticulture or pastoralism, or agriculture). While industrialism produced wealth for some and at least elevated the standard of living for others, it also destroyed traditions and entrenched ways of life. In short, the social organizations of societies undergoing modernization were altered, superseded by a new type of organization.

In those societies where modernization occurred over several generations, the existing social structure was able to accommodate it with relative ease. But even under these conditions, change could create turmoil. In Britain, the earliest industrial nation in Europe, farmers and serfs had to learn to become industrial workers. They moved to urban centers where industries were located, learned to work in exchange for wages, to accept a secondary relationship with their employers, and to live without the moral support of an extended family. None of these learning experiences were easy or rapidly acquired, and dislocations and disorganization were widespread. However, because of the relatively slow rate at which modernization occurred, new patterns had an opportunity to become crystallized. New values, new political and economic systems, even new personalities resulting from different methods of socialization became reasonably integrated in the society. Individuals adjusted to the new social order, even though such adjustment is never perfect in any society.

In other societies, where social change in the form of modernization has occurred rapidly, through diffusion instead of evolution, events have proceeded less smoothly. Dislocation and strain evidence themselves in rootlessness, anomie, and often violence. Societies that are colonized and used by more technologically advanced nations as sources of cheap labor and raw material or markets for manufactured products are often prey to such negative reactions. On gaining political independence, these nations generally attempt to modernize their economies as rapidly as possible, frequently unleashing conflict when forces of tradition clash with those of modernization. In most, serious political instability persists, which different groups periodically try to remedy by coups d'etat and the violent overthrow of governments in order to install military dictatorships. In others a variety of social movements are common. Some seek a return to previous political prominence; others stress millenarian religions promising a future paradise; still others work to foment revolutions aimed at establishing new social and economic systems or use nationalism as a bond to unite their populace.

Social and Cultural Change: Processes

Change occurs on both societal and cultural levels. In society this is reflected as some alteration in the patterned system of interaction among individuals and groups; certain members assume new statuses and play new roles. The abolition of slavery, for instance, represented social change in that it gave former slaves a new status—that of free persons—in which they could play new roles as the equals of other free members of society. This kind of **social change** occurs through planning, reform, or revolution.

Culture, on the other hand, comprises the norms, values, beliefs, and material objects produced by society. Change in these is referred to as **cultural change** and occurs as a result of scientific discoveries, technological inventions, new achievements in the arts, shifts in religious doctrine, and so on. In Western civilization, dramatic cultural changes have occurred: The belief that slavery was justified has given way to the notion that it is reprehensible; the assumption that the earth is flat has given way to the discovery that it is round; the invention of the automobile has profoundly affected sexual mores, family traditions, and humankind's perception of the world.

Just as society and culture cannot exist independently, social and cultural change cannot occur separately and distinctly. Social changes effect cultural changes and vice versa. The two overlap and are viewed separately only for purposes of analysis. Social scientists use the term *sociocultural change,* or simply change, to refer to both social and cultural change.

Social Change: Planning, Reform, Revolution

Planning is a self-explanatory process in which humans are constantly engaged. Planning by governments at all levels results in continuous though gradual social change.

Reform involves efforts by either citizens or governmental agencies to correct laws or institutions. During the Great Depression, laws were reformed to provide citizens with jobs, to furnish the wherewithal for their survival during unemployment, to help with health care, and so on. In 1954, the law permitting racial segregation was reformed. Abortion and divorce laws have undergone the same process.

Revolution is change achieved through violent means when a nation's government ceases to be responsive to its people's needs. Revolution will be analyzed in the context of social movements in the following chapter.

Cultural Change: Innovation and Diffusion

Cultural change, though characteristic of every society, occurs in different ways at different rates in different societies. Because people are creatures of habit, they conservatively resist giving up old beliefs, values, and customs—aspects of nonmaterial culture—in favor of new ones. Nonetheless, certain cultural changes necessitate such an exchange. Processes of cultural change include **innovation** (discovery and invention) and **diffusion.**

Innovation   Innovations produce new elements, or new combinations of old ones, to be absorbed into the culture. They take the form of discovery or invention. Innovations are always cumulative. Whether in music, painting, or state-of-the-art space technology, innovations invariably rest upon foundations erected earlier. Innovations may be arrived at through either discovery or invention.

A **discovery** represents a new perception of an existing fact or relationship. Principles of physics and chemistry predated humanity, yet it was centuries before men and women perceived or understood them. The circulation of blood, the presence of microbes, and the organization of the solar system are other examples of discoveries. In order for a discovery to effect sociocultural change, it must be put to some use. A society must possess the necessary technological know-how to support it and must value and have a need for the finished product. The principle of the steam engine, for instance, was known to the Greeks 2000 years ago but was not put into practice because societies of the time did not possess the necessary technology. Parts that would make the engine workable did not exist. And there was little justification for the need for rapid transportation.

An **invention** is a way of putting existing knowledge to new use. Ideas or objects present in a culture are combined to produce results more significant than the sum of their parts. Knowledge of the boat and the principle of the steam engine, for instance, existed separately in many societies. However, when combined to produce the steamboat, they provided a more effective mode of transportation than the earlier rowboat. In turn, the steam engine joined to the four-wheeled carriage produced the train, a much faster vehicle than the horse-drawn carriage. And when still later the four-wheeled carriage was united with the internal combustion engine, the resultant automobile became an indispensable mode of modern transportation.

Nonmaterial culture also provides a basis for inventions. Old ideas, connected in new ways, yield new ideas. The U.S. Constitution may be seen as a

Levi jeans are being advertised in this French town. At work is the process of cultural diffusion, which spreads material and nonmaterial culture traits from one society to another.

cultural invention combining the philosophical traditions of western Europe with the experience of the colonists in the New World.

Diffusion **Diffusion** is a process whereby cultural traits from one society are spread to another and within society from one group to another. Diffusion represents an important factor in cultural change: Spaghetti, brought to the United States by Italian immigrants (as it had been brought to Italy from China), is today considered as American as apple pie. Anthropologists claim that the content of complex cultures is primarily the product of diffusion.

Diffusion tends to be reciprocal; cultures in contact each give something to the other, although not always in the same proportion. As a rule a simple culture borrows more elements from a complex culture than vice versa. In addition, the borrowing culture is generally selective, accepting only certain traits of the new. Japan has readily accepted Western technology and music, but is only slowly adopting Western values in other areas. Similarly, Americans borrowed the idea of representative government from the British but did not assign it parliamentary form. Finally, the traits a society borrows tend to be modified: Native Americans smoked tobacco in pipes as a ritual, but the settlers eventually converted the product to cigars and cigarettes, and the practice from a ceremonial to a social one.

Change, as noted above, may be willed or planned. It may also be borrowed or imitated from other societies. Or phenomena may be discovered and technologies invented. But change also springs from other sources.

In the first place, the physical environment, over which we have little control, directs the cultural development of a society and the creation of its social structures. It also promotes some and limits other changes. Earthquakes, volcanic eruptions, repeated flooding, and severe droughts may effectively alter the lives of an area's inhabitants, sometimes eliminating them altogether. Even environmental forces that are not so dramatic interact with social forces to produce change. In fact, change occurs more rapidly and more consistently in societies that are geographically at a crossroads, where each is exposed to the culture of the other. Conversely, little change occurs in geographically isolated societies due to the absence of opportunity for cultural diffusion.

Population migrations, as well as increases and decreases in their size, also provide sources of change. A decrease in size or slow rate of growth can threaten a society with extinction. Rapid increases, on the other hand, can create grave problems, straining societal resources to the breaking point. This can provoke internal conflict as members compete for scarce supplies, or warfare, as they seek solutions through migration. Population changes can also alter social relationships. In small societies, relationships tend to be primary: Members know each other personally and interact on a face-to-face basis. Large societies engender secondary relationships: New institutions and agencies of social control are created, and formal organizations take the place of informal groups. Finally, changes in the size of a population or its structure promote social changes that may have dramatic consequences. The baby boom following World War II required the construction of many new schools and the development of youth-directed industries. The same generation today creates special demands in jobs and housing, and in future will form a society top-heavy with older members. This will affect the entire society: schools will have to be closed and new nursing homes opened.

Social change may additionally originate in ideas or belief systems, also known as ideologies. A number of social thinkers have speculated about which came first—the social reality or the ideology promoting it. While Marx believed that ideology derived from social conditions, Weber maintained that social conditions are shaped by particular ideologies. He noted that beliefs embodied in the Protestant ethic created a propitious climate for the development of capitalism. Émile Durkheim, while admitting that social conditions may beget certain ideologies, also believed that the ideologies themselves become independent social facts that in turn act upon social conditions, creating social change. The American Revolution may be seen as a triggering mechanism for social change: The economic hardships of dependence on England created the notion that Americans ought to be independent; on the basis of this belief, the Revolution was fought.

Finally, random events and individual acts may also lead to sociocultural change, although such phenomena cannot be subject to scientific inquiry. The assassination of a president, resulting in a vice president's taking over the helm of a nation, can have dramatic consequences, as can the judgment of a general who loses a significant battle. Individuals themselves can profoundly influence the course of events in society, although the effect of a single member on social change is always difficult to ascertain.

Technology

Logic suggests that an increase in the rate of technological progress triggered the chain of events leading to modernization. Modernization has included such events as a tremendous growth in population, rapid rates of urbanization and industrialization, and the increase of bureaucratic organizations in mass societies. These changes have been neither wholesale nor total. Many have occurred against a backdrop of stability—people still live in families, profess religious beliefs, celebrate major events in their lives, and so on, just as they did before modernization took place.

Technological Revolutions

Technology includes all methods, devices, and artifacts made by humans to help manage and control their environment. For prehistoric humans, technology meant the use of sharpened sticks and stones. For their contemporary counterparts, it includes everything from simple shovels to sophisticated mainframe computers.

Some technological discoveries or inventions have been so significant in terms of sociocultural change that they have been termed technological revolutions. One such revolution occurred during the Neolithic, or New Stone Age (between 5000 and 3000 B.C.), when, for the first time in history, people changed from food gatherers to food producers. Animals were domesticated and put to use. The plow was invented. People began using four-wheeled vehicles. Later, they added the solar calendar, writing, and arithmetic, and began to use bronze. Finally, irrigation, sailboats, looms, bricks, glazing, and the great architectural invention of the arch were brought into existence.

Results of the First Technological Revolution   Tilling the soil and keeping flocks provided men and women with a fairly dependable food supply, even an occasional surplus. As the rate of starvation was drastically reduced, populations boomed. No longer engaged in a constant search for food, groups began to settle permanently in one spot. A rooted existence promoted the development of institutions, and custom and tradition solidified in the family, religion, education, government, and the economy. In time, these pivotal institutions grew more complex. Temporary settlements became permanent villages and towns. Work was divided for the sake of efficiency. Goods and services began to be exchanged with other communities. New ways to control the environment accumulated.

For the next several thousand years, sociocultural changes abounded in the world's societies. Villages grew into towns and then cities, eventually becoming city-states and nation-states. Religions progressed from the belief in magic to more sophisticated forms such as monotheism (belief in one god). The family underwent a number of changes, taking on different forms in different societies.

The Industrial Revolution

Not until the mideighteenth century did another technological revolution trigger a new cycle of sociocultural change. The year 1750 is a somewhat arbitrary date to mark the beginning of this revolution; what is known today as the Industrial Revolution actually had its roots in much earlier events.

Inventions and Discoveries of the Industrial Revolution   The Industrial Revolution may be said to have begun with (1) the invention of a limited number of basic machines; (2) the invention and discovery of certain new materials; and (3) the discovery of new sources of power. The wide-ranging effects of these discoveries and inventions included the mechanization of agriculture and manufacturing; the application of power to manufacturing; the development of a factory system; a tremendous increase in speed of transportation and communication; and dramatic changes in economic systems.

Among the most crucial machines invented during the first phase of the Industrial Revolution were the pendulum clock, the spinning wheel, the power loom, the blast furnace, and the steam engine. During the second phase, thought to have begun about 1860 and still continuing, the dominant invention was the combustion engine. Steel was substituted for iron as the basic material of industry, and coal was replaced by gas and oil as principal sources of power (current attempts to harness atomic energy as a source of power are a further development in this area). Electricity became a major form of industrial energy. Automatic machinery was developed, and labor became highly specialized.

Automation came into existence around the 1930s. Basically, automation involves a process in which machines control other machines, as contrasted with *mechanization,* the substitution of machines for human and animal muscle power. Not all effects of automation have yet been measured. Some welcome the process as simply a further development of basic mechanization and foresee few problems in human adjustment. Others view automation as the beginning of another technological revolution. Such a revolution may be said to have begun after 1945 with the rise of computers. In addition to creating their own spin-off, computer science, computers are responsible for a knowledge explosion that has virtually doubled our ability to store and access information in the last 20 years. There is little question that computers have ushered in a new era.

Industrialism   The system of production that has come to be known as industry represents a radical departure from previous methods of manufacturing goods. In the Middle Ages, artisans or craftsmen organized into guilds (types of unions) produced entire articles and sold them directly to buyers. As commerce expanded, some craftsmen began to rely on merchants to dispose of their merchandise rather than waiting for customers to come to their shops. Eventually craftsmen interacted with merchants much as employees do today, allowing them to control most of the production process, from supplying raw materials to selling the finished product.

As their need for workers increased, merchants began to employ entire families to manufacture finished products out of raw or unfinished materials, and to be paid by the piece for their services. This system, alternately termed the piece, domestic, or putting-out system, became the foundation of the English woolen industry. Farm families supplemented their small earnings by spinning the yarn that merchants brought to their cottages (hence the name cottage industry). Eventually, as more and more articles were produced, the piece system became increasingly specialized. The production of an article was divided into several steps that different members of a family or apprentices could easily perform, initiating specialization and division of labor, particularly efficient methods of organizing production.

With the implementation and increased use of machinery in manufacturing, convenience dictated the housing of both workers and bulky machinery under one roof. Thus the factory system was introduced as the basis of industrialism. Former merchants—now called entrepreneurs and employers—had much more control over their workers when all stages of production were housed in one location. They could pace the work of their employees—decide how many pieces had to be finished per hour or per day. And they could use their capital much more effectively when everything needed for production was at their disposal.

The Industrial Revolution reached the United States in the early part of the nineteenth century. It spread to western Europe in the middle of the century and to Japan some decades later. After the revolution of 1917, Russia began serious efforts at industrialization, as did in succession China, India, and South America.

The Industrial Revolution continues today; none can foresee where and when it will end, although some maintain that we already inhabit a postindustrial era. However, the sociocultural changes wrought by the Industrial Revolution are readily apparent: tremendous increases in population; a move toward the city, or urbanization; and almost complete dependence on industry as the prime mover of the economy. These changes in turn have created social conditions that are frequently problematic.

Technology and Social Change

Technology may be defined as the practical application of knowledge that builds on existing knowledge and previous technology. Therefore, the more technologically advanced a society, the more rapid is its technological progress. Needless to say, technological progress leads to social change; the faster the progress, the faster the pace of change.

Modern industrial societies are characterized by more rapid rates of change than any heretofore known. While for most of history the lives of children were almost identical to those of their parents, each new generation's experience is now different, sometimes in dramatic ways. Younger generations are future-oriented, accustomed to constant change, expectant of progress. In fact, technological progress is equated with improvement in one's material well-being.

Technology has radically altered people's lives, transforming both social reality and cultural values. More of us live longer; machines do formerly backbreaking work; and a constant demand exists for education and training in order to cope with ever-accumulating information and technology. More importantly, due to the widespread availability of mass media (radio, television, records, newspapers, and so on), information is immediately available to every member of society. Incidentally, this wealth of information and rapid rate of change pose problems in socialization, first because certain information becomes obsolete before it can be passed on, and second because it is difficult to prepare young people for a future that can only be vaguely imagined.

Technology is now so vital to our lives that certain social thinkers maintain it actually determines a society's culture, social structure, and much of its history. This view is termed *technological determinism,* and elements of it appear in the works of Marx, Thorstein Veblen, and William Ogburn (1950). Ogburn, for example, argues that the invention of the cotton gin led to a continuation of slavery in the United States by increasing the productivity and profits of the textile industry, necessitating more plantations and thus more slaves. Ogburn further maintains that change tends to occur first in material cultures, since people accept such transformations much more readily than they do alterations in values, ideas, and norms. Consequently, there is always a **culture lag** as nonmaterial aspects of culture attempt to catch up to material ones. This lag produces social problems and disorganization in society.

The cultural lag theory enjoyed popularity for a time, but the weakness of technological determinism in general lies in the assumption that specific changes are attributable to particular technological innovations. Change does not occur in isolation, but rather within the context of a number of social phenomena. In addition, technology results from many simultaneous cultural forces, so that the innovations it brings cannot be attributed to any single cause.

Population

The biblical injunction to be fruitful and multiply seems to have been heeded by the majority of the world's people. Today, most societies, especially the poorest, are plagued by overpopulation, and major catastrophes are periodically predicted if humans do not mend their ways and curb their growth.

However, if the world population were evenly distributed over the earth's surface, only about 55 people would occupy each square mile. Thus the real problem is **population density,** which varies from 0 in some uninhabited regions of Antarctica to an average of 77,000 per square mile on the island of Manhattan.

The distribution of population is a vital issue as the welfare of a society often depends on such factors as its birthrates, death rates, sex ratios, age groups, marriage incidence, divorce frequency, and mobility. The gathering and interpretation of statistics in these areas is a function of the discipline of **demography.**

Population Density

Population density can be measured in a variety of ways. In continental terms, 76 percent of the human population lives in Eurasia, 9 percent in North America, 10 percent in Africa, and 5 percent in South America and the Pacific islands. In political terms, 22 percent reside in the People's Republic of China, 15 percent in India, 6.5 percent in the Soviet Union, 5.5 percent in the United States, and the rest in much smaller percentages throughout the remaining countries of the world. The western, southern, and eastern edges of the Eurasian continent are densely settled; two-thirds of the human population is concentrated in areas that run through the southern half of Japan, the plains and hills of eastern China, the coasts and the Ganges River plain of India, and the industrial districts of Europe. The only other densely settled areas of the world are the highly industrialized sections of the United States and the irrigated farmlands along the lower Nile River in Africa.

Birthrates

Birthrates, an important demographic concept, represent the number of births occurring per 1000 persons in a specific population per year. Related concepts are those of **fertility rates,** the number of actual births per year per 1000 women between the ages of 15 and 44, and **fecundity rates,** the biological potential for reproduction (how many births per 1000 women of that age group could occur).

Birthrates do not generally correspond to population density. In fact, densely populated areas such as Western Europe and Japan experience low birthrates, while in sparsely settled regions such as Arabia and interior Africa the rates are extremely high. From an economic perspective, high birthrates seem to occur in less industrialized and less urbanized countries, the so-called underdeveloped nations. Conversely, highly industrialized and urbanized nations experience the lowest birthrates. Social scientists view the birthrate as the best single socioeconomic variable differentiating developed from underdeveloped nations. This distribution of birthrates is comparatively new: between 1840 and 1930, the population of Europe grew from 194 million to 463 million, approximately double the rate for the world as a whole.

Death Rates

Death rates, also called **mortality rates,** represent the number of deaths per 1000 people of a given country per year. On a world basis, death rates are highest in tropical Africa, whereas urban, industrial nations have low death rates in addition to low birthrates. However, certain less urban and industrial nations such as Thailand, Turkey, and Ecuador also exhibit low death rates even though their birthrates are moderate or high.

Death can result from a number of causes: traffic accidents, suicide, disease, or starvation. But the great leveler of death rates has been western medical technology, which in this century has reached almost every corner of the world, dramatically decreasing death rates, even in areas where they had formerly remained stubbornly high. Decreasing death rates, in fact, are a major source of excessive population growth in Third World nations.

Population Crisis

The "crisis" in population frequently alluded to in the media refers to the **geometric progression** (a progressive doubling, by 2,4,8,16,32, etc.) in the world's population at increasingly shorter intervals of time. At present, world population doubles every 35 years, each year heralding about 75 million more births than deaths. This is in contrast to the past, when from A.D. 1 to the mideighteenth century the birthrate doubled only once every 500 years. Figure 9.1 reflects this change.

Figure 9.1 The accelerated rate at which world population has been growing since the mid-1800s is visually apparent in this graph. Note: *U.N. medium projection variant. *Source:* From presentation by Werner Fornos, President, Population Institute, in testimony before the House Committee on Foreign Affairs, March 24, 1983.

World Population Growth: Past and Projected

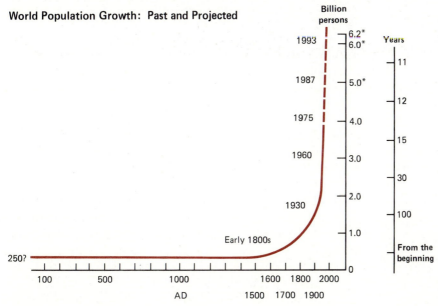

The increase in this rate of doubling is responsible for the overpopulation problem. As early as two centuries ago, certain forecasters realized that the earth would experience overpopulation and insufficient resources unless birthrates were curbed. The best known of these was Thomas Malthus, who published his treatise, *An Essay on the Principles of Population,* in 1798. Malthus asserted that whereas under favorable circumstances populations increase by geometric progression, the corresponding food supply increases only by **arithmetic progression**—by 1,2,3,4,5, and so on. Eventually, therefore, the food supply is destined to become exhausted, causing an increase in the death rate through starvation. Although quite pessimistic about the possibility of reversing this trend, Malthus did suggest the use of preventive checks to control fertility. Later marriage and enforced celibacy were the curbs he favored, neither a particularly realistic alternative. The gloom of Malthusian prophecy has thankfully been tempered by great advances in technology, agriculture, and methods of birth control. Nonetheless, his prophecy still holds relevance, particularly for developing nations in which, largely as the result of lowered death rates, population growth does indeed outpace food production.

Demographic Transition

Demographers have calculated that if current rates of growth remain unabated, in a few centuries the population of the world will reach such levels that each of us will have only a single square foot of land area at our disposal. Of course none could live in such minuscule space. Moreover, most experts do not expect that growth rate to remain constant but to level out at some point between 8 and 15 billion. This leveling off will take place through zero population growth (where the population only replaces itself) worldwide, or through the continued functioning of the demographic transition theory.

As noted, for most of human history, the rate of population growth was barely sufficient for people to replace themselves. A high birthrate was necessary to compensate for the extremely high death rate. In addition, famine, disease, and wars periodically decimated much of the world population.

The Industrial Revolution with its technological innovations changed all this. In the West, populations began to explode around the mideighteenth century, but despite Malthus's warnings this uncontrolled growth failed to alarm those who felt that continued technological progress would always ensure an adequate food supply. Additionally, population growth at the time was accompanied by an increase in the standard of living. Many interpreted this correlation to mean that rapid growth was actually needed for economic expansion: More people consume more products, thus requiring more workers in order to produce still more articles for consumption. In reality, rapid population growth erases any gains derived from improvements in agricultural and industrial technology.

In the past 200 years, the Western world has undergone what demographers term a *demographic transition*. Essentially, this means that Western societies have gone from high to low mortality and fertility rates. Populations grew

It is to be hoped that Third World nations will arrive at the third stage of the demographic transition model just as the developed nations have.

rapidly for a time, and death rates dropped before birthrates. Soon, however, birthrates also fell off, and population growth began to stabilize at a relatively low level.

In the belief that this transition represents a general pattern, demographers have pieced together a conceptual model of population growth. According to the model, societies pass through three basic stages: In the first, birthrates and death rates are both high, leading to a balance achieved through cycles of growth and decline. In the second, death rates decline but birthrates remain high, leading to unchecked population growth. In the third, birthrates decline, leading to stabilization of population. The model allows for shifts in population growth following unusual events such as wars and depressions.

Applying this model, we may interpret tropical Africa, tropical South America, and the eastern and middle sections of Asia as currently undergoing the first stage. Parts of North Africa, the temperate part of South America, India, the People's Republic of China, and several other Third World nations can be viewed as having entered the second stage, while the United States, Australia, New Zealand, Japan, Canada, the United Kingdom, and northern and western Europe have theoretically reached the third and final stage. Figure 9.2 illustrates how much lower the population growth rates are in the developed regions of the world than in the developing ones.

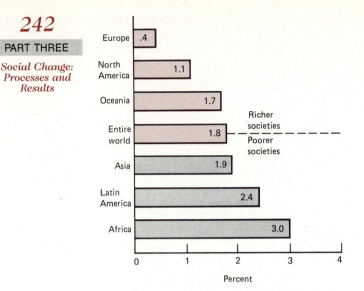

Figure 9.2 The rates of population growth in the industrialized regions of the world are below the world average; the opposite is true for Third World regions. *Source:* United Nations, 1983.

Zero Population Growth

Zero population growth refers to a situation in which the number of births equals the number of deaths in a specific society. At the end of 1972, the United States Bureau of the Census issued new, extremely low projections of future population size in America. These were based on the declining fertility rate, which in that year dropped for the first time below the replacement level to between 2.08 and 2.04. (The replacement level is 2.11, 2 representing the rate of simple population replacement and 0.11 taking into account those who remain childless.) This lower fertility rate can be best appreciated by recalling that as recently as 1961 Americans produced well over 3.6 children per family.

In attaining zero population growth, the United States follows the lead set by other urban, industrial nations. Conditions in cities, where most of the population of these nations is concentrated, do not lend themselves to the creation of large families. Housing is scarce, industrial employment unavailable to children, and education and health protection expensive. Thus urban families, regardless of religion and culture, tend to curb their fertility. Ireland, France, and Italy, for instance, are all Roman Catholic nations whose religion forbids birth control. Yet the birthrate in these countries is among the lowest in the world and is still declining.

Currently, American women each bear an average of 1.8 children, well below the replacement level. However, this situation may readily change, particularly if the so-called baby boom generation produces larger families. In addition, in spite of the efficacy of contraceptive devices, a number of unintentional births still occur every year. Finally, due to habits of high consumption, Americans use up more than one-third of the world's energy and material resources, even though they comprise less than 6 percent of the world's population. Thus any increase in United States population—and Americans are expected to increase by 50 million by the year 2000—has a tremendous impact on the world.

In spite of optimism engendered by the demographic transition model and the achievement of zero population growth in a number of nations, the danger of overpopulation cannot be ignored. The human race is multiplying extremely rapidly, particularly, according to the United Nations and Population Reference Bureau, in poor, underdeveloped nations where food, housing, sanitation, and economic opportunities are already stunted; if present trends continue, these institutions claim, worldwide zero growth can be anticipated no sooner than the year 2040, at a peak population total of more than 14 billion.

Urbanization

Urbanization refers to the growth of cities and their suburbs at the expense of rural areas. Industrial nations experience urbanization because industry attracts labor to cities, and since larger populations require additional services, commercial enterprises increase as well. In addition, an industrial economy can support densely populated areas, whereas rural areas must use available land for agriculture rather than to accommodate people and commerce.

Urbanization, however, does not explain city growth entirely. Due to increased birthrates, decreased death rates, or immigration from abroad, cities may grow without a parallel decrease in rural population. Or they may reflect an overall population growth in both rural and urban areas. Such has been the case in developing nations where the death rates have been reduced through improved hygiene and medical findings, but values regarding birth control have not kept pace.

The shift from rural to urban living began in Britain with the Industrial Revolution. Factories located in cities attracted large numbers of people who were no longer able to make their living on the land. Science and technology had improved agricultural methods, and iron and steel plows, reapers, threshers, harvesters, tractors, and combines did much of the work formerly accomplished by humans. Crop rotation, chemical fertilizers, irrigation, and insect and disease control increased yields per acre without necessitating additional human labor.

With continued improvements in agricultural methods, rural populations have suffered a consequent decline. In the United States the average farm worker in 1820 produced enough food to feed four people. By 1950, one worker could produce enough to sustain 15 ½ others, and by 1969, enough for 47. Such superefficiency in food production has resulted in the disappearance of the small farmer, forcing many to abandon the rural in favor of the city way of life. At the same time, commercial agriculture has created a demand for agricultural machinery produced in urban centers, adding still more to the urbanization trend. Urbanization, then, has been the hallmark of all industrial and industrializing nations. Table 9.1 illustrates the shift from rural to urban life experienced by the United States in the period from 1790 to 1984.

The Urban Population of the United States, 1790–1984

	TABLE 9.1	
Year	Population (millions)	Percent Urban
1790	3.9	5.1
1800	5.3	6.1
1820	9.6	7.3
1840	17.1	10.5
1860	31.4	19.7
1880	50.2	28.1
1900	76.0	39.7
1920	105.7	51.3
1940	131.7	56.5
1960	179.3	69.9
1980	226.5	73.7
1984	236.7	76.2

Source: U.S. Bureau of the Census.

A city, as defined by the United States Bureau of the Census, represents any locality with a minimum population of 2500. Sociologist Louis Wirth, member of the so-called Chicago School (for the University of Chicago) mainly responsible for delineating urban sociology, defined a city as "a relatively large, dense, and permanent settlement of socially heterogeneous individuals" (1938, 3). Wirth saw the task of urban sociologists as an investigation into the forms of social action and social organization that typically emerge in such settlements. Contemporary sociologists use the term *ecological city* to describe a central city (or the city proper), the suburbs that surround it, and satellite settlements that depend socially and economically upon it.

The extent of urbanization in the United States is made clear by the examination of a few statistics. According to the first census in 1790, 95 percent of the American population lived in rural areas and only 5 percent in cities. In 1981, 75 percent resided in urban areas (*World Population Data Sheet,* 1981). However, a countertrend is also apparent. In the decade of the 1970s, rural areas gained 8.4 million people, representing a 15.4 percent increase over the previous decade. At the same time, cities grew by only 9 percent (*Newsweek,* 1981, 32).

In spite of the interrelationship of industrialization and urbanization, cities existed centuries before such terms had even been coined. Permanent settlements were usually built in fertile areas, on natural transportation routes such as rivers, lakes, bays, or between mountains. The earliest known permanent farming community, located in the Fertile Crescent, was inhabited from about 7000 to about 6500 B.C. The development of larger, more complex human settlements, more accurately described as towns or cities, followed people's need to defend themselves from marauding nomads. Defense requirements necessitated the creation of rudimentary political organizations as well as centralized military establishments (Gold, 1982, 32–33). A number of cities through the ages grew strong and powerful: One might mention Athens, Rome, or Venice. But these also often reverted to rural status following wars and invasions.

The urban trend initiated by the Industrial Revolution was of a different nature, however, resulting in the congregation of astonishingly large numbers of people in cities because they had nowhere else to earn a living. People became concentrated in relatively small areas, making interaction among different groups unavoidable. Such contact led to the development of new forms of social organization. Life in cities strengthened the importance of economic and political institutions while weakening those of religion and primary group ties. Class structure grew more flexible as fortunes were made or lost and not merely inherited, and urban residents began to experience social mobility.

Urbanism

In contrast to urbanization, which represents an ongoing process, **urbanism** is a condition, a set of attitudes, a quality, or a way of life distinct from the rural. It reflects the replacement of the traditional rural values of predominantly agricultural societies by modern urban values. Moreover, these urban values are spread through the mass media, so that all modern industrial nations have begun to look and think alike.

Traditional values centered on the intimacy and security provided by large, extended families, close rapport with one's neighbors, friendships maintained throughout a lifetime, and opinions developed and shared through attending the same schools, churches, and clubs. Such values produced a stereotype in the minds of Americans which depicted rural residents as honest, trustworthy, neighborly, and helpful. However, this fantasy was exploded in a classic sociological study (Vidich and Bensman, 1958) which found conditions in rural areas far from ideal. On the contrary, it appeared that the flattering image of the rural population was a figment of the news media's imagination. In reality, rural residents depended largely on cities for new technology and accepted the sociocultural changes of the urban environment. Instances of political machines and corrupt governing bodies indicated rural residents to be no more virtuous than their urban neighbors.

The stereotype of rural as good and urban as evil has had its effect on American politics as well. Proponents of popular democracy like Thomas Jefferson and other early observers of the American scene held great faith in the rural population, believing that these simple folk, through direct participation in the democratic processes, would keep the system alive. This tradition resulted in the failure of many states to revise legislative and congressional districts in accordance with population shifts toward cities. Thus for a long time rural residents had greater representation in state and federal legislatures than their numbers warranted. This situation was finally corrected by the *Baker* v. *Carr* Supreme Court decision, but the justice of having two senators to represent both densely populated and sparsely inhabited states is still subject to debate.

Because cities have tended to grow rapidly, little planning has gone into their physical shape, and their social structure has also created occasional problems. The large concentration of people in cities requires housing in the form of many-storied buildings situated close together. Without proper planning, this condition can lead to ugliness, to lack of green and open spaces, to the oft-mentioned "asphalt jungle." Modern-day city planners are aware of this need for attention to appearance; the cities of the future will thus no doubt be far more attractive than those of the past.

Of greater interest to sociologists are the urban mores that these environments produce. Wirth and others hypothesize that the shift from rural to urban societies produces change in almost all phases of human existence. With the increase in size, density, and heterogeneity of city populations, the division of labor has become more complex, the bonds between residents weaker and impersonal, and the nature of urban dwellers more rational, sophisticated, and anonymous.

In fact, the transition from rural to urban residence has required certain adjustments that have profoundly affected personality and social organization. First, the family became a nuclear one, as only parents and their children

In the Gesellschaft society of the city, the bonds between residents are weak, impersonal, and anonymous. Thus, this passerby can callously walk past the panhandling street person without worrying how she will survive.

could live together in small city dwellings. As a consequence the support network offered by the extended family of grandparents, aunts, uncles, and cousins was missing, and the small family had to stand on its own. Friends and neighbors that rural residents knew intimately and talked to daily were replaced by strangers busy with their own concerns. In essence, urban dwellers experienced a transition from a Gemeinschaft (folk, traditional) society to a Gesellschaft (associational) society (see Chapter 2).

Separation from the ties of the primary group has in turn had mixed effects. For one, it has led to an increase in individual freedom of action. But freedom of action in anonymous circumstances can result in behavior regarded as deviant or antisocial. Without the imposition of primary-group norms, an individual may feel confused, no longer certain of right and wrong. Even worse than the perplexity of normlessness is the discomfort of not belonging to any definite group. In sociological terminology, such an individual becomes a victim of anomie and alienation.

Anomie and alienation in turn may trigger the onset of mental illness, contribute to delinquent or criminal behavior, provoke a search for escape through drugs or alcohol, or drive people to seek aid in psychoanalysis or fundamentalist religious movements. Some even respond by assuming a callous, indifferent, dehumanized mask of self-defense which they present to the world.

In practical terms, the decrease in informal controls by the primary group necessitates an increase in formal controls by secondary groups. Laws are passed and police departments formed to enforce them. The activities of urban residents are increasingly structured by codes and regulations. The urban resident thus pays the price for freedom from primary group interference by increasing bureaucratization and an impersonal life-style.

Wirth and his colleagues from the Chicago School displayed an underlying pessimism about life in the big city as conducive to social disorganization and the source of a variety of social problems. However, contemporary urban sociologists tend to believe that more organization than disorganization prevails in city life, and that a large variety of people with different life-styles living so closely together creates an atmosphere that facilitates creativity and productivity.

Suburbia

From the midnineteenth century until well into the 1950s, populations gravitated toward urban areas. Since then, the trend has moved outward and away from the city toward suburbanization and metropolitanization, although not back toward the country. The most significant growth has occurred in the **suburbs,** small communities on the outskirts of a central city and somewhat dependent on it. Suburban residents now outnumber central-city ones.

This movement to the suburbs has a variety of causes. First, the expansion of industry and business into residential areas forced people to move ever farther from the city center. Second, a general increase in standards of living stimulated the construction of larger, more comfortable homes on land cheaper than could be found in the city. City dwellers began to want to escape the dirt, crime, and noise of urban areas. Finally, the widespread use of the automobile permitted commuting to jobs farther from home.

As cities did before them, the suburbs have spawned their own particular life-style, revolving around the absence of the father for long portions of the day, the necessity for private vehicles and the chauffeuring of children to various activities, as well as the patronage of local shopping centers, a focus of recreation for suburbanites.

Originally, the suburbs attracted young married couples planning large families—the parents of the baby boomers born in the wake of World War II. The postwar economy increased individual incomes and the availability of mortgage money so that home ownership for the first time became a dream almost all could afford. Most early suburbanites were between 25 and 45, with children ranging in age from infancy to teens. As a group they were predominantly white, middle-income, high-school graduates, politically conservative, and morally "proper." From these beginnings developed the stereotype of the suburbs as bedroom communities of identical homes and "square" values.

Today, the suburbs are increasingly characterized by a heterogeneity formerly associated with cities. Increasing rates of divorce have led to as many single-parent homes in the suburbs as in the city. Generalizations formerly made by urban residents about the suburbs have largely been proven wrong (Berger, 1961, 38–49). In addition, whereas suburbanization originally rep-

Suburbs, like city neighborhoods, reflect the social class of their residents.

resented a movement of white middle or upper middle class inhabitants, leading to high degrees of racial segregation, since the 1970s an increase in minorities flocking to suburban homes has reversed this trend (Sternlieb and Hughes, 1978). Social class appears to play a deciding role in this change as middle-class blacks seek refuge from urban conditions much as their white counterparts did a decade or two earlier.

For a while, suburbs depended on the central city for commercial, cultural, and recreational activities. Later, city and suburbs became interdependent, the suburbs providing the labor force for business and industry still housed in the city. Increasingly, however, suburbs are becoming completely independent of the city. Business and industry have relocated to large suburban shopping malls and professional complexes, offering locally available jobs and facilities to suburban residents.

This mushrooming has occurred at the expense of the central city, which loses important tax bases when people, commerce, and industry move away. Without tax money, cities cannot provide important facilities, thus forcing more people, commerce, and industries to leave. As a consequence, the city may be left with a run-down transportation system, outmoded physical facilities, inadequate police protection, and poor schools, so that only those who cannot afford to move out remain.

Metropolitanization

Some suburbs grow so large that they become towns and cities in their own right. Such small cities, smaller suburbs, and the central city around which they cluster make up the ecological city, or metropolitan area. The United States Bureau of the Census uses metropolitan areas as the basis for measuring units of population. The **Standard Metropolitan Statistical Area** (SMSA) consists of one or more counties containing at least one city of over 50,000 or two cities totaling that number. As of 1980, there were 288 such SMSAs in the United States.

The large number of metropolitan areas has led to a new phenomenon in the United States, that of urban sprawl, known by the term of **megalopolis.** In a megalopolis, one metropolitan area is joined to another without interruption. One such complex is the Great Lakes chain, beginning in Buffalo and continuing solidly to Milwaukee and farther west. By the year 2000 an estimated 40 million will be housed in this complex alone. Another megalopolis, the Boston–Washington chain, will contain around 80 million inhabitants.

The growth of metropolitan areas has created large concentrations of people in comparatively small areas. This trend generates political problems since each municipality, county, township, city, and village within the metropolitan area maintains its own government. In such a bureaucratic maze, agencies and officials of neighboring governments are often at odds, leading to the squandering of money and resources. Urban specialists have long favored some form of metropolitan government, but federal studies have concluded that nothing short of broad regional governments will relieve the chaotic situation of metropolitan areas.

U.S. Population: A Portrait in Numbers

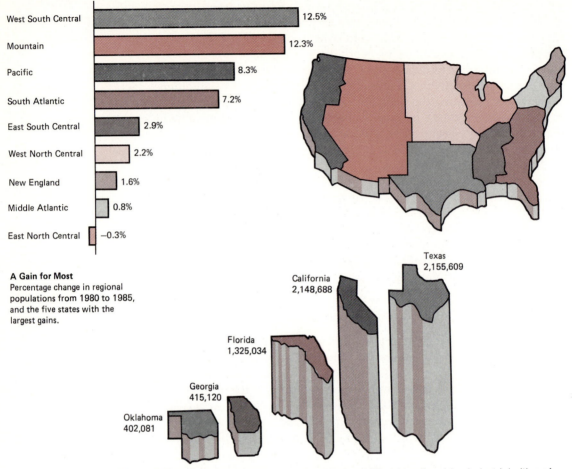

Region	Percentage change
West South Central	12.5%
Mountain	12.3%
Pacific	8.3%
South Atlantic	7.2%
East South Central	2.9%
West North Central	2.2%
New England	1.6%
Middle Atlantic	0.8%
East North Central	−0.3%

A Gain for Most
Percentage change in regional populations from 1980 to 1985, and the five states with the largest gains.

Texas 2,155,609
California 2,148,688
Florida 1,325,034
Georgia 415,120
Oklahoma 402,081

Figure 9.3 The population of the United States is shifting from the older, industrial cities of the Northeast and North Central regions to the South and Southwest, where the new information industries are located. *Source:* From the *New York Times*, April 28, 1985. Copyright © 1985 by The New York Times Company. Reprinted by permission.

The Urban Crisis

The modern afflictions of American cities have been well publicized in the media. Two separate components are involved in this crisis. First, suburbanization has left cities struggling to provide necessary services. Added to that, the departure of many upper-middle-class families, in addition to businesses and industries, has created a loss of tax revenues. Second, a shift has occurred in the regions of the country that are experiencing growth: The older, larger cities in the northeastern and north central areas are losing population as industrial jobs become scarce, while southern and southwestern cities, many of them new, are growing faster than the national average. Figure 9.3 illustrates this development.

Urban Ecology

Cities do not consist of haphazard collections of residential, commercial, and industrial buildings. Both buildings and people are distributed according to interdependent patterns within a geographic area. The study of distributive patterns and their interdependence is known as **urban ecology.** Three major models have been developed by urban ecologists in an attempt to explain the arrangement of people and facilities in American cities.

The *concentric-zone* model stresses the relationship between social status and distance from the center city: The higher the social class of residents, the farther they are likely to live from the central business district. The *sector model examines the tendency of cities to spread in wedge shaped areas extending* from center to outskirts, or along river valleys, water courses, and railroad lines. The *multiple-nuclei* model places less importance on the central business area, suggesting instead that cities consist of a number of nuclei, each of which forms the center of a specialized area.

These models, although descriptive of the processes that structure a city, overlook significant noneconomic forces. Zoning restrictions, the construction of highways or freeways, even the placement of their entrance and exit ramps influence the way a city develops.

One consequence of the flight to suburbia, for instance, has been the expansion of inner-city slums and ghettos. A slum refers to an area that has deteriorated from its previous form but has not yet attained a new one. Residents of slums tend to be recent immigrants, either from abroad or from

The flight to suburbia has left in its wake entire sections of older cities looking like war zones. But most cities are waging a valiant battle to reclaim these neighborhoods.

native rural areas, who can afford housing only in old, often decaying areas since they are unskilled and employed at menial jobs. Many depend on welfare, are victims of discrimination and segregation, and remain unfamiliar with cultural and physical aspects of the larger city.

Following the influx of blacks from the rural South during and after World War II, most central urban areas became ghettos. Ghettos are similar to slums in their origins, conditions, and problems, but are generally restricted to particular racial or ethnic groups. Often, residents are members of the so-called underclass (those chronically unemployed or underemployed), mothers with dependent children, the elderly, and the disabled.

Attempts to Reclaim the City

The critical condition of American cities, abandoned by the middle and working classes, by businesses, professionals, and industrial complexes, bereft of a tax base and thus unable to provide necessary services to their remaining populations, appears dismal. However, many are fighting back vigorously. By continuing to offer desirable activities and jobs, many attract a substantial number of people. Young professionals often prefer to live in central districts, near jobs and entertainment. Even married couples with children frequently find real estate in cities more within their means than in the suburbs. Instances of **gentrification,** the reclaiming of decaying neighborhoods by middle-class, professional families, are on the rise. Gentrification, however, has also encountered criticism. Former residents of these neighborhoods claim to be victimized as they are evicted from housing they could afford into even worse areas.

Urban Renewal   Similar criticism was leveled at government attempts to resolve the plight of the cities through **urban renewal** programs. Urban slums, a reality in industrial societies since the Industrial Revolution drew rural inhabitants into the cities, always contained at least one group who, for a variety of reasons, could not find work, and were thus condemned to live, with government assistance, on the fringes of society. Following World War II, however, in addition to simply aiding the urban poor, the American government began to provide loans for construction of low-cost urban dwellings and later for slum clearance and public housing.

Unfortunately, these programs never worked. Slum clearance resulted in shunting the urban poor from one neighborhood to another, with benefit only to those involved in clearance and construction businesses. Public housing enjoyed equally little success. Due to the stigma attached to living in such quarters, residents tended to display minimal pride of ownership, and their property, built shoddily and without consideration of human interests and needs to begin with, soon fell prey to vandalism and wanton destruction.

Government attempts to offer subsidies so that those with insufficient incomes may compete in the private housing market have also met with little success. Owners of rental property discriminate against large families or those headed by women or disabled fathers. The fear of neighborhoods being overrun by "undesirable" elements persists. For the same reason, suburbs and small towns have effectively kept out public or federally subsidized low-rent housing.

Urban renewal is thus an ineffective remedy of the urban crisis. Original residents living in renovated buildings will benefit from the improvements but remain unable to pay higher city taxes. On the other hand, slum areas cleared in favor of new, expensive housing, commercial buildings, or shopping centers, benefit the city by providing good tax bases, but not the former residents, who are displaced in the process. In such instances, however, middle- and upper-class residents and even shoppers from the suburbs are attracted to the newly refurbished apartments, stores, theaters, and restaurants, thereby creating jobs for city residents.

In 1978, a new urban policy, national in scope, was formulated, stressing the need for cooperative efforts among federal, state, and local governments, as well as the help of neighborhood associations. Its goal is less focused on clearance and renewal than on the preservation, revitalization, and conservation of cities and their neighborhoods. Special concern is expressed for the needs of the poor and minorities in areas of health, employment, and social services. Of course, the formulation of such a policy is only a first, easy step and does not necessarily guarantee any action.

The Natural Environment

Populations and the physical and social structures which they erect exist within the framework of a natural environment, the total complex of natural conditions and resources occurring in specific areas. This environment consists of such elements as landforms, climate, natural vegetation, soils, native animal life, underground and surface waters, and mineral resources. Such elements do not remain static but vary from time to time and from area to area around the world.

A reciprocal relationship exists between the environment and people and their cultures. The environment affects nearly every facet of human life, shaping traditions and institutions; in turn, it is affected, often negatively, by its inhabitants. However, the relationship is neither simple nor direct. People live differently in similar environments, even differently at different times in the same environment. And the same type of physical environment may be dealt with in varying ways by those with divergent perceptions about land use.

The Ecosystem

The use of the very technology that allowed a reduction in the death rate, prompted spurts in population, and crowded large numbers into cities in search of industrial jobs now endangers human life on earth by ignoring or despoiling the natural environment. Such neglect is not new; early humans, however, saw themselves as insignificant inhabitants of a natural world to which they were related and on which they remained dependent. The complex technology that produces myriad articles for easing life today has inspired in contemporary humans the notion that they are in control of the world and perhaps the universe. The humble attitudes of our primitive ancestors who tried to appease the spirits of plants and animals they thought responsible for their existence have been replaced by an arrogant confidence that nothing is impossible for human beings, an attitude which poses grave threats to the ecosystem.

The **ecosystem** is the manner in which living things interact and interrelate with each other and their environment. Ideally, this interaction maintains a balance and permits life to continue. People, land, animals, vegetation, atmosphere, and social processes are so interdependent that slight alterations in one necessarily affect the others. The photosynthetic activity of green plants, for example, produces the oxygen needed for human life and also the machinery of the industrial system. Without plants, animals, and the microorganisms that live in them, pure water in lakes and rivers could not be found. Without certain processes taking place within the earth, we would reap no food crops, mine no oil or coal. The ecosystem represents, in short, our biological capital: human productivity depends on it, and the most advanced technology will be useless if it is destroyed (Commoner, 1971, 16–17).

The ecosystem has been the focus of attention in recent years as concern about the environment continues to grow. The discipline of **ecology,** which studies interrelationships in nature, has played a prominent role in making people aware of environmental developments.

In ecological terms, there are various levels of ecosystems: A particular swamp or river is a local ecosystem; an ocean a regional ecosystem; the planet a global ecosystem.

An ecosystem is delicate and unstable; unforeseen events often disturb its balance. Fires destroy forests; floods and droughts affect the soil, as do gradual climatic changes, population explosions, and the disappearance of particular species. But any ecosystem tends to return to a balance. For instance, imagine a forest inhabited by two species of animals, one of which feeds off the other. If one species is decimated because of disease, the other will experience population growth, feeding easily off sick and dying members of the first. But the diminished numbers of the afflicted group result in less competition and more food, and so the group replenishes itself. Meanwhile the second group will suffer a subsequent reduction in numbers since there is less for it to eat, and the equilibrium of the ecosystem will be reestablished.

The harmony of the human ecosystem can be disturbed by overpopulation, environmental pollution, and environmental depletion. Overpopulation results from increases in the birthrate without a corresponding increase in death rates. Environmental pollution refers to the degradation of air, land, and water, as well as physical aspects of the environment leading to visual and noise pollution. Environmental depletion represents a decrease in natural resources in proportion to their increased demand (as has occurred in the case of energy).

Overpopulation   Obviously, when large numbers occupy an area, the environment will be radically altered. In fact overpopulation and the ecological crisis—the destruction of the environment—are closely related, the first resulting in the second. A team of researchers (Brown, McGrath, and Stokes, 1976, 238–245) has pinpointed 22 dimensions of overpopulation's effect on the environment, maintaining that population growth results in a growth of illiteracy; a decline in worldwide fishing; overcrowding in recreational centers; worsening pollution; a growth in inflation, as increased demand leads to higher-priced goods and services; increased illness; increased hunger owing to low rates of world food supplies; the inability of new housing to keep pace with need; climate changes in densely populated areas; overgrazing of cropland, as more cattle are needed for increased consumption; crowding of people living too close to each other; a decline in income; urbanization; deforestation in the wake of increased lumber needs; conflicts within and between nations; depletion of minerals; inadequate health services; inadequate or polluted water; unemployment; extinction of certain plant and animal species; energy shortages; and threats to individual freedom.

Environmental Pollution   **Pollution** is the result of human actions, a tampering with the environment that leads to harmful consequences. Pollutants are sometimes unforeseen and unwanted by-products of human activities, or the residue of products made, used, and thrown away.

Pollution may affect the air, water, or land, and may also involve our senses of sight and hearing. Every year, millions of tons of pollutants are sent into the air, the by-products of fossil fuels (oil, natural gas, and coal). Among the worst consequences are acid rain, caused by sulfur dioxide emissions from coal-burning plants, and an increase in lower-level ozone, a form of oxygen normally found in the upper atmosphere, where it absorbs the ultraviolet radiation of the sun. Acid rain kills fish, reduces crop yields, and damages buildings. Ozone is harmful to eyes, throats, and lungs. Human activity has reduced the amount of ozone in the stratosphere and increased it on the ground. A reduced upper ozone layer may result in a vastly changed climate on earth, in the destruction of certain animal and plant life, in a greater incidence of skin cancers, in smaller crop yields, and in the possibility of genetic damage to plants, animals, and humans (Brodeur, 1979, 18).

Water is polluted by the dumping of wastes, which have made many beaches unsafe for swimming, as well as by occasional oil spills. From the cleaning of the bilges of tankers alone an estimated 22 million barrels of oil are dumped annually into the oceans. Other kinds of water pollution include organic sewage, overfertilization by excess nutrients, water-borne bacteria or viruses, and organic chemicals such as insecticides, pesticides, and detergents. All are toxic to aquatic life.

In a number of locations the soil is being polluted as well by pesticides, herbicides, chemical wastes, radioactive fallout, and garbage. Some pollutants, harmful to humans, must be used in increasing amounts to control pests which have become resistant to earlier chemicals. Residues of such chemicals remain in the soil, sometimes for years after they have been banned.

Prolonged exposure to intense noise not only damages hearing but increases irritability and prevents sleep. A noise level of 80 decibels is annoying to most people, yet the sound level in a third-floor apartment adjacent to a freeway

Arrogance and irresponsibility have characterized our attitudes toward the environment, and we are now paying the price in undrinkable water and unswimmable streams.

registers about 87 decibels. In addition, decaying property, smog, noxious odors, and inhibited visibility all detract from our enjoyment of the environment.

Environmental Depletion   Polluted air, water, and land can be cleaned up, but a depleted resource is gone forever, leaving the need to find some alternative. No nation in the world is completely self-sufficient in terms of its natural resources. In 1978, for instance, the United States imported 100 percent of the mica, 93 percent of the bauxite and alumina, 81 percent of the tin, and 29 percent of the iron ore used in the country. A particular source of concern is the import of oil, due to rapid increases in the consumption of energy since the turn of the century. Demand for electrical power has also increased, tripling between the 1940s and 1970s. Some experts maintain that nuclear sources of energy provide our only hope for the future, but others point out that these have severe limitations; their safety is dubious and they pose potential environmental hazards.

To summarize, the human species is faced with a threat to its physical and mental well-being, with an ecological imbalance and the consequent disappearance of entire species of animals and plants, and with a hazard to world peace due to imbalance in the standards of living between developed and developing nations. Environmental problems, unfortunately, hold low priority among political leaders and the public in general. Yet owing to the complexities involved, any solution to these must involve governmental action. The establishment of the Environmental Protection Agency and the passage of the Clean Air Act have been steps in this direction, but these policies have been fraught with difficulties. It is likely that certain cultural values must be changed before people can learn to appreciate their environment to a greater extent than is true at present.

The Chapter in Brief

Change is an integral part of nature and of all living things, although a degree of stability is equally characteristic of individuals, societies, and cultures. The mechanisms of sociocultural change are easier to determine than its cause. Principal processes of **cultural change** include **innovation** (**discovery** and **invention**) and **diffusion**. On the other hand, change in the structure of society— **social change**—occurs through planning, reform, and revolution. Sources of change include technology, the physical environment, the size and structure of populations, ideology, events, and individuals.

Sociocultural change has been triggered chiefly by technological progress. **Technology** includes all methods and devices that help humans manage and control their environment. The first technological breakthrough was the invention of agriculture. A second was the advent of the machine era, or the Industrial Revolution. Although this movement accelerated in the middle of the eighteenth century in Great Britain, its roots go back several centuries, and its effects continue to be felt today. The most significant changes wrought by the Industrial Revolution are a surge in the growth of population; industrialization, or the dependence of the economy on industry; and **urbanization**, or the growth of cities at the expense of rural life.

Modernization represents one form of change, encompassing the transition from preindustrial to industrial modes of production. The process has been difficult in all societies. Where it has occurred slowly, over a number of generations, it has eventually been integrated into existing social orders. Rapid modernization, on the other hand, has led to great political instability and other forms of dislocation. In modern industrial societies technological progress has occurred at the most rapid rate in history. Technology has radically altered people's lives, both physically and in terms of cultural values, so significantly that certain thinkers maintain it determines a society's culture, structure, and history. This view, known as technological determinism, was held by Karl Marx. William Ogburn maintained that change was always easier to accept in material culture than nonmaterial, and a **cultural lag** inevitably results when nonmaterial aspects try to catch up with material ones. This lag may also create problems and disorganization.

Population density varies dramatically, with two-thirds of humanity concentrated in an area encompassing the southern half of Japan, the plains and hills of eastern China, the coasts and Ganges River plain of India, and the industrial districts of Europe and the United States. **Birthrates** and **death rates** are calculated on the basis of how many occur per 1000 people in a given year. High birthrates are characteristic of less industrialized and urbanized nations. This fact has engendered the demographic transition model which holds that societies pass through three basic stages of population growth. Stabilization occurs in the third stage, when birthrates decline. Lowering a population's birthrate is a cultural, not a technical, matter.

The United States reached **zero population growth** in 1972, but the birthrate could increase at any time. Urban industrial nations, however, tend to curb and stabilize their populations owing to the difficulty of supporting large families in such societies.

The rapid growth of population, or population explosion, was predicted by Thomas Robert Malthus, who warned that overpopulation would become a threat to humanity, since populations increase by **geometric progression** while food production increases **arithmetically,** at a much slower rate. The Malthusian prophecy holds little relevance for developed nations, but it may be applied to developing nations where population does indeed exceed food production.

The mechanization of agriculture and the factory system have led many people to move from the country to city in search of jobs. City life has given rise to a life-style and tradition which, circulated through the mass media, are becoming dominant in the national culture. Secondary relationships, formal organizations, and the institutions of the economy, government, and education have been strengthened, at the expense of primary relationships and the institutions of the family and religion.

One development in urbanization is the trend toward suburbanization. **Suburbs** grew as people fled to them to escape urban problems. Today, however, suburbs resemble the cities themselves. Cities have suffered from the exodus to the suburbs due to decreased tax bases and the consequent difficulty in providing services to their remaining residents. **Metropolitanization,** the growth of cities and suburbs to a point where they follow each other without interruption over great distances, represents another current problem. Large metropolitan areas, also called **megalopolises,** suffer unique problems such as the need for expanded governmental bureaucracy. Although such programs as **urban renewal** and **gentrification** have attempted to remedy the plight of the inner cities, such areas are still plagued with problems, basically because they remain home to those who cannot afford to move out of them.

Overpopulation and urban life have engendered problems that threaten the environment. First, natural resources are finite and cannot support dramatic increases in population. Second, our careless disregard for the environment threatens to destroy it through various forms of **pollution** and waste. Humans are only one element in the global **ecosystem;** their arrogance, however, is such that they believe themselves the center of creation. Cultural values must almost certainly change before the pollution of air, land, and water as well as the wasting of natural resources is reversed.

Terms to Remember

Arithmetic progression   Single-digit progression: by 1, 2, 3, 4, 5, etc. Refers to world food supply.

Birthrate   The number of births per 1000 persons in a specific population per year.

Cultural change   Change in values, beliefs, and norms which may be effected by scientific discoveries, technological inventions, new achievements in the arts, or shifts in religious doctrine.

Culture lag   A condition occurring when different segments of a culture change at different rates of speed, creating dislocations and disorganization in the society. Associated with William Ogburn.

Death rate   The number of deaths per 1000 persons in a specific population per year. Same as mortality rates.

Demography   The study of the growth or decline of populations, their distribution throughout the world, and their composition.

Diffusion   A process of cultural change in which the traits of one society's culture are spread to another (or from one group to another within a society).

Discovery   A process of cultural change whereby an existing fact or relationship is newly perceived.

Ecology   The study of the relationship between living organisms and their environments.

Ecosystem   The way living and nonliving entities interact and maintain a balance that permits life to continue.

Fecundity rates   The biological potential for producing offspring.

Fertility rates   The number of actual births per 1000 women per year between the ages of 15 and 44.

Gentrification   The reclaiming of decaying neighborhoods by middle-class, professional families.

Geometric progression   A progressive doubling: 2, 4, 8, 16, etc. Refers to world population growth.

Innovation   Cumulative discoveries or inventions that produce new elements or new combinations of old elements to be absorbed into the culture.

Invention   A process of cultural change in which existing ideas or objects are combined in new ways to produce ideas or objects more significant than the sum of their parts.

Megalopolis   The condition in which one metropolitan area follows another without interruption. Also called urban sprawl.

Metropolitanization   The tendency of suburbs, small cities, and surrounding rural areas to cluster around a central city and be considered a single unit.

Modernization   The sociocultural change that transforms small preindustrial societies into large industrial ones.

Mortality rates   See death rates.

Pollution   The degradation of air, land, and water, as well as the aesthetic aspects of the environment.

Population density The ratio of population to land area.

Social change Change in the patterns of social interaction in which a substantial number of societal members assume new statuses and play new roles. Occurs through planning, reform, and revolution.

Standard Metropolitan Statistical Area (SMSA) Term used by the United States Bureau of the Census to designate units of population consisting of a county or counties that include a city of 50,000 or more.

Suburbs Smaller communities on the outskirts of central cities and somewhat dependent upon them.

Technology All the methods and devices that help humans manage and control their environment.

Urban ecology The study of distributive patterns of buildings and people in cities, and their interdependence.

Urbanism A condition, set of attitudes, quality, or way of life distinct from the rural.

Urbanization A population trend in which cities grow at the expense of rural areas.

Urban renewal Attempts by the federal government to help cities by providing loans for construction of low-cost, urban dwellings, slum clearance, and public housing.

Zero population growth A condition in which each person replaces only himself or herself (a replacement level of 2.11), thus equalizing the birthrate and death rate.

Suggestions for Further Reading

Geist, William. 1985. *Toward a safe and sane Halloween and other tales of suburbia.* New York: Times Books. A journalistic view of suburban living, including the effect of shopping malls on American culture.

Nam, Charles B. and Susan Gustavus Philliber. 1984. *Population: A basic orientation.* Englewood Cliffs, N.J.: Prentice-Hall. A recent and basic textbook in the field of demography, stressing world population trends.

Peterson, Paul E., ed. 1985. *The new urban reality.* Washington, D. C.: Brookings Institution. A collection of essays focusing on the reasons for the decline of central cities in the United States.

The World Bank. *World Development Report 1984.* 1984. New York: Oxford University Press. This report centers on the interrelationship of demographic and economic issues, especially in the nations of the Third World.

Simon, Julian L. 1981. *The ultimate resource.* Princeton, N. J.: Princeton University Press. The author presents the controversial thesis that resources are limitless because of human ingenuity and continued technological progress.

Bushmen

JOHN YELLEN

Nowhere are changes wrought by the passage of time and interaction with more advanced societies more dramatic than in the case of preliterate hunting and gathering groups who come into contact with the twentieth century. Such has been the case with a group of Bushmen in the Kalahari Desert. John Yellen, an anthropologist and director of the National Science Foundation, has returned to the Kalahari numerous times, where he and his colleagues have been able to witness personally the nature of this change.

In the mid-1960s, the South African government had decided to accurately survey the Botswana border, mark it with five-strand fence, and cut a thin firebreak on either side. At intervals they constructed survey towers, strange skeletal affairs, like oil drilling rigs, their tops poking well above the highest mongongo trees. It was to one of these that Dau led me across the border, through the midday sun. Although he would not climb it himself, since it was a white man's tower, he assumed I would. I followed his finger, his chain of logic as I started rather hesitantly up the rusted rungs. I cleared the arrow grass, the acacia bushes, finally the broad leafy crowns of the mongongo nut trees. Just short of the top I stopped and sat, hooked my feet beneath the rung below, and wrapped my arms around the metal edges of the sides.

For the first time from the tower, I could see an order to the landscape. From up there on the tower, I could see that long thin border scar, could trace it off the horizon to both the north and south. But beyond that, no evidence, not the slightest sign of a human hand. The Bushmen camps were too few in number, too small and well-hidden in the grass and bush to be visible from here. Likewise, the camp where we anthropologists lived, off to the east at the Dobe waterhole, that also was too small to see.

In those first years with the Dobe Bushmen, I did gain at least a partial understanding of that land. And I learned to recognize many of those places, the ones that rate no name at all but are marked only by events—brief, ephemeral happenings that leave no mark on the land. I learned to walk with the Bushmen back from a hunt or a trip for honey or spear-shaft wood and listen. They talked, chattered almost constantly, decorating the bush, these no-name places as they went, putting ornaments of experience on them: "See that tree there, John? That's where we stopped, my brother and I, long before he was married, when he killed a kudu, a big female. We stopped under that tree, hung the meat up there and rested in the shade. But the flies were so bad, the biting flies, that we couldn't stay for long."

It took me a long time to realize that this chatter was not chatter at all, to understand that those remarks were gifts, a private map shared only among a few, an overlay crammed with fine, spidery writing on top of the base map with its named waterholes and large valleys, a map for friends to read. Dau would see a porcupine burrow, tiny, hidden in the vastness of the bush. And at night he could sit by the fire and move the others from point to point across

Source: Adapted by permission of SCIENCE 85 © 1985 by the American Association for the Advancement of Science.

the landscape to that small opening in the ground.

But as an archeologist, I had a task to do—to name those places and to discover what life had been like there in the past. "This place has a name now," I told Dau when I went back in 1976. Not the chicken camp, because when I was there I kept 15 chickens, or the cobra camp, for the cobra we killed one morning among the nesting hens, but Dobe Base Camp 18. Eighteen because it's the eighteenth of these old abandoned camps I've followed you to in the last three days. See? That's what goes into this ledger, this fat bound book in waterproof ballpoint ink. We could get a reflector in here—a big piece of tin like some metal off a roof and get some satellite or a plane to photograph it. We could tell just where it is then, could mark it on one of those large aerial maps down to the nearest meter if we wanted.

What appealed to me about the Dobe situation, why I followed Dau, walked out his youth and his early manhood back and forth around the waterhole was the neat, almost laboratory situation Dobe offered. A natural experiment. I could go to a modern camp, collect those discarded food bones even before the jackals and hyenas had gotten to them, examine and count them, watch the pattern emerge. What happened then to the bones after they'd been trampled, picked over, rained on, lain on the ground for five years? Five years ago? Dobe Base Camp 21, 1971. I could go there, dig up a sample and find out.

What went on farther and farther back in time? Is there a pattern? Try eight years ago. 1968, DBC 18. We could go there to the cobra camp and see. Thirty-four years ago? The camp where Tsaa with the beautiful wife was born. One can watch, can see how things fall apart, can make graphs, curves, shoot them back, watch them arc backwards beyond Dau, beyond Dau's father, back into the true archeological past.

We dug our way through the DBCs, back into the early 1940s, listening day after day to the South African soap operas on the short-wave radio, and our consumption of plastic bags went down and down. Slim pickings in the bone department. And the bones we did find tended to be rotten: They fragmented, fell apart in the sieve.

So we left the 1940s, collapsed the bridge table and the folding chairs and went to that site that played such a crucial role for anthropologists: DBC 12, the 1963 camp where those old myths about hunters and gatherers came up against the hard rock of truth.

They built this camp just after Richard Lee, the pioneer, arrived. They lived there through the winter and hunted warthog with spears and a pack of dogs so good they remember each by name to this day. Richard lived there with them. He watched them—what they did, what they ate, weighed food on his small scale slung with a rope from an acacia tree. He weighed people, sat in camp day after day with his notebook and his wristwatch and scale. He recorded times: when each person left camp in the morning, when each returned for the day.

In this small remnant group, one of the last in the world still living by hunting and gathering, it should be possible, he believed, to see a reflection, a faint glimmer of the distant universal past of all humanity, a common condition that had continued for millions and millions of years. He went there because of that and for that reason, later on, the rest of us followed him.

What he found in that desert camp, that dry, hard land, set the anthropological world back on its collective ear. What his scale and his wristwatch and his systematic scribbles showed was that we were fooled, that we had it all wrong. To be a hunter and gatherer wasn't that bad after all. They didn't work that hard, even in this land of thorns: For an adult, it came to less time than a nine-to-five office worker puts in on the job. They lived a long time, too, didn't wear out and die young but old-looking, as we had always thought. Even in this camp, the camp with the good hunting dogs, it was plants, not meat, which provided the staff of life. Women walked through the nut groves and collected nuts with their toes, dug in the molapos and sang to each other through the bush. Unlike the game, which spooked so easily and followed the unpredictable rains, the nuts, roots, and berries were dependable, there in plenty, there for the picking. Another distinguished anthropologist, Marshall Sahlins, termed those DBC 12 people "the original affluent society"—something quite different from the traditional conception of hunting and gathering as a mean, hard existence half a step ahead of starvation and doom.

Over the years that name has held—but life in the Kalahari has changed. That kind of camp, with all the bones and mongongo nuts and dogs, is no more.

By the mid-1970s, things were different at Dobe. Diane Gelburd, another of the anthropologists out there then, only needed to look around her to see how the Bushman lifestyle had changed from the way Richard recorded it, from how Sahlins described it. But what had changed the people at DBC 12 who believed that property should be commonly held and shared? What had altered their system of values? That same winter Diane decided to find out.

She devised a simple measure of acculturation that used pictures cut from magazines: an airplane, a sewing machine, a gold mine in South Africa. (Almost no one got the gold mine right.) That was the most enjoyable part of the study. They all liked to look at pictures, to guess.

Then she turned from what people knew to what they believed. She wanted to rank them along a scale, from traditional to acculturated. So again she asked questions:

"Will your children be tattooed?"

To women: "If you were having a difficult childbirth and a white doctor were there, would you ask for assistance?"

To men: "If someone asked you for permission to marry your daughter would you demand (the traditional) bride service?"

Another question so stereotyped that in our own society one would be too embarrassed to ask: "Would you let your child marry someone from another tribe—a Tswana or a Herero—a white person?"

First knowledge, then belief, and finally material culture. She did the less sensitive questions first. "Do you have a field? What do you grow? What kind of animals do you have? How many of what?" Then came the hard part: She needed to see what people actually owned. I tagged along with her one day and remember the whispers inside one dark mud hut. Trunks were unlocked and hurriedly unpacked away from the entrance to shield them from sight. A blanket spread out on a trunk revealed the secret wealth that belied their statements: "Me? I have nothing." In the semidarkness she made her inventory. Then the trunks were hastily repacked and relocked with relief.

She went through the data, looked at those lists of belongings, itemized them in computer printouts. Here's a man who still hunts. The printout shows it. He has a bow and quiver and arrows on which the poison is kept fresh. He has a spear and snares for birds. He has a small steenbok skin bag, a traditional carryall that rests neatly under his arm.

He also has 19 goats and 2 donkeys, bought from the Herero or Tswana, who now get Dobe Bushmen to help plant their fields and herd their cows. They pay in livestock, hand-me-down clothing, blankets, and sometimes cash. He has 3 large metal trunks crammed full: One is packed to the top with shoes, shirts, and pants, most well-worn. He has 2 large linen mosquito nets, 10 tin cups, and a metal file. He has ropes of beads: strand upon strand—over 200 in all, pounds of small colored glass beads made in Czechoslovakia that I had bought in Johannesburg years earlier. He has 4 large iron pots and a five-gallon plastic jerry can. He has a plow, a gift from the anthropologists. He has a bridle and bit, light blankets, a large tin basin. He has 6 pieces of silverware, a mirror and hairbrush, two billycans. His wife and his children together couldn't carry all that. The trunks are too heavy and too large for one person to carry so you would have to have two people for each. What about the plow, those heavy iron pots? Quite a job to carry those through bush, through the thick thorns.

But here is the surprising part. Talk to that man. Read the printout. See what he knows, what he believes. It isn't surprising that he speaks the Herero language and Setswana fluently or that he has worked for the Herero, the anthropologists. Nothing startling there. A budding Dobe capitalist. But then comes the shock: He espouses the traditional values.

"Bushmen share things, John. We share things and depend on each other, help each other out. That's what makes us different from the black people."

But the same person, his back to the door, opens his trunks, unlocks them one by one, lays out the blankets, the beads, then quickly closes each before he opens the next.

Multiply that. Make a whole village of people like that, and you can see the cumulative effect: You can actually measure it. As time goes on, as people come to own more possessions, the huts move farther and farther apart.

In the old days a camp was cosy, intimate and close. You could sit there by one fire and look into the other grass huts, see what the other people were doing, what they were making or eating. You heard the conversations, the arguments and banter.

We ask them why the new pattern?

Says Dau: "It's because of the livestock that we put our huts this way. They can eat the grass from the roofs and the sides of our houses. So we have to build fences to keep them away and to do that, you must have room between the huts."

I look up from the fire, glance around the camp, say nothing. No fences there. Not a single one around any of the huts, although I concede that one day they probably will build them. But why construct a lot of separate small fences, one around each hut? Why not clump the huts together the way they did in the old days and make a single large fence around the lot? Certainly a more efficient approach. Why worry about fences now in any case? The only exposed grass is on the roofs, protected by straight mud walls and nothing short of an elephant or giraffe could eat it.

Xashe's answer is different. Another brief reply. An attempt to dispose of the subject politely but quickly. "It's fire, John. That's what we're worried about. If we put our houses too close together, if one catches fire, the others will burn as well. We don't want one fire to burn all our houses down. That's why we build them so far apart."

But why worry about fire now? What about in the old days when the huts were so close, cheek by jowl? Why is it that when the huts were really vulnerable, when they were built entirely of dried grass, you didn't worry about fires then?

You read Diane's interviews and look at those lists of how much people own. You see those shielded mud huts with doors spaced, so far apart. You also listen to the people you like and trust. People who always have been honest with you. You hear their explanations and realize the evasions are not for you but for themselves. You see things they can't. But nothing can be done. It would be ludicrous to tell these brothers: "Don't you see, my friends, the lack of concordance between your values and the changing reality of your world?"

Now, years after the DBC study, I sit with data spread out before me and it is so clear. Richard's camp in 1963: just grass huts, a hearth in front of each. Huts and hearths in a circle, nothing more. 1968: more of the same. The following year though the first *kraal* appears, just a small thorn enclosure, some acacia bushes cut and dragged haphazardly together for their first few goats. It's set apart way out behind the circle of huts. On one goes, from plot to plot, following the pattern from year to year. The huts change from grass to mud. They become larger, more solidly built. Goats, a few at first, then more of them. So you build a fence around your house to keep them away from the grass roofs. The *kraals* grow larger, move in closer to be incorporated finally into the circle of huts itself. The huts become spaced farther and farther apart, seemingly repelled over time, one from the next. People, families move farther apart.

The bones tell the same story. 1947: All the bones from wild animals, game caught in snares or shot with poisoned arrows— game taken from the bush. By 1964 a few goat bones, a cow bone or two, but not many. Less than 20 percent of the total. Look then at the early 1970s and watch the line on the graph climb slowly upwards— by 1976 over 80 percent from domesticated stock.

But what explains the shattering of this society? Why is this hunting and gathering way of life, so resilient in the face of uncertainty, falling apart? It hasn't been a direct force—a war, the ravages of disease. It is the internal conflicts, the tensions, the inconsistencies, the impossibility of reconciling such different views of the world.

At Dobe it is happening to them all together. All of the huts have moved farther apart in lockstep, which makes it harder for them to see how incompatible the old system is with the new. But Rakudu, a Bushman who lived at the Mahopa water-

hole eight miles down the valley from Dobe, was a step ahead of the rest. He experienced, before the rest of them, their collective fate.

When I was at the Cobra Camp in 1969, Rakudu lived down near Mahopa, off on his own, a mile or so away from the pastoral Herero villages. He had two hats and a very deep bass voice, both so strange, so out of place in a Bushman. He was a comical sort of man with the hats and that voice and a large Adam's apple that bobbed up and down.

The one hat must have been a leftover from the German-Herero wars because no one in Botswana wore a hat like that—a real pith helmet with a solid top and a rounded brim. It had been cared for over the years because, although soiled and faded, it still retained the original strap that tucks beneath the chin. The second hat was also unique—a World War I aviator's hat, one of those leather sacks that fits tightly over the head and buckles under the chin. Only the goggles were missing.

I should have seen then how out of place the ownership of two hats was in that hunter-gatherer world. Give two hats like that to any of the others and one would have been given away on the spot. A month or two later, the other would become a gift as well. Moving goods as gifts and favors along that chain of human ties. That was the way to maintain those links, to keep them strong.

When I went to Rakudu's village and realized what he was up to, I could see that he was one of a kind. The mud-walled huts in his village made it look like a Herero village—not a grass hut in sight. And when I came, Rakudu pulled out a hand-carved wood and leather chair and set it in the shade. This village was different from any of the Bushman camps I had seen. Mud huts set out in a circle, real clay storage bins to hold the corn—not platforms in a tree—and *kraals* for lots of goats and donkeys. He had a large field, too, several years before the first one appeared at Dobe.

Why shouldn't Bushmen do it—build their own villages, model their subsistence after the Herero? To plant a field, to tend goats, to build mud-walled houses like that was not hard to do. Work for the Herero a while and get an axe, accumulate the nucleus of a herd, buy or borrow the seeds. That year the rains were long and heavy. The sand held the water and the crickets and the birds didn't come. So the harvest was good, and I could sit there in the carved chair and look at Rakudu's herd of goats and their young ones and admire him for his industry, for what he had done.

Only a year later I saw him and his eldest son just outside the Cobra Camp. I went over and sat in the sand and listened to the negotiations for the marriage Rakudu was trying to arrange. His son's most recent wife had run away, and Rakudu was discussing a union between his son and Dau the Elder's oldest daughter who was just approaching marriageable age. They talked about names and Dau the Elder explained why the marriage couldn't take place. It was clear that the objection was trivial, that he was making an excuse. Even I could see that his explanation was a face-saving gesture to make the refusal easier for all of them.

Later I asked Dau the Elder why he did it. It seemed like a good deal to me. "Rakudu has all that wealth, those goats and field. I'd think that you would be anxious to be linked with a family like that. Look at all you have to gain. Is the son difficult? Did he beat his last wife?"

"She left because she was embarrassed. The wife before her ran away for the same reason and so did the younger brother's wife," he said. "Both brothers treated their wives well. The problem wasn't that. It was when the wives' relatives came. That's when it became so hard for the women because Rakudu and his sons are such stingy men. They wouldn't give anything away, wouldn't share anything with them. Rakudu has a big herd just like the Herero, and he wouldn't kill goats for them to eat."

Not the way Bushmen should act toward relatives, not by the traditional value system at least. Sharing, the most deeply held Bushman belief, and that man with the two hats wouldn't go along. Herero are different. You can't expect them to act properly, to show what is only common decency; you must take them as they are. But someone like Rakudu, a Bushman, should know better than that. So the wives walked out and left for good.

But Rakudu understood what was happening, how he was trapped—and he tried to respond. If you can't kill too many goats from the herd that has become essential to you, perhaps you can find something else of value to give away. Rakudu thought he had an answer.

He raised tobacco in one section of his field. Tobacco, a plant not really adapted to a place like the northern Kalahari, has to be weeded, watered by hand, and paid special care. Rakudu did that and for one year at least harvested a tobacco crop.

Bushmen crave tobacco and Rakudu hoped he had found a solution—that they would accept tobacco in place of goats, in place of mealie meal. A good try. Perhaps the only one open to him. But, as it turned out, not good enough. Rakudu's son could not find a wife.

Ironic that a culture can die yet not a single person perish. A sense of identity, of a shared set of rules, of participation in a single destiny binds individuals together into a tribe or cultural group. Let that survive long enough, let the participants pass this sense through enough generations, one to the next, create enough debris, and they will find their way into the archeological record, into the study of cultures remembered only by their traces left on the land.

Rakudu bought out. He, his wife, and his

two sons sold their goats for cash, took the money and walked west, across the border scar that the South Africans had cut, through the smooth fence wire and down the hard calcrete road beyond. They became wards of the Afrikaaners, were lost to their own culture, let their fate pass into hands other than their own. At Chum kwe, the mission station across the border 34 miles to the west, they were given numbers and the right to stand in line with the others and have mealie meal and other of life's physical essentials handed out to them. As wards of the state, that became their right.

When the problems, the contradictions of your life are insoluble, a paternalistic hand provides one easy out.

Dau stayed at Dobe. Drive there today and you can find his mud-walled hut just by the waterhole. But he understands: He has married off his daughter, his first-born girl to a wealthy Chum kwe man who drives a tractor—an old man, more than twice her age, and by traditional Bushmen standards not an appropriate match. Given the chance, one by one, the others will all do the same.

Collective Behavior and Formal Organizations in Mass Society

As the previous chapter made clear, the chief thrust of modernization was to transform relatively simple societies with agrarian economies into highly complex, technologically advanced, industrial societies. Such transformation, which in centuries past followed the standard processes of sociocultural change, was dramatically accelerated by several crucial technological revolutions, chiefly those of agriculture and industrialism. The Industrial Revolution heralded a surge in population growth and the prominent trend toward urbanization. In time, the population explosion, urbanization, and industrialization began to threaten societies with overpopulation, pollution and other degradations of the environment, and resource depletion. The growth of cities prompted large numbers to congregate in relatively compact areas. Cities became metropolitan areas, requiring the efficient production of goods and services and rapid transportation for distribution of these to consumers. Industrial growth has also resulted in a vast number and variety of products which the consumer must be enticed to buy. In short, the larger size and greater complexity of societies has necessitated the creation of systems according to which activities may be organized to prevent chaos and confusion.

Modernization has also been hastened by a movement toward rationalism, the dependence upon reason rather than mystery or magic. As science has unraveled the secrets of many previously mysterious phenomena, human thought has shifted from a preoccupation with symbolic meanings and spiritual values to a concern for concrete, empirical matters. While earlier historical eras were governed by the philosophies of religious prophets and spiritual thinkers, the modern era is the domain of scientists and engineers. Earlier eras strove for the truth through faith or belief in revelation, an attempt which, in the modern era, has given way to scientific investigation. In a secular, materialistic time, goals must be achieved primarily through organization. The complex societies of our modern age, then, may be described as resembling the model of mass societies in which formal organizations with bureaucratic administrations predominate, and in which forms of collective behavior abound.

Mass Society

A society need not be large in order to be termed a mass society, though sizeableness does predispose a society toward massification. In essence, a **mass society** is composed of large numbers of members (masses) who are widely distributed and anonymous rather than well integrated into the social system. As a consequence, the system is loosely organized, even somewhat disorganized. Masses may react to the same stimuli—may watch the same news on television, for instance—but do so separately, without reference to one another. In contrast to individuals or groups, masses do not participate in any broad social grouping, not even that of social class. "The mass merely consists of individuals who are separate, detached, anonymous, and thus homogeneous as far as mass behavior is concerned" (Blumer, 1969, 86–87).

French social commentator Alexis de Tocqueville, who visited the United States in the early nineteenth century, predicted the transition there from a society of individuals and distinctive social classes to one composed of an undifferentiated mass. Since such a society could be easily manipulated by a ruling elite prepared to satisfy its whims, the mass represented, in Tocqueville's eyes, a potential threat to democracy.

Modern societies, especially those of the United States and the USSR, have often been described by the term "mass." To some people's minds, in fact, the terms modern society and mass society are synonymous. But while definitely a consequence of modernization with its new technologies, forms of organization, and ideologies, the term "mass" society is *not* interchangeable with "modern" society.

Mass society may be more exactly described as the model of a society at the farthest end of the continuum from Gemeinschaft to Gesellschaft—traditional to associational (see Chapter 3). As such, it represents the final stage in the transition from primary to secondary relationships. Modern societies inevitably drift toward this model, characterized by anonymity, mobility, specialization of roles and statuses, and a lack of individual integration in the social structure. In such societies, individuals make choices independently, without regard to common customs, traditions, norms, or values.

Mass society is perceived as being divided into two factions: an organized elite and an unorganized, diffused mass. The elite may be influenced by the mass; in democracies, for instance, the mass elects the elite by ballot, while in other political systems it may use violence or noncooperation to bring in a ruling segment or to overthrow it. Contrary to past circumstances, the modern elite is no longer insulated from the mass, due to the pervasive nature of mass media, which enables the elite and the mass to communicate directly and immediately. But the elite easily mobilizes the mass, organizing and manipulating propaganda, for instance, to its own benefit (Kornhauser, 1959).

In mass society, behavior frequently tends to be collective: unorganized, unstructured, uncoordinated. A mass is also more susceptible to invoked action, including violence, especially under the command of a charismatic leader. The work of such leaders is greatly simplified by selective use of the mass media in communication.

Mass Communication

Communication represents a fundamental element of culture building. Norms, values, traditions, myths, attitudes, as well as material objects, come into existence and are disseminated by transmitting and diffusing knowledge. In folk societies of the distant past, communication occurred among members on a face-to-face basis. Such societies relied on oral traditions to transmit historical events and legends, through memory and recitation, from one generation to the next. An oral tradition, however, can reach only a small number of people; equally limited are forms of communication other than speech, such as paintings in caves or the beating of drums. As a result, folk societies generally remained static and traditional, lacking the potential for cultural and social change since ideas could not be dispersed among a sufficient number.

The invention of writing broadened the communication of knowledge immensely. But not until the first part of the fifteenth century, when Johannes Gutenberg invented the printing press, did a real breakthrough occur in communications technology. The printing press revolutionized human societies: a single message could be communicated simultaneously to thousands (later to millions). No longer was there any need for intermediaries like priests and clerics to interpret, and possibly modify, messages or information.

Such direct communication revolutionized old social structures. The elite of the stratification system now had direct access to the mass below, with little further need for those in between. As pamphlets, newspapers, and magazines swept through societies, spreading information and ideas to increasing numbers, established institutions began to be seen as imperfect, and subject to attack. In this manner the printing press affected religion, politics, and culture in general.

Mass communication can be distinguished from face-to-face communication in several important ways. First, it exposes large, heterogeneous, anonymous audiences to symbols transmitted by impersonal means from an organized source personally unacquainted with audience members (Larsen, 1964, 348). Second, information is public, rapid, transient, and one-sided (since the audience cannot respond to the message nor can the communicator sense their reaction). In short, mass communication prohibits normal interaction, resulting in potential frustration for all involved and the possibility of unforeseen consequences.

Another source of frustration resides in the superabundance of information caused by the spread of communications media. Newspapers, television, radio, tapes, films, books, music, graffiti, and dozens of other assorted attacks of daily messages generate such a tremendous explosion of knowledge that the sheer input of information can be overwhelming. The knowledge explosion introduces another paradox: On the one hand, direct access to necessary knowledge conveys power on the recipient; on the other, a flow of information understood by only a small segment of the population enables these few people, through their ability to control it, to manipulate the rest.

Collective Behavior

In addition to the strong tendencies toward the mass model, industrial urban societies exhibit to a much greater extent than traditional preindustrial or agrarian ones a type of behavior known to social scientists as collective. Collective behavior differs from the interactive behavior characteristic of social groups, even though both involve reactions by members to the same situations. As noted in Chapter 2, most human behavior follows regular patterns, and so is predictable to a degree. In fact, such regularity makes life in society possible: Members interact in the context of statuses and roles within the framework of a normative system that is more or less shared.

When humans are suddenly thrust into foreign situations, for which no precedent exists in their experience, they may find themselves lacking societal norms or guidelines to follow. For instance, if a person Christmas shopping in a department store suddenly hears another customer yelling "Fire!" that person may well be unsure about how to behave. In such circumstances, people are likely to act spontaneously, perhaps even illogically or irrationally, following the influence of those who happen to be near at the time. This type of behavior is termed collective, and tends to occur in crowds, mobs (giving rise to riots or lynchings), certain kinds of sports events or musical concerts, and religious revival meetings. Collective behavior also occurs when members of a society follow fashions, fads, or give in to a craze; make up a public or an audience; act on public opinion, propaganda, and rumors; or work together in social movements toward the attainment of certain goals.

Sociologists define **collective behavior** as actions that take place unplanned, without clear-cut direction from a culture's normative system, and with unforeseen effects. In sum, collective behavior represents spontaneous, unstructured ways of acting, thinking, or feeling engaged in by large numbers of people in situations where they do not know how to act, what to expect of others, or what others expect of them. Under such circumstances, they tend to improvise and follow each other's example. Since the usual regulating cultural norms do not apply, collective behavior tends to be unpredictable and contain a high degree of emotional charge.

In spite of this lack of pattern, however, rarely is there a complete lack of structure in the behavior of an aggregate of people. Only when one's life is threatened is one likely to act with complete absence of awareness of others. Thus, in most situations, collective behavior is partly structured and partly unstructured. For instance, although a department-store crowd does not form a group in the sociological sense, a great deal of awareness of others nonetheless exists, a certain amount of interaction takes place, and the crowd behaves in accordance with general norms. Should such norms be deliberately flaunted—should a customer get up on a counter and start to undress—negative sanctions would be rapidly applied: The customer would be asked to leave the store. But because such a crowd is not a cohesive group, its behavior can, without too much difficulty, grow disorganized and unpredictable. A cry of "Fire!" in such a crowd may easily precipitate panic, and the crowd become a mindless, destructive mob. In more cohesive groups—a classroom, for instance—people would be more likely to line up in front of a fire escape and listen to directions from those in charge.

Some situations of collective behavior start out fairly structured and end up completely disorganized. An audience at a rock concert may at the end of the show surge forward, jump on the stage, and destroy musical instruments. Other situations may start out disorganized and end up structured. Many social movements—the labor movement, for one—begin as nothing more than disorganized protests, and only later develop definite goals, apply ranked roles to their members, and evolve norms and techniques for social control such as characterize any organized group.

Because of its unpredictability, collective behavior is a subject of great fascination to social scientists. This type of action characterizes periods of rapid social change when cultural norms are in transition or poorly defined. Sociocultural change and new values and norms are in fact often triggered by spontaneous, unstructured, unpatterned behaviors of large numbers of people. Many social movements, several religious denominations, and numerous governments owe their origin to some form of collective behavior. The United States itself represents such an example, originating when large numbers of settlers grew dissatisfied with British rule and sought change through revolution.

Kinds of Collective Behavior

Collective behavior, as noted above, occurs most frequently among crowds. A *crowd* refers to a temporary collection of people responding to the same stimulus. Different kinds of crowds include: *casual*— those who come together

Even happy crowds are potentially dangerous since they are temporary and individuals remain anonymous.

by accident, waiting for example at a red light to cross the street; *organized*—those who come together for specific events such as concerts or football games; *expressive*—those who gather to express their emotions, as in a protest rally or religious revival meeting; and *acting*—those who come together to act out emotions, usually of a hostile nature, as exemplified by mobs, riots, and violent protest meetings. Any crowd, even a casual one, may, given the proper stimulus, evolve into a panic crowd, mob, or riot, although organized crowds are more receptive to mob behavior.

People in crowds tend to develop a common mood. Emotions reach a high pitch, and a shared conception of what constitutes proper behavior emerges. Crowds may also engage in unpredictable behavior, often of an antisocial nature, due to a lack of definite norms and the temporary removal of its participants from most kinds of social control; since individuals in crowds do not personally know their neighbors, it is easy for them to shed their identities and act anonymously. In this way, they need not feel guilty about their actions: They can simply explain that "the crowd did it."

Still, even though a crowd represents more than the sum of its individuals (explaining thus the long history of crowd violence, lynchings, and massacres in every society), limits exist on how far a crowd will tolerate antisocial behavior. Seldom will crowds do anything individual members profoundly oppose. Crowd violence is rarely random, but rather directed against persons or institutions perceived as unjust or oppressive. Even then a destructive crowd will only temporarily commit actions strongly forbidden by societal norms.

Rumors   Rumors are the unsupported reports of events or projected events that often spark riots, panics, or mobs. These reports are not backed up by facts, but continue to spread by word of mouth or through the mass media. An example of a widespread and damaging rumor involves the alleged association with Devil worship recently attributed to a major company, as described in Box 10.1.

Rumors may prove helpful in times of stress, when accurate information is not readily available. But because they are usually at least partially false, they may also court disaster. In accepting rumors, people generally hear what they want to hear in order to rationalize their participation in crowd behavior or simply to clarify a confused situation.

Fashions, Fads, and Crazes   These collective behaviors differ from those described above in that they are less temporary or action-directed. *Fashions* refer to manners of dress, architecture, or house decor and reflect the interests, values, and motives of a society at a given time. *Fads* and *crazes* are minor fashions that are more irrational and short-lived. Some groups add variations in slang and labels to fashions in clothes and fads in appearance, as well as in values (see Box 10.2). Crazes have a slightly more obsessive character. *Mass hysteria* is the ultimate fad or craze, compulsive and irrational. These types of collective behavior begin as departures from tradition, but often end by giving birth to new varieties of their form.

BOX 10.1

By Rumor Possessed

*T*rue, not many consumers think that their boxes of Pampers or Duncan Hines cake mix are possessed by the Devil. But to rid itself of that bizarre rumor once and for all, the Proctor & Gamble Company, the maker of those and other popular household products, performed a marketing exorcism last week.

The Cincinnati-based company announced that its products would no longer bear its century-old trademark, which shows a bearded Man in the Moon and 13 stars enclosed in a circle. According to rumors that started about five years ago, the symbol is the "mark of Satan."

One anonymous leaflet noted that, in a mirror, the curlicues in the Man in the Moon's beard appear as 666, the sign of the Antichrist. Another claim has it that Proctor & Gamble executives tithe to the Devil. And there have been calls for a boycott.

The company has tried everything to squelch the stories. It set up a toll-free recorded message ("We are not connected to any Satanic church or organization whatsoever"), and sued six people for spreading "false and malicious" rumors. The libel suits were settled out of court when the defendants retracted their statements. But the rumors that began in the West and South recently surfaced in the Northeast, and the company has been receiving 5,000 inquiries a month about its relationship with the Devil.

A spokesman, who said the controversy had hurt sales, denied the company was "bowing to pressure" in phasing out the logo over the next few years; it will still appear on company buildings and letterheads.

But, she said, "there seems to be little advantage to having it on products. As we added more information, the trademark has gotten smaller and smaller."

Source: Copyright © 1985 by The New York Times Company. Reprinted by permission.

Theories of Collective Behavior

Because collective behavior has always struck observers as very much out of the ordinary, explanations of the phenomenon have been offered by many social thinkers. French sociologist Gustave LeBon speculates that a process emerged in crowds that made individuals forget their rational faculties and become impulsive, irritable, incapable of reasoning and judging—in short, like savages (1960). LeBon adds that crowds are suggestible and easily led, as participants readily imitate one another's behavior.

The idea of *contagion* operating in a crowd is echoed by contemporary sociologists. Herbert Blumer maintains that contagion results from a reflex chain reaction that may overcome rationality (1946, 170). As one person in a crowd imitates the action of another and sees his own action imitated by others, he is further stimulated to even more outrageous acts. This initiates a chain reaction where behavior departs ever farther from the norm.

Other theorists disagree, stressing that collective behavior merely brings into the open feelings already present in the individual members of a crowd or aggregate. The *convergence theory* focuses on the fact that a collective

BOX 10.2

Beatniks, Preppies and Punkers—The Love Affair With Labels

Americans throughout history have pigeon-holed their fellow citizens into categories with unique names. It doesn't matter that these labels haven't always been accurate or logical, people still insist on "brandishing terms," says folklorist Peter Bartis of the Library of Congress. Among the labels that have come into use since the 1940s:

Bobby-soxers, early 1940s. Rolled anklet socks became the trademark for teenage girls who cried and swooned when Frank Sinatra and other crooners sang during live engagements.

Silent Generation, early 1950s. First used by *Time,* the term describes the majority of Americans during the Eisenhower years, people content with quietly following the prevailing rules of business and society. Portrayed in Sloan Wilson's *The Man in the Gray Flannel Suit.*

Beatniks, mid-1950s. An outgrowth of the "beat generation" described in Jack Kerouac's *On the Road.* The era's drifters, a small group more interested in music and poetry than jobs or social conformity.

Hippies, late 1960s. Known also as flower children, hippies got their name from a San Francisco political organization known as H.I.P. (Haight-Ashbury Independent Proprietors). Preaching love and peace, the group protested the Vietnam War.

Yippies, late 1960s. Members of the Youth International Party organized by Jerry Rubin and Abbie Hoffman. Known for civil disobedience and Vietnam protests.

Silent Majority, 1969. Richard Nixon first used the term to describe the segment of the population he considered his backers—people "whose individual opinions are not colorful or different enough to make the news, but whose collective opinion, when crystallized, makes history."

Me Generation, 1976. Writer Tom Wolfe's label depicting those young Americans who put their social consciences aside and plunged headlong into a quest for self-fulfillment.

Preppies, late 1970s. Forerunners of the yuppies. Neat, buttoned-down people with the "Ivy League" look who were popularized in Lisa Birnbach's 1980 book, *The Official Preppy Handbook.*

Punkers, late 1970s. Teens and young adults who by their bizarre dress, hairstyles, and strident music advocated social nonconformity and even violence and anarchy. The term was first used to describe a segment of the British lower class.

Valley Girls, 1981. Originating in California's San Fernando Valley, the label describes fun-loving teens with materialistic values and their own style of dress (leg warmers, cut-out sweatshirts) and lingo ("fer shurr," "tubular," "grody"). Subject of a 1982 pop hit by Moon Unit Zappa.

Underclass, 1982. Writer Ken Auletta's book *The Underclass* was among the first to treat a part of the American population seemingly mired in poverty.

Yuppies, 1984. Marissa Piesman and Marilee Hartley outlined the consumerist lifestyle of the "young upwardly mobile professionals" in *The Yuppie Handbook.*

situation may simply bring together people with similar tendencies, allowing them to do collectively what each has wanted to do individually.

A third group of scientists favors the *emergent norm theory,* according to which collective behavior is indeed governed by norms, even though these may not be the prevailing ones of society. In the opinion of these theorists, collective behavior takes place when satisfactory rules for behavior are lacking in the society. In the process, new norms emerge as individuals arrive at new definitions and agreements on how to behave. Although members of a collectivity do not necessarily share opinions, a majority usually prevails, since those who perceive themselves a minority fail to act or speak out.

To sum up, contagion and convergence theories assume that the crowd becomes homogeneous in its behavior, whether by the mechanisms of contagion or the expression of preexisting desires. Emergent norm theory, on the other hand, recognizes that a variety of opinions may exist in a crowd; nonetheless, the power of social control is such that dissenters remain silent and passive, giving the illusion that the crowd acts as one.

Publics and Public Opinion

Collective behavior works in publics as well. A *public* is defined as a scattered collection of people sharing common interests or concerns or affected by a common occurrence. The readers of the *New York Times,* university students, moviegoers, voters, or members of a Michael Jackson fan club are all examples of publics. The bond holding a crowd together is emotion, whereas that holding a public together is intellect. A crowd gathers in one place, while a public is dispersed, each member able to communicate directly only with a fraction of others, or, as in the case of television, to receive communication but not respond to it. Nevertheless, the mass media help to create and consolidate publics.

Some publics are temporary in nature, with rapidly changing compositions. Those watching a television program at 7:30 on a Saturday night, for example, constitute a public. But at 8:00 on the same night, some members may decide to go out to eat; others, disgusted by television fare, may prefer to read a book; still others will opt for a visit with friends. No longer will they constitute the public of half an hour earlier. A public may thus be redefined as an unstructured collectivity, with a portion of its members continuously losing interest in the event that brought them together and just as continuously being replaced by others.

Publics are more characteristic of complex societies than simple ones, since complex societies, being heterogeneous, contain members with innumerable and varying interests. These individuals are unceasingly confronted with endless issues, both local and national in nature. Many such issues may be at odds with one another. One group may want to preserve our national forests; another may want to hunt game or to log timber in them. One may propose building a new gym for a local high school; another may oppose the move as wasteful and unnecessary. In less complex societies, many such issues are not likely to arise, since norms and values are shared to a greater extent by all, and very few individuals question traditional methods.

Public Opinion

The large variety of publics, each concerned with its own issue, activity, attitude, and beliefs, gives rise to a system of thought known as public opinion. **Public opinion**, a generic term, refers to the attitude or judgment of a substantial number of people on a specific issue. It may be regarded as the dominant opinion on an issue among a specific population, or as the position taken by the general public on a particular issue.

Public opinion holds a special meaning in mass societies, where it is diffused through the mass media. In traditional societies, as noted above, conflicting issues do not normally arise, and since governments and economies are run according to tradition, leaders care little for individual societal members' opinions on specific issues. In industrial societies, predominantly democratic and consumption-oriented, leaders and industrialists must take into consideration public opinion on their style of leadership (if they wish to be reelected) or their products (if they wish them to sell).

The strongest influence on public opinion is exerted by the mass media, one reason why candidates for political office take great care in creating an image they can sell to the public. Those with local or national prestige and power may also affect public opinion. Individuals themselves create it through interaction, molding each other's opinions according to their social background and membership in specific groups.

Propaganda and Censorship

The power to manipulate public opinion greatly benefits certain individuals and groups in society. Car manufacturers want to persuade the public to buy their products. Political candidates want to be elected. Teachers want their salaries increased. Administrations in office want their citizens' support. Parents want their children to do as they are told. All these groups, and countless more, exert influence on specific public opinion through propaganda and censorship.

Propaganda   **Propaganda** represents a deliberate attempt on the part of an individual or group in power to convince a public to accept a particular belief uncritically, or to make a certain choice rather than another. Advertising, sales promotions, public relations, political campaigns, fund-raising drives, billboards, even Sunday school lessons use propaganda.

Propaganda is a manipulative device depending on emotional appeal, and frequently playing on fears and anxieties. Advertisements for cosmetics, deodorants, and toothpaste promise to make people attractive and young-looking, characteristics the public wants to possess and fears it does not. Propaganda also relies on the "good old values" of the past ("Grandma's apple pie") and on the human desire to belong or be popular ("Everybody's doing it").

Propaganda is quite successful when it does not attempt to change opinions too drastically. However, in democratic societies, those involved in propaganda face much competition. Education and sophistication on the part of the public further limit the effectiveness of this tool. Finally, although strong trends in sociocultural evolution may be temporarily thwarted by propaganda, they are not ultimately affected by it.

Censorship   Propaganda, by giving a one-sided interpretation of an issue or showing only the plus side of a product, distorts information available to the public. **Censorship,** on the other hand, deletes all or part of such information. Many important institutional organizations use censorship: The government and military institutions withhold information in the name of national security and defense; families and religious organizations tend to censor certain information about sex; political candidates are selective in the information they disseminate about themselves and their intentions once in office; manufacturers choose not to disclose that the car or refrigerator they sell is characterized by a built-in obsolescence that will necessitate its replacement every few years; and the mass media report some and fail to report other news.

Both propaganda and censorship are necessary, to a degree, in a large, complex society. In and of themselves, they are neither good nor bad. But either may be put to uses that are beneficial or detrimental to society.

Social Movements

Social movements are defined as "collective enterprises to establish a new order of life" (Blumer, 1951, 200) as well as collective efforts to either change, the sociocultural order or resist such change (Killian, 1964, 430). This type of collective action represents the personal involvement of individuals and their intervention in directing, redirecting, furthering, or resisting change.

All forms of collective behavior reflect social change. In addition, collective behavior creates change through its alteration of individual perspectives, introducing new lines of action and laying the groundwork for new institutions. Historically, sociocultural change has occurred whenever group identity has changed, as when group loyalty shifted from a religious to a national base. Such a shift was most likely initiated by some form of collective behavior.

When conceptions of reality are modified, sociocultural change often results. Europeans could not travel to the Americas before changing their ideas about the structure of the world: They had first to accept the reality that the earth was round rather than flat, and that they could continue sailing toward the horizon without falling off.

Ideology in Social Movements

Changes in perspective and group identity can be lengthy and involve tense periods during which people seek systematic ways of interpreting emerging

281

CHAPTER 10

*Collective
Behavior and
Formal
Organizations in
Mass Society*

The ideology of Marxism-Leninism, brought in by a nationalistic revolutionary movement, is
thoroughly entrenched in the Soviet Union.

realities. During such periods, members of society are receptive to *ideology,*
a system of beliefs or doctrines that provides a basis for collective action
(Mannheim, 1936).

Ideologies tend to develop around a central value, such as equality, or racial
purity. Those espousing a particular ideology claim to speak for major social
groups: Marxists for the working class, feminists for all women. Some ideologies defend or rationalize the status quo, others criticize it and exhort change.
All ideologies maintain that only they give a true picture of world reality. As
a result ideologies represent important facets of social movements.

First, ideologies explain the causes of events and situations. Second, they
reinforce participants' beliefs, clarifying and incorporating them into a program for action. Third, they direct members to behave in ways that will effect
the desired change. Finally, they educate members of the social movement
and society at large as justification for their actions.

In spite of their important function in social movements, ideologies often
distort the truth. They also tend to make "true believers" of their followers,
supporters who are blindly loyal to them, and the kind of fanaticism blind
loyalty evokes does not generally respect the truth.

Rise of Social Movements

A collective action may be considered a social movement when the following factors are present: (1) a specific ideology; (2) a strong sense of idealism and solidarity, involving dedication and loyalty in followers; (3) an orientation toward action; and (4) a significant number of people involved.

Although some social movements are almost totally devoid of organization, most are pursued in voluntary groups or associations. These are secondary groups (see Chapter 2 and this chapter below) organized for attaining a definite goal. Both social movements and voluntary groups are characteristic of urban industrial societies experiencing rapid social change. In some nations, social movements develop into political parties, pursuing their goals by attaining political power.

Marxism represents an example of an ideology that has prompted social movements in a number of societies. In some—such as the United States—its goals are pursued in voluntary associations. In others—France, Italy, Portugal—Marxism has become a political party. Finally, in the USSR and the People's Republic of China, the movement has become the party in power (although with alterations in ideology), while in Chile it came to power and was subsequently overthrown.

Conditions for the Rise of Social Movements

Social movements are sometimes called institutions in the making, their ultimate aim being to affect change to the extent that it becomes institutionalized—the usual and traditional way of doing things. In this, such movements are often successful; many political parties, international ideologies (such as socialism and communism), women's suffrage, and some nations started as social movements.

Social movements flourish in societies undergoing rapid social change. A society in transition from an agrarian to an industrial economy will inevitably experience disorganization. Formerly held norms and values are questioned, and members become subject to feelings of anomie and alienation. *Anomie*, described in more detail in Chapter 5, refers to a feeling of normlessness, of not knowing which behavioral guidelines to follow when several conflicting sets of norms coexist. *Alienation* is a feeling of separateness from society, of powerlessness and isolation leading to a conviction of one's incapacity to influence one's own fate. Social movements attract those who suffer from anomie and alienation, as well as those who are dissatisfied on a variety of grounds, who are restless and confused, or who crave focus in their lives.

A particular source of dissatisfaction in society is *relative deprivation*. People feel relatively deprived when they compare themselves with others and find they suffer by comparison. The *failure of rising expectations* is related to dissatisfaction based on relative deprivation. Rising expectations are experienced when the standard of living goes up in a society. However, when that standard fails to rise fast or high enough for a particular group, that group will experience frustrated expectations, and dissatisfaction will result.

It is worthy to note, however, that not only the downtrodden or underdogs of society join social movements. On the contrary, often those from solidly middle-class, comfortable backgrounds become most intensely involved. One explanation for this is that lower-class persons spend most of their time and energy providing the bare necessities for themselves and their families and have little left for pursuing ideological commitments. Since upper-class individuals generally benefit from the status quo, they too seldom participate in social movements. It is the middle-class member who possesses the will, the opportunity, and the time, and is willing to expend the effort to be active in social movements.

Kinds of Social Movements

The two social movements that have had the most influence on societies and their governments have been the revolutionary and the reform.

Revolutionary movements consider the present social order so inadequate, corrupt, unjust, and beyond salvation that its total removal and substitution are seen as the only solution. In effecting such absolute change, revolutionary movements must often resort to violence. In **nationalistic revolutionary movements,** a predominantly foreign government is overthrown and replaced with a native one. **Class revolutionary movements** substitute one ruling class for another in the same society. The American Revolution was nationalistic, whereas the French, Russian, Chinese, and Cuban were all class revolutions. Revolutionary movements should not be confused with revolts, or coups d'etat, which merely replace individual members of the ruling class. True revolutions change the very structure of major social institutions.

Reform movements attempt to change some feature of an existing social order without resorting to destruction of the entire order. Such movements are most successful in democratic societies where relative freedom exists to criticize institutions and channels are available through which such reforms can be put into effect. Recent reform movements in the United States include the women's movement, the civil rights movement, and the movement for removing the social stigma of homosexuality.

Revolutionary movements receive considerable notoriety by reflecting the discontent of those who believe change is occurring too slowly. However, certain movements reflect the belief of some groups that change is occurring too fast. These movements are called **change-resistant,** their purpose being to stop or eradicate certain changes in society. The Ku Klux Klan is one example among many of a change-resistant movement.

Formal Organizations and Bureaucracy

Although collective behavior characterizes most modern industrial societies, organization, the opposite kind of behavior, is equally a feature of such societies. Organization, in the sense of order, distinguishes most enterprises in

The Ku Klux Klan is an example of a change-resistant movement. Members want to bring back a mythical past and resist sociocultural change, particularly where race and religion are concerned.

which humans participate. Communication in the form of speech necessitates the organization of sounds. Music represents organization of tones. Teams consist of organized players. Through constant repetition, all human interaction, in fact, acquires some structure or organization.

Formal Organizations

Organization as a process reaches its highest development in formal organizations, associations deliberately brought into existence to enable people unacquainted with one another to carry on complicated relationships for the purpose of attaining specific goals. It is through these formal organizations that large, complex societies carry out most necessary activities. For example, the business of governing is executed by a network of formal organizations known as the government. Educating each new generation is the task of formal organizations called schools. Production, distribution, and trade occur through countless formal organizations referred to as corporations.

An important distinction must be made between formal organizations and institutions (which will be discussed in the following chapter). An *institution* represents a procedure, an established process of action, a pattern of behavior, a deeply ingrained societal custom (see also Chapter 3). Institutions are not groups of people. One cannot join an institution: One can merely do things in an institutionalized way. When two people marry, they engage in a human activity—establishing a paired relationship—in an institutionalized way. If a couple simply live together, they carry out that activity in a noninstitution-alized way.

On the other hand, formal organizations do consist of groups of people. One may join a formal organization or have dealings with its members or employ-ees. The institution of government refers to the regular and established meth-ods by which political decisions are made, laws enacted, and order maintained in society. A particular government, on the other hand, is a formal organization consisting of large numbers of highly structured and hierarchically ranked individuals elected, appointed, or hired to carry out activities involved in the governing process.

Characteristics of Formal Organizations

Formal organizations originate when certain individuals band together for the purpose of reaching particular objectives. Thus corporations like General Motors came into being when a number of entrepreneurs decided to organize for the purpose of making a profit by manufacturing automobiles. All their subsequent activities revolved around this objective, engendering a policy to guide their progress, and a force of executives, administrators, and laborers to carry out needed tasks.

Formal organizations display the following characteristics: First, they pos-sess a *formal structure*. Goals and methods by which these goals are to be achieved are formally stated in policy guidelines, constitutions, and other bylaws. Such organizations include a body of officers whose relations with one another and with other members of the organization are specified in writing.

Second, formal organizations are meant to be relatively *permanent*. Some, especially those established for profit making, may prove temporary; but the expectation is that the formal organization will last as long as it performs the tasks set for itself.

Third, authority is organized in a *hierarchical order,* giving rise to a bu-reaucracy. The leadership of the organization consists of individuals progres-sively ranked. High-ranking individuals make decisions and give orders, and each lower rank executes these.

Fourth, formal organizations have a *formal program*. Members of the or-ganization use the program as a guide in attaining their goals. Relationships among such members are systematic and complex, following bureaucratic principles and guidelines specified in the program.

Voluntary Associations

People join certain formal organizations out of necessity; if, for instance, they want a job, they may have to become employees of a corporation. But other formal organizations are joined by choice. These are referred to as **voluntary associations** and consist mainly of spare-time volunteers, although most such organizations also have a core of full-time, paid, professional employees. Ex-amples of voluntary associations are church organizations, professional groups such as the American Medical Association, and recreational associations like the American Contract Bridge League.

Americans are known as joiners and patronize a great number of voluntary associations. In reality, however, only a minority are active in this way, generally urban residents in their middle years, married and with children, socially and economically upwardly mobile or already at a high socioeconomic level, residentially stable, and well educated. More Jews and Protestants than Roman Catholics join voluntary associations, as do more whites than blacks (Berelson and Steiner, 1964, 379).

Voluntary associations bring together those whose particular interests are not universally shared throughout a society; for instance, not all Americans are concerned with planned parenthood, yet the concept represents the goal of a good many. Supporters of planned parenthood are better able to work for their cause when organized into a voluntary association and may even manage to convince an indifferent or hostile majority of the value of their goal. Thus voluntary associations often provide testing grounds for social programs still too controversial to be handled by institutional organizations. They also offer a channel through which private citizens can share in the decision-making process of society, a situation of particular importance to interest groups, political parties, and social movements.

Bureaucracy

Large-scale formal organizations are administered according to the principles of bureaucracy. **Bureaucracy** is a hierarchical system for rationally coordinating the work of many through division of labor and chains of authority. In other words, a bureaucracy is a group of people organized in pyramid fashion, whose aim is to administer large-scale organizations in the most efficient and intelligent manner.

Characteristics of a Pure Bureaucracy In analyzing bureaucratic organization, eminent sociologist Max Weber used the method of constructing an ideal type of a social phenomenon (Weber, [1925] 1947, 334), highlighting and accentuating certain features of this phenomenon and permitting greater comprehension of its underlying concepts. The ideal type, or pure, bureaucracy that Weber describes does not correspond to any real organization; rather, it illustrates how a bureaucracy *ought* to function. A pure bureaucracy, then, is characterized by:

1. Specialization, or division of labor. Activities are assigned to specialized individuals who then assume responsibility for their performance.

2. A chain of command, or a hierarchy of authority. Each individual is responsible to the person above, and each in turn is responsible for subordinates. The scope and limits of individual authority and responsibility are clearly defined.

3. A body of rules. The activities of bureaucracies are governed by specific rules that define the functions and roles of every person holding a position

in the organization. These rules are abstract and apply to the position, not the person who holds it; they are binding regardless of who fills the position; and they are designed to guarantee the behavior of the employee, facilitating the continuity of operation.

4. Impersonality. Each function is performed impersonally, that is, without allowing personal considerations to enter into interpersonal dealings. Efficiency is guaranteed by impartiality and the equitable treatment of all concerned.

5. Selection based on merit and job tenure. Selection of an employee for a given position is made strictly on the basis of merit, and not due to any personal considerations. This ensures employee competence. If job performance is considered satisfactory by superiors, the employee obtains job tenure and is promoted to higher levels of the hierarchy. Such an employee may expect to become a career bureaucrat.

In Weber's view, a bureaucratic organization is one in which goals can be attained efficiently and with a minimum of conflict among people. Individual personalities are irrelevant to the organization since each position consists of activities which remain constant regardless of who fills the position. Such formality gives the organization stability, predictability, and continuity. Bureaucratic organizations work equally well for private and public associations, and in fact for all associations designed to serve the people.

The Reality of Bureaucratic Organization

Weber knew that bureaucracy would not work as well in reality as in the ideal form he described. Unfortunately bureaucracies, originally intended to serve people, often frustrate them instead. The average bureaucracy is resistant to change and the bureaucrats within it inclined to believe that its rules are ends in themselves. Blind loyalty to rules results in the familiar red-tape phenomenon, as well as in the stifling of personal initiative on the part of bureaucrats. The latter often prefer to "pass the buck," finding it easier to shift the responsibility for decision making to someone higher in the hierarchy so that person can be blamed if the decision turns out to be wrong. In addition, bureaucracies have a nasty habit of becoming devoted to their own welfare and perpetuation rather than to the ends for which they were created. Both government agencies and corporate departments often outlive their usefulness, simply because employees wish to hang on to their jobs.

Oligarchy Most systems are organized in oligarchical fashion, with a small elite governing the vast majority of rank and file members. The democratic ideology challenged the assumption of oligarchy as the optimum leadership by suggesting that power should emanate from all members of an organization (or society, in the political sphere) through a system of representation.

In democratic societies, attempts were made to organize formal associations according to democratic principles, giving members control over their organization. After a time, however, effective control seemed to drift back into the

Collective Behavior and Formal Organizations in Mass Society

hands of a few leaders. European social scientist Robert Michels set out to discover the source of these authoritarian tendencies (Michels, 1949, 342). He came to the conclusion that neither lust for power nor the immaturity of the members caused the control of an organization to gravitate to a handful. Rather, the situation resulted from inevitable patterns emerging in all organizations. Michels called the emergence of such patterns the **iron law of oligarchy.**

An oligarchy develops, according to Michels, when patterns of participation are such that rank and file members attend meetings infrequently and are consequently poorly informed about activities in the organization. The few individuals who do become knowledgeable and are willing to invest their time in the organization then take the opportunity to assume control. They may do so not out of greed or hunger for power, but simply because no one else chooses to.

Large, formal organizations with complex bureaucratic structures are particularly likely to develop oligarchies, and once installed, these are difficult to dislodge. Oligarchs have considerable means at their disposal to maneuver events effectively in their favor. The movement toward oligarchy can be interrupted only by an active and interested membership interacting on a primary level within strong local units of the organization.

The Dynamic Aspect of Bureaucracies

In spite of its several shortcomings, bureaucracy maintains a certain dynamic quality enabling it to respond to changing societal conditions. Sociologists Blau and Meyer note that bureaucracies have been changing for a number of reasons (1971, 139–143): First, employees in developed nations are more prosperous and less dependent on their superiors. Second, the general willingness to accept authority is on the decline; coercive authority and illogical use of power are no longer meekly accepted, and skepticism and lack of credibility are frequent responses of ordinary citizens toward their governments and leaders. Finally, the advanced technology of modern societies requires technical specialists like scientists and technicians who have usurped much of the real power from bureaucratic managers (whose lack of technical knowledge puts them at a disadvantage).

In some respects, bureaucracies may be instrumental in promoting societal innovation. Blau and Meyer also suggest that the ideas of scientists alone could not lead to inventions that trigger social change (1971, 105). In today's complex societies, bureaucratic machinery is needed to translate these ideas into products, and to furnish laboratories and environments in which scientists can collaborate on new developments. The authors conclude that the "deliberate introduction of a social innovation . . . depends on bureaucratic methods of administration."

Informality in Bureaucracy

In addition to the formal and structured nature of bureaucracy, there exists an informal component made up of networks of personal relationships among employees. These networks are occasionally responsible for accomplishment achieved through the influence of individuals instead of through regular channels. Sometimes the informal structure, in bypassing the rules of the formal structure, actually defies the purpose of the formal bureaucracy (as when dissatisfied workers sabotage operations). In the long run, however, such actions may help the formal organization to reach its goals. One example occurs in war movies when the hero disregards his commanding officer's orders and successfully guides his unit through an "impossible" action, thus turning the tide of the battle. In sum, informal networks within formal organizations are actually crucial to their survival. And by making experiences within formal organizations more personal, they boost employee morale, thus assuring productivity and continuity within the organization.

The Chapter in Brief

The technological revolutions collectively known as modernization have propelled advanced societies toward a model to be found at the extreme end of the continuum from Gemeinschaft to Gesellschaft societies. This is the model of **mass society.** Mass societies, although not necessarily large in numbers, show evidence of social disorganization characterized by a loosely integrated social organization, by anonymity, mobility, specialization of roles and statuses, and secondary relationships. The masses are easily manipulated by an organized elite or a charismatic leader and thus pose a potential threat to democracy.

The tendency toward mass society is reinforced by a system of **mass communication.** Communication is essential to all culture building; with the present technology, the same message can be transmitted directly, rapidly, and simultaneously to millions of people, thus dramatically altering old societal structures.

Technologically advanced societies are also more subject to various forms of **collective behavior.** Collective behavior occurs in situations that are highly emotionally charged and in which the usual norms do not apply. Such situations include crowds (riots, mobs, panics), rumors, fashions, fads, crazes, publics and audiences, public opinion, propaganda and censorship, and social movements. Collective behavior is relatively unpatterned and unstructured. Its mechanisms are described by the contagion theory (which proposes a process in which moods, attitudes, and actions are communicated by chain reaction to the collectivity); by the convergence theory (which stresses that collective behavior brings into the open feelings already present in individual members of the collectivity); and by the emergent norm theory (which views collective behavior as governed by new and different norms generated by the situation at hand).

Publics—scattered collections of people who temporarily share a common interest or concern—also represent a form of collective behavior. The large number of publics in advanced societies generates **public opinion,** the attitude or judgment of many on a specific issue. Public opinion is especially significant in democratic societies and greatly influenced by mass media. The latter sometimes use **propaganda** and/or **censorship** to manipulate public opinion. Propaganda is a deliberate attempt to persuade others to accept a belief uncritically or make a specific choice. Censorship distorts information by partial or complete suppression or deletion.

Social movements are collective attempts to establish a new order of life—either by changing the old social order or resisting changes already in effect. Important factors in social movements include evolving perspectives and ideologies. Social movements are rooted in discontent, and flourish when a society experiences anomie, alienation, relative deprivation, and rising expectations; their goals, however, are long-range solutions, their ultimate aim being to effect change to the point where it becomes institutionalized. Social movements may attempt reforms by trying to change only selective features of an existing social order, or they may be revolutionary, seeking the removal of a present order and its substitution by a new one.

All human activities are somewhat ordered and structured. In complex societies, **organization** occurs on a large scale; groups of people who are not personally related must carry on complicated relationships in order to attain specific goals. Most activities of modern societies are performed in such groups, called **formal organizations** or associations. These are usually extensive and highly organized in administrative patterns termed bureaucracies. Formal organizations have a formal structure, a degree of permanence, a hierarchical order of authority, and fixed relationships among members.

Voluntary associations bring together people with similar interests. Although Americans are known as joiners, in reality only a minority are active in such groups.

Bureaucracy is a hierarchical arrangement based on division of labor and a chain of authority for the purpose of rationally coordinating the work of many. Its ideal or pure form seldom corresponds to the real functioning of the bureaucracy: it tends to resist change; its rules become rigid and ends and means get confused; it stifles personal initiative; and it makes employees indecisive. At the same time, bureaucracy is often dynamic enough to respond to change and promote innovation in society.

Terms to Remember

Bureaucracy   The hierarchical system of administration prevalent within a formal organization. This hierarchy depends on job specialization, a set of rules and standards to promote uniformity, and an attitude of impersonal impartiality.

Censorship   A method of control used to limit the information available to the public.

Change-resistant movement   A social movement reflecting the discontent of those who believe that change is occurring too rapidly and want to stop it.

Class revolutionary movement   A revolutionary social movement in which one ruling class is replaced by another in the same society.

291

CHAPTER 10

*Collective
Behavior and
Formal
Organizations in
Mass Society*

Collective behavior A type of behavior that tends to occur in crowds, mobs, fashions, fads, crazes, rumors, panics, and in publics, public opinion, and social movements. Collective behavior is characteristic of a collectivity of people who respond to a common stimulus under conditions that are usually temporary, unstable, unstructured, and unpredictable, so that existing norms do not apply.

Formal organizations Large-scale associations of people through which most activities of complex societies are handled. These are highly organized groups displaying a formal structure, a body of officers, the expectation of permanence, and a hierarchical organization of authority (bureaucracy).

Iron law of oligarchy Robert Michels's formulation that even in the most democratic organizations, leadership eventually drifts into the hands of a few interested individuals willing to work for the goals of the organization.

Mass communication The relatively simultaneous exposure of large heterogeneous audiences to symbols transmitted by impersonal means from organized sources with whom audience members are personally unacquainted.

Mass society The model (theoretical construct) of society toward which postindustrial societies are drifting. The mass society consists of an undifferentiated mass and an elite capable of dominating and manipulating it. Highly urbanized and industrialized, mass society displays secondary relationships, a lack of traditional values, alienation, anomie, pressure to conform, and susceptibility to manipulation through mass media.

Nationalistic revolutionary movement A revolutionary social movement in which a predominantly foreign government is overthrown and replaced with a native one.

Organization A formal process that deliberately brings into existence a group of people organized to perform tasks directed toward achieving specific goals. The process of organization allows people unacquainted with each other to cooperate effectively on complex projects.

Propaganda A deliberate attempt to persuade a population to uncritically accept a particular belief or make a certain choice.

Publics and public opinion Persons in society who are geographically dispersed but share a common interest, express that interest, and know that others are aware of their interest. Public opinion represents the totality of opinions, attitudes, and judgments expressed by publics.

Voluntary associations Formal organizations joined by choice rather than out of necessity.

Suggestions for Further Reading

Gitlin, Todd. 1980. *The whole world is watching: Mass media in the making and unmaking of the new left*. Berkeley, Calif.: University of California Press. The importance of the mass media in furthering the message of a social movement.

Kanter, Rosabeth Moss. 1977. *Men and women of the corporation.* New York: Basic. A well-known work analyzing formal organizations by a sociologist who has become a consultant to a number of the largest American organizations.

Koenig, Fredrick. 1985. *Rumor in the marketplace: The social psychology of commercial hearsay.* Dover, Mass.: Auburn House. The psychology of rumors, and how they can damage a corporation.

Miller, David L. 1985. *Introduction to collective behavior.* Belmont, Calif.: Wadsworth. A general text on the subjects of collective behavior and social movements.

Walton, John. 1984. *Reluctant rebels: Comparative studies of revolution and underdevelopment.* New York: Columbia University Press. Revolutionary social movements in world perspective, with particular stress on nations of the Third World.

Westrum, Ron and Khalil Samaha. 1984. *Complex organizations: Growth, struggle, and change.* Englewood Cliffs, N.J.: Prentice-Hall. A fairly comprehensive and readable text on the subject of formal organizations. In paperback.

Blood in the Stands

RICHARD LACAYO

The rational individual has little difficulty understanding, sometimes even sympathizing with, a crowd of protesters if the latter have been notoriously oppressed or mistreated. Secretly, most of us may even admire the French peasants who beheaded their aristocratic rulers after their pleas for bread were answered by the cynical "Let them eat cake!" But it is harder to comprehend the violence of an organized crowd that gathers for an event designed to entertain and give pleasure, namely a football (soccer) match. Yet, violence—and the death of 38 persons— is exactly what such a crowd engendered on one such occasion.

The trouble began in Section Y on the northeast end of Heysel Stadium in Brussels. In the stands thousands of fans were waiting for the opening of the European Cup Final between Britain's Liverpool and Italy's Juventus of Turin. About 45 minutes before the scheduled 8:15 P.M. kickoff, the mostly young Liverpool fans began to taunt the Juventus followers. Emboldened by alcohol, many backed up their insults by hurling rocks and bottles over the wire fence that separated them from the Italians. Suddenly, as if acting on some invisible signal, the screaming British crowd exploded across the standing-room terraces. They swarmed into the adjoining section, heaving rocks and bottles. The human tide crushed and maimed people in scenes of sheerest horror. Television cameras provided watching millions with close-up pictures of fans caught beneath a human pile; of hands held out in vain supplication; of the injured and dying crying out pitifully for help.

By the time the riot had subsided and the wave of raw violence had passed, 38 people lay dead; more than 400 had been injured. Amid the scene of death and destruction, people wandered aimlessly about the field, injured and in shock. "I've seen too much," moaned one bloodied Italian fan, tears streaming down his cheeks. "I've seen death."

The 30th annual playing of the European final was one of the bloodiest sporting events in modern memory. It outraged Europeans and raised agonizing questions about why Europe's soccer stadiums are increasingly coming to resemble gladiator pits. The behavior of the English fans, who were blamed for starting the riot, resulted in much soul searching in Britain about why a land famous for patience and civility produces the most violent soccer crowds. A shocked and angry Prime Minister Margaret Thatcher declared that the country was "worse than numb" over the riot. Said she: "Those responsible have brought shame and disgrace to their country."

The rampage began as 60,000 spectators were filling the 55-year-old stadium, five miles from the center of Brussels, to witness one of the premier events of the international soccer calendar. An estimated 400 million viewers in Europe and Africa were tuned in for what promised to be a feast of first-class football, as soccer is known outside North America. Many of the Liverpudlians, dressed in the bright red colors of their home team, were gathered in Section Y, separated by a flimsy wire fence and a stairway from the mostly Italian spectators in Section Z, an uncovered sloping stand. The Liverpudlians, many of them drunk, began pushing against the fence. Suddenly, weakened by the weight of several hundred heaving bodies, the divider collapsed. "It was like watching guerrillas in a battle," recalled Giampietro Donamigo, an Italian fan. "They came forward in waves toward the fence, throwing bottles. . . . Some answered back with threats, but most of us were terrified. We tried to move away."

As the Liverpool crowd poured across the stand, the Juventus fans panicked. Hundreds made a rush for the nearest exit, beyond a low wall at the bottom of the sloping spectator terrace. Some managed to clamber over the wall, dropping to the ground on the other side. Hundreds more were trapped, crushed by the weight of the crowd. Then, with a sickening crack, the concrete wall collapsed, killing some and spilling others onto the field in a murderous cascade of bodies and fractured concrete.

"There was a mass of crushed bodies," said Renzo Rocchetti, a Juventus supporter from Milan. "I saw people trampled to death under the feet of the frightened mob stepping on their bodies, including many babies and children." Remarked an off-duty British policeman among the Liverpool supporters: "Those poor bloody Italians went down like a pack of cards."

Most of the 1,000 Belgian police assigned to the game were outside, trying to control drunken groups still attempting to pour into the stadium. Inside, helmeted Red Cross medics dodged bricks, bottles, and smoke bombs as they worked among the dying and injured, frantically trying to resuscitate people who had been suffocated beneath piles of bodies. It was 30 minutes before ambulances arrived, and at first the dead were carried out of the stadium on sections of crowd-control barriers, some covered with flags and banners that only minutes earlier had been waved by cheering fans. The dead, their faces and limbs a grotesque purple, were taken to a makeshift mortuary outside the stadium, where priests administered the last rites.

In Turin, the home city of at least 10,000 Juventus supporters in Brussels, there was an outpouring of grief. Among the dead was Restaurant Owner Giovacchino Landini, 49. "Why did it have to be him?" cried his daughter Monica, 22. "He was too passionately fond of Juventus." Of the dead, 31 were Italians, including a ten-year-old boy and a woman. Also killed were four Belgians, two Frenchmen and a Briton who was a resident of Brussels. All the dead were asphyxiated or crushed. Ten spectators, all British, were arrested, none for alleged offenses committed inside the stadium.

Fearful of triggering an even more terrible riot if they called off the match, Belgian officials and members of the Union of European Football Associations decided that it should be played. "Call it a surrender to fear if you wish," said Association Treasurer Jo Van Marle. Italian Prime Minister Benedetto ("Bettino") Craxi, in Moscow for discussions with Soviet Leader Mikhail Gorbachev, telephoned Belgian Prime Minister Wilfried Martens after the riot to protest the decision. Said Martens: "I told him that the decision to begin play was taken purely for reasons of security." The crowd, which was largely unaware of the magnitude of the tragedy, watched the macabre match as helmeted riot-control police stood guard and ambulance sirens wailed.

Across Europe, along with the grief and shock, came the recriminations. In an editorial, the *Times* of London declared: "It is hard to resist the conclusion that the game of soccer is as good as dead." Some laid the blame for the Brussels tragedy squarely on the estimated 16,000 Liverpool followers at the match. Many had spent the afternoon before the game drinking in the streets and bars of Brussels. The Belgian government acted swiftly by banning all British teams—from England, Wales, Scotland and Northern Ireland— from competing in Belgium—"until further notice." England's Football Association then announced that it was withdrawing all English soccer teams from European competition for the season starting in September. "It is absolutely unbearable to continue to admit the English hordes on soccer grounds," said Jean-Michel Fournet-Fayard, president of the French Football Federation.

While not underplaying the responsibility of the British fans for the tragedy, commentators and sports officials charged that Belgian police had been lax in preparing for the possibility of violence, especially considering the reputation of British club followers. (Last year, for example, an English fan was killed by an irate bar owner and 141 were arrested in disturbances connected with a match in Brussels.) The police were also criticized for not segregating the fans of the opposing teams more effectively and for not searching more thoroughly for weapons as the crowd entered Heysel Stadium. Others claimed that there had been too few police on hand, even though 1,000 would seem to be adequate by the standards of most sports events. To many watching the rampage on television, the police in the stadium appeared somewhat lame and ineffectual. Said one Liverpool fan: "The police were just too scared."

Soccer, the world's most popular sport, for decades had unleashed ferocious scenes. In 1945 George Orwell, deploring the bloodlust of soccer crowds, wrote that "serious sport" is "war minus the shooting." In Lima in 1964, some 300 spectators were killed in riots sparked by a disputed referee's call. In China, where civil disorder is rare, hundreds of fans rioted in the streets of Peking last month after the home team was knocked out of the World Cup by Hong Kong. Even as crowds were headed for the stadium in Brussels, families in Mexico City were mourning the victims of a stadium riot last week in which eight people, two of them children, were crushed to death.

The penchant of English fans for rock-hurling mayhem has become an increasing problem at home, and one of the country's sorriest exports. In the past three months alone, England has witnessed three major soccer riots that have left one dead and scores injured. At matches abroad, rampaging fans have become ambassadors of bad will, bashing heads in France, trading tear-gas volleys with police in Italy and urinating on spectators in Spain. In 1975 Leeds United, a team whose followers have one of the worst reputations, was barred from playing on the Continent for four years after Leeds fans raised a storm of violence at the European Cup Final in Paris. In 1977 Manchester United was briefly kicked out of the European Cup Winners competition after its fans rioted during a first-round match in St. Etienne, France.

Prime Minister Thatcher responded to the violence in Brussels by summoning a number of her country's football officials to confer with her on the problem of fan violence. She announced that Britain would be contributing $317,500 to a special fund for victims of the riot and families of the dead. Last March, Thatcher set up a panel that included members of her cabinet to study soccer violence after fans went on a rampage in Luton, England. The Prime Minister said last week that she will now meet sooner than planned with the group to review progress on implementing some of the measures that have already been agreed to, including a voluntary ban by clubs on the sale of alcohol in stadiums. A similar measure has led to a sharp de-crease in violent episodes over the past five years in Scotland, where soccer brawls were once a favorite pastime. Faced with declining attendance and rising demands for expensive security precautions, team owners in England have so far been unwilling to give up the revenues from drink concessions. Now that the teams are banned from European competition, their losses are certain to be even greater.

Stadium design has also been cited as a reason for the frequency of English soccer violence. Trouble at games often starts among the working-class youths who fill up the low-cost, standing-room areas known as terraces, similar to the areas occupied by the Liverpool and Juventus fans in the Brussels stadium. Sir Philip Goodhart, a Conservative Member of Parliament, believes that one reason there is less fan mayhem at sporting events in the U.S., a nation that many Britons regard as violence prone, is that its stadiums have fewer standing-room sections. Says Goodhart: "It is very difficult to riot when you are sitting down."

To be sure, there are those who feel that soccer violence is largely a symptom of deeper social and economic problems, perhaps even a direct result of Britain's 13.5% unemployment rate. In Liverpool, for example, 25% of the labor force is out of work. "We have football," says psychologist Peter Marsh. "Other societies have street gangs." A 1980 study of soccer hooliganism in Britain found that four-fifths of those charged with soccer-related crimes were either unemployed or manual workers. Says sociologist John Williams of the University of Leicester: "We must go into the community to find out why young people find status in this kind of violence."

A different picture of some soccer rowdies emerged two weeks ago in a British courtroom, where 25 supporters of Cambridge United were sentenced to prison terms of up to five years for soccer-related assaults. Members of a "hooligan army," as they were called by the press, they were organized into a paramilitary group and were affluent enough to buy "uniforms" consisting of costly designer sweaters, jeans, and track shoes. Indeed, much of the trouble at soccer games seems to be started by similarly well-organized gangs of about 200 members that attach themselves to their home teams. Many of the groups have their own chants, symbols, and even weapons of choice. The infamous Bushwackers of Millwall, a tattered docklands area of London, wear surgical masks during matches to hide their identities and favor small Stanley cutting tools to carry out their assaults. Some Liverpool supporters who attended the Brussels game insist that many fans dressed in the crimson of Liverpool spoke in the Cockney accents of Chelsea and West Ham, London neighborhoods whose clubs are known for their marauding followers. In fact, Liverpool fans had a reputation among the British for relative propriety.

As the search for causes of the violence in Brussels went on, those touched by the tragedy made an effort to come to terms with their feelings. At a Requiem Mass held in Liverpool's Roman Catholic cathedral, the Archbishop of Liverpool, Derek Worlock, summed up the feelings of shocked and puzzled citizens. "If it comes to responsible human conduct and moral behavior," he said, "the answer lies in ourselves." At a service held in a hangar at a Brussels military airport on Saturday, Belgian Prime Minister Martens paid his final respects to 25 of the riot victims. He spoke of the need "to put an end to this mad race toward violence." Then, as more than 100 relatives of the dead tearfully filed past the coffins covered with flowers, three priests gave their blessings. Unless ways are found to ensure that such tragedies do not recur, those flowers could become a memorial for European soccer itself.

Cultural Patterns: Pivotal Institutions

PART

Four

The Family, Religion, and Education

*C*ulture, discussed earlier in Chapter 3, is the most important product of the social way of life—the only way in which humans can sustain life. Often called the cement that holds the social bond together (known in the context of this book as the social web), culture represents the distinguishing factor separating humans from other living creatures. In particular, the normative component of culture is central to human life, providing a design for living: the first "how to" guide ever produced, and a best-seller still. The most vital components of the normative system, in turn, are its institutions.

Institutions are defined as patterns of behavior that help fulfill pressing human needs and become habitual through repeated use. The most fundamental of these needs is the propagation of the species. Reproduction must therefore somehow be controlled, since infants need adults to take care of and nurture them until they reach adulthood, and reproduction without certain controls would be too haphazard to ensure this. Children, for example, would not know their fathers. Mothers without the support of the males who impregnated them would find it difficult to maintain tolerable living conditions for themselves and their infants, and thus might abandon their young, who would then face ensuing death. Allowing men and women to mate promiscuously and without regulation would lead to chaos and violence, as men fought for the privilege of mating with a particular woman, or women fought to mate with an especially gifted male. In the meantime, the children of such sporadic unions would remain uncared for, running wild if they survived infancy, with ties to no particular parents, and would be likely to make very unsatisfactory adults themselves.

Other essential human needs include the need to eat and drink at regular intervals; the need to live in relative peace and to defend oneself from hostile neighbors or strangers; the need to teach new generations how to live; and the need for accepted authorities to answer such enigmatic questions as: What is the meaning of life? What happens after death? How did it all begin? And how will it end?

All human societies must provide means of satisfying these universal needs; due to potential disorganization and mass confrontation, they cannot afford to let individual members fend for themselves. If each member of society, for instance, had to satisfy his hunger by stealing his neighbor's food, or his sex drive by grabbing any available mate; if parents were too lazy to teach their children useful knowledge; if neighbors had to sleep with one eye open to listen for hostile intruders; if each individual were permitted to believe and act as he chose in matters concerning life and death, society would grow too disorderly to survive for long.

To avoid such havoc, each society devises patterns, known to social scientists as **institutions,** to fulfill these essential needs in orderly ways. The institution of the family ensures the continuation of the species; education serves to transmit societal knowledge; religion answers transcendental questions; the economy provides a system for feeding and clothing societal members; and the political institution, or government, keeps the peace within society and keeps outside enemies away. These five institutions, apparent in every known human society, are referred to as pivotal: they form the most significant of human constructs, around which other institutions, as well as folkways, mores, and laws, accumulate.

Institutions are *durable* in the sense that each generation faces the same basic problems and maintains ties with both past and future through parents and offspring. But though established institutional patterns are followed, new ones continually emerge, since members never totally conform to existing models. Thus the form of the enduring institutions remains constantly in flux.

Institutions are *interdependent:* One tends to support the others and is in turn supported by them. At the same time, they exhibit tensions between stability and change. Institutions that are stable and durable tend to become rigid, and while rigidity maintains social stability, it also imprisons things as they are, leading to a degree of stagnation. As new methods of accomplishing goals appear and are judged workable, these challenge the status quo, forcing rigid institutions to accept change.

Finally, it must be stressed that institutions are simply abstract concepts of organized habits and standardized methods of behavior. They are not tangible objects: We cannot see them. But we can see what they produce: families, schools, banks, federal buildings, churches, and so on. While institutions give form to individual behavior, it is individuals who give institutions their form.

The Basic Institution: The Family

The family is considered the oldest and most basic social unit, traces of which can be found in all societies, past and present. In spite of controversies that have flared around it in technologically advanced societies, the structure of the family remains strong.

The origins of this institution are long forgotten, but sociologists generally believe that the family instigated the cycle of institution building. Thus, in the course of human history, in all known societies, the family has provided the individual with an identity, a social status, and physical as well as moral support. Other pivotal and less important institutions gradually emerged out of the family, remaining dependent upon it for a long time. The family has continued as a pervasive force in human life, the most relevant of primary groups, and the most important element of the socialization process.

To attest to the universality of this institution, anthropologist George Murdock studied 250 societies and found evidence of a nuclear family in every one (1949). Murdock speculated that the family's universality stemmed from its functional nature with respect to four fundamental dimensions of social life: the sexual, the economic, the reproductive, and the educational.

The functional interpretation has been challenged on several grounds. The functionality of the family, according to some critics, is limited to some, not

The family is a universal institution, although its form and structure varies around the world.

all, members of society, and certain family-related services can be provided by other agencies. Others have noted universal functions that may be considered effects, rather than causes, of the family arrangement, namely the positioning of individuals within the social system and the regulation of social alliances between family units (Coser, 1964, xiv).

Family Forms

Although the institution of the family is a universal one, its forms vary from society to society. All families, however, as social groups, share certain common features: They originate in marriage; they consist of husband, wife (or wives), and children born of their union (in some forms other relatives are included); they include members connected by legal, economic, and religious bonds as well as by duties and privileges; they provide a network of sexual privileges and prohibitions, as well as varying degrees of love, respect, and affection (Levi-Strauss, 1971, 56).

Historically, the family has adopted two chief forms, the extended and the nuclear. The **extended,** or **consanguine** ("belonging to the same blood"), family includes not only husband, wife, and their offspring, but a number of blood relatives with their mates and children who live together and are considered a family unit. This form is typical of traditional, agricultural societies, where cooperation is advantageous in securing a better livelihood. Psychologically, an extended family provides certain benefits: child rearing is a communal responsibility and children form affectionate relationships with many persons, relieving parents of the entire burden of socialization. Physical neglect or

Extended, or consanguine, families are typical of primarily agricultural societies. They are dysfunctional in urban industrial societies.

mistreatment (child abuse) are virtually unheard of in extended families. On the other hand, since the welfare of the family unit takes priority over that of the individual, personal goals and desires must often be stifled. Finally, extended families exhibit a well-defined hierarchy of authority to which individual members are subservient.

The **nuclear** family form, also known as the **conjugal** ("joined, or united"), includes the nucleus (center) of father, mother, and their children. Children regard their family as consanguine since they and their parents are related by blood ties. The parents consider it **procreative,** their relationship centering on the production of children.

The nuclear family is typical of urban industrial societies where significant geographical and social mobility exists. Under such conditions, individuals are attracted to urban centers and better jobs, where they form new family units, leaving behind their original families. Moreover, in industrial societies, many functions originally performed by primary groups are transferred to secondary ones. Protection, education, health care, money lending, nursing, and so on, are taken over by separate institutions. The large extended family unit, almost totally self-sufficient in agrarian societies, finds little place in industrial societies; in urban environments where housing is scarce and education expensive, the form can actually prove counterproductive. Finally, in industrial societies achieved status carries more weight than ascribed status; what a person does through his or her own effort is more important than the family's social position (Goode, 1963), making the process of leaving the extended family behind even simpler. In short, the life-style of the nuclear family is compatible with the values of industrial societies and their open stratification systems. As a result, the nuclear family has become the norm in so-called developed nations and will eventually predominate in many developing societies as well.

Kinship Systems

A number of people related by common descent, marriage, or through adoption form a kinship system. Kinship systems vary from society to society: The number of marriage partners, who may marry whom, where newlyweds live, and relevant authority patterns all vary tremendously across cultures.

Marriage

The basis of every kinship system is marriage, traditionally a union of man and woman or various combinations thereof living together in a sexual relationship with the expectation of producing offspring (today this definition is frequently amended as certain couples eliminate having children as a prime purpose of marriage). This relationship is defined and sanctioned by tradition and law, which provide guidelines for behavior in matters of sex, obligations to offspring and in-laws, division of labor within the household, and other duties and privileges of marital life.

Most societies encourage marriage, and give high status to married persons. They also distinguish between unions sanctioned by society (marriages) and those that are not (couples living together).

Although every society encourages marriage as opposed to unregulated sex, the relationship may take various forms in different societies. Two broad subdivisions are monogamy and polygamy. **Monogamy** describes the union of one man with one woman. **Polygamy** is the term for plural marriage, which can in turn be subdivided into *polyandry,* the union of one woman with several men, *polygyny,* the union of one man with several women, and group marriage, involving several men living with several women.

Historically, monogamy has represented the most common form of marriage, probably due to the simultaneous maturation and availability for mating of an approximately equal number of males and females. Polygyny is the more common form of polygamy. Once widely practiced, particularly in Muslim societies, the custom is today more limited, both due to the diffusion of Western values and the expense of maintaining several wives and their attendant children. Polyandry is an uncommon form of marriage, practiced chiefly in areas where physical existence is difficult and seminomadic, so that more than one husband is required to support a wife and her children. Group marriage, though it does exist, has never been practiced consistently or extensively in any known society.

Limitations on Marriage Every society regulates the choice of mates between members by specifying whom they may marry and whom they may not. All societies, for instance, prohibit marriage within a certain group, whether family, clan, tribe, or village. In Western societies people are forbidden by laws based on deep-seated tradition to marry blood relatives such as parents, sisters, brothers, and in some localities first cousins. The limitation requiring that marriage occur outside particular groups is called *exogamy.* A universal example of exogamy is the **incest taboo,** or prohibition of sexual relations between mother and son, father and daughter, or sister and brother. This taboo, although occasionally broken for specific reasons in some societies, and broken today in more American families than we care to admit, is clearly enforced in every known society. Many anthropologists believe the taboo originated because incest is counterproductive to society. Incestuous relationships tend to damage family structure: Relationships become extremely tangled, rivalries and conflicts among family members abound, and families are forced to absorb new children instead of providing economically valuable adults. Marrying outside the family builds bonds of dependence among non-related groups, establishing a cohesive society and ensuring the creation of new families (Levi-Strauss, 1971, 55). The incest taboo, then, may have arisen in prehistoric times as a means of gaining cooperation with competing hunting bands. The exchange of mates between groups no doubt helped ensure friendly relations and prevent excessive conflict over hunting territory (Washburn and DeVore, 1961, 96–100).

At the same time, societies require their members to marry within other specified groups. In traditional societies, individuals are encouraged to choose their mates from members of their clan, tribe, or village. In Western societies, more subtle pressure exists on members to marry within their race, religion, and social class. Except in South Africa, where marrying outside one's race ceased being a crime only in 1985, the prohibitions are usually not couched in the context of the law. Still, informal sanctions in this area are strong. Such limitation on marriage is called *endogamy,* or the requirement that marriage occur within the group.

Family Functions

As noted earlier, many of the family's former functions have been taken over by modern institutions. Nevertheless, in traditional or "alternative" forms, the family continues to fulfill certain important functions: it regulates sex, controls reproduction, acts as the principal agent of socialization, and provides affection and companionship.

Regulation of Sex No known society leaves the regulation of sex to chance. All attempt to channel the human sex drive into relationships between persons whose access to each other is legitimized through marriage or other legal bonds.

Most societies encourage marriage, giving high status to married couples and making a further distinction between unions sanctioned by society and those entered into by consenting partners without such sanction. In general, societies discourage the single state. In some societies, there are no unmarried adults at all, as provisions are made for each individual to enjoy a full sex life in spite of personal shortcomings that might make it difficult to find a marriage partner.

Reproduction A fundamental function of the family since its beginning has been to ensure the process of reproduction and continuation of the species. In many societies, an individual is not considered an adult until he fathers or she gives birth to a child. Some cultures attach no stigma to children born out of wedlock, making provisions instead for their incorporation into the family. However, reproduction outside the family is not sanctioned in any society. In the United States, change in the institution of the family has led to increasing numbers of single mothers. Though some unmarried career women now deliberately choose to be unwed mothers, most single parents are teenage girls whose pregnancies are unwanted and unplanned. The large increase in such pregnancies is partly the result of liberalized sex norms without a consequent adjustment in values.

Socialization As outlined in Chapter 4, most societies depend on the family to socialize their young. Those which have attempted to transfer this function to other agencies have had mixed results at best. In the USSR, the policy of allotting the socialization of children to preschools was rapidly reversed, as such action failed to produce the type of individual the government had hoped for. On Israeli kibbutzim, socialization has also reverted to families. Communally reared children apparently considered the entire kibbutz as their family, to the point of going out of their way to marry outside the group. Thus the family was not dispensed with, only extended (Spiro, 1971, 501–508).

Although the function of socialization has therefore remained basically within the family, schools and peer groups have assumed a large portion of the process. The importance of the family as an agent for establishing individual identity and readying children to function as adults in the wider society has nonetheless grown considerably. Socialization within the family is particularly influential in the area of mate selection, because it is within the family that attitudes on race, politics, and class are passed on without being consciously taught.

Affection and Companionship The need for human affection and companionship appears fundamental. Numerous studies have indicated that lack of affection in the development years may lead to an antisocial personality and even to physical illness. Children who receive faultless physical care but no affection often become ill or even die (Spitz, 1945, 53–57, a classic study on the subject; many others have since replicated these findings).

While groups outside the family may provide companionship, affection is more likely to be limited to those within it, and increasingly within the nuclear family, since most people get together only occasionally with their extended families, often having little in common with them beyond a last name. The nuclear family's responsibility to satisfy all of an individual's emotional needs, however, frequently becomes a burden it cannot sustain, leading to a breakdown of the fragile bonds that tie it together.

Love and Marriage in America

Love as a prerequisite for marriage is a modern invention. In preindustrial societies, marriage served as an economic arrangement between families. Love between partners did not enter into such alliances. With modernization and the ability of young adults of both sexes to find wage-paying work came the freedom to make one's own marital choices. Naturally, those able to choose their mates select partners who are appealing, attractive, and with whom they feel at ease and share a number of interests—at least at first. Hence the introduction of romance as a preamble to courting and inspiration for marriage.

Yet even though free choice exists in American society, that choice is much more socially determined than is first obvious. Not only are endogamy and exogamy at work—spouses are chosen within certain groups and outside others—but people overwhelmingly marry mates very much like themselves. This tendency is called *homogamy,* while its opposite, marrying a person with different traits, is referred to as *heterogamy.* Homogamy occurs when people meet and develop relationships with those who live in the same neighborhoods, attend the same schools, churches, or synagogues, or frequent the same recreational facilities. Those who meet at work also tend to share educational backgrounds and interests. In short, social factors evident in homogamy include age, residence, race and ethnicity, religion, education, social class, and family influence. The best evidence of homogamy may be found in statistics: As a percentage of all married couples in the United States, interracial couples constitute about 1 percent. In other words, over 99 percent of

Interracial Married Couples: 1970 to 1984

TABLE 11.1

Item	1970	1980	1984
Total married couples	44,597	49,714	50,864
Interracial married couples	310	651	762
All Black-White married couples	65	167	175
Husband Black, wife White	41	122	111
Wife Black, husband White	24	45	64
Other interracial married couples	245	484	587
Husband Black	8	20	17
Wife Black	4	14	6
Husband White	139	287	340
Wife White	94	163	224

Note: In thousands. 1970, 14 years old and over; 1980 and 1984, 15 years old and over. 1970 data as of April. 1980 and 1984 data as of March and based on Current Population Survey.

Source: U.S. Bureau of the Census, *Census of Population: 1970, Marital Status,* PC(2)-4C; *Current Population Reports,* series P-20, No. 398, and earlier reports.

white husbands, 96 percent of black husbands, and 82 percent of other husbands are married to women of similar race (U.S. Bureau of the Census, 1984, Table 16). However, the *rate* of interracial marriages is growing, as illustrated by Table 11.1. In addition, 92.6 percent of American Protestants marry other Protestants, 82 percent of Catholics marry Catholics, and 88.2 percent of Jews marry Jews (Glenn, 1982, 555–566); white ethnic groups of English, German, Irish, Italian, Swedish, and Polish descent marry about 75 percent of the time within their own groups of descent.

Changing Marital Patterns

Modernization and the general affluence of industrial societies greatly changed the structure and substance of family life. Almost equally dramatic changes have occurred in this century alone, particularly in the past few decades. Improved birth control, liberalized sex norms, and the entrance of women into the work force have resulted in a sharp decline in America's birthrate (from 3.7 children per family in 1955–59 to 1.8 in 1981), voluntary childlessness has increased, and the divorce rate has skyrocketed.

Divorce   The most notorious modern change in the marital pattern is the recent frequency and acceptance of divorce. High divorce rates in urban industrial societies, as illustrated in Figure 11.1, reflect (1) the separation of marriage from religion; (2) the emancipation of women; and (3) a change in values stressing a new emphasis on individuality and personal happiness.

   The link between industrialization and increasing divorce is widespread and consistent. In the United States, where marriage rates have remained stable since the turn of the century, divorce rates have increased from .9 per thousand in 1910 to 5.3 per thousand in 1980. A majority of divorces is granted to those between 20 and 35 who have been married only briefly or who married

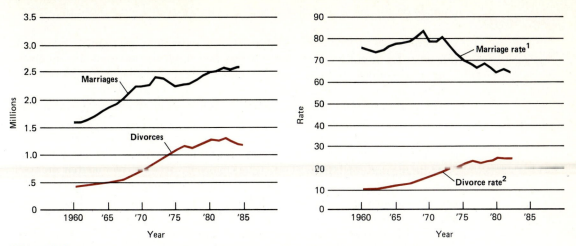

Marriages and Divorces: 1960 to 1984

Figure 11.1 The U. S. divorce rate began climbing steadily in 1960, but it has recently experienced a dip, which began in 1982. Still, it is the highest rate in the world. *Notes:* [1]Rate per 1000 unmarried women, 15 years old and over; [2]Rate per 1000 married women, 15 years old and over.
Source: Chart prepared by U.S. Bureau of the Census.

when either spouse was a teenager. In 80 percent of cases both partners remarry, although divorce occurs more frequently among couples married more than once. About 6 percent of married couples have been married three or more times. The frequency of divorce and remarriage has led analysts to refer to these unions as *serial* or *throwaway.*

Marriage itself is a highly prized status. Second and third remarriages clearly indicate that it is the partner, not the institution, that is spurned, and often due more to high expectations than any other factor.

Divorce as the New Norm The prevalence of divorce has greatly increased its acceptability. Growing numbers recognize divorce as a natural product of social change, and a majority even consider the divorced status as normal. Polls show that divorce is widely regarded as an acceptable solution to an unacceptable marriage. Married couples today are more skeptical about the institution and less willing to put up with unpleasant situations. An increasing number of women now work outside the home and are thus freed from economic dependence on their husbands. The women's movement has popularized the right of women to be independent and assertive and not necessarily dependent on men for their happiness. All these factors have made it increasingly easier for both partners, and women especially, to seek divorce rather than remain in an unhappy marriage.

In addition, divorce laws have recently become much simpler. Almost half the states have adopted no-fault divorce, in which neither party must prove the other is to blame. Finally, support systems have sprung up to assist couples with emotional, financial, and legal difficulties connected with divorce. Books about how to handle the process abound on library shelves, colleges offer courses on the subject, and counseling is freely available to those in need.

Consequences of Divorce   Despite its frequency and "normality," divorce is not easy for a couple, and less so for any children that may be involved. Numerous studies on the subject have indicated that women suffer more stress and trauma from divorce than do men (Albrecht, 1980, 59–68).

The reason may be that men generally enjoy better economic positions that facilitate their postdivorce adjustment. In fact, a majority of women report that their income following divorce considerably decreases. From this perspective, divorce is much easier for the man. However, their psychological adjustment may be harder: Four times more divorced than married men kill themselves (Moffet and Scherer, 1976); and men who are not remarried within six years following divorce have higher rates of car accidents, alcoholism, drug abuse, depression, and anxiety (Brody, 1983, C1 +). A much better adjustment is made by couples who remain childless and divorce after a few years: These rejoin the ranks of the singles with little trace of their former status. Not so for those who have been married long, or who have had children: They remain forever the "formerly married" (Hunt and Hunt, 1980, 340–354).

The effects of divorce on children are more difficult to evaluate although a large number are fated to go through the experience of parental divorce—an estimated one-third of American children under 18 by 1990 (Kurdek, 1981, 856–866). Although all children report being traumatized, nine- and ten-year-olds whose self-concept depends on having parents physically present in the household are especially shaken (Wallerstein and Kelly, 1983, 438–452). However, most youngsters maintain that the conflict preceding divorce is much worse than the action itself. Thus difficulties associated with children of divorce are probably more correctly the result of years of parental fighting (Luepnitz, 1979, 79–85).

Alternatives to Traditional Marriage

We may safely say that the American family, like other contemporary institutions, is still undergoing the aftereffects of modernization. Social scientists have focused much attention on this evolution, since the changes in question have been unusually visible, particularly from midcentury on. Infected by the ideological ferment of the 1960s, many young people began to see the family as a repressive breeding ground of under-the-surface conflicts. Alternative lifestyles became fashionable, and many drifted into communal living arrangements. Communes are not new; they sprout in each generation, but none seem to survive for more than the span of that generation (with the exception of the Israeli kibbutzim which continue to exist in a modified form). Nonetheless, the general and widespread interest in communal living pointed to a certain vacuum the family had failed to fill.

An alternative that did take hold was the option of simply remaining single. Though always available as a choice, in the past this status carried a much greater stigma; the bachelor uncle or maiden aunt were regarded as misfits who lived at the margin of a relative's family. In extended families there was always room and a function for these "unfortunates," whereas in nuclear families there was not.

Forms of the New American Family

The stereotype of the nuclear family consisting of father, mother, two children, and a dog no longer corresponds to reality. With the high incidence of divorce and subsequent remarriage, American families appear substantially different than they did twenty years ago. Although a majority of children still grow up in a two-parent family, an increasing number become part of alternative structures.

The Single-Parent Family   One of the fastest-growing modifications of the family consists of one divorced parent with a child or children. Although in the past that parent was almost exclusively the mother, fathers increasingly request and receive custody. Divorce, though a predominant cause, is not the only source of single-parent families; death, ill health, or institutionalization also contribute to its numbers. In addition, unmarried women are now much more likely to keep their illegitimate children rather than give them up for adoption.

Single-parent families tend to be temporary, ending either when the child reaches majority age and moves out or when the parent remarries (if widowed

As a result of the frequency of divorce, the single-parent family is now a growing form of the American household.

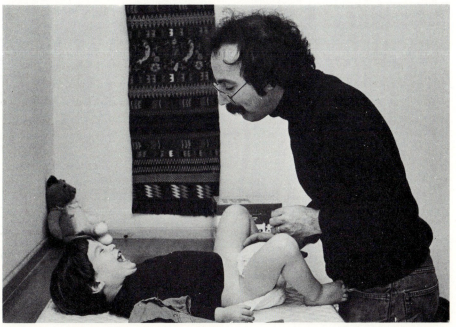

or divorced) or marries for the first time. However, the number of single-parent households in all three major American ethnic groups has seen a dramatic increase, as illustrated in Figure 11.2. In the decade from 1970 to 1982, the number of children under 18 living in single-parent households rose from 12 to 22 percent of the total American households containing children of that age group (U.S. Bureau of the Census, *Marital Status and Living Arrangements,* March 1982, Table E). More than 90 percent of these households, moreover, are headed by women, whose lower income compounds the problems of caring for children single-handedly. Not only do women earn less than men, but single-parent households must rely on a single income, women with small children may be able to work only part-time, and women who head families tend to have less education than the average American female (40 percent have not graduated from high school). Additional difficulties encountered by such households revolve around the lack of time and the need for the single parent to play the roles of mother *and* father in the face of fatigue and worry over money matters. This situation is particularly regrettable in light of new research that suggests that poor parenting, regardless of family structure, is primarily responsible for deviant behavior among children (Patterson, 1980).

The Blended or Reconstituted Family   A common form created as a result of remarriage is the blended or reconstituted family. This household type consists of two remarried partners, the children of either previous marriage, and sometimes those born to the couple.

Figure 11.2   A dramatic shift in the American family has been the trend, among all ethnic groups, toward single parenthood.   *Source:* From the *New York Times,* November 4, 1984, p. E5. Copyright © 1984 by The New York Times Company. Reprinted by permission.

Family Life

Single–parent families as a percent of families with children

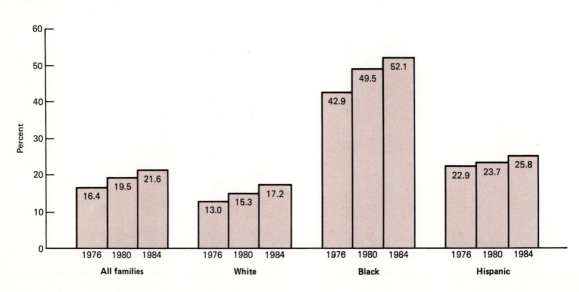

Blended families have been described as representing the wave of the future, especially if the high divorce rate continues. Such families contain their own sets of problems. Relationships are multiplied—one may have several sets of siblings, grandparents, children, and other relatives. Occasions for jealousy and rivalry are increased. Because women tend to get custody, a remarried man will often have children of his own who do not live with him, while living with children not biologically his. Some research seems to indicate as well that girls residing in households with stepfathers experience higher incidences of sexual activity, drug involvement, and school-related problems than those who live with both natural parents or just their mother (Cherlin, 1981). These findings, however, are not meant to establish a cause-and-effect relationship; that is, all girls who live with their mothers and stepfathers will not necessarily engage in undesirable behavior. The findings do point, however, to a potential for problems in a household where conflict and tension are present, or where a child suffers from hostility and resentment.

The Small, Childless, or One-child Family   Since the Industrial Revolution, families in the Western world have been growing smaller. In 1930, the average family in the United States consisted of 4.11 persons; in 1983, 3.26 (U.S. Bureau of the Census, 1983, 3). But the trend toward childless marriages or those producing a single child is fairly new in American society. Between 1970 and 1980, for instance, the number of children aged fourteen and under declined by more than 6.5 million. In addition, a study conducted in 1980 revealed that each 1000 women between 18 and 34 had borne a total of 1127

Figure 11.3   More women have had to join the work force in order to maintain a satisfactory living standard. This trend has resulted in a smaller number of children per family. *Source:* From *Newsweek,* September 10, 1984, p. 16. Compiled by the U.S. Bureau of the Census. Reprinted by permission.

Two-Job Families

In millions

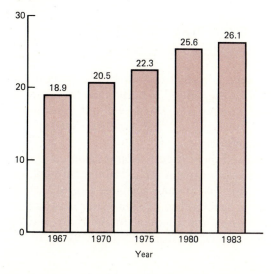

babies and expected to bear 932 more (U.S. Bureau of the Census, 1981, 20). This represents a rate of 2.06 per mother, less than the replacement rate of 2.2. Young single women have an expectation rate of 1.8 babies each; 21.4 percent of women polled indicated they expected to have no children at all.

Some reasons for the decline in the number of children per family are economic in nature. Since more women must work in order to maintain a comfortable standard of living (see Figure 11.3 for a breakdown of the recent increase in two-career families), extended leaves of absence represent hardships for the family. Women who want careers may worry about missing promotions if they are frequently absent to care for ill children. The widespread availability of contraceptives, abortion, and sterilization also make remaining childless or having only one child relatively easy. Finally, due to the highly publicized opinion of behavioral scientists that parents largely determine their children's characters, many couples fear to undertake such momentous roles. At the same time, a countertrend is discernible: Increasing numbers of women in their thirties and forties who have pursued successful careers and now feel their biological clock running out are deciding to have children while they still can. This trend has become so apparent the media has labeled it an impending "baby boomlet," one which may keep the birth rate from seriously declining.

Tomorrow's Family   There is little doubt that the family institution is changing. Just as the nuclear model followed dramatic changes in society in the wake of industrialization and urbanization, so new forms will take shape in response to the postindustrial information society currently in the making. Since families nevertheless continue to provide the emotional center of human life, it is highly unlikely that the institution will disappear altogether. In spite of its numerous weaknesses, it still functions as the most efficient and satisfactory transmitter of culture and socializer of children yet contrived. Thus as long as humans continue to perpetuate their species by raising new generations, the institution of the family will endure.

Pivotal Institutions: Religion

Among separate institutions that have absorbed certain former functions of the family, religion probably ranks as the oldest. In early agrarian societies, each family took care of religious worship and rituals without resorting to such intermediaries as priests; in many societies, each family claimed its own particular deities to protect and benefit it.

Social scientists who initially focused their attention on religion commonly regarded it as an attempt by primitives to explain reality. Nineteenth-century French sociologist Auguste Comte felt that human societies passed through three stages: In the first two religion was used to explain many natural phenomena to which humans did not know the answers. In the third, religion would be replaced by science. Other social thinkers, notably E. B. Tylor and

Herbert Spencer, sought to explain religion in terms of a universal concern with the soul, originating among primitives' supposedly mistaken interpretations of dreams and death. Religion, in short, was viewed as the relic of an era when men and women lived in a state of ignorance about their world.

Karl Marx added an economic twist to the interpretation of religion's role in human life, stating that the institution originated in a fear of natural phenomena and thus was fated to eventually disappear. In the meantime, according to Marxist economic determinism, religion was viewed as a masquerade for class interest. The ruling classes used it as the prevailing ideology of society (the "opiate of the masses") and were thus able to manipulate and control those beneath.

An alternative view was expressed by French sociologist Émile Durkheim, who suggested that religion dealt with sacred matters, to be distinguished from the profane ([1912] 1947, 209). The **sacred** remains separate from everyday experience; in its representation of the unusual, inexplicable, mysterious, and powerful, it therefore deserves reverence and respect. The **profane**, on the other hand, includes objects and events of everyday life that are usual, explicable, and repetitive.

Durkheim also speculated that primitives were keenly aware of a force greater than themselves which had to be obeyed and on which they depended for survival. But unable to understand the nature or origin of such a force, they invented deities with supernatural power and control over human life. They also invented rituals intended to appease these deities and make them well-disposed toward humans. Primitive people arrived at their concept of the divine by imagining that the divinity possessed the characteristics of society: society has moral authority over the individual and often demands behavior that goes against the wishes of the individual; society requires obedience and sometimes sacrifices of its members; and society is more powerful than the single individual. At the same time, society helps individuals cope with their lives (through institutions) and offers a collective power (against outside enemies, or evil, for instance) that individual members could not wield on their own.

Because of these similarities in character between societies and divine beings, Durkheim maintained that religious beliefs and practices were not rooted in ignorance and superstition, as others asserted. Rather, they dealt with a very real object—human society. In Durkheim's view, then, religion represented the expression of human solidarity, the individual awareness of the social system and the web of relationships occurring within it, and finally, the recognition of one's dependence on this system despite its occasionally dictatorial nature.

The Functions of Religion

Durkheim's insights provided a framework for contemporary social scientists who conjecture that religion's universal existence in society reflects the important functions it performs. Humans live in perpetual uncertainty—at any moment accidents may maim or kill them; they are able to control their environment only minimally—a tornado or tidal wave can destroy entire communities; and most live in conditions of scarcity, where necessary or desired resources are never sufficient. As a result, a mechanism is required to help them adjust to frustrating but inevitable facts of existence. Religion gives the faithful a means to reach beyond their ordinary experience and establish a link with the sacred through the ritual of worship.

More specifically, religion performs the following functions: (1) it helps ease personal doubts about security and identity; (2) it clarifies the physical world, making it understandable, familiar, and meaningful; (3) it supports societal norms and values by transforming them into divine laws; (4) it helps individuals face life at critical stages—entering adulthood, contracting marriage, undergoing the birth of children, and so on; and (5) it helps men and women deal with guilt over their transgressions, offering a way back to a constructive life.

Most people consider these functions to be positive. But conflict theorists point out that in supporting the norms and values of society, religion also supports the status quo—in short, it represents a conservative force opposed to change. Marx, too, felt that religion had an alienating effect on people: Conflicts arose between those of different religions, and the institution was used by the dominant class to justify injustice and inequality and repress the anger of the exploited lower classes by offering future rewards in an afterlife instead of their rightful share in the present.

Marx was partially right; however, religion also stimulates social change. Numerous examples exist of religions, through the sacrifice of certain faithful, improving the lot of the oppressed. In the United States, for instance, religion played a part in abolishing slavery and in passing civil rights legislation, thus providing the impetus for radical social change.

Religion in America

All religions comprise belief, ritual, and organization. Belief is often spelled out in doctrine or articles of faith. Ritual provides an important practice in its representation of correct forms of behavior toward the sacred. In modern times, the role of belief is emphasized more than that of ritual, which perhaps explains the attraction of so many young people to more colorful religious expressions. Religious organization reflects the classification into church, sect, or cult.

A **church** is a religious organization that is thoroughly institutionalized and well integrated into the social and economic order of society. The Roman Catholic Church, Protestant churches (such as the United Methodist, the National and Southern Baptist, the Church of Jesus Christ of Latter-Day Saints), the Greek Orthodox, and the Jewish congregations are all churches in the United States. Churches are differentiated into the *ecclesia,* the official state religion to which most members of a society belong, and the **denomination,** not officially linked to any state or national government. (The United States, of course, has no ecclesia, but contains many denominations, sects, and cults.) A **sect** is usually a breakaway movement, a rebellion against conservatism in the established church, although successful sects in turn become denominations of the latter. **Cults** are the least conventional and institutionalized forms of religious organizations. They are temporary and tend to revolve around a charismatic leader.

Religion in the United States possesses characteristics that distinguish it from those in other societies. The United States, for example, has never adopted a state religion to which its citizens are expected to belong. On the contrary, the separation of church and state is a firmly ingrained principle in the society. Moreover, due to the coexistence of many denominations—approximately 85 according to the 1984 U. S. Bureau of the Census and as many as 1200 as reported by Melton (1978)—religious organizations, like secular ones, must compete for attention and attract as many faithful as possible. Thus religion has been forced to adopt practices of the economic marketplace and, practiced in the context of voluntary organizations, often appears secular or worldly rather than spiritual. Church buildings are used for recreational purposes—cards and bingo—and as forums for discussion of politics and sex. In other words, religion has become highly bureaucratized, specialized, and efficient.

Religious affiliation is somewhat related to ethnic group (as illustrated in Figure 11.4) and social class. The relationship between membership in particular denominations and social status may be credited both to the effects of the Protestant ethic and to historical circumstances. Historically, immigrants have generally been thrust upwards in the stratification system by the arrival of those behind them. Thus the earliest American settlers, who were Protestant, automatically formed the upper strata. Protestant denominations have moreover been divided along class lines from the beginning, whereas the Catholic religion has traditionally embraced all social strata, as has the Jewish.

Although class differences among members of different churches and denominations exist, such data must be interpreted with caution. In a very general sense, Roman Catholicism has been associated with urban, industrial masses. Protestantism draws its members from business and professional communities on the one hand and rural farmers and the urban middle classes on the other. Small Protestant denominations such as Quakers, Congregationalists, Unitarians, and Christian Scientists tend to attract middle- and upperclass members on a local basis. Working-class Protestants are more apt to gravitate to the colorful rituals of radical sects (Baltzell, 1968, 312–313).

A quantitative study of religion by Gerhard Lenski attempted to test the hypothesis that Protestants, who are more indoctrinated into the Protestant ethic of rewards accruing from hard work and frugality, should thus prove more upwardly mobile than Catholics, whose orientation leans toward rewards in an afterlife (1961). In fact, Lenski did find that more white Protestants entered or remained in the middle class, while Catholics tended to enter or remain in the lower half of the working class. Later studies, however, contradict these findings, showing no direct relationship between Protestant or Catholic religious beliefs and socioeconomic status (Riccio, 1979, 199–231).

Measured in terms of church participation rather than membership, those at both extremes of the stratification system (the upper and lower class) have

Religion in the United States

Question: What is your religious preference? Is it Protestant, Catholic, Jewish, some other religion, or no religion?

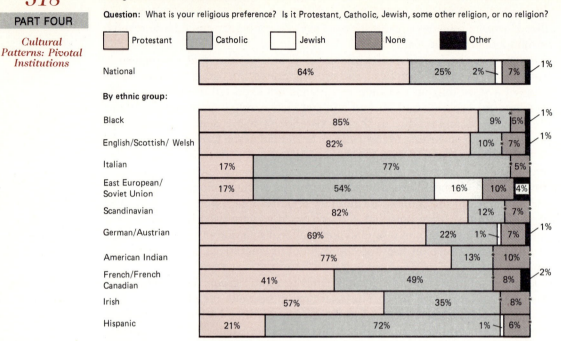

Figure 11.4 Religious affiliation is related to ethnicity and social class. A majority of Americans belong to one of the Protestant denominations, some of which rank high on the stratification ladder. *Note:* *Less than .5%. 1982, 1983, 1984 combined. *Source:* From surveys by National Opinion Research Center, General Social Surveys. (*Public Opinion*, October/November 1984, p. 20). Reprinted by permission.

been shown to engage in very little church activity. The most active participants in church affairs are chiefly from the upper lower or lower middle classes. Among these strata, church activism and doctrinal belief are most intense. The upper middle class also shows a high degree of participation, but one motivated more by the desire for social recognition, for "doing the right thing," than by any moral conviction (Glock and Stark, 1965, 20–21).

The Sanctification of the American Way of Life

Has the function of religion diminished in contemporary society? Statistics indicate that at least in the United States it has not. Although church attendance in this country has dropped in the past 20 years, it remains one of the highest in the industrial world. Surveys indicate that 95 percent of Americans believe in God or some universal force or spirit, as compared to only 88 percent of Italians, 76 percent of Britons, and 65 percent of Scandinavians. Moreover, 56 percent of Americans characterize religion as very important in their lives as compared to only 36 percent of Italians and Canadians, 23 percent of Britons, and 17 percent of West Germans, Scandinavians, and Japanese (Gallup, 1984). On the surface, then, Americans appear to be a very religious people. But statistics do not tell the whole story, for the difficulty lies in the definition of religiosity. While attendance at religious services and belief in God could indicate a high degree of religiosity, the facts that only two-thirds of Americans claim to believe in an afterlife and only half of American adults claim to pray at least once a day point to the conclusion that they may be classified as marginally, and not profoundly, religious.

In his classic work, *Protestant, Catholic, Jew* (1955), sociologist Will Herberg notes, however, that although membership in American churches and synagogues has increased, congregants are less committed to religious beliefs and ethics than to the idea of belonging to specific religious communities. In other words, establishing places for themselves in society as members of a particular church is a prime motivator. Through the use of religion for social purposes, beliefs themselves have declined in significance. In fact, Americans tend to embrace the secular principles of democracy, the so-called American way of life, as a type of religion. To Herberg, such a manipulation of religion is equivalent to idolatry. Sociologist Robert Bellah expands this view by positing the existence in the United States of a "civil religion" that sanctifies the American political system, past and present leaders, and the American mission in the world, as well as the ultimate position the nation will assume in history (1970). Such statements as "One nation under God" and "In God We Trust" lend legitimacy to ideals of democracy. Traditional churches, nonetheless, do not view civil religion as a threat since it makes no claims of doctrinal merit and no effort at general organization.

Civil religion thus represents a variety of things to a variety of people. Bellah maintains that its emergence is one further indication of the positive function of religion as an integrating element of society. Without a general religious adherence, a society may lose direction and fall prey to social disintegration.

Contemporary Trends

Social scientists have generally assumed a dominant trend in contemporary religions toward secularization, away from the stress on the supernatural, spiritual, traditional version of a faith in the direction of a more worldly, practical, and rational version. On the surface, such secularization might be assumed to lead to the end of religion. Most established denominations, in fact, *are* losing members and suffering waning attendance. But the trend is not unidimensional. Religious bodies that have not yielded to secularization, that may even have originated as a reaction to secularization, are thriving. Sociologists Stark and Bainbridge point out that the need for the supernatural has not diminished in contemporary societies, despite their rationalistic basis (1981). Not only are many convinced of the relevance of astrology or Zen, most Americans raised in homes where religion played a minor role or was nonexistent eventually join some type of denomination. Finally, evangelical and fundamentalist sects and denominations are flourishing. Stark and Bainbridge conclude that when religious bodies grow too secularized, sects break away and attempt to revive old traditions. Secularization, in the opinion of these sociologists, is a self-limiting process that prompts religious revival and innovation (1985). Just as centuries ago Christianity, Judaism, Islam, and Buddhism originated as cults to counteract weaknesses in the dominant creeds of their day, so today new cults are acquiring power as established religions are losing it.

In the last two decades, in fact, numerous religious groups have appeared in the United States. These stress personal religious experience and commitment and deemphasize rational, bureaucratic religious organization. Accurate conclusions about the roots of such groups are difficult to formulate. Some include the fact that a complex and diversified society spawns complex and diversified belief systems; that such groups represent a search for meaning, or identity; that they represent a reaction against the materialism and militancy of the mass society; or that they attempt to inject a concrete value system into what is perceived as a climate of moral ambiguity.

Religion, like other pivotal institutions, occurs universally in societies as an agent for satisfying basic, essential human needs. Although science has clarified much mystery surrounding the human condition and given us a measure of control over our environment, certain needs persist that science will never satisfy. So long as humans ponder the meaning of life or experience disappointments, suffering, and death, they will gravitate toward religion to still their fears.

Education

Since humans lack highly developed instincts, any knowledge they accumulate about survival in groups, as well as the technology necessary to simplify life, must be transmitted as each new generation reaches adulthood. In traditional, preindustrial societies, such transmission of culture occurs within the family and consists mainly of imparting necessary survival skills as well as knowledge of ritual and religious myths. This information is easily absorbed as children follow and try to imitate their parents in the course of their everyday lives. Most such learning takes place in the context of informal socialization.

When modernization takes place and societies grow more complex, specialists become necessary to act as administrators and executives of the increasingly formal organizations established to care for the business of the society. Informal socialization systems are no longer adequate. Children are unable to follow their parents to the workplace. Some work, in fact, is so abstract and technical that a parent's explanation would be incomprehensible to a child. More formal methods of teaching must then be implemented, in which specially trained individuals instill skills, values, and a concrete body of knowledge to the young. The habits and traditions that evolve around this formalized type of socialization have become the institution we call education.

The educational institution has grown increasingly important with the passage of time. The economy of preindustrial societies depended primarily on those who performed manual labor. Education was therefore reserved for a small elite of future rulers, clergy, and occasional administrators. The economy of contemporary societies depends on those who can use their brains rather than their brawn. Uneducated individuals are largely unproductive in the national economy, whereas in preindustrial societies the educated person was unproductive. As a result of this shift, the goals of education have changed. In preindustrial societies, the aim of education was to produce a cultivated individual knowledgeable in many areas, conversant in many languages, and familiar with the history of many nations. Such an individual, it was hoped, could make enlightened decisions. In contemporary societies, such a wealth of information and a proliferation of specialized occupations exist that training for them has taken the place of cultivation. The earlier system of apprenticeship is inadequate to all but the least-skilled jobs; education has thus largely appropriated the task of producing experts specialized in limited areas of knowledge or technology.

Education in America

The first 12 years of the American educational system are open and universal, in sharp contrast to elitist systems still largely prevalent in other nations. The goal of a universal system is to provide equal educational opportunities to a society's children regardless of social class, race, sex, ethnicity, physical condition, and intellectual ability. The goal of an elitist system, on the other hand, is to educate the more talented or privileged in society for positions of leadership.

Universal or Mass Education   In the United States, compulsory mass education was instituted in the latter half of the nineteenth century, when large waves of immigrants began pouring into American cities, many of whom spoke no English and could neither read nor write. In order to make them fit citizens of the nation it was therefore necessary to "Americanize" them. The idea of educating immigrants to be literate in English was reinforced by the demands of new industries for skilled laborers to handle increasingly complex technologies. A certain level of education, first represented by an eighth-grade and later by a high-school diploma, became a prerequisite for all but the most menial jobs. During this period, schooling provided the means for each American to become self-supporting.

Of late, much criticism has been heaped on American public schools, most of it focusing on the decline of standards. But standards have fallen primarily due to the success of universal compulsory education. When those spread over an entire spectrum of intelligence and social background must be educated, teaching will be inevitably and ultimately geared to the learning capacities of average to slower students. Otherwise only a minority would be able to pass through the system.

As a society, the United States has been deeply committed to the principle of universal education. (As indicated in Figure 11.5, the percentage of adults who reach higher levels of education has steadily increased over the past three decades, though blacks still lag behind whites in this department.) The framers of the Constitution were convinced that democracy required a literate and

Percent of Adults Who Have Completed Four or More Years of High School
1950 to 1982

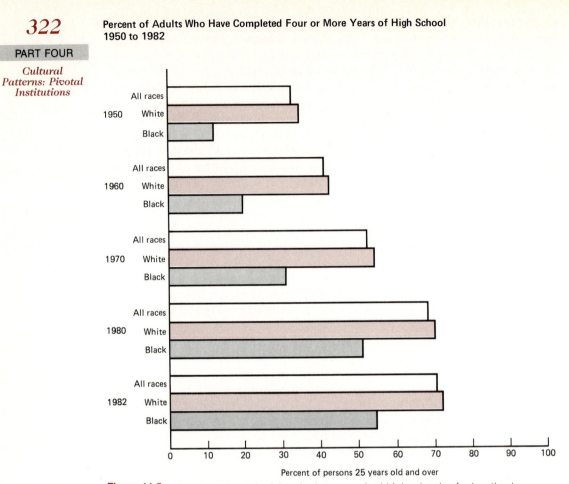

Figure 11.5 The percentage of adults who have acquired higher levels of education has been steadily increasing, but blacks still lag behind whites. *Source:* From chart prepared by U.S. Bureau of the Census.

well-informed electorate. And widespread belief persists about the value of education as an asset to the society as a whole. As a result, education in the United States is supported by taxation on all citizens, and parents are legally bound to send their children to school until at least age 16.

Local Control American education is characterized by its schools being subject to community control. Local school districts are created in each community, and children residing in that community attend schools within the district. The district's board, elected by local residents, makes decisions regarding the schools. This zealously guarded tradition has contributed to a variety of standards in the nation's schools and also to inequalities in funding (wealthier states donating more generously than poorer ones). Most other nations manage to avoid such disparities by controlling funding through central governments.

Upward Mobility as a Cure-all for Social Problems   An especially characteristic trait of American education is its reputation as a first, necessary step toward economic and thus social upward mobility. In fact, as Figure 11.6 illustrates, there are spectacular differences in income between those who fail to finish grade school and those who finish college. To this end American schools often stress training, the transmission of skills and information to be used in the performance of a job, at the expense of education, the development of creative and critical abilities. Repeatedly, American parents have declared their desire to have their children properly schooled to obtain better jobs, not particularly to stimulate their mental powers or develop any potential creative talents. Most parents also believe schools should instill in students a respect for law and authority and shy away from subjects that prompt controversy.

Due to the strong belief that education is necessary to produce good American citizens, the institution is frequently viewed as a cure-all for all manner of social problems. In response to an increase in traffic deaths, schools institute driving education programs; if society suffers from alcohol and drug abuse, schools provide for drug education programs; if too many unwanted teenage pregnancies occur, schools establish sex education programs. While such intentions are noble, little proof exists that these programs significantly affect any social problems.

The Functionalist View of Education

The structural-functionalists view education in terms of the institution's effect on society. From this perspective, education holds both manifest or intended functions and latent or unintended ones.

Figure 11.6   Education appears to be a prime factor in enhancing a person's upward social mobility—the more education, the higher one's income.   *Source:* U.S. Bureau of the Census, *Statistical Abstract of the United States*, 1985, p. 443.

Education and Income

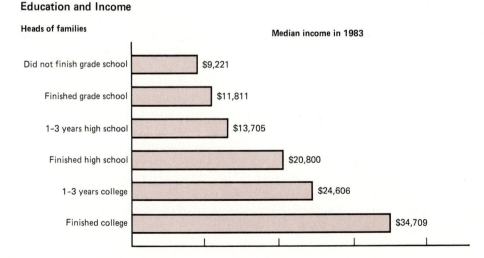

Heads of families

Median income in 1983

Did not finish grade school	$9,221
Finished grade school	$11,811
1–3 years high school	$13,705
Finished high school	$20,800
1–3 years college	$24,606
Finished college	$34,709

Manifest Functions   The overall manifest function of the educational institution is to supplement the socialization process begun in the family. Specifically, manifest functions may be summarized as follows:

Transmission of Culture. Schools teach students how to read, write, and compute; such basic facts as the history of their own and other countries of the world; and the essential laws governing physical phenomena. By exposing pupils to the history and literature of their society and Western civilization, schools help preserve a nation's cultural heritage. They also impart the values, beliefs, and attitudes of the society, thus reinforcing values acquired earlier through family socialization.

Recruitment and Preparation for Roles. Schools function to help select, guide, and prepare students for the social and occupational roles they will eventually fill. These roles are acquired through socialization that stresses personality traits necessary for the society. American school children thus learn to be competitive, to value success, to be hardworking, and to conform to group norms. They also learn what tasks they may grow up to perform in society. This last function is especially important in industrial societies.

Cultural Integration. Schools reinforce the values and norms prevalent among the majority. During the influx of large masses of immigrants, children from different backgrounds were taught that becoming American involved memorizing and reciting the pledge of allegiance, learning to play baseball, finding out why Americans celebrate Thanksgiving, and so on. The intention of such experiences was to give students a common ground and to foster their sense of national unity and solidarity. Within the last decade, this function has been severely criticized as an attempt to enforce the supremacy of white middle-class values and norms on all students, rather than stressing the pluralism of the society.

Innovation. In addition to preserving and disseminating past and present cultural knowledge and teaching skills, schools also function to generate new knowledge. This is especially true of higher education, which consists of seeking new ideas, techniques, or inventions to facilitate human life. Genetic engineering, cures for cancer and other diseases, as well as many unknown factors of human behavior are all pursued in university laboratories.

Latent Functions   An unintended function of education is the reinforcement of a society's stratification system. Schools sort students into different categories, in theory according to ability and talent, so that each may fulfill his or her potential as a productive and creative person. The unintended effect on this process is the assignment of middle-class students to academic, college preparatory courses and lower-class and minority ones to general and vocational study programs. The issue is of course not so simple: Numerous reasons exist why middle-class students are better prepared to attend college and go on to professions. But schools do appear to play their part in perpetuating this reality.

Schools also perform custodial functions. With children in school, both parents are able to work. The general acceptance of this function and the growing demand for child-care centers to accommodate younger children after school indicates the general belief that the state should contribute toward the care of its future citizens.

The bringing together of students for long periods of time, some for better than twenty years, contributes to the formation of youth subcultures, which occasionally may become deviant or countercultural. All exert great influence on the young and can create generational conflicts. At the same time, such interaction among young adults often initiates relationships that lead to romance and marriage.

Finally, education affects attitudes. Studies indicate that high-school graduates are more tolerant of political and social nonconformity than those who fail to complete their secondary education. College graduates in turn are more tolerant than high-school graduates. Education thus wields a positive effect on such values as egalitarianism, democratic principles, and tolerance of minority and opposition views, though we do not know as yet whether these effects remain permanent.

The Conflict View of Education

Recalling that conflict theorists view society as experiencing perpetual turmoil, with a variety of groups constantly at odds, one would suspect them to view education in a similar light. Conflict theorists predictably charge that the educational system is used by the elite to manipulate the masses and maintain its power in society (Bowles and Gintis, 1976; Collins, 1979). In particular they claim that the real purpose of education is to allocate a given social status to people. To that purpose, a hidden curriculum exists alongside the visible one, a subtle instruction in the arts of competitiveness, obedience, and patriotism, values elites need to imbue in those being prepared to fill certain jobs.

Thus the ethics of those in power are passed on uncritically in schools: the supremacy of the United States and its founders and leaders is stressed, and the capitalist system which allows citizens to accumulate wealth and pass it on to their heirs is praised and inculcated. Furthermore, not all students are taught the same values. Those in schools attended by upper-class children are taught the importance of being civic-minded, of voting, and of participating in the democratic process. Those in schools attended primarily by lower-class children are instructed in the efficacy of the American government, with little mention of the importance of power and group struggles in the political process (Litt, 1963, 69–75). Minimum information is revealed that would show other societies and socioeconomic systems in a positive light. Conformity is instilled by stressing obedience to rules: standing in line, raising one's hand to talk, and so on. Finally, competition is valued, and those who compete the hardest— getting better grades, more attention, and special privileges—excel in the system, while those who fail to compete may be labeled as slow and kept back.

Such competition is also unfair because it reflects the norms of the middle class. Teachers, generally drawn from this class, thus favor students whose socialization accords with their own values and make use of teaching methods understandable to middle-class students, but which may be lost on lower-class, ethnic, or minority pupils.

The upshot of these true functions of the educational system, according to conflict theorists, is that the credentials, diplomas, and degrees conferred by schools on students who have performed well in their systems are not really necessary in the execution of most jobs. *Credentialism,* the practice of requiring degrees for certain high-paying and prestigious jobs, is a way of ensuring that only those with families of a high social position remain in that social stratum. Credentials are said to represent artificial barriers erected by those in power to ensure that certain others (such as the lower classes and minorities) do not enter high-paying, prestigious occupations. One sociologist has contributed the insight that levels of education (high-school graduate, college graduate, Ph.D.) in themselves constitute social statuses, giving the educational institution the power to grant such statuses to individuals and teach them the appropriate roles (Meyer, 1977, 55–77). So strong is the socialization schools impart with regard to statuses and roles that its influence does not end when the student leaves school: Rather, individuals continue to act the roles connected with their educational status throughout adult life, regardless of occupational statuses attained. Finally, education actually creates new occupations and installs selected people within them, increasing the number of specialized and elite positions. For example, economists, sociologists, geneticists, and football coaches did not exist before universities implemented these specialized bodies of knowledge and forms of athletics. Such actions have helped create more positions at the top of the occupational ladder while restricting those at the bottom.

As usual, functionalist and conflict theorists view the same reality from opposite sides and thus arrive at different conclusions. The truth is likely to lie somewhere in the middle; that is, education certainly performs some very positive functions in society but at the same time may create negative repercussions for certain groups.

Education and Social Class

As mentioned earlier, the United States set out on a course of educating each of its members, and in some respects it succeeded in its goal. Almost 90 percent of Americans now graduate from high school, 50 percent begin some form of education beyond high school, and 30 percent complete a four-year college degree. Mass education, however, does not mean equal education, nor do large numbers graduating from high school and attending college necessarily signify high intellectual achievement.

The dilemma faced by American schools involves credentialism, the need for conferred degrees as access to the professions and other high-paying jobs. Courses of study leading to such degrees are not equally attainable to all students. Differences in intellectual abilities naturally affect the outcome of some educational careers. But perhaps of greater impact are factors related to social class and race that tend to impede the progress of certain students.

For a variety of reasons schools seem unable to work to the advantage of all enrolled. One is the extremely bureaucratized structure of American schools, which often alienates those from lower-class and minority homes. The stress on order and regularity, on silence and lesson plans and staying in line is further sharpened by the attitudes of teachers, most of whom hail from middle-class backgrounds, and who often subtly communicate to lower-class students the unlikelihood of their academic success equaling that of their classmates from higher social classes. This self-fulfilling prophecy usually comes true.

The extensive testing that students continually undergo, although supposedly adjusted to be objective and fair, frequently discriminates against lower-class children, whose culture and experience do not prepare them for competitive test-taking. Such tests are generally given in standard English and deal with subject matter more familiar to middle-class students. Since test scores are given much weight when it comes to channeling students into either college preparatory or vocational programs, ultimately a student's future is affected. Finally, students who consistently test low acquire a low self-image, coming to believe that they are not intelligent and cannot achieve academically. Again, the self-fulfilling prophecy tends to prove them right.

It must be emphasized that neither administrators nor teachers purposely or consciously discriminate against certain students. The nature of the system is simply self-perpetuating. Teachers, successful products of these schools, find it difficult to know how to reach students from backgrounds where education does not hold significant value, where books, magazines, or newspapers are unknown, where parents are perennially frustrated and worried about money problems, where homes provide no quiet corners in which to study, and most importantly, where neither hope nor expectation exists that a successful school career will lead to a better life.

The Role of the Family   The most important determinant of scholastic success is the family. Familial values, attitudes, and behavior are directly related to future academic success for several reasons. First, middle- and upper-class families foster the viewpoint that occupational success is desirable and attainable through educational achievement. Parental and peer pressure to do well in school is strong. Teachers, too, may unconsciously express higher expectations with regard to these students' success. Family backgrounds of students from higher social classes generally include college-educated parents, homes filled with books and magazines, and activities such as trips to theaters and museums, and riding, music, or dance lessons; in short what is generally considered an enriched environment. Not the least consideration is the fact that middle- and upper-class families can afford high tuitions and room and board at prestigious universities.

Students from lower classes, on the other hand, often have little experience with the collegiate scene. Teachers and guidance counselors sometimes fail to supply them with necessary information for college admission, assuming these students will not wish to continue their education. Values and expectations of lower-class families and peer groups are not on the whole conducive to academic success. Lower-class families, for instance, aware of their lack of opportunities, value education less as an avenue toward upward mobility than as a training ground for the habits of conformity, obedience to rules, and neat grooming in preparation for blue-collar jobs where orders must be taken from a variety of superiors. At the lower socioeconomic end, families also tend to be larger, with both parents and older siblings at work most of the day. Verbal skills of the parents are probably limited since they are likely to have interrupted their educations sometime in their teens. Most of the expensive trappings of the enriched environment are lacking. None of these features promotes success in the academic portion of schooling.

Education, Race, and Ethnicity   Since certain racial and ethnic groups still generally remain at the lower end of the stratification system, they can be assumed to have encountered less success in their scholastic experience. With the exception of Asian Americans and Jews, who have taken full advantage of the upward mobility made possible by becoming credentialed professionals, most current minorities have not been well served by American schools.

Initially, schools were segregated because students attended neighborhood schools, and neighborhoods were segregated. Blacks and Hispanics who lived in inner-city neighborhoods and attended inner-city schools generally completed fewer years of school and obtained lower grades and lower achievement and IQ test scores than suburban white students. To find out why, sociologist James Coleman and a group of associates undertook an exhaustive research project to compare the facilities of schools in white and black neighborhoods (1966). They found that the schools differed little in physical facilities: They were approximately the same age, possessed the same library and laboratory equipment, and spent the same amount of money per pupil. In addition, teacher qualifications and class size were similar. Coleman and his associates concluded that variations in achievement between white and black and Hispanic students were primarily accounted for by family background and the fact that minority students had little sense of control over their environment. Coleman also found that black students attending school with whites in a harmonious desegregated situation exhibited improvement in their school performance. He speculated that this pattern was due to a middle-class atmosphere which permeated the schools and exerted a positive influence on minority students without lowering the performance of whites.

Chiefly as a result of this research, busing to achieve racial integration was instituted in a number of large urban districts. In some, busing has been successful. In others, it has been greeted with hostility and remains a source of tension.

A new study by Coleman (1981) concluded that private schools do a better job of educating students than public ones, and that Roman Catholic schools in particular come closest to the American ideal of similar education for all. The reason that students learn more in private than public schools (regardless of background factors such as family income, parents' education, race, number of siblings, and whether the mother worked while the child was in elementary school) is that these are more apt to provide the safe, disciplined, and well-ordered environment that is conducive to learning.

Education and Social Change   Education has been hailed as the foremost step to upward mobility by both social scientists and the public at large. Increasingly, however, the optimistic notion of education as the gateway to upward mobility has been strained. For one thing, factors other than education exert just as powerful an influence on the jobs people take. Family background rather than the amount of education obtained is responsible for more sons entering the same occupation as their fathers (Jencks, 1979). In short, although highly educated people indeed earn more than those with little education, many other factors distinguish the rich from the poor. Even though schools represent a way out of poverty for some, they also reflect social inequality and in many ways reinforce it.

Success and Failure of Education   Judged by the number of high-school and college graduates, by the number of Ph.D.s awarded annually, and by the number of people (about one-fourth) currently enrolled in some kind of school, American education appears to be a smashing success. Yet, judged by the sliding SAT scores, by the high dropout rates of black and Hispanic students, by the functional or total illiteracy of many who have gone through the system, by the complaints from colleges that entering students do not possess even the minimal tools to ensure successful completion of courses of study, and by criticism from the marketplace that high-school and even some college graduates lack the skills and information to perform adequate jobs, American education stands accused of failure.

Through the years, schools have attempted to respond to such criticism by instituting a variety of reforms. Unfortunately, most have met with little success, perhaps as a result of poor unity among educators regarding the goals of education; many reforms have even worked at cross-purposes. The cry of the 1980s is "Back to basics," as pressures from the labor market mount, insisting that new employees upgrade such basic skills as reading, writing, and arithmetic.

In the past two or three decades, schools have attempted to contend with the lack of background and poor motivation of students. But a decreased dropout rate accomplished by lowering standards and passing students through the system despite little actual learning is no advantage to those unable to obtain jobs with their meaningless high-school diplomas. The greatest challenge continues to face American schools: to make universal mass education a reality.

The Chapter in Brief

The culture that each society produces becomes a blueprint for the behavior of each new generation. An important element of culture is the **institution,** a collection of habits or traditional pursuits that eventually crystallizes into a pattern of behavior. Institutions develop around certain essential human needs. The five pivotal human institutions are the family, religion, education, the economy, and government.

The family is the oldest of societal institutions. Most of its functions in modern industrial society concern the control of reproduction and sex, the socialization of the young, and the provision of affection and companionship.

As a result of modernization the family has undergone changes in form, becoming **nuclear** and more egalitarian, with **monogamy** as the preferred form of marriage. Although marriage partners are not chosen by parents, as they are in traditional societies, even in urban industrial societies mate selection is not random. It is influenced by endogamy, or marriage within one's group, and homogamy, marriage to partners with similar traits. In most marriages, partners are of the same race, religion, and social class, as well as similar in age, physical appearance, education, and residence.

The nuclear family is better adapted to life in urban industrial societies than is the **extended** family since it allows members more freedom to pursue upward social mobility. Its isolation from the support system of an extended family and the intensity of the emotions constrained within it, however, make it particularly susceptible to conflict and disintegration. Divorce and desertion are two prominent results, as are child and mate abuse. Divorce is also a corollary of liberalized sexual norms and changing attitudes toward marriage. As the need to produce several children declines, the focus of marriage shifts from the duty to marry and replenish society to a desire for affection and companionship.

Religion has been viewed as an attempt by humans to explain a reality they did not understand. Émile Durkheim proposes that religion deals with the **sacred,** and the model of its beliefs and practices is society itself. Functionalists have incorporated this viewpoint, assuming that the functions of religion include relief of frustration, explanation of the physical world, support of societal norms and values, provision of a means for repentance, and help during critical stages of life. Conflict theorists view religion as a divisive ideology used by the elite to manipulate the masses.

Religions display beliefs, rituals, and organization. Religious organizations are divided into **church, sect,** and **cult.** Religion in America is **denominational,** and the methods of the marketplace are used to recruit and hold members.

Modern trends in religion include secularization and bureaucratization, leading religious organizations to resemble other voluntary associations that deal with mental health, family togetherness, and social welfare. A reaction to the subsequent lack of spirituality may be seen in the emergence of a number of sectarian movements of a pentecostal and evangelical nature.

The transmission of knowledge from one generation to the next is the primary function of education. Education also serves to recruit and prepare students for social and occupational roles in the outside world, to integrate into the wider culture its various subcultures, and to generate new knowledge through research. Schools, finally, perform custodial functions, contribute to the formation of a youth subculture, and sometimes effectively change attitudes.

The best predictor of academic success is socioeconomic status, a function of the family. This does not entail a direct economic relationship but rather depends upon such factors as family life-styles, styles of communication, values and expectations of parents, and so on. Middle-class families prepare their children for successful school experiences where they are taught by middle-class teachers with similar cultural goals and expectations. Life in the lower-class family is not likely to adequately prepare a child for a successful school experience, and since most minorities still predominantly fall into lower-class backgrounds, they too have been least successful in academic pursuits.

Although education has been considered the gateway to upward mobility—and for many has proved so—the recent increase in the number of high-school and college graduates has begun to alter this relationship. Many other elements appear to contribute to the kinds of jobs people acquire; a rethinking of our educational goals is thus in order.

Terms to Remember

Church A religious organization that is institutionalized and well integrated into the socioeconomic life of a society, and in which participation by members is routine.

Consanguine Another term for the extended family. Also, the way parents are related to their children, i.e. by blood ties.

Cult The least conventional and least institutionalized of religious organizations, consisting of groups of followers clustered around a leader whose teachings differ substantially from the doctrines of the church or denomination.

Denomination A subdivision of the church that is considered as equally valid as the church.

Extended family A form of the family consisting of the nucleus— two spouses and their children—and other blood relatives together with their marriage partners and children. Common in preindustrial societies.

Incest taboo An almost universal prohibition of sexual relations between mothers and sons, fathers and daughters, sisters and brothers, and other relatives as specified by society.

Institution A pattern of behavior (culture complex) that has developed around a central human need.

Monogamy The most common form of marriage, consisting of the union of one man with one woman.

Nuclear or conjugal family A form of the family consisting of two spouses and their children living together as a unit.

Polygamy A form of marriage in which multiple spouses—either wives or husbands—cohabit as units.

Profane The objects and events of everyday life that are common, usual, explainable, and repetitive.

Sacred   Objects, events, or persons distinct from the profane, that is, uncommon, unusual, unexplained, mysterious, powerful, and therefore deserving of reverence and respect. Religion deals with the sacred.

Sect   A religious organization, characterized by a revolutionary movement away from the church or denomination, that stresses the spirit, rather than the letter, of religion.

Suggestions for Further Reading

Berger, Brigitte, and Peter L. Berger.   1983. *The war over the family: Capturing the middle ground.* Garden City, N. Y.: Anchor/Doubleday. Two well-known sociologists critique both the liberal and the conservative approaches to the family institution.

Blumstein, Philip, and Pepper Schwartz.   1983. *American couples: Money, work, and sex.* New York: Morrow. A wide-ranging survey of American couples, mostly white and middle class, who express their approach to contemporary relationships.

Clark, Reginald M.   1983. *Family life and school achievement: Why poor black children succeed or fail.* Chicago: University of Chicago Press. A study purporting to show that race and poverty can be overcome and that success in school can be achieved in spite of those hostile variables.

Douglas, Mary, and Steven M. Tipton, eds.   1983. *Religion and America: Spirituality in a secular age.* Boston: Beacon. A number of essays by social scientists who discuss current trends in American religion.

Goodland, John I.   1984. *A place called school: Prospects for the future.* New York: McGraw-Hill. A number of research findings are presented to illustrate the status of contemporary American public schools.

Kozol, Jonathan.   1985. *Illiterate America.* Garden City, N. Y.: Anchor/Doubleday. This book focuses on the amazing extent of functional illiteracy in the United States, its causes, and its effects.

Macklin, Eleanor D., and Roger H. Rubin, eds.   1983. *Contemporary families and alternative lifestyles.* Beverly Hills, Calif.: Sage. A collection of readings illustrating the large variety of current alternative arrangements to the traditional family.

Families in Trouble

ELEANOR HOLMES NORTON

In times of rapid social change, institutions take the brunt of the disorganization of the transitional period. In this generation, although all institutions have felt some shock waves, the family has been at the epicenter of the quake. The author of the following article argues that the disruption of the black family is only an exaggerated microcosm of what has happened to the American family in general.

What would society be like if the family found it difficult to perform its most basic functions? We are beginning to find out. Half of all marriages in this country end in divorce, and half of all children will spend a significant period with only one parent.

Startling and unsettling changes have already occurred in black family life, especially among the poor. Since the 1970s, birthrates among blacks have declined, but two out of every three black women having a first child are single, compared to one out of every eight white women. Today, 57% of black children in this country are born to single women. Why are female-headed households multiplying now, when there is less discrimination and poverty than a couple of generations ago, when black family life was stronger?

The disruption of the black family today is, in exaggerated microcosm, a reflection of what has happened to American family life in general. Public anxiety has mounted with the near-doubling of the proportion of white children living with one parent (from 9% to 17%) since 1970. Single parents of all backgrounds are feeling the pressures—the sheer economics of raising children primarily on the depressed income of the mother (a large component of the so-called "feminization of poverty"); the psychological and physical toll when one person, however advantaged, must be both mother and father; and the effects on children.

While families headed by women have often proved just as effective as two-parent families in raising children, the most critical danger facing female-headed households is poverty. Seventy percent of black children under the age of 18 who live in female-headed families are being brought up in poverty. In 1983, the median income for such households was $7,999, compared to almost $32,107 for two-parent families of all races when both spouses worked. Without the large increase in female-headed households, black family income would have increased by 11% in the 1970s. Instead, it fell by 5%.

As recently as the early 1960s, 75% of black households were husband-and-wife families. The figure represents remarkable continuity—it is about the same as those reported in census records from the late 19th century. Indeed, the evidence suggests that most slaves grew up in two-parent families reinforced by ties to large extended families.

The sharp rise in female-headed households involves mostly those with young children and began in the mid-1960s. The phenomenon—by no means a trend that permeates the entire black community—affects a significant portion of young people today, many of whom are separated economically, culturally, and socially from the black mainstream. They have been raised in the worst of the rapidly deteriorating ghettos of the 1960s, 1970s, and

1980s, in cities or neighborhoods that lost first the white and then the black middle and working classes. Drugs, crime, and pimps took over many of the old communities.

The emergence of single women as the primary guardians of the majority of black children is a pronounced departure that began to take shape after World War II. Ironically, the women and children—the most visible manifestations of the change—do not provide the key to the transformation. The breakdown begins with working-class black men, whose loss of function in the post–World War II economy has led directly to their loss of function in the family.

In the booming post–World War I economy, black men with few skills could find work. Even the white South, which denied the black man a place in its wage economy, could not deprive him of an economic role in the farm family. The poorest, most meanly treated sharecropper was at the center of the work it took to produce the annual crop.

As refugees from the South, the generation of World War I migrants differed in crucial respects from the World War II generation. The World War I arrivals were enthusiastic, voluntary migrants, poor in resources but frequently middle-class in aspiration. They were at the bottom of a society that denied them the right to move up very far, but they got a foothold in a burgeoning economy.

Family stability was the rule. According to a 1925 study of black families in New York City, five out of six children under the age of 6 lived with both parents. In the nation a small middle class emerged, later augmented by the jobs generated by World War II, service in the armed forces, and the postwar prosperity that sometimes filtered down to better-trained urban blacks.

Today's inner-city blacks were not a part of these historical processes. Some are the victims of the flight of manufacturing jobs. Others were part of the last wave of Southern migrants or their offspring, arriving in the 1950s and 1960s. They often migrated not because of new opportunities but because of the evaporation of old ones. Mechanized farming made their labor superfluous in agriculture, but unlike the blacks of earlier generations and European immigrants, later black migrants were also superfluous in the postwar cities as manufacturing work for the less-skilled and poorly educated declined. Today's post-industrial society, demanding sophisticated preparation and training, has only exacerbated these problems.

This permanent, generational joblessness is at the core of the meaning of the American ghetto. An entire stratum of black men, many of them young, no longer performs its historic role in supporting a family. Many are unemployed because of the absence of jobs, or unemployable because their ghetto origins leave them unprepared for the job market. Others have adapted to the demands of the ghetto—the hustle, the crime, the drugs. But the skills necessary to survive in the streets are least acceptable in the outside world.

The macho role cultivated in the ghetto makes it difficult for many black men, unable to earn a respectable living, to form households and assume the roles of husband and father. Generationally entrenched joblessness joined with the predatory underground economy form the basis of a marginal lifestyle. Relationships without the commitments of husband and father result.

The transformation in poor black communities goes beyond poverty. These deep changes are anchored in a pervasively middle-class society that associates manhood with money. Shocking figures show a long, steep, and apparently permanent decline in black men's participation in the labor force, even at peak earning ages. In 1948, before the erosion of unskilled and semiskilled city and rural jobs had become pronounced, black male participation in the labor force was 87%, almost a full point higher than that of white males. In the generation since 1960, however, black men have experienced a dramatic loss of jobs—from 74% employment to 55% in 1982, according to the Center for the Study of Social Policy in Washington, D.C. While white male employment slipped in that period, much of the white decline is attributed to early retirement. Since 1960, the black male population over 18 has doubled, but the number employed has lagged dramatically.

Yet, the remedy for ghetto conditions is not as simple as providing necessities and opportunities. Just as it took a complex of social forces to produce ghetto conditions, it will take a range of remedies to dissolve them. The primary actors unavoidably are the government and the black community itself.

The government is deeply implicated in black family problems. Its laws enforced slavery before the Civil War and afterward created and sanctioned pervasive public and private discrimination. The effects on the black family continue to this day. Given the same opportunities as others, blacks would almost certainly have sustained the powerful family traditions they brought with them from Africa, where society itself is organized around family.

Quite apart from its historical role, the government cannot avoid present responsibility. Although programs capable of penetrating ghetto conditions have proved elusive, the current government posture of disengagement is folly. With the poor growing at a faster rate than the middle class, the prospect is that succeeding generations will yield more, not fewer, disadvantaged blacks. An American version of a lumpen proletariat (the so-called underclass), without work and without hope, existing at the margins of society, could bring down the great cities, sap resources and strength from the entire society and, lacking the usual means to survive, prey upon those who possess them.

Perhaps the greatest gap in corrective strategies has been the failure to focus on prevention. Remedies for deep-rooted problems—from teenage pregnancy to functional illiteracy—are bound to fail when we leave the water running while we struggle to check the overflow. A primary incubator for ghetto problems is the poor, female-headed household. Stopping its proliferation would prevent a spectrum of often-intractable social and economic problems.

Remedies often focus at opposite ends—either on the provision of income or of services. Neither seems wholly applicable to entrenched ghetto conditions. Public assistance alone, leaving people in the same defeatist environment, may reinforce the status quo. The service orientation has been criticized for using a disproportionate amount of the available resources relative to the results obtained.

More appropriate solutions may lie between income and service strategies. Programs are likely to be more successful if they provide a rigorous progression through a series of steps leading to "graduation." This process, including a period of weaning from public assistance, might prove more successful in achieving personal independence. Such programs would be far more disciplined than services to the poor generally have been. They would concentrate on changing lifestyles as well as imparting skills and education.

The welfare program—a brilliant New

Deal invention now stretched to respond to a range of problems never envisioned for it—often deepens dependence and lowers self-esteem. Reconceived, public-assistance program could reach single mothers and offer them vehicles to self-sufficiency. The counterparts of young women on welfare are working downtown or attending college. Far from foreclosing such opportunities because a woman has a child, public assistance should be converted from the present model of passive maintenance to a program built around education or work and prospective graduation.

Studies of the hard-core unemployed have shown women on welfare to be the most desirous of, open to, and successful with training and work. Some, especially with young children, will remain at home, but most want work or training because it is the only way out of the welfare life. Some promising experiments in work and welfare are under way in such cities as San Diego and Baltimore. Gainful employment, even in public jobs for those unaccommodated by the private sector, would have beneficial effects beyond earning a living. Jobs and training would augment self-esteem by exposing women to the values and discipline associated with work, allowing them to pass on to their children more than their own disadvantages.

The ghetto, more than most circumscribed cultures, seeks to perpetuate itself and is ruthless in its demand for conformity. However, it contains the institutions of the larger society—schools, churches, community groups. With minor additional resources, schools, for example, could incorporate more vigorous and focused ways to prevent teenage pregnancy. If pregnancy occurs, girls could be motivated to remain in school, even after childbirth, thus allowing an existing institution to accomplish what training programs in later life do more expensively and with greater difficulty.

Schools and other community institutions also need to become much more aggressive with boys on the true meaning and responsibilities of manhood, and the link between manhood and family. Otherwise, many boys meet little resistance to the ghetto message that manhood means sex but not responsibility.

Most important, nothing can substitute for or have a greater impact than the full-scale involvement of the black community. Respect for the black family tradition compels black initiative. Today, blacks are responding. Many black organizations are already involved. In 1983, the country's major black leaders endorsed a frank statement of the problems of the black family and a call for solutions. The statement, published by the Joint Center for Political Studies, a black research center in Washington, represented the first consensus view by black leadership on the problems of the black family. Significantly, it went beyond a call for government help, stressing the need for black leadership and community efforts.

With the increase in the number of black public officials, many black mayors, legislators, and appointed officials control some of the resources that could help shape change. Although they cannot redesign the welfare system by themselves, for example, some are in a position to experiment with model projects that could lead to more workable programs—such as supplementing welfare grants with training or work opportunities for single mothers; promoting family responsibility and pregnancy prevention for boys and girls through local institutions, and encouraging single teenage parents to finish school.

The new black middle class, a product of the same period that saw the weakening of the black family, still has roots in the ghetto through relatives and friends. From churches, Girl Scout troops, and settlement houses to civil rights organizations, Boys Clubs and athletic teams, the work of family reinforcement can be shared widely. Most important is passing on the enduring values that form the central content of the black American heritage: hard work, education, respect for family and, notwithstanding the denial of personal opportunity, achieving a better life for children.

The Economy and Government

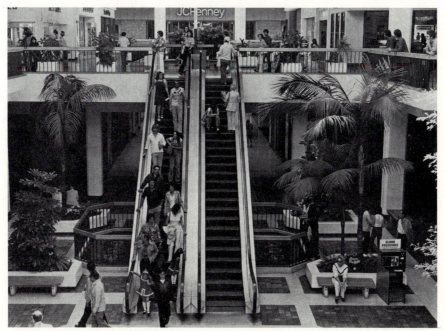

A fundamental prerequisite of human biological organisms is a daily supply of water and food and some covering and shelter from the elements. Achieving these is a fairly simple endeavor when people live in small groups of a dozen or so and when good sources can be found in nearby forests and streams. Certainly some division of tasks takes place under such circumstances, the men hunting small game, the women gathering berries and seeds, the children trying to catch slow-moving fish in a stream; but when there is little to do and still fewer items to divide, very little conflict ensues as to who does and who gets what.

But what happens when the groups become hundreds, then thousands? What if food is grown, not simply found? Who determines what crops to sow, where to plant them, how to divide the harvest? Who decides what is to be done with the surplus? Who ensures conflicts between neighbors do not end in bloodshed? Who makes provision for the defense of the group and its territory from hostile strangers who wish to usurp it?

The answers to these questions should be obvious to those students who have read this far. The growing size and complexity of groups necessitate the development of organizational patterns to cope with the need for a steady supply of food and shelter and for order and defense. Eventually, these patterns crystallize into the institutions of the economy and government while social change transforms the societies from Gemeinschaft to Gesellschaft groups.

The Economy

Certain elements essential to human survival are freely available: the air we breathe, for instance. But food, shelter, and protective coverings have been scarce resources in most societies. In some geographical locations they occur more abundantly than in others, but in all locations, efforts must be made to accumulate adequate supplies for survival. The patterns of behavior that have emerged over time to help obtain scarce resources needed for survival make up the institution of the economy, one of the five pivotal human institutions.

The primary function of the economy is to provide a blueprint demonstrating to members of a society how to produce, distribute, exchange, and consume the resources available to them in the most efficient way. The economy, then, is in essence a system of behavior through which members adapt to their environment by making decisions and choices aimed at satisfying their needs and combating the problem of scarcity.

The first decision a society must make concerns the need for production. This may involve hunting and bringing an animal back to camp; sowing and harvesting a field; or turning a bolt on the assembly line. Societies must somehow motivate their members to perform these tasks in order that they may eat, cover themselves, and enjoy a safe place in which to be protected from the elements.

The next decision concerns the need to distribute what has been produced. When no surplus is involved, this is a relatively easy task: Whatever is produced is equally distributed and consumed. But once a surplus is created, the question "Who gets what, and how?" becomes more difficult to resolve. Without fail, some will accumulate more than others. This gives them an extra edge, making them stronger or healthier or wealthier than the rest, and their advantage is multiplied when such excess is passed on to their children. Eventually, the result is a stratified society in which methods of distribution include barter, gifts, dowries, monetary systems, wages, investments, and so on.

The final issue in the economy is consumption. Consumption, again, presents no problems in simple societies: What little is produced is immediately distributed and consumed. In more complex societies, however, people tend to develop needs not strictly related to survival. They crave more variety in food, more colorful clothing, more comfortable or even luxurious housing. In industrial societies, moreover, consumption is encouraged since it makes the economy grow; however, on occasion, consumption must be limited when certain resources become temporarily scarce (as when gasoline had to be rationed).

The study of the structure, functions, and general operation of the economy belongs to the discipline of another social science, economics. However, because the economy consists of the interactions of people, and because the institution itself is interdependent with other institutions, sociologists are equally involved in its analysis. In particular, sociologists examine the various types of economic systems: the size, functions, and power of the formal organizations in which economic activities take place; and occupations, work, and leisure, as these affect members of a society.

Economic Decision Making

As noted above, the fundamental economic problem facing every society is the scarcity of resources necessary for survival. Even in developed nations, although basic needs for food and shelter are met for the majority, other needs, some artificially inspired, are not. In fact, these social needs seem to be never ending; no economy has ever been able to satisfy them all.

The basic questions economic systems in every society must decide include the following:

1. Which commodities should be produced, and in what quantities?

2. How should these commodities be produced with greatest efficiency?

3. For whom should these commodities be produced, and how should they be distributed?

Different societies solve these questions in different ways. In some, solutions rely entirely on custom and tradition. Specific crops are grown or articles manufactured simply because of long-established patterns. In others, decisions are made by command. A ruler or body of representatives decides that such and such crops will be grown or such and such articles made. Such rulings may also be based on tradition, or may be enforced for reasons of personal aggrandizement, or even because they are perceived (or alleged) to be beneficial to the community. Finally, in some societies, answers to the questions above are decided according to the machinations of a market that depends on supply and demand, on prices, profits, and losses. For example, in these so-called free-market, private-enterprise economies, if people need and want shoes (resulting in a great demand), the price of shoes goes up. This means more profits for manufacturers, who then work doubly hard to produce more shoes. Eventually, the supply meets the demand. When the quantity of shoes exceeds the need, the price goes down. At this point, manufacturers no longer rake in profits, and so they slow down their production of shoes.

Very few modern economies are based entirely on one of the systems described above. Most are a mixture of two, even all three. In the American economy, for instance, both private and public (governmental) organizations exercise economic control. Moreover, supply and demand never function in as clear-cut a manner as the example above might suggest. Ways of creating demand and limiting supply to keep prices artificially high are sometimes enforced. Both the market and the command system are used to make economic decisions in Western industrial societies.

Basic Elements of the Economy

The goods and services produced in each society derive from resources found naturally within it. (Of course, when barter and trade come into being, resources may be imported from and exchanged between other societies.) *Resources* are defined as everything needed for the production of goods and services. They include human energy used in producing goods and services as well as material objects. In economic terms, human energy is referred to as *labor*. Material objects may be found in nature or made by people. Those found in nature, such as land, minerals, and water, are collectively called *land* by economists. Those made by humans, such as machinery, factories, shoes, and pencils, are known as *capital*. Labor, land, and capital, in addition to *entrepreneurship,* are the *factors of production* and form the basic elements that must be combined in the production of goods and services. For example, when building a house, individuals are impelled by the spirit of entrepreneurship to use human energy—labor—to put a structure on a lot—land—using both natural material objects—wood and stone—and human-made material objects—nails, hammers, bricks, and so on. In economic terms, the result is a product which can be personally used or sold or traded for another product.

In addition to these basic factors, *technology, time,* and *efficiency* play important parts in production. The greater a society's skill and knowledge (its technology), the more effective its production of goods and services. Time is an economic resource that is scarce and precious: If production is to be effective, it must occur within reasonable time limits. If it takes five years to produce one hundred cars in a society of over two hundred million inhabitants,

Once a society experiences surpluses, it can barter and trade with others, increasing its resources and the standard of living of its members.

those cars will be of little value: The need is for immediate transportation. Efficiency, the ability to obtain the highest output from a given combination of resources in the least amount of time, is also an important factor.

Resources are versatile; they can be put to many uses. Land can be used to grow crops or for building factories, apartments, or shopping centers. Labor can be employed to harvest crops, to develop complex data systems, or to teach. But resources are also finite. Once used up or destroyed, they cannot always be replaced. Societies must therefore conserve resources and try to replace those depleted through production.

Contemporary Economic Systems

Economic institutions constitute both social and cultural systems: social systems because people within them hold specific statuses and play corresponding roles, and cultural systems because patterns of behavior, values, and expectations emerge around a system of production. Such patterns are then made legitimate by a philosophy or ideology workers accept as valid. In modern industrial societies, the three prevailing economic patterns of behavior and legitimating ideologies are capitalism, socialism, and communism.

A society's economic system is largely determined by its concept of property. *Property* is defined as the rights an owner holds to an object as compared with the rights of those who are not its owners. The concept of property arose in response to the scarcity of resources and the profitability of ownership. In most societies, ownership takes one of three forms: communal, private, or public. In the communal form, property belongs to the community. Any member may use but may not own it. In the *private* form, property belongs to the individual, and unless permission is given may not be used by others. In the *public* form of ownership, the state or officially recognized political authority owns property in the name of the public. Schools and highways, parks and public transportation systems are generally publicly owned.

Although the manner in which property is owned determines a society's economic system, no group is limited strictly to one form. All recognize some private ownership, and a degree of public ownership is essential to all. The extent to which one or another form dominates serves to differentiate one system from another.

Capitalism

Capitalism is based on the premise that private ownership of property and the means of production and distribution lead to maximum efficiency in economic functioning and ultimately serve the best interests of all. In a capitalist system, resources are considered the private property of individuals and families. The purpose of owning property is to invest it and, through work and enterprise, accumulate more; that is, to make a profit. This is accomplished by supplying the best product at the least cost to the greatest number of people; that is, through competition. The cornerstone of capitalism, then, includes private property, profit, and competition.

The capitalist system, as described in its early years, was intended to function according to a mechanism known as the *invisible hand*. This term was coined by Scottish professor of philosophy Adam Smith, in his treatise *The Wealth of Nations* (1776). The invisible hand referred to actions in the marketplace derived from individual self-interest, which Smith believed to be a natural human sentiment. The pursuit of self-interest in the long run theoretically benefits the entire society. For instance, members of society require certain goods: food, clothing, and appliances, to name a few. To satisfy these needs, manufacturers produce food, clothing, and stoves and refrigerators, but only insofar as they can make a profit. In order to do so, they develop better and less expensive methods of production and manufacture only those goods for which a great demand exists. When demand for an item slackens, they discontinue production. This pattern has come to be known as the law of supply and demand. In turn, consumers purchase the choicest merchandise at the cheapest prices, so that manufacturers who do not seek efficient means of production are unable to sell their products. In short, competition and supply and demand, in the absence of government intervention or control, presumably lead to the greatest good for the greatest number, or, according to Smith, the most desirable system of economic progress. The system was referred to as the free and open market, and the noninterventionism advocated by Smith has come to be known as the laissez-faire (leave it alone) policy.

The free market has never functioned as perfectly as Smith envisioned it. Today, his concept of the free market is known as classical capitalism and has long been discarded in favor of a *mixed economy* in which government intervention plays a substantial role. However, the principles of self-interest and competition survive as ideals of economic behavior in a capitalist system.

Socialism

Socialism is an economic system whose premises differ quite radically from those of capitalism. Whereas the capitalist system is chiefly concerned with the attainment of individual success and comfort, socialism maintains a preoccupation with the welfare of society as a unit and the belief that all members are entitled to the necessities of life. Individuals are not left to their own devices in the competition for survival. Accordingly, in socialist societies, most property is publicly owned, and the government levies high taxes to help redistribute wealth more equitably, basically taking from those who have accumulated wealth and giving to those who have not been able to. Property may be privately owned, but only if such ownership does not deprive others in any way. Essential industries are owned and operated by the government in the name of all, and the government controls and directs the economy in general.

Long-range plans of socialist economies include the coordinated planning of all sectors of the economy through government regulation of industry, agriculture, commerce, and the professions. Production in such an economy is not undertaken for profit but in response to the needs of the people. Workers and professionals are expected to be guided not by the profit motive but by the desire to serve society and express themselves through their work. The ultimate objective is total redistribution of income.

Democratic Socialism A socialist economy occurring within a democratic political system is referred to as democratic socialism. Great Britain and the Scandinavian countries are prominent examples of democratic socialist societies. These societies, also called welfare states, have no interest in using revolutionary means to attain power. Rather, they prefer to work within a democratic system, generally parliamentary in nature, using the electoral system to obtain governmental representation. Economic policies in these societies are implemented by those elected to public office rather than by the owners of the means of production. In addition, ownership of the means of production does not necessarily lie in the hands of the state. A mixed economy, in which businesses are both privately and publicly owned, is a more common feature of welfare states (a system frequently referred to as welfare capitalism).

A number of enterprises remain in private hands, but are forced through government intervention to be responsive to the nation's welfare.

Communism

Two of the goals of socialism—total government control of the economy and total income redistribution—also represent the goals of communist societies. (True **communism** remains a theoretical political and economic order.) Such societies are determined to eliminate the profit motive entirely as well as economic individualism of any sort. Members are encouraged to think and labor for the collectivity and strive for the even distribution of resources, in the hope of eventually attaining a classless society. In communist economies, the state is the sole producer, distributor, and consequently the sole employer. Private ownership of business is discouraged or forbidden. Economies are thoroughly planned in the upper echelons of government, which assumes total responsibility for its people, providing nurseries and day-care facilities for infants and children and exhaustive social services for the rest. Figure 12.1, a comparison of the two types of economies, shows that, in spite of such planning, the total wealth of the capitalist economies is far higher than that of socialist ones.

Socialism and what passes for communism are outgrowths of the doctrines of Karl Marx and other utopian thinkers of the nineteenth century (Marx considered socialism an interim stage on the road to communism). However, practitioners of these ideologies have had to digress from a strict interpretation

In spite of central planning, the economies of the Eastern bloc Communist nations have not been resounding success stories.

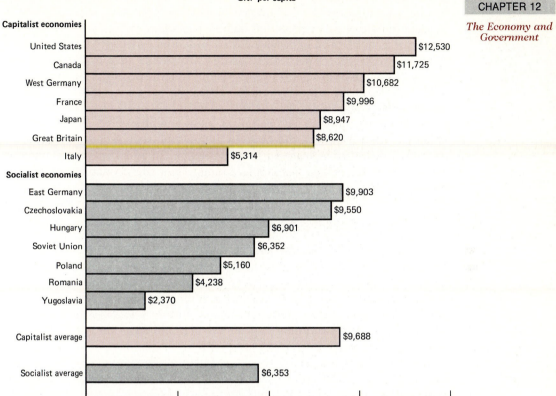

GNP per capita

Capitalist economies	
United States	$12,530
Canada	$11,725
West Germany	$10,682
France	$9,996
Japan	$8,947
Great Britain	$8,620
Italy	$5,314
Socialist economies	
East Germany	$9,903
Czechoslovakia	$9,550
Hungary	$6,901
Soviet Union	$6,352
Poland	$5,160
Romania	$4,238
Yugoslavia	$2,370
Capitalist average	$9,688
Socialist average	$6,353

Figure 12.1 The thoroughly planned economies of the so-called Communist bloc fall considerably behind the capitalist economies of the West when comparisons are made of the GNP per capita. *Source: The World Factbook: 1984* (Washington, D.C.: U.S. Government Printing Office, 1984).

of Marxist doctrines in favor of practical considerations. Socialism, under the banner of communism, has been embraced by underdeveloped nations with agricultural economies, usually following the termination of colonial rule. (This reality is contrary to the expectations of Marx, who believed the system would be implemented by industrial workers in technologically developed nations rebelling against the abuses of capitalism. Thus, socialism has acted as the harbinger of industrialization, when Marx intended it to be a corrective against this movement.)

Moreover, certain self-proclaimed communist societies have begun to stray from the Marxist prescription of how an economy ought to function. Having found a strictly centralized, planned economy difficult to manipulate, these have adopted, to a limited degree, the capitalist mechanisms of profit motive and market-based price setting. Socialism in fact seems to be drawing nearer to capitalism, while the latter, due to growing government regulation, is beginning to resemble socialism.

Communism has traditionally found followers among the peasants or agricultural workers in undeveloped nations. Democratic socialism, on the other hand, seeks support from a wide spectrum of the population, particularly from salaried middle-class workers and highly specialized technicians. The goal of democratic socialism is to provide certain essential services to those who need them and distribute wealth more justly than occurs in a capitalist system. The goal of communism is to transfer wealth from the private to public domain.

All three systems are situated at varying points on an ideal continuum, differentiated from each other by the extent to which government intervenes in the economy. In modified capitalism, government involvement is minimal, although recently on the increase. In democratic socialism, government interferes in essential industries. In communism (in effect socialism), government totally determines economic action. Thus the economies of modern societies reflect matters of degree rather than kind.

Theoretical Perspectives on Economic Development

Social philosophers have long sought to establish the origin of these different economic systems and the reasons for their persistence. Although capitalism evolved as the prevailing economic system in Europe during the initial stages of the Industrial Revolution, economic systems throughout recorded history have taken basically capitalist or socialist forms. The explanation for this consistency differs according to whether one embraces the structural-functionalist or the conflict perspective.

The structural-functionalist theory, as noted on previous occasions, stresses that social systems emerge to meet basic social needs and reflect fundamental values of the society. The freedom of the individual in all areas, including the liberty to accumulate property, was highly valued in Great Britain, where capitalist ideas developed. It was and still is valued in the United States, a country to which those in search of political freedom have flocked in great waves. The desire of individuals to determine their personal economic welfare is simply an outgrowth of their desire to determine their political fate. Such ideas received a kind of official sanction in Adam Smith's demonstration of the elegant balance apparent in the capitalist system, where individual greed and self-interest work to the advantage of society through the functioning of the law of supply and demand.

Beginning with the Great Depression, structural-functionalists have been forced to admit that certain individuals and groups nonetheless fail to achieve success within a capitalist system. Although the system itself may not be at fault, dysfunctions in the society act to deny such individuals and groups equal access to the benefits of capitalism.

Conflict theorists accept Marx's interpretation of the rise of capitalism: With the growth of industrialization came economies based on money, or capital. As people accumulated capital, they were able to buy up larger portions of factories and machines, the means of production. Others, who did not own capital, were forced to sell the only commodity they did possess—their labor. As workers eventually came to outnumber owners, Marx theorized, competition for jobs would force wages down to the point where workers would become an impoverished class. At this point they would revolt, overthrow the owners, and establish an economic system based on communal notions (communism). Marx erred on this last point when instead of revolting, workers united (in the union movement) and were eventually able to protect their wages and obtain other benefits that kept them from being exploited.

Contemporary conflict theorists are concerned with the alienation experienced by many industrial workers in jobs that offer little fulfillment. They also decry the bureaucratization of corporations which dehumanizes relations among people, and the expansion in size of such organizations which endows them with undue advantage and power.

Western Economies in Historical Perspective

The economies of the Western world are mostly modified capitalist, mixed-market institutions whose roots hark back to a momentous transformation that occurred in western Europe as it was emerging from the Middle Ages. This transformation, revolving around the transition from chiefly agricultural to chiefly industrial modes of production, was marked by conflict due to fundamental changes in class structure and societal values and beliefs. In agrarian societies, wealth, power, and status had been the monopoly of those who owned land: in feudal Europe, the landed aristocracy; in pre–Civil War America, plantation owners and other large landholders. When industry became the chief mode of production, status and power shifted to those who controlled industrial and financial capital.

Industrialization followed the creation of a middle class (or bourgeoisie) whose values and beliefs facilitated the accumulation of capital and its continued reinvestment. The establishment of the value of the individual and of personal fulfillment was initially necessary for this shift in economic emphasis. In order to participate fully in a capitalist system, workers had to aspire to the rewards of a better social status, wealth, and prestige which could be acquired through hard work. To this end the profit motive and the work ethic were assigned positive social value.

This transformation of values and beliefs coincided with the circulation in Europe of certain religious ideas, put in motion by the Protestant Reformation. These new doctrines extolled hard work, thrift, and denial of sensual pleasure, and thus seemed to go hand in hand with certain notions of capitalism. (The relationship between the new religious ideas and the emergence of capitalism is analyzed by Max Weber in his classic work, *The Protestant Ethic and the Spirit of Capitalism* [1930].) Such doctrines appealed especially to the emerging merchant classes in England and Holland who came to be known as the Puritans. This group, convinced that its way of life was particularly pleasing to God, was especially receptive to the new capitalist system and eventually imported it to the New World.

Capitalism at first required a rearrangement of concepts regarding the function of an economy. Instead of gold and silver, the basis of wealth became ownership of the elements of production—land, labor, capital—and the spirit of entrepreneurship. These factors of production were abstracted, dehumanized, objectified, and bought and sold in the marketplace. In particular, labor, once supplied to landowners in exchange for food, shelter, and protection, could now be exchanged for wages with the highest bidder. Wealth shifted from owners of land to those who owned or controlled the means of production—the machines, tools, and materials of the merchant middle classes, who were employing freemen, rather than serfs or vassals, to perform the labor needed for production.

The new economic system greatly increased production of goods and services, placing them within reach of substantially more societal members. The once poor and powerless but sheltered and protected serfs and apprentices became the working class (in Marxian terms, the proletariat). In exchange for wages, they surrendered individual responsibility for their work to their employers.

During the nineteenth century, capitalism in Western societies was made manifest in a factory production system, the factories being owned by a few powerful individuals and families. Toward the end of the century family capitalism began to decline, to be replaced by finance and industrial capitalism.

The American Economy

The emergence of the corporation chiefly distinguished this new type of capitalism. A **corporation,** a public institution, is sold in shares to the public instead of belonging to one individual or family; the owners of such an enterprise are therefore those who buy stock in it. Managers are hired by representatives of the owners in the form of a board of directors. The foremost advantage of the public corporation lies in its ability to accumulate vast amounts of capital over a short period of time. Its most relevant characteristic is the separation of ownership from control. Thus, in theory, control of the corporation is in the hands of the stockholders who elect the board of directors and vote during annual meetings on company policy. In practice, most stock is owned by other corporations rather than private individuals, and most decisions concerning the corporation are arrived at daily by managers and simply rubber-stamped by the board of directors.

Some of the biggest stockholders are corporate executives and directors themselves, who are thus able to wield effective financial control. Moreover, directors often also serve as key executive officers in their own companies, or are members of management in one company while sitting on the board of directors of another, a condition called *interlocking directorates*. Finally, even a small-percentage share in their own companies may give director-owners controlling interest and may involve significant amounts of money. This situation seems to support the assertion of sociologist C. Wright Mills that the corporate elite—the one-half percent of the adult population who are owners, directors, and managers of the corporate world—controls the majority of corporate and privately owned wealth in the nation (1953, 101).

Oligopoly   In the United States a few corporations have tended to increase in size and consequently in economic power, effectively curtailing competition. Whole industries and markets are thus dominated by a small number of large corporations. The 200 largest possess more than one-fourth of income-producing national wealth. The 100 largest, which make up only 0.01 percent of all corporations in the nation, own more than half the total assets derived from manufacturing. Many of the largest American corporations have annual revenues that exceed the gross national products of many countries. Such immense power, exerted by so few, is termed **oligopoly**. Oligopoly wields a significant effect in society to the extent that powerful corporations may exert their power to influence political decisions: to see that legislation passed is in their favor; that taxes levied by the government do not overly burden them; and that steps to curb their further growth and power will not be taken. In turn, because corporations employ so many and produce so much of the national wealth, government often cooperates in keeping them profitable.

From Competition to Advertising   The oligopolistic nature of corporations has also altered the classic capitalist ideology that the consumer is king in a free market where many producers compete for his or her business by offering high quality at a low price. When a few corporations own a lion's share of the market, little need exists for competition. Instead corporations spend large sums on advertising, hoping to sway the consumer to purchase essentially the same product their competitors offer.

Advertising creates artificial demands for unnecessary products; many food-manufacturing corporations, for example, concoct new products yearly, several of which are derived mostly from chemicals and do not exist in nature. The public is saturated with advertising until it becomes convinced that the new product is indispensable. Or manufacturers deliberately create shoddy merchandise (planned obsolescence) and then use advertising to induce customers to replace such equipment more frequently.

Advertising as a method of increasing consumption has been immensely successful, so much so that it has become a profitable industry in its own right. The American public has become so convinced of the necessity of a substantial number of superfluous goods that it is more willing to spend money on these than on taxes, which would allow the government to provide much-needed public services. This situation has prompted critics to describe American life as offering private affluence but public squalor— fine automobiles are available to those who can afford them, but mass transit systems for those who cannot are sorely inadequate. Of course, advertising is not solely responsible for this situation: The capitalist system itself convinces people that individual effort will bring personal affluence, thus leaving them less concerned about public needs.

Diversification and the Multinational Corporations   Two increasingly criticized features of modern corporations are the tendencies toward diversification and multinationalism. Diversification refers to a corporation's acquisition of controlling shares in other corporations, often in altogether different industries. A cosmetics corporation which owns a movie-producing company as well as another that makes computer software is thus diversified.

Many corporations, in addition, build industries in foreign countries, or take over foreign companies, thus vastly broadening their markets. Their profits often greatly exceed the budgets of their host nations, and their power derives from providing jobs for thousands while remaining subject to little government control. Criticism of these corporations centers on their alleged abuse of this power, often in the form of bribing foreign officials to gain favorable government policies or contracts. The multinationals are thus potentially able to use vast concentrations of economic power to further their own ends. At the same time, however, they often stimulate foreign economies as well as benefit their own.

Work in the Industrial Society

In all societies except the very simple, obtaining the necessities for survival has involved some form of work. Workers are employed in one of three economic sectors: In the *primary sector,* they extract and process raw material through agriculture, fishing, mining, and forestry. In the *secondary sector,* they work at manufacturing and construction, turning raw materials into finished products. In the *tertiary sector,* they render services to society, such as maintaining automobiles, selling merchandise, remodeling homes, teaching, or healing the sick.

When a society becomes industrialized, a dramatic switch occurs in the sectors in which most workers are employed. In preindustrial societies, a large majority is employed in the primary sector. During the U.S. colonial period, 95 percent of workers were employed in agriculture, whereas today the figure is less than 4 percent. The secondary sector showed a steady increase from 1900 to 1950, but since then has exhibited a steady decline. Today, as illustrated in Figure 12.2, the majority of workers are employed in the tertiary sector, and predictions indicate that the trend away from blue-collar and primary-sector employment toward professionalization will continue. This shift demonstrates an important change in the occupational structure of society: More workers are becoming professionals, managers, or technicians as the need for unskilled or semiskilled occupations wanes, leading to changes in the stratification system and chronic unemployment for the segment of the population unable to attain professional status.

Work in industrial societies displays several distinctive characteristics. First, only about 10 percent of workers are self-employed. The remainder work for others, in the majority of cases formal organizations like corporations, which are highly bureaucratized. Bureaucracy, as noted earlier, can be an efficient form of organization but can also breed dissatisfaction and frustration when

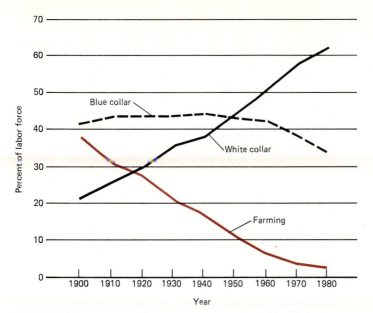

Figure 12.2 Industrial societies experience a dramatic shift in the sectors of the economy in which workers are employed. This graph illustrates the decline of farming (primary sector) and blue-collar work (secondary sector), and the spectacular rise of white-collar employment (tertiary sector). *Source:* U.S. Bureau of the Census, 1984.

action is drowned in a sea of red tape and decisions postponed by "passing the buck."

Since individual workers often feel powerless in the face of bureaucratic organizations, they frequently seek protection through labor unions and professional organizations. Unions have strengthened the position of their members and provided effective methods for negotiating with huge bureaucracies of corporate employers so that workers have never become the exploited class of Marx's prediction. Nonetheless, unions themselves have in recent years become heavily bureaucratized and been criticized for not truly representing the interests of the rank and file. In the true spirit of the iron law of oligarchy, union leaders have attempted to solidify and perpetuate their existence, attaining the status and adopting the roles of the corporate managers with whom they are expected to bargain. As heavy industry declines in importance and society enters a postindustrial era, unions are losing their function and therefore their members.

At the height of the industrial era, workers were said to suffer from alienation and anomie. Alienation, the concept used by Marx to signify estrangement from work due to limited roles in production, stems from the fact that workers in industry are not expected to use their capabilities or talents but rather to repeat a single boring action innumerable times every day. Under such circumstances they easily lose sight of the total product and their role in producing it.

As previously discussed, French sociologist Émile Durkheim maintained that modern industrial societies, characterized by vast differences in activity and the heterogeneity of members, evoke a state of anomie, or normlessness. In economic terms, the growing division and specialization of labor induces industrial workers to feel detached from one another and pursue individual goals with little concern for the welfare of society at large. Many workers are overqualified for the jobs they perform; specialization restricts their ability to acquire a wide range of skills; and the assembly line division of labor promotes both boredom and anger.

This general dissatisfaction manifested itself over several recent decades in high rates of absenteeism, high job turnover, industrial sabotage, lack of interest, use of alcohol and drugs on the job, and sheer negligence in job performance. However, after a period of prolonged recession when many workers lost their boring, unfulfilling jobs, much less emphasis has been given to workers' feelings about their jobs, and much more to the ability of the economy to furnish them with jobs in the first place.

The Role of Government

In socialist and communist nations, the role of government in the economy is accepted as a given. In fact, in these nations the government controls the economy. In the United States, the role of government is still being debated. In a pure free-enterprise system, government intervention is not an issue. Such a system no longer exists, if it ever did, and government intervention in the American economy keeps steadily increasing. The government enforces laws against misrepresentation of products; prohibits undue growth of monopolies; inspects food and drug companies; licenses doctors, pilots, and teachers; issues permits to build public structures and drill for oil; gives subsidies to farmers, temporarily depressed industries, schools, and highway systems; and presides over labor disputes. The American government also serves as one of the world's largest employers, engaging the services of lawyers, scientists, doctors, teachers, social workers, and other professionals. It also runs several industries of its own: the postal system, forests, parks, museums, a publishing industry (the Government Printing Office), a huge library (the Library of Congress), and a complex insurance system (social security).

Many Americans believe that the encroachment of government represents a threat to personal and civil freedom. Others welcome the expansion of government functions and would be glad to accept a more complete system of health care and coverage in other areas. (See Figure 12.3 for a breakdown of attitudes on this issue.) Social problems created by a lack of centralized planning, such as the unbridled growth of suburbia and the decline in quality of mass transit, are eroding public trust in the old principle that the self-interest of some will necessarily work for the good of all.

On the other hand, societies whose governments assume central roles in planning are far from ideal. Great Britain, for instance, suffers from an economy in turmoil, with excessively high rates of unemployment and inflation that the government has been unable to control despite centralized planning

Government Obligation vs. Personal Initiative

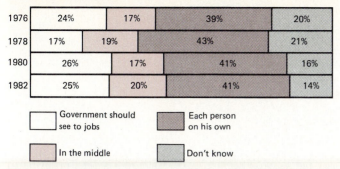

Figure 12.3 Some people feel it is the government's obligation to provide everyone with a good job and a satisfactory standard of living. Others think people should try to get ahead on their own. This graph shows the percentage of people favoring each side. *Source:* From the *New York Times,* November 4, 1984, p. E5. Copyright © 1984 by The New York Times Company. Reprinted by permission.

and the nationalization of much of British industry. Additionally, Eastern Bloc nations, whose very essence revolves around centralized planning of the economy, are chronically subject to shortages and instability.

Future Trends of the American Economy

According to several economists and social commentators, a profound restructuring of the economy is beginning to take place in America. In *Megatrends,* John Naisbitt maintains that the first element of this restructuring occurring at the present time, involves the shift from a national to a global economy (1982). In practical terms, this means that the so-called smokestack industries—automobiles, steel, appliances, textiles, apparel, and shoes—will be taken up by Third World countries as developed countries go on to newer tasks. In global terms, what is happening is a re-sorting of who makes what; in this process, the developed nations are deindustrializing because newly developed or still-developing countries are performing industry-based work more effectively—they have newer plants and facilities and, in the case of Japan, a stronger work ethic.

Naisbitt notes that in 1950, 65 percent of the U. S. work force was engaged in industrial occupations, whereas today only 27 percent is similarly engaged. Conversely, while in 1950 only 17 percent was engaged in information-related jobs—creating, processing, and distributing information—today that figure has grown to 58 percent. Information jobs are located in such fields as publishing, education, the media, banking, the stock market, insurance, and government. In this sense, while capital represents the strategic resource in industrial societies, the strategic resources of postindustrial informational societies are knowledge and data. Since the latter lend themselves more easily to small entrepreneurial enterprises, Naisbitt claims, access to upward mobility is facilitated.

In the interim period, society will be faced with a number of problems,

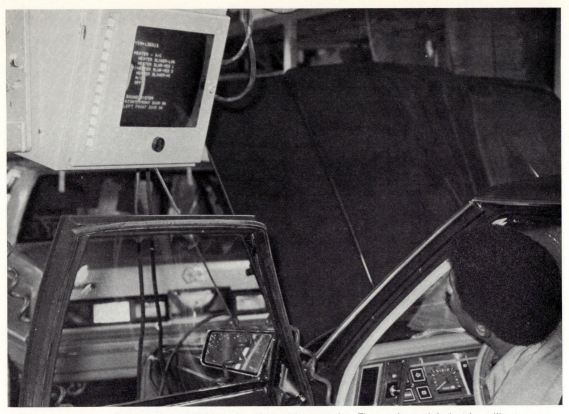

A restructuring is taking place in world economies: The smokestack industries—like car manufacturing—are being taken up by Third World countries, while the developed nations go on to new tasks.

central among which will be the reallocation of the blue-collar segment of the work force when its corresponding industries are phased out. Many of these workers are too old to be retrained, particularly in high-technology fields where future jobs lie. Unemployment and the wholesale displacement of a portion of the work force will probably force the government to intervene even more profoundly, especially since those unemployed or displaced cannot be left to fend for themselves.

Government and Politics

Whereas decisions about who gets what in a society are inherent in the institution of the economy, implementation of these is left to another pivotal institution, government. In other words, since what is good for the collectivity and what is good for the individual often collide, a leader or body of representatives must exist with sufficient power to see that decisions concerning the operation of a society are respected and obeyed. In most modern societies, the state is the source of ultimate political power since it holds a monopoly on the use of force within its borders. The state, however, is an abstract concept, and the real, day-to-day exercise of power is performed by government, a body consisting of a number of individuals who hold power in the name of the state. The process by which people and groups acquire and maintain power is known as politics.

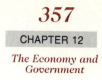

The institution of government may be defined as that pattern of statuses and roles a society develops to fulfill the need for order within and the need for defense against threats from without. It includes a system of norms, values, laws, and general patterns of behavior that legitimize the acquisition and exercise of power. The government also determines its own relationship to members of society.

Purpose of Government

Societies require government insofar as any group way of life demands a degree of social order. There are certain actions people must take and others they must refrain from taking in order to prevent chaos and maintain relative peace. In small societies, the family institution maintains social control over its members by exercising moral control. Moral control, essentially cultural learning, lies within the individual, having been internalized through socialization. As societies grow large and complex, other institutions—religion, education, and government—must appropriate certain functions of maintaining social order by exercising social control. *Social control* is the process by which a group induces or forces the individual to behave in a designated way, and government represents the ultimate source of social control. In short, in large societies, moral control must be supplemented by political control. *Political control* is social control exerted by forces outside the individual, such as laws and the agencies in charge of punishing those who violate them.

Functions of Government

As noted, government's most important function is the implementation of social control: maintaining order, settling disputes, and coordinating the activities of a society's members. In addition, government must protect its citizens from external threats. It accomplishes this by creating and maintaining armies, by manufacturing armaments for their provision, and by securing strategic military installations. In some societies, the military institution itself acts as the government. In most, however, civilians remain in charge of the government and the military is subordinate to it.

The government is also in charge of planning and maintaining facilities and activities involving large portions of the population. Government agencies regulate the economy, build highways, are in charge of traffic regulation, fund schools, maintain national parks and museums, help run certain hospitals, provide a degree of health care, and so on. Government also subsidizes activities valued by society that the private sector does not pursue, such as the arts. The above functions are *manifest,* or deliberate.

The unintended, or *latent,* functions of government often include a great deal of repression. In the United States, governmental repression has fortunately been minimal. Latent functions of American government have included the formation of party machines, common in the past, as well as the creation of alleged power elites which act to maintain the status quo, including a system of social stratification. Even in nations that consider themselves classless, administrative and managerial elites arise; the relationship between political power and socioeconomic status can thus be regarded as universally entrenched.

Political Power: Legitimacy and Authority

Power is central to the political process; whoever exerts social control in a society must have the means to do so. As a concept, power is difficult to define. Max Weber described it as "the probability that one actor within a social relationship will be in a position to carry out his own will despite resistance" (1957, 152). Power plays a significant role in all social interaction: Parents hold power over their children, professors over students, employers over employees, and so on. Individuals possess greater or lesser degrees of power according to the statuses they occupy in society and the roles they fill.

Power relationships are always somewhat reciprocal. That is, the child exerts some power over the parent: It can throw a temper tantrum or refuse to eat or breathe until the parent gives in. In short, ways exist of sabotaging the powerful individual in most interactions.

Power can be asserted in a number of ways. One is by promising rewards in return for compliance. Another is through coercion, the threat of punishment to individuals who do not comply. Finally, power can be asserted through influence, the ability to manipulate information, values, attitudes, and feelings. Television commentators and popular authors have widespread power because their statements are accepted as authoritative by a large public. Political leaders have a similar effect.

Legitimacy Political power represents power exercised by the state through its government. The reason the state can wield power is that its citizens accept its authority. Power held by an individual or group unacceptable to members of society is considered illegal and illegitimate. Weber defined this kind of power as coercion. An example is the control an armed thug possesses over an unarmed pedestrian when he demands the latter's wallet. Such power lacks legitimacy.

Authority Power, to be legitimate, must have authority. Authority represents a form of control socially accepted as right and proper. A police officer holding a gun to a suspect's head while trying to make an arrest is not considered to be acting coercively. The officer is within the rights of the authority vested in his or her status.

In order to be accepted, a government must possess legitimate authority. That is, citizens must believe "that the existing political institutions are the most appropriate ones for the society" (Lipset, 1963, 64). No political system, not even one born of violence and functioning through force, can survive very long without legitimacy. When citizens question the legitimacy of their government, a situation known as a *crisis of legitimacy,* the conflict is usually resolved with the overthrow of those in command.

Types of Legitimate Authority

How does an individual or group acquire authority? In other words, how does power become legitimized? In a classic thesis, Weber maintains that the sources of authority lie in tradition, the law, and charisma (1957, 324–369).

Traditional Authority   The oldest type of power known is that which depends on tradition. The legitimization of power in this regard depends on the past. The authority of a person or group is accepted because it always has been. The religious authority of churches and the political authority of government rest heavily on traditional sources.

Traditional authority tends to prevail in relatively homogeneous, nontechnological societies where citizens experience similar group identification and share the same values, beliefs, and attitudes. However, even in heterogeneous and highly technological societies traditional sources of authority may prevail. The U.S. Constitution, for example, is accepted by most Americans as a near-sacred document that forms the basis of the political and governmental system. Legislation that runs counter to the letter of the Constitution is considered illegitimate.

Legal-Rational Authority   This type of authority is based on rules arrived at in a rational manner. Systems depending on legal-rational authority are organized in a bureaucratic fashion due to the limitations in exercise of power this pattern of social organization fosters. In a bureaucracy, power resides in social position and role rather than in any specific individual. In addition, a bureaucratic pattern of organization defines and specifies the exact amount of power each role entails. Authority is based on obedience to the rule of law rather than on loyalty to an individual.

Legal-rational authority appears in complex, multigroup societies where members are heterogeneous and belong to many subcultures. Such societies usually experience rapid social change, resulting in lack of uniformity of values, attitudes, and beliefs. Legal-rational authority is accepted because societal members are convinced that those with authority employ rational methods for the benefit of all. Social change, moreover, is reflected in frequent modifications to the law.

Charismatic Authority   One type of authority does not rest either on tradition, reason, or law. Instead, **charismatic authority** derives from the personality of an exceptional leader. It may appear either in a society with a traditional base of authority or one that has a legal-rational base. Charismatic leaders seem to possess special qualities, often described as magnetic, fasci-

Both of these leaders wield a legal-rational type of authority: Their power resides in their status and role, not in their being specific individuals.

nating, and extraordinary by their followers. Leaders such as Mao Ze-dong, Hitler, Martin Luther King, and John F. Kennedy have all been described as charismatic.

Charismatic authority, however, does not encourage stable social organization. It provides no system of rules, either traditional or rational, with which to guide behavior. Charismatic authority, in fact, resists attempts at routinization or bureaucratization, and consequently does not encourage the development of a stable political system. Stability can only be established if a system based on the charismatic authority of a leader evolves into one of the other two systems of authority.

The State and Its Government

The terms state and government are frequently misunderstood and confused. Government is the institution that develops as a consequence of the need to maintain social order in a society. Government is a *process*, but also includes those who exercise political power in a society.

The **state,** on the other hand, is the abstract embodiment, or symbol, of the political institution. Government provides social control through its political processes, through the laws it establishes and implements, and through the work of its separate agencies. The state is the formal representation of government. The functions of the state are carried out by the government; thus, government represents the working, active arm of the state. Individuals and groups that form the government—together with the laws they pass and procedures they establish—change over time and with each new administration. But the state goes on.

In some societies, differentiating between the state and its government is simple, due to the offices of the head of state and the head of government being held by two different persons. In Great Britain for instance, the queen is the head of state, whereas the prime minister is the head of government. In the United States, on the other hand, both offices inhere in the position of president.

The state differs from other institutions in two essential ways. First, membership is compulsory for all living within its territorial limits, with the exception of those designated as aliens or temporary visitors. Second, unlike other forms of social organization, the political control it exerts is complete. The state and the state alone can seize one's property, deprive one of freedom through imprisonment, or, as a last resort, take one's life as punishment for a capital crime.

These two conditions are necessary if the state is to exercise effective, organized political control. Individuals able to resign from the state within whose geographical limits they lived would be relieved of all obligation to obey its laws. Moreover, since the state bears the duty of enforcing certain patterns of behavior on those within its boundaries, its government must hold the authority to employ whatever sanctions are necessary to achieve this purpose. The state must possess *sovereignty,* or supreme political power, which derives from its capacity to monopolize the use of force within its borders. A state's sovereignty is recognized by both its own citizens and by other states.

The basic components of the state are territory, government, sovereignty, and population. Within its territory, through its government, on the basis of its sovereignty, and for the benefit of its people, the state performs certain functions and deals with other states.

Theoretical Views of the State

The fundamental raison d'être of the state is the maintenance of social order. Theorists who see life from a functionalist perspective naturally accept the idea that the institution originated to perform this specific function. One of the older expressions of this notion may be found in the writings of Thomas Hobbes (1588–1679), an English philosopher who speculated that the state emerged as the result of a "social contract" made by the people in order to end their existence in a "state of nature" in which life was "solitary, poor, nasty, brutish, and short." Modern functionalist sociologists perceive the state as a functional institution necessary for maintaining law and order.

Additionally, the state acts to arbitrate conflicts among individuals, to plan with the official goal of providing the greatest good for the greatest number, and to maintain relations with other states. Thus the state allocates scarce resources, regulates the economy, funds new research, protects those unable to work, looks out for the environment, and generally provides for the needs of members of society. It also makes trade agreements, political alliances, or war with other states. All of these functions require a centralized source of authority.

Theorists who view life from a conflict perspective maintain that the state emerged to protect the rights of a privileged few. The conflict view derives from the work of Jean-Jacques Rousseau (1712–1778), who disagreed with Hobbes, believing instead that before the emergence of the state people lived as "noble savages" in peace and harmony. According to Rousseau, only when the idea of private property developed did people begin to fight among one another and had need to resort to a central authority to restore peace. This central authority was not impartial, but rather served the interests of the upper classes, keeping the majority poor and oppressed.

These ideas were pursued by Karl Marx, who believed that all but the most primitive societies consisted of at least two classes. Of these, one dominated and exploited the rest by the manipulation of social institutions. The state became an instrument in the service of the ruling classes. Marx concluded that the state would cease to exist only when the final stage of social evolution was reached. In the classless society that followed communism, the state would "wither away," since in such a society there was no need to safeguard the interests of any group.

Marx had a point in his contention that the state tends to protect the interests of the ruling class, since historically those in positions of political power have also enjoyed economic power. He failed to see, however, that the state also performs positive functions unrelated to class conflict. As always, both the functionalist and the conflict perspectives show only one version of reality. It may be argued that the state maintains the status quo and with it some instances of social inequality. It may equally be argued that large, complex, heterogeneous societies cannot function without a central body with the authority to make certain vital decisions.

The Nation-State

The increasing growth and complexity of societies led members to seek political organization first in clans based on kinship, later in tribes that were collections of clans, and finally in city-states. Around the fifteenth century, city-states gradually emerged as nation-states.

A **nation** refers to a culture group residing within the territory of a political state. A group is considered a nation if (1) members live within specific geographic boundaries, generally set off by mountains, rivers, or the sea; (2) they develop commercial ties throughout this area; and (3) they speak or are familiar with a common language. When such a group submits to the jurisdiction of a central government, a situation eventually emerges in which older loyalties are subordinated to the new political order and a common literature, history, and sense of a shared future develop. Ultimately a nation will develop a "we against them" attitude, a sense of unity so strong that in spite of lack of cultural uniformity, members consider themselves as separate from others (then designated as foreigners).

The development of nation-states has proved vitally important in the modern world. Principally, the loyalties and beliefs of nationalism have served as motivating forces for the organization of complex technological societies in the urban-industrial era. These forces have also been instrumental in establishing and maintaining international antagonisms based on variant ideologies.

Nationalism may be defined as a set of beliefs regarding the superiority and distinction of one's own nation, and a defense of its interests above all others. Individual identification with the nation, its culture, its interests, and its goals is implicit in such a stand. Nationalism can be described as a form of ethnocentrism that cuts across all other loyalties to stress emotional adherence to the national group.

Historically, nationalism represents a new movement, first appearing only in the second half of the eighteenth century. Previously, in the aftermath of the feudal era, the Western world was relatively unified in culture and religion. Rulers of most Western nations constituted an international society of governing classes due to frequent intermarriages and kinship relations. Events following World War I, particularly the rise of a number of communist and fascist regimes, effectively destroyed this unity. These new regimes stressed nationalism because they believed that a drive for national supremacy would strengthen them internally. Their goal was the creation of a monolithic state whose people had only one allegiance—to the government—and one overwhelming sentiment—patriotism.

Political Ideologies

People accept the authority of the state because they agree with its underlying ideology. An **ideology** is a system of values, ideas, beliefs, and attitudes that a society, or groups within it, share and accept as fact. Political ideology, more specifically, represents a system of beliefs that explains, interprets, and rationalizes why a particular political order is best for the society. This political order may already exist, or may be still in the planning stage. Political ideology offers a definite strategy for attaining or maintaining the preferred political order, including processes, institutional arrangements, and other programs. It is comparable to a blueprint for the good society.

Those who embrace a given ideology are expected to become totally committed to it. A political ideology should result in political behavior and its ideas should be translated into action. Political parties, social movements, interest groups, and the political system itself are all motivated by ideologies.

Although in pluralistic societies a variety of ideologies, some conflicting, coexist, most members are socialized into accepting one over the others. Few are even aware of the multiplicity of ideologies open to them. In democratic societies, the variety of ideologies deemphasizes their importance; societies whose governments permit only one official ideology punish individuals who hold conflicting ones.

Even so, ideologies are not monolithic. Democracy, for example, can be divided into democratic capitalism and democratic socialism, while communist nations such as the Soviet Union and China disagree about the interpretation of Marxism.

Democracy

The two prevailing political ideologies in the world may be broadly divided into democracy and autocracy. A basic assumption of **democracy** is the value of the individual as the primary unit of society. From this assumption, it follows that in the democratic frame of reference, the ultimate purpose of the state is to ensure the self-fulfillment of each individual. The ideology of democracy derives from beliefs about human nature, specifically that men and women are free, rational, moral, equal, and possess certain rights. Equality does not imply equivalency, but rather refers to universal possession of particular moral and rational faculties by virtue of which each individual is entitled to the same freedoms and rights as all others.

Following logically is another fundamental democratic principle, the belief that each human being is entitled to freedom and the opportunity to pursue individual goals. Applied to political systems, this involves the guarantee of (1) the right to vote; (2) the assurance that political information is freely accessible; (3) the freedoms of speech, of the press, of religion, of movement, and of assembly; (4) the right to seek public office; (5) the right to criticize public officials and programs; and (6) the freedom from arbitrary persecution.

Democratic ideology is based on the principle of popular sovereignty, the notion that ultimate power resides in the people. That one is not subject to any authority but one's own and is capable of directing one's own behavior is a basic article of democratic faith.

Popular sovereignty yields another democratic principle, that the only legitimate basis of rule is the consent of the governed. The state, in other words, acts as the trustee of powers given it by the people and holds no purpose or authority other than that assigned it. In short, the state and its government are instruments created and maintained for the sole benefit of their subjects.

Autocracy

The ideology most directly opposed to democracy holds that government should be in the hands of one or more individuals who wield supreme power over the populace. This ruler or ruling body is not accountable to anyone for any actions: Its decisions are made without being subject to law. In effect, the ruler *is* the law. This ideology is termed **autocracy**, and through the ages has taken such forms as primitive kingship, despotism, tyranny, and absolutist monarchy. In this century, military dictatorships and other forms of temporary or emergency rule are autocratic in nature.

Totalitarianism   Traditional autocracies in this century have been replaced by ideologies of the right or left in a system known as **totalitarianism**. Total-

The totalitarian leftist ideology of the USSR is based on modern technology and mass legitimization.

itarian regimes are based on modern technology and mass legitimization (Friedrich and Brzezinski, 1966, 4). Their ideology encourages revolt against present society and idealistic hopes for a future one of perfect men and women. Most importantly, such ideologies are totalist, embracing all facets of human life. They deal with the total individual and attempt total reform. Thus they prescribe a life-style not only in the political sphere, but in social, religious, educational, and economic domains as well.

Another important feature of totalitarian regimes is their maintenance of a single political party functioning as the organization through which their ideology is presented and kept alive. The party is frequently—at least initially—led by a charismatic leader and hierarchically arranged into a political elite that is either superior or equal to governmental bureaucracy. The leader (dictator) or the oligarchy (small elite) interprets the ideology to the masses.

Other characteristics of the totalitarian state include the existence of an all-pervasive secret police, an almost total control of the mass communications media, a monopoly on arms, and an economy centrally planned and controlled. These traits allow the totalitarian state complete and unprecedented power over the individual.

Authoritarianism   The ideologies of some types of autocracies in existence today can be best described as reflecting **authoritarianism**. In these regimes, power is held by either an absolute monarch or dictator or a small elite. But such power is limited to the political sphere, with no attempt made on the part of the ruler to invade other areas of human life. These regimes resemble the totalitarian model and in time may become more or less totalitarian themselves.

Political Power in the United States

In the classic conception of democracy, individual participation in government decisions is a chief postulate, based on the premise of personal dignity and the natural law that guarantees each life, liberty, and the pursuit of happiness. This goal is achieved by allowing the majority to make decisions regarding public policy (majority rule) with simultaneous respect for the rights of minorities (which can attempt to influence decisions or even become the majority themselves). The freedom of dissent and opposition and the right to run for political office are additionally guaranteed to all. Moreover, classical democratic ideology includes the principle of political equality; that is, each individual, regardless of social position, economic class, creed, or race has an equal opportunity to influence public policy, as expressed in the motto "one person, one vote."

These concepts appear to imply that Americans actively participate in governmental matters. Clearly, however, popular participation has never been a reality in the political life of this nation, and the larger and more complex the society becomes—the more it approaches the mass society model—the more popular participation dwindles.

Who Governs?

If the people do not govern this nation, who does? Two opposing schools of thought prevail with respect to power distribution in the United States. One is that of political pluralism, or broker rule (rule by compromise). The other is elitism.

Pluralism   From this point of view, power is diffused among numerous interest groups rather than being concentrated in any single person or group. Interest groups continually compete with one another but also unite in coalitions when such unity works to their advantage and attempt to find compromise solutions to problems encountered in the decision-making process.

The model of political pluralism includes these assumptions and arguments: (1) the basis of politics involves the struggle for power between organized interest groups; (2) the stability of the political system is actually promoted by the great number and diversity of these groups. Stability is ensured by an underlying consensus (agreement on basic issues and ideology) that acts to restrain group conflicts. Stability is further enhanced by the role of politicians as brokers; by overlapping memberships in varying interest groups; and by the possibility of continual formation of new groups. Change is provided through the emergence of such new groups. Although group bargaining is performed by elites—small groups of individuals given the power to make significant decisions—these elite are responsive and accountable to the people through elections (Livingston and Thompson, 1971, 107). In sum, according to the pluralist model, power and governmental decision making occurs through the "steady appeasement of relatively small groups" (Dahl, 1956, 146).

Elitism Proponents of this school of thought maintain that power in this society belongs to a limited number of individuals or groups. The late sociologist C. Wright Mills was a prominent twentieth-century exponent of this view. Mills believed that the most significant decisions, including those concerning war and peace, are made by a handful who represent the corporate rich, the upper echelons of the military, and the political directorate. In Mills's view, the consensus that supposedly exists in the nation is, in reality, brought into existence by elites who manipulate the masses through mass communication. Competition, as examined in the pluralist model, occurs only when issues are minor. The interaction of innumerable interest groups results in no real diffusion of power (1956). Another sociologist, William Domhoff, maintains that power wielded by the elite is in effect monolithic since members resemble one another in social background and have developed a community of interests and values. Consequently, they tend to act in unison (1967).

As usual, the reality lies somewhere between these two views. Mills's views are too extreme to accurately reflect reality, but the pluralist position also appears somewhat romantic. Compromise is not easy to attain, and consensus not always present; thus conflict is also part of the political process.

Conflict and Consensus In spite of the fact that conflict exists in society—since politics inevitably revolves around who will have power—the political system continues to function when there is at least a consensus on how conflict should be mediated. In other words, most people agree on the rules of the game. The true argument concerns which element predominates in American society—conflict or consensus? The pluralist school favors consensus, stating that even those in conflict with each other remain in fundamental agreement with the principles of liberal democratic capitalism (Hofstadter, 1954, 7). Elitists tend toward the conviction that force alone holds society together, even though this is seldom displayed by the elite. Instead, force is disguised by an ideology that supports the status quo. Thus, from the elitist view, consensus in the society is artificial, forced on the masses by a manipulative elite.

Political Processes

Politics, or the competition for the power to make decisions affecting society, possesses several distinctive characteristics in the United States. Public policy—that which government does or fails to do—is influenced by interest groups, political parties, and individual voters.

Interest Groups **Interest groups** are coalitions of individuals with similar attitudes and interests who attempt to influence public policy. In their goal, they resemble political parties; interest groups, however, do not present candidates for public office, nor do they aim for complete control of the government.

Interest groups are peculiar to the American system owing to their vast numbers and staggering variety. They function to provide group representation above and beyond that offered by elected officials in Congress. The latter represent constituents according to geographical region, whereas interest groups reflect individual economic, occupational, religious, moral, ethnic, and myriad other interests. Specifically, they help clarify opinions, stimulate discussions, debate various aspects of issues, and educate the public, helping to achieve consensus. Some interest groups "lobby" or seek to influence the enactment or defeat of specific legislation.

Interest groups may prove genuinely helpful to both government and those they represent. First, as the best-informed sources on the issues around which they are organized, they are able to enlighten legislators and the public in general. They may also act as checks on other groups and individuals in public office, bringing to attention abuses that otherwise may be ignored. Of course, they may also serve to promote the narrow interests of their constituents to the detriment of Americans at large.

Political Parties **Political parties** represent the third base of democracy (the other two comprising a system of representation and the right to participate in government by voting). The establishment of political parties derives from the right to organize an opposition for the purpose of gaining access to the power of governmental decision making. Framers of the U.S. Constitution made no provision for political parties, believing that popular elections would offer citizens a direct voice in government; it soon became apparent, however, that more effective organization was needed, and political parties came into being to offer leadership and to speak for those who opposed the government in power, as well as those who supported it.

The democratic system of government requires unanimity only on the desirability of the system itself. In all other areas, conflicts are to be mediated by instituting a government of temporary coalitions or alliances for joint action (Riker, 1965, 88). The task of placing a particular coalition in power is left to political parties.

Consequently, the fundamental purpose of political parties is to gain control of government and take on the responsibility for conducting its affairs—in short, to seize and exercise political power by legal means. Political parties in democracies must win elections in the name of the electorate, whose interests the parties loosely represent. Different parties strive to determine and define the ideals of the people, clarifying them as issues and ideologies, and organizing them into a platform. This platform is presented to the electorate together with various candidates who support it. The party that wins the election attempts to execute the policies of its platform by making them the policies of the government.

By nominating, electing, and recruiting public officials, political parties also provide the personnel necessary to run a government. Those not in power adopt the role of the "loyal opposition" or critics of the party in control. They also attempt to modify through compromise the innumerable wishes and interests of different groups. Thus American political parties play a unifying rather than divisive role in society, unlike many of their counterparts in other societies.

Another uniquely American characteristic is the existence of only two major parties (most democratic societies support a wide variety of parties, while totalitarian regimes permit only one). These two parties, because they must represent a broad spectrum of interests, cannot afford to embrace extremist positions if they wish to win the support of the majority of voters. As a result, they have adopted moderate, middle-of-the road positions, enabling them to unite a very heterogeneous group of supporters.

Critics have observed that, as a consequence, Democrats and Republicans are almost indistinguishable. In very general terms, the middle classes and conservative elements of the population have tended to vote for the Republicans, while working-class and liberal elements vote for the Democrats. Still each must try to "convert" enough electors from the opposing camp to win a majority, a situation which effectively blurs social-class differences in voting patterns. Lipset notes that individuals in lower social classes prefer to identify with the party that represents a higher social class and are also more prone to accept the conservative values that schools, mass media, and churches transmit. Middle-class voters, on the other hand, are more open to radical or leftist influences transmitted through universities and portions of the news media (1967, 463).

Political scientists Dye and Ziegler maintain, on the same subject, that the American party system is designed to serve those who embrace middle-class values (1972, 209). Those who refuse to accept such values are excluded from participation in the system, their beliefs finding little expression in the platforms of either party.

Finally, contemporary American political parties differ from others in not being based on any particular doctrine or ideology. In addition, party leaders and members never share complete agreement on any given principle. Within each party a vast spectrum of opinion on specific issues prevails. But both parties agree on certain premises and goals: the value of the democratic system, the Constitution, and capitalism.

Participation in the Political Process: Voting and Public Opinion

Although the United States was one of the first nations in the world to implement universal adult suffrage, only about 60 percent of its citizens vote in presidential elections. Local elections sometimes draw out only 10 percent of the electorate, and during off years in which all representatives, one-third of senators, and almost half the governors are chosen, the turnout is around 50 percent of all registered voters.

Poor voting records can be attributed to apathy and political alienation. Apathetic voters feel that since little difference on issues exists between the two parties, it remains irrelevant which one wins. The feeling among the politically alienated is that conventional political participation is meaningless because no action on the part of the individual can alter the course of political events.

The lowest voting record belongs to those who did not finish high school and who hold unskilled jobs. These tend to be rural residents, under 25, and members of minority groups. The highest voting record is found among college-educated, professional-managerial and white-collar citizens, who tend to be urban and suburban residents, over 25, and members of many voluntary organizations.

Voting, however, does not represent the only form of citizen participation in the political process. To vote is to act on the basis of a political opinion. While not everyone chooses to act this way, almost everyone holds such opinions.

Opinions in general are learned through interaction and in the socialization process. They are based on attitudes, which are acquired tendencies or predispositions that remain essentially unexpressed. Opinions represent the expression of attitudes.

Public opinion comprises the totality of opinions expressed by members of a community on any given issue that touches it. Political opinion, on the other hand, is the totality of opinions expressed by members of a community on political issues alone. Political opinions are influenced by family and peer groups, as well as by schools (particularly the level of schooling achieved), race, religion, and region. Increasingly, mass media, chiefly television, play an important role in opinion formation. Children in industrial nations cite television as their primary source of information, whereas parents are mentioned in this regard in less industrial nations.

The danger in overreliance on mass media is that in the process of communicating information, interpretation becomes necessary. News is relayed by third parties who may not have witnessed specific events firsthand. A reporter's goal may be complete objectivity, but a degree of bias will always creep in. Finally, only selected events are brought to the public's attention: The very process of choosing which to report implies that objectivity cannot be total.

In the United States, the state and its government have remained a fairly stable institution. Even during the unrest of the 1960s and 1970s when Americans expressed widespread dissatisfaction with their government on the issues of civil rights and the country's presence in Vietnam, the institution managed to survive these challenges to its legitimacy. Today, it appears that the basic system is no longer being challenged, only the fact that it operates better for some segments of the population than for others. Still, although less vocal, dissatisfaction remains, and perhaps discontent with government is part of the human condition. Because we live in groups, and especially because modern societies are large, heterogeneous, and complex, bodies with binding authority are a must. But because we are individuals and our groups are often in conflict, such authority must inevitably be resented from time to time.

The Chapter in Brief

To sustain human life, a constant supply of food, sufficient shelter, and clothing for protection from the elements are necessary. These goods are scarce and require effort to obtain. The institution of the economy consists of those patterns of behavior that revolve around obtaining these scarce and necessary resources.

Essentially, societal members must decide what to produce, how to distribute and exchange produced goods, and in what manner to consume them. These decisions are made either by relying on custom and tradition; by the command of a leader or group of leaders; or by the functioning of a market dependent upon supply and demand, prices, profits, and losses. Most modern economies make use of a variety of these methods in decision making with regard to resources and production. Resources include labor, land, capital, and technology. Resources are versatile, but finite; they must be conserved.

Modern industrial economies are characterized by (1) large amounts of capital; (2) extreme specialization and division of labor, methods for producing more with less effort; and (3) the use of money as the chief medium of exchange. Economic systems are both social and cultural, and legitimized by an **ideology** accepted as valid by most members of the society. **Capitalism, socialism** (in both democratic and nondemocratic forms), and **communism** represent the three ideologies underlying most modern industrial economies.

The chief element of capitalism is the concept of the free market which works on the basis of supply and demand, is regulated by competition, and founded on a desire for profit. A modified version of capitalism prevails in the American economy, characterized by a work force largely employed in the tertiary sector, that is, in supplying services rather than extracting new material or turning it into finished products. This shift has resulted in changes in the occupational structure of society, and consequently in the stratification system, creating a trend toward professionalization and the existence of a permanently unemployed or underemployed underclass.

The **corporation** is the most important product of capitalist economies. A corporation is an organization in which ownership is separate from control: Corporations are owned by stockholders and controlled by boards of directors. In practice, much stock is held by other corporations and effective control exerted by management. The trend has been for a few corporations to grow very large and powerful—engaging in **oligopoly**—through the use of advertising to market their products instead of through competition. Some corporations have constructed plants in other nations—the multinationals—which has created a potential for abuse.

In industrial societies, workers frequently suffer from alienation and anomie due to rigid divisions of labor and specialization. Alienation stems from the limited role workers are forced to play in production, and anomie, or norm-lessness, is a reaction to the dehumanized nature of the secondary relationships prevalent in industrial societies.

The institution of government arises out of humanity's need for social order. When social control can no longer be administered within the family because of the size and complexity of a society, some body with the authority to make decisions binding on that society becomes essential.

To be acceptable to societal members, government must possess authority. Authority may have its basis in tradition, in reason and the law, or in the charisma of a leader, and may be defined as legitimate power. **Power** is the ability of one person or group to influence the behavior of another person or group in a desired direction. Force or the threat of force frequently underlies power.

The **state** is the formal abstract structure representing government. Its elements are territory, population, government, and sovereignty. The chief aim of the state is to impose organized political control over its citizens, which it does by the use of a monopoly over the legitimate employment of force within its territory.

The organization of societies into nation-states is a comparatively recent event in history. Inhabitants sharing similar characteristics in a particular territory overseen by a central government develop a sense of unity and nationhood. **Nationalism,** the ideology behind the nation-state, may be defined as a set of beliefs concerning the superiority of one's own nation and a defense of its interests above all others.

According to democratic ideology, individuals participate in decisions of government. But since personal participation is impossible, the function of governing is taken over by competing **interest groups** or by an elite, depending upon which theory or perspective one chooses to embrace. Pluralist theory maintains that power is diffused among multiple interest groups. The elitist view states that a handful of people make significant decisions for a society with the threat of force concealed to appear as consensus.

Political parties place particular groups in power; they gain control of government and take on the responsibility for conducting its affairs. They also define and clarify issues, organize these into a platform, and provide the personnel to run the government. The two major parties in the United States are ideologically similar due to the need of both to appeal to the greatest number of people. Interest groups voice their concerns through lobbying and sometimes protest. Ordinary citizens participate in decision making principally by voting. However, only about 60 percent of the electorate vote in presidential elections and even fewer in nonpresidential election years. Those who vote are predominantly college-educated, middle-aged professionals of urban or suburban residence. Those who fail to vote are less-educated, low-income segments of the population thought to be apathetic and convinced their vote will have a negligible impact on the system. Though they may not choose to vote, most people hold political opinions formed during socialization and greatly influenced by the media.

Authoritarianism A type of autocracy in which power is held by an absolute monarch, a dictator, or small elite. Power, however, is limited to the political sphere.

Autocracy An ideology directly opposed to democracy according to which government rests in the hands of one individual or group which holds supreme power.

Capitalism An economic system in which property belongs to private individuals, in which production is engaged in for a profit motive, and in which prices, wages, and profits are regulated by supply and demand and by competition. The welfare of the individual is the chief concern.

Charismatic authority According to Max Weber, a type of authority based on the leadership of a person with charisma. A charismatic leader is thought to possess special gifts of a magnetic, fascinating, and extraordinary nature.

Communism An economic and political system whose goals are total government control of the economy and total income redistribution with the ultimate aim of a classless society. The state is the sole employer, producer, distributor, and planner in the economy; it also assumes total responsibility for the survival of the individual in society. According to Marx, communism was the final stage of societal evolution.

Corporation A form of enterprise organized for large-scale production in which ownership and control are separated and in which large amounts of capital can be easily accumulated. One of the most successful products of capitalism.

Democracy An ideology, and the political system based on it, that stresses the value of the individual, as well as his or her rationality, morality, equality, and possession of specific rights.

Ideology A system of values, ideas, beliefs, and attitudes that a society or groups within it share and accept as true.

Interest groups Coalitions of individuals with similar interests who compete with each other for their share of political power, attempting to influence legislation in their favor.

Legal-rational authority According to Weber, a type of authority accepted by members of society because it is based on rational methods and laws and is exerted for their benefit.

Nation A culture group residing within the territory of a political state.

Nationalism The ideology behind the nation-state. A set of beliefs about the superiority of one's own nation and a commitment to the defense of its interest above all others.

Oligopoly The domination of an industry or market by a few large and powerful corporations.

Political party An organization that brings diverse elements of the general population into a coalition whose primary purpose is to seize political power through legal means and exercise it for a specified term.

Politics   The forces that make up and direct the government of the state, its policies, and its actions.

Power   The probability that one individual in a social relationship will carry out his or her own will despite resistance. The ability of one person or group to direct the behavior of another person or group in a desired direction, under the ultimate, though not always obvious, threat of force.

Socialism   An economic system based on concern for the welfare of the collectivity. Under democratic socialism, essential industries are owned and operated by the government in the name of the people and high taxes are levied to redistribute wealth more equitably. Under totalitarian socialism, economies—and most individuals' lives—are centrally planned.

State   The formal, abstract symbol of government.

Totalitarianism   A kind of modern-day autocracy, of the left or right, characterized by a totalist ideology, a single party, a secret, government-controlled police, and a monopoly over mass communications, weapons, and the economy by the ruling elite.

Traditional authority   According to Weber, authority based on reverence for tradition.

Suggestions for Further Reading

Bell, Daniel.   1976. *The coming of post-industrial society: A venture in social forecasting.* New York: Harper Colophon. A classic analysis of the emerging postindustrial society from the perspective of an eminent contemporary sociologist.

Dahl, Robert A.   1982. *Dilemmas of pluralist democracy: Autonomy and control.* New Haven, Conn.: Yale University Press. An examination of the pluralist model of social power in the United States.

Domhoff, G. William.   1983. *Who rules America now? A view of the 80s.* Englewood Cliffs, N.J.: Prentice-Hall. The elitist model of social power by a sociologist who had analyzed it some twenty years earlier.

Fuchs, Victor R.   1983. *How we live: An economic perspective on Americans from birth to death.* Cambridge, Mass.: Harvard University Press. An examination of the effect of the economy on individual choices in education, work, family, and health.

Ginsburg, Helen.   1983. *Full employment and public policy: The United States and Sweden.* Lexington, Mass.: Lexington. The reasons for the disparity in unemployment rates in a socialist and capitalist economy, as well as the effects of unemployment in the United States, are thoroughly analyzed.

Gregory, Paul R., and Robert C. Stuart.   1985. *Comparative economic sys-*

tems. 2nd ed. Boston: Houghton Mifflin. An economics text that presents an overview of capitalism and socialism focusing on a number of world societies and their economies.

Page, Benjamin I. 1983. *Who gets what from government.* Berkeley: University of California Press. The effect of government policies on the American public, and the influence on such policies exerted by political parties, interest groups, and public opinion.

Meet Today's Young American Worker

MICHAEL BRODY

The transformation of the serf or peasant of medieval Europe into the industrial worker of eighteenth-century England brought with it social conflict and disorganization, and untold misery to the new workers themselves. So traumatic were the birth pangs of a new social class that Marx was not alone in predicting a bloody upheaval in which the workers of the world would unite and tear off the chains that bound them to their oppressors. But Marx was wrong, and though the industrial workers of the West never achieved financial parity with their employers, they nonetheless managed to live comfortably once they succeeded in organizing unions. But now a postindustrial era beckons. Once again momentous changes threaten the work force unless it acquires new skills, is trained in new technologies, and responds to a new work ethic. For the workers near the end of their working careers, this period is tragic. But the new American worker, young, better-educated, prepared to move from place to place and job to job, seems to be responding to the challenge eagerly and enthusiastically.

*I see you on the street and you look so
    tired,
Girl, I know that job you got leaves you so
    uninspired,
When I come back to take you out to eat,
You're lying all dressed up on the bed,
    baby, fast asleep.*
                Bruce Springsteen, "Jersey Girl"

Rock powerhouse Bruce Springsteen's passionate young losers, picking up girls at union hall dances in dying industrial towns, have become the 1980s images of working-class youth. But the working girls and guys who pack his pounding rock concerts in Oakland, Pittsburgh, and Chicago have money enough for the $17.50 tickets—and cassette tapes, and car stereos, and the cars from which the music blasts. In fact, most workers 18 to 35 are making

Source: From *Fortune,* November 11, 1985. © 1985 Time Inc. All rights reserved.

anywhere from $14,000 to $40,000 a year as skilled machinists, medical technicians, telephone equipment repairmen, and computer operators. Springsteen's wild kids, scraping a living from dead-end jobs and trying to outrun state troopers across industrial New Jersey's lunar landscapes, have a gut appeal even for listeners no longer adolescent. But they have as much to do with the reality of most young workers' lives as the angry rebels portrayed by James Dean did with the square, crew-cut kids of the Eisenhower era.

The attitudes of America's young working class are critically important to managers who have to find people to man an increasingly high-tech, service-based economy. Half the U.S. work force is now under 35, up from just over a third at the end of the 1950s. Whether their collars are blue, white, or pink, most of these are non-supervisory—47 million, vs. 10 million supervisors, managers, and professionals of the same age whose own careers will turn at least partly on their ability to manage these increasingly well-educated and skilled people.

Fortune reporters have interviewed upwards of 100 young workers across the U.S.—in factories, offices, bars, and unemployment lines. They range from nurses to garbagemen to robotics technicians to construction roustabouts. Many seem not even to recognize the hallowed term "blue collar," so much has the workplace changed in the 1970s and 1980s. Indeed, many have made their way up and out of low-skilled, low-paying white-collar jobs at the checkout counter or filing cabinet to more highly skilled, higher-paying blue-collar work.

Their plans for the future match the needs of corporations for flexible, mobile, highly skilled workers like the machinist who is as familiar with computer controls as with the milling machines they drive. From auto parts plants in Ohio's rustbelt to

the high-tech, union-free industrial "campuses" of Texas, young workers are intensely aware of the changes that have been taking place in the labor markets. Traditional wage structures have broken down, old-line industries have disappeared, to be replaced by others. Some young workers can't find jobs—the unemployment rate for people under 35 is 9.3%, twice that of older workers. And the jobs young workers do find sometimes prove evanescent. "I've worked for many different contractors in the Houston area, but most of the jobs don't last more than a few months," says an unemployed 23-year-old.

Partly in response, young workers have become avidly interested in acquiring new skills, even when their companies pay little extra for their additional knowledge. Almost two out of five have at least some college training—double the proportion among their parents—and many are going back to night school and technical college for more.

While they would be quite willing to change jobs and relocate to seize opportunities, they also tend to speak highly of their current employers. Oh, they have their gripes, all right: their most common beefs are about excessive overtime and the failure of managers to tell them what's going on. They are not hostile to unions in principle, but most seem indifferent to them. Only a small minority are union members, and those who are often find union seniority rules, which protect older workers at their expense, infuriating. To anyone who worked in plants in the bitter Vietnam years and remembers the angry, violent, drug-ridden young Luddites of the GM Lordstown plant, which symbolized that era, their successors seem like a manager's dream.

Many of their work attitudes, in fact, hark back not 15 years to Lordstown but 30 years to the post-Depression work ethic of their parents. In this respect, young workers are also far removed from the "I'm entitled" ethos often attributed to the much-hyped elite of their generation, the young urban professionals; many are working at high-skill, high-stress jobs that pay less than some garbagemen's.

However much new technology may be changing their jobs, members of the new working class live, like their parents before them, in that world described by Carl Sandburg, "where nobody works unless they have to, and they nearly all have to." They work for the rent money, the grocery money, the diapers and children's shoes, and for the down payment on a two-bedroom frame house not too far from the plant. Many have something going on the side, "off the books" and invisible to the tax man, like the house-cleaning supervisor at a hospital near San Francisco who also works as an auto mechanic at a friend's garage.

Young workers clearly perceive economic reality—the Japanese threat, the decline of industries that were organized labor's strongholds—and they're adapting to it. Today many of the steel mills up and down the Monongahela River valley winding southeast from Pittsburgh are mothballed hulks. This is Springsteen country; in Pittsburgh for a concert, the singer gave $10,000 to Steelworkers Local 1397, which has been struggling to force the reopening of shuttered plants.

But those who appear hardest hit by the closings are the older workers, unwilling to consider leaving the Mon Valley, as they call it. Younger workers like Arthur Pepper, 31, an electrician laid off from U.S. Steel's closed Duquesne mill, shrug off the union militants' Save the Mon campaign and instead talk about jobs available out of state. "They can buy the plant. I'm not," says Pepper. "It's been let go so many years, I don't see how it can be done. I don't think you can compete with foreign imports, anyhow. There's no future here. Lots of people are

moving; I have one friend who left for Florida today."

Not that they have to move terribly far. Jobs can be had across the industrial Midwest by young people prepared to work for less than the rates the unions once enforced. GM's Packard Electric division has 18 plants, employing some 9,000 hourly workers, in and around Warren, Ohio, about 10 miles northwest of hard-hit Youngstown. Last year GM and the International Union of Electrical Workers agreed on a new contract to give older workers "lifetime" job security, Japanese-style, in exchange for sharply lower wages for new hires. Since that agreement, about 300 new workers have been hired.

Young workers on Packard Electric's assembly lines plugging wires into electrical harnesses for automobiles are skeptical about how Japanese a company like GM can afford to be under the onslaught of Japanese competition. Janiece Walters is 27 and black; she tried to make it as an actress in New York City before coming back to Warren and getting a job at Packard. "A lot of people can't believe the lifetime job security," she says. "The company has to sell cars to keep people working." She notes that tension has come between some new hires and those like herself who voted to approve the two-tier wage system. "Some of them have an attitude about it, but we tell them: 'Hey, you could be making the minimum wage,'" she says. "But most of them are happy to have the job." And whether at the higher or the new lower wage rate, the contract also offers younger workers, like Karen Pacifico, 27, special benefits. A tuition refund program is paying for her computer technology degree at Kent State.

Across the U.S., companies moving to make old plants competitive are getting little but praise from workers who have grown up with the idea that the Japanese are invading U.S. markets, that Japanese employees work for less, and that Japanese plants are newer and cleaner and more efficient. "A very clean people," says Orlando Davila when the subject of Japanese plants is raised. "A very smart people. Maybe too smart." Davila, 30, a Puerto Rican who grew up in Chicago, works on the packaging line at an aging Purex bleach and detergent plant in industrial South Gate, near Los Angeles.

Purex Corp. was recently acquired by Greyhound, a move that has elicited a cautious welcome from workers, who see the need for more aggressive management. "They're doing a lot of cleanup," says Alphonse Sheffield, 35, a soft-spoken black lead-man on the line. "They're planning to put in a lot of new machinery, to get things up to date—they're putting money into it, which Purex didn't. Most of the machinery there is about, I'd say, 25 to 30 years old—tied down, wired down, tape, rubber bands, whatever it takes to get it running." Most workers are members of the United Auto Workers, making around $11 an hour. But a new two-tier pay system, cutting the wages of new hires by $2, went through in last year's contract.

Perhaps as a result of rapid change, young workers want their employers to keep them clued in, probably more than their predecessors did. Unetta Jones, 30, is a service assistant at AT&T in Morristown, New Jersey; she helps out junior operators with customer problems. Jones says flatly, "The problem with AT&T is they just don't *communicate*."

The elimination of some 24,000 jobs announced by Ma Bell in August won't cut into the ranks of operators and telecommunications technicians, but the operators are worried about being bumped from daytime shifts by workers with greater seniority as offices are consolidated. AT&T, they note, still has lots of ladies on its switchboards with 40 years' seniority and no plans to leave. (Despite the efforts of fem-inists, working-class women across America, young and old, still resolutely refer to themselves as ladies.)

Most young workers have no plans to remain phone company operators for 40 years. Their commitment to getting up and out is plainly evident. Michelle Pond, 25, works days as an AT&T operator and then works four hours a night as a computer programmer for another company. In the rest of her waking hours she tries to find enough time to complete an AT&T home study course that will allow her to qualify as a computer technician. Maurice Woodward, 29, who started out as an operator, taught himself electronics with Heathkit sets and passed an AT&T exam to qualify for training as a technician repairing electronic switching equipment—a job that can pay as much as $40,000 a year with overtime, compared with $26,000 or so for operators. AT&T pays the tuition of workers going back to school to acquire high-tech skills.

Especially across the Sunbelt, high-tech companies determined to remain non-union aren't waiting for organizers to push such demands; they are promoting education and upward mobility themselves. In the Research Triangle Park outside Raleigh, North Carolina, Northern Telecom, a powerhouse in telephone switching technology, offers its non-union work force generous educational benefits, not to mention lunch in an elegant atrium with trees and flowers; a working environment of spotless conveyor lines, IBM robot arms, and computer terminals; and for end-of-the-day workouts, exercise equipment on the premises.

Northern's young workers have seen the future and seem to think it works. Shirley Davis, 30, makes $6.70 an hour feeding tiny electronic parts into a machine that places them on printed circuit boards. "From this job I want to go into operating computers," she says. Joyce Massey, 22, makes $10 an hour as lead hand on a line using computers to test systems and has a two-year associate in applied science degree in electronic engineering from a local technical college. She's making enough to have bought, with her boyfriend, a Cablevision technician, a $10,000 powerboat they use for water-skiing. "I'm the captain of the ship," she says. "He knows I drive better. He does the skiing."

Construction laborers doing dirty jobs in the open air probably come as close to matching up with Bruce Springsteen's young roustabouts as any workers we spoke with. But even they have far more going in their lives than the adolescent rebels in his ballads. Like many other young workers, they display a passionate avidity for work—they will go to great lengths, and put up with a lot, to find a job and stick with it.

David Byers is a 29-year-old ironworker who had to leave his wife and two children in depressed eastern Ohio to find work in New York City. He returns home every other weekend. Byers did a lot of ironwork in steel mills in and around Wheeling, West Virginia, but there's no work left there now. In New York, where Manhattan is still in the midst of an office construction boom, he hasn't missed a day's work for several months.

Byers finds it tough living apart from his family, but there is no way they could join him: he's living in a Howard Johnson motel, along with nine other men from Ohio, only half of them registered at the front desk. "The work is all right," he offers. "I guess I'm stuck with this until I retire—or unless I win the lottery." He says he'll stay in New York "until things pick up back home."

That is the true voice of the American worker. Across an ocean to the west, big chunks of Japan's notoriously industrious work force are locked in place by the almost feudal loyalties of a system where young workers straight out of school commit themselves for life to a single corporation. Across an ocean to the east, European job markets are only beginning to thaw from decades of labor legislation and welfare state policies that have frozen labor mobility. In the U.S., the labor market, never anywhere near as unionized or as regulated, has become a wide-open free-for-all. And a generation of young workers who have grown up with kaleidoscopic change are in the middle of it, learning whatever new skills they have to learn, moving a hundred or a thousand miles to find a job, and keeping the wheels of the economy turning.

References

A boom in small towns. 1981. *Newsweek,* 16 March, 32.

Adorno, T. W. et al. 1950. *The authoritarian personality.* New York: Harper.

Albrecht, Stan L. 1980. Reactions and adjustments to divorce: Differences in the experiences of males and females. *Family Relations* 29 (January): 59–68.

Allport, Gordon. 1954. *The nature of prejudice.* Reading, Mass.: Addison-Wesley.

Archdeacon, Thomas J. 1983. *Becoming American: An ethnic history.* New York: Free.

Aries, Philippe. 1962. *Centuries of childhood.* New York: Knopf.

Baltzell, E. Digby. 1968. Religion and the class structure. In *Sociology and history: Methods,* ed. Seymour Martin Lipset and Richard Hofstadter, 310–325. New York: Basic.

Becker, Howard S. 1963. *Outsiders: Studies in the sociology of deviance.* New York: Free.

Bellah, Robert N. 1970. *Beyond belief.* New York: Harper.

Belsky, Jay, and Laurence D. Steinberg. 1978. The effects of day care: A critical review. *Child Development* 49: 929–949.

Berelson, Bernard, and Gary A. Steine. 1964. *Human behavior: An inventory of scientific findings.* New York: Harcourt.

Berger, Bennet M. 1961. The myth of suburbia. *Journal of Social Issues,* 17: 261–270.

Berger, Peter L. 1963. *Invitation to sociology.* Garden City, N.Y.: Doubleday.

Berger, Peter L., and Thomas Luckmann. 1966. *The social construction of reality: A treatise on the sociology of knowledge.* Garden City, N.Y.: Doubleday.

Blau, Peter M., and Otis Dudley Duncan. 1967. *The American occupational structure.* New York: Wiley.

Blau, Peter M., and Marshall W. Meyer. 1971. *Bureaucracy in modern society.* New York: Random.

Blumer, Herbert. 1946. Collective behavior. In *Principles of sociology,* ed. Alfred McClung Lee, 165–222. New York: Barnes.

———. 1951. Social movements. In *Principles of sociology,* ed. Alfred McClung Lee, 99–120. New York: Barnes.

———. 1962. Symbolic interaction. In *Human behavior and social process,* ed. Arnold M. Rose, 19–22. Boston: Houghton.

———. 1969. Collecive behavior. In *Principles of sociology,* ed. Alfred McClung Lee, 65–121. New York: Harper.

Bowles, Samuel, and Herbert Gintis. 1976. *Schooling in capitalist America: Educational reform and the contradictions of economic life.* New York: Basic.

Brodeur, P. 1979. Aerosol sprays: A planetary time bomb. *National Parks and Conservation Magazine.* (February).

Brody, Jane E. 1983. Divorce's stress exacts long term health toll. *New York Times,* 13 December, C1.

Brown, Lester R., Patricia L. McGrath, and Bruce Stokes. 1976. The population problem in 22 dimensions. *Futurist* 10 (October).

Caplow, Theodore. 1968. *Two against one: Coalitions in triads.* Englewood Cliffs, N.J.: Prentice-Hall.

Cherlin, Andrew J. 1981. *Marriage, divorce, remarriage.* Boston: Harvard UP.

Cloward, Richard A., and Lloyd E. Ohlin. 1960. *Delinquency and opportunity: A theory of delinquent gangs.* New York: Free.

Cohen, Albert K. 1955. *Delinquent boys: The culture of the gang.* New York: Free.

Cohn, Werner. 1958. The politics of American Jews. In *The Jews: Social patterns of an American group,* ed. Marshall Sklare. Glencoe, Ill.: Free.

Coleman, James S., et al. 1966. *Equality of educational opportunity.* Washington, D.C.: GPO.

———. 1981. *High school achievement: Public, Catholic, and private schools compared.* New York: Basic.

Collins, Randall. 1979. *The credential society: An historical sociology of education and stratification.* New York: Academic.

Commoner, Barry. 1971. *The closing circle.* New York: Knopf.

Cooley, Charles Horton. 1909/1910. *Social organization: A study of the larger mind.* New York: Scribner's.

———. [1909] 1964. *Human nature and the social order.* New York: Schocken.

Coser, Lewis A. 1956. *The functions of social conflict.* New York: Free.

Coser, Rose Laub, ed. 1964. *The family: Its structure and functions.* New York: St. Martin's.

Cumming, Elaine, and William E. Henry. 1961. *Growing old: The process of disengagement.* New York: Basic.

Dahl, Robert A. 1956. *A preface to democratic theory.* Chicago: U of Chicago P.

Dahrendorf, Ralph. 1959. *Class and class conflict in industrial society.* Stanford, Calif.: Stanford UP.

————. 1959. Conflict groups, group conflicts and social change. In *Class and class conflict in industrial society,* 202–223. Stanford, Calif.: Stanford UP.

————. 1964. Towards a theory of social conflict. In *Social change,* ed. Amitai Etzioni and Eve Etzioni, 100–124. New York: Basic.

Davis, Kingsley, and Wilbert Moore. 1945. Some principles of stratification. *American Sociological Review.* 10. (April): 242–249.

Deck, Leland. 1971. Short workers of the world unite. *Psychology Today,* August, 102.

Domhoff, William G. 1967. *Who rules America.* Englewood Cliffs, N.J.: Prentice-Hall.

Durden-Smith, Jo, and Diane deSimone. 1983. *Sex and the brain.* New York: Arbor House.

Durkheim, Émile. [1912] 1947. *The Elementary forms of religious life.* Repr. New York: Free.

————. [1897] 1951, 1966. *Le suicide: Etude de sociologie,* trans. J. A. Spaulding and George Simpson. New York: Free.

Dye, Thomas R., and L. Harmon Ziegler. 1972. *The irony of democracy.* 2d ed. North Scituate, Mass.: Duxbury.

Erikson, Erik. 1968. *Identity, youth and crisis.* New York: Norton.

Erikson, Kai T. 1964. Notes on the sociology of deviance. In *The other side: Perspectives on deviance,* ed. Howard S. Becker, 15. New York: Free.

Farnia, Amerigo, et al. 1977. Physical attractiveness and mental illness. *Journal of Abnormal Psychology* 86: 510–519.

Fogel, Robert William, and Stanley L. Engerman. 1974. *Time on the cross: Evidence and methods—a supplement.* Boston: Little.

Ford, Clelland S., and Frank A. Beach. 1951. *Patterns of sexual behavior.* New York: Harper.

Friedrich, Carl J., and Zbigniew Brzezinski. 1966. *Totalitarian dictatorship and autocracy.* New York: Praeger.

Fromm, Erich. 1944. Individual and social origins of neurosis. *American Sociological Review* 9: 380–384.

Gerth, H. H., and C. Wright Mills, eds. 1946. *From Max Weber: Essays in sociology.* New York: Oxford UP.

Glenn, Norval D. 1982. Interreligious marriage in the United States: Patterns and recent trends. *Journal of Marriage and the Family* 44 (August): 555–566.

Glock, Charles Y., and Rodney Stark. 1965. *Religion and society in tension.* Chicago: Rand.

Glueck, Sheldon, and Eleanor Glueck. 1956. *Physique and delinquency.* New York: Harper.

Goffman, Erving. [1956] 1959. *Presentation of self in everyday life.* Repr. Garden City, N.Y.: Doubleday (Anchor).

————. 1961. *Asylums: Essays on the social situation of mental patients and other inmates.* Garden City, N.Y.: Doubleday.

Gold, Harry. 1982. *The sociology of urban life.* Englewood Cliffs, N.J.: Prentice-Hall.

Goode, William J. 1963. *World revolution and family patterns.* New York: Free.

Gordon, Leonid A., and Eduard V. Klopov. 1975. *Man after work,* trans. John Bushmess and Kristine Bushmess. Moscow: Progress.

Greeley, Andrew M. 1974. *Ethnicity in the United States.* New York: Wiley.

Gross, Jane. 1985. Against the odds: A woman's ascent on Wall Street. *The New York Times Magazine,* 6 January.

Gutman, Herbert G. 1976. *The black family in slavery and freedom, 1750–1925.* New York: Pantheon.

Harlow, Harry. 1966. Learning to love. *American Scientist* 54 (September): 224–272.

Hauser, Robert M., and David L. Featherman. 1977. *The process of stratification: Trends and analysis.* New York: Academic.

Herberg, Will. 1955. *Protestant, Catholic, Jew.* New York: Doubleday.

Herbert, Wray. 1982. Sources of temperament: Bashful at birth? *Science News.* 16 January 16: 36.

Hofstadter, Richard. 1954. *The American political tradition.* New York: Vintage.

Horn, Joseph M., et al. 1976. Heritability of personality traits in adult male twins. *Behavior Genetics* (January): 17–30.

Hunt, Morton, and Bernice Hunt. 1980. Another world, another life. In *Family in transition,* ed. Arlene Skolnick and Jerome H. Skolnick, 340–354. Boston: Little.

Janowsky, Oscar. 1945. *Nationalities and national minorities.* New York: Macmillan.

Jencks, Christopher, et al. 1972. *Inequality.* New York: Basic.

———. 1979. *Who gets ahead? The determinants of economic success in America.* New York: Basic.

Juel-Nielson, Neils. 1980. *Individual and environment: monozygotic twins reared apart.* New York: International Universities P.

Kagan, Jerome, Barbara Hosken, and Sara Watson. 1961. Child's symbolic conceptualization of parents. *Child Development* 32: 234–263.

Kagan, Jerome. 1964. Acquisition and significance of sex typing and sex role identity. In *Review of child development research,* ed. M. S. Hoffman and L. W. Hoffman, 137–167. New York: Russell Sage Foundation.

Kennedy, Ruby Jo Reeves. 1944. Single or triple melting pot? Intermarriage trends in New Haven, 1870–1940. *American Journal of Sociology* 49 (January): 331–339.

Killian, Lewis M. 1964. Social movements. In *Handbook of modern sociology,* ed. Robert E. Faris, 426–455. Chicago: Rand.

Kluckhohn, Clyde, and Henry A. Murray, eds. 1953. *Personality in nature, society, and culture.* New York: Knopf.

Kohlberg, Lawrence. 1966. A cognitive developmental analysis of children's sex-role concepts and attitudes. In *The development of sex differences,* ed. Eleanor E. Maccoby, 82–172. Stanford, Calif.: Stanford UP.

Kornhauser, William. 1959. *The politics of mass society.* New York: Free.

Kurdek, Lawrence A. 1981. An integrative perspective on children's divorce adjustment. *American Psychologist* 36 (August): 856–866.

Larsen, Otto N. 1964. Social effects of mass communication. In *Handbook of modern sociology,* ed. E. L. Faris, 349–381. Chicago: Rand.

Le Bon, Gustave. 1960. *The Mind of the Crowd.* New York: Viking.

Lenski, Gerhard. 1961. *The religious factor.* New York: Doubleday.

———. 1966. *Power and privilege: A theory of social stratification.* New York: McGraw-Hill.

———. 1970. *Human societies.* New York: McGraw-Hill.

Levi-Strauss, Claude. 1971. The family. In *Family in transition,* ed. Arlene S. Skolnick and Jerome H. Skolnick, 55–63. Boston: Little.

Liazos, Richard. 1972. The Poverty of the sociology of deviance: Nuts, sluts, and perverts. *Social Problems* 20: 103–120.

Lieberson, Stanley. 1980. *A piece of the pie: Blacks and white immigrants since 1880.* Berkeley: U of California P.

Lipset, Seymour Martin, and Reinhard Bendix. 1959. *Social mobility in industrial society.* Berkeley: U of California P.

———. 1963. *Political man.* Garden City, N.Y.: Doubleday.

Lipset, Seymour Martin. 1967. Political sociology. In *Sociology: An introduction,* ed. Neil J. Smelser, 461–473. New York: Wiley.

———. 1976. Equality and inequality. In *Contemporary social problems.* 4th ed., ed. Robert K. Merton and Robert Nisbet, 305–353. New York: Harcourt.

Litt, Edgar. 1963. Civic education, community norms, and political indoctrination. *American Sociological Review* 28 (February): 69–75.

Livingston, John C., and Robert G. Thompson. 1971. *The consent of the governed.* New York: Macmillan.

Lombroso, Cesare. 1911. *Crime: Its causes and remedies.* Boston: Little.

Luepnitz, Deborah. 1979. Which aspects of divorce affect children? *The Family Co-ordinator* 28 (January): 79–85.

Lynd, Robert S., and Helen M. Lynd. 1929. *Middletown.* New York: Harcourt, Brace and World.

———. 1929, 1937. *Middletown in transition.* New York: Harcourt.

Mannheim, Karl. 1936. *Ideology and utopia.* New York: Harcourt.

Marx, Gary T. 1967. *Protest and prejudice.* New York: Harper.

Mead, George Herbert. 1934. *Mind, self, and society.* Chicago: U of Chicago P.

Mead, Margaret. 1935. *Sex and temperament in three primitive societies.* Magnolia, Mass.: Peter Smith.

Melton, J. Gordon. 1978. *Encyclopedia of American religions.* Wilmington, N.C.: McGrath.

Merton, Robert K. 1938. Social structure and anomie. *American Sociological Review* 3: 672–682.

———. 1968. *Social theory and social structure,* 2nd ed. New York: Free.

Meyer, John W. 1977. The effects of education as an institution. *American Journal of Sociology* 83: 55–77.

Michels, Robert. 1949. *Political parties: A sociological study of the oligarchical tendencies in modern democracy.* New York: Free.

Miller, Walter B. 1958. Lower-class culture as a generating milieu of gang delinquency. *Journal of Sociological Issues* 14: 5–19.

Mills, C. Wright. 1953. *White collar.* New York: Oxford UP.

———. 1956. *The power elite.* New York: Oxford UP.

———. 1959. *The sociological imagination.* New York: Oxford UP.

Moffet, Robert K., and Jack F. Scherer. 1976. *Dealing with divorce.* Boston: Little.

Monahan, Thomas P. 1976. An overview of statistics on interracial marriage in the United States, with data on its extent from 1963–1970. *Journal of Marriage and the Family* 38 (May): 223–231.

Money, John, and Anke Erhardt. 1972. *Man and woman, boy and girl.* Baltimore: Johns Hopkins P.

Murdock, George Peter. 1949. *Social structure.* New York: Macmillan.

———. 1957. World ethnographic sample. *American Anthropologist* 59: 664–687.

Naisbitt, John. *Megatrends.* New York: Warner.

Nisbett, Robert A. 1970. *The social bond.* New York: Knopf.

Ogburn, William F. 1950. *Social change.* New York: Viking.

Owen, D. R. 1972. The 47 XYY male: A review. *Psychological Bulletin* 78 (September): 209–233.

Patterson, Gerald R. 1980. Children who steal. In *Understanding crime: Current theory and research,* ed. Travis Hirschi and Michael Gottfredson, 73–90. Beverly Hills: Sage.

Population Reference Bureau. 1981. *World population data sheet.* Washington, D.C.: GPO.

Quinney, Richard. 1970. *The social reality of crime.* Boston: Little.

Riccio, James. 1979. Religious affiliation and socioeconomic achievement. In *The religious dimension: New directions in quantitative research,* ed. Robert Wuthnow, 199–231. New York: Academic.

Riesman, David, et al. 1961. *The lonely crowd.* New Haven.: Yale UP.

Riker, William H. 1965. *Democracy in the United States.* New York: Macmillan.

Schlapentokh, Vladimir. 1984. Many Soviet males not fit to be tied. *The Plain Dealer* 10 February, p. 13b. (Originally appeared in The New York Times).

Schur, Edwin. 1965. *Crimes without victims: Deviant behavior and public policy.* Englewood Cliffs, N.J.: Prentice-Hall.

Sears, Robert R., Eleanor E. Maccoby, and Harry Levin. 1957. *Patterns of child rearing.* New York: Harper.

Sheldon, William H. 1940. *The varieties of human physique.* New York: Harper.

Sheldon, William H., et al. 1949. *Varieties of delinquent youth.* New York: Harper.

Shelley, Louise I. 1981. *Crime and modernization: The impact of industrialization and urbanization on crime.* Carbondale, Ill.: Southern Illinois UP.

Simmel, Georg. [1905] 1956. *Conflict and the web of group affiliation,* trans. Kurt H. Wolff. Glencoe, Ill.: Free.

Simon, William, and John H. Gagnon. 1976. The anomie of affluence: A post-Mertonian conception. *American Journal of Sociology* 82 (2): 356–378.

Simpson, George E., and J. Milton Yinger. 1972. *Racial and cultural minorities: An analysis of prejudice and discrimination.* New York: Harper.

Skinner, B. F. 1971. *Beyond freedom and dignity.* New York: Bantam/Vintage.

Spiro, Melford. 1971. The Israeli kibbutz. In *Family in transition,* ed. Arlene S. Skolnick and Jerome H. Skolnick, 501–508. Boston: Little.

Spitz, Rene A. 1945. Hospitalism. In *The psychoanalytic study of the child.* Vol. 1, 53–57. New York: International Universities P.

———. 1964. Hospitalism. In *The family: Its structure and functions,* ed. Rose L. Coser, 399–423. New York: St. Martin's.

Stark, Rodney. 1985. *Sociology.* Belmont, Calif.: Wadsworth.

Stark, Rodney, and W. S. Bainbridge. 1981. Secularization and cult formation in the jazz age. *Journal for the Scientific Study of Religion* 20 (December): 360–373.

———. 1985. *The future of religion: Secularization, revival and cult formation.* Berkeley: U of California P.

Statistical Abstract of the United States: 1982–83, 1983–84, 1984–85. Washington, D.C.: GPO.

Sternlieb, George, and James W. Hughes. 1978. *Current population trends in the U.S.* New Brunswick, N.J.: Center for Urban Policy Research.

Sutherland, Edwin H. 1949. *White collar crime.* New York: Dryden.

Swafford, Michael. 1978. Sex differences in Soviet earning. *American Sociological Review* 43: 657–673.

Sweden discourages full-time housewifery. 1985. *The Plain Dealer,* 7 July, p. 25P.

Taylor, Ian, Paul Walton, and Jock Young. 1973. *The new criminology: For a new theory of deviance.* New York: Harper.

Tiger, Lionel, and Joseph Shepher. 1975. *Women in the kibbutz.* New York: Harcourt.

Tönnies, Ferdinand. [1887] 1957. *Community and society.* New York: Harper.

Turnbull, Colin. 1973. *The mountain people.* New York: Simon.

U.S. Bureau of the Census. 1982. *Money, income, and poverty.* Washington, D.C.: GPO.

———. 1983. Fertility of American women. In *Current population reports,* Series P-20, No. 382. Washington, D.C.: GPO.

———. 1985. Consumer income. In *Current population reports,* Series P-60, No. 149. Washington, D.C.: GPO.

Vidich, Arthur J., and Joseph Bensman. 1958. *Small town in mass society.* Princeton, N.J.: Princeton UP.

Wagley, Charles, and Marvin Harris. 1958. *Minorities in the new world.* New York: Columbia UP.

Wallerstein, Judith S., and Joan B. Kelly. 1983. The effects of parental divorce: Experiences of the child in later latency. In *Family in transition,* ed. Arlene S. Skolnick and Jerome H. Skolnick, 438–452. Boston: Little.

Warner, W. L., and Paul Lunt. 1941. *The social life of a modern community.* New Haven, Conn.: Yale UP.

Washburn, Sheldon L., and Irven DeVore. 1961. Social behavior of baboons and early man. In *Social life of early man,* ed. S. L. Washburn, 96–100. Chicago: Aldine.

Weber, Max. [1925] 1947, 1957. *Theory of social and economic organization,* trans. A. L. Henderson and Talcott Parsons. New York: Free.

Weitzman, Lenore J., and Deborah Eifler. 1972. Sex role socialization in picture books for preschool children. *American Journal of Sociology.* 77 (8): 1125–1149.

Weitzman, Lenore J. 1975. Sex-role socialization. In *Women: A feminist perspective,* ed. Jo Freeman, 4–6. Palo Alto: Mayfield.

Whiting, B. 1963. *Six cultures: Studies of child rearing.* London: Wiley.

Wilson, William Julius. 1984. The black underclass. *The Wilson Quarterly* 8 (2): 88–99.

Wirth, Louis. 1938. Urbanism as a way of life. *American Journal of Sociology* 44 (July).

Wrong, Dennis H. 1961. The oversocialized conception of man. *American Sociological Review* 26: 183–193.

Yetman, Norman R., and C. Hoy Steele, eds. 1971. *Majority and minority.* Boston: Allyn and Bacon.

Photograph
Credits

Index

Study Guide
to accompany

Perry & Perry:
THE SOCIAL WEB

An Introduction to Sociology
Fifth Edition

Rollie E. Dorsett

Austin Community College

Contents

A Note to the Student

This Study Guide contains no gimmicks or busy-work activities. It is designed to help you grasp the facts and concepts contained in *The Social Web*, Fifth Edition. The Study Guide, if utilized properly, will help you pass the course with a good grade.

It is recommended that you proceed as follows:

Step 1. Read the GOALS for the chapter.

Step 2. Read the SYNOPTIC OUTLINE of the chapter so that you will get an idea of what the chapter is about.

Step 3. Read the chapter in the text and carefully review the terms to remember at the end of the chapter.

Step 4. Write out the answers to the LEARNING OBJECTIVES for the chapter.

Step 5. Take the SELF-TEST for the chapter. If you miss any questions, go back to the text and look up the answers.

If you do these five steps prior to class discussion of the chapter, your comprehension of the material covered will be significantly increased.

Chapter 1
Sociology: Science and Art

Goals

After you read the chapter, study the learning objectives, and take the self-test, you will be able to:

1. Understand the meaning of the scientific spirit.
2. Comprehend the use of the scientific method.
3. Define the social sciences.
4. Define sociology.
5. Recognize the major theoretical models used in sociological study.
6. Give the definitions of the major terms used in the chapter.

Synoptic Outline

I. **The Scientific Method:** A way of acquiring knowledge based on verifiable empirical evidence rather than intuition, common sense, the word of authority, or traditional assumptions.

   A. *The scientific spirit*: An attitude that underlies the scientific method. The four principles of the scientific spirit are:

      1. Doubt and skepticism.
      2. Objectivity.
      3. Ethical neutrality.
      4. Conclusions are relative and subject to change.

   B. *The scientific method*: A systematic observation that is:

      1. Accurate and precise.
      2. Conducted under controlled conditions.
      3. Performed by a trained observer.

   C. The steps of the scientific method are:

      1. Formulation of a *hypothesis* that can be tested.
      2. Collection of data.
      3. Data classification.
      4. Data analysis.
      5. Verification.
      6. Generalization.

II. **Sociology:** The systematic and scientific study of human social behavior and of all the social systems that such behavior creates.

III. **Sociological Perspectives**

    A. *Evolutionary perspective*: The earliest model. Society is analogous to a living organism passing through progressively more complex stages of development. It is also analogous to species evolution in that societies adapt "naturally" to environmental changes.

    B. *Functionalist perspective*: By analogy with a living organism, it holds that all social institutions are functional and form a complex, interlocking, life-maintenance system for the whole.

    C. *Conflict perspective*: Holds that conflict is the most important and universal characteristic of societies as well as the prime cause of social change. Conflict between the individual and the group, between group and group, and between institutions and groups leads to social change, followed by regrouping, followed in turn by new conflicts. Karl Marx, the most famous of the conflict theorists, held economic disparity to be the fundamental conflict. His model projects a time of economic parity when all conflict will cease.

    D. *Symbolic-interactionist perspective*: Holds that the development of the self and socialization derive from the internalization of communal symbols. The individual learns from those around him or her the symbolic meanings of language, gesture, actions. Thus the individual's cognitive world necessarily correlates with the external world.

    E. Other perspectives include: *Ethnomethodology, sociobiology,* and *humanistic sociology*.

IV. **The Scientific Method in Sociology**

    A. *Concepts*: Generalized ideas about people, objects, and processes that are related to one another. Concepts are abstract ways of classifying things that are similar.

    B. *Theories*: Sets of concepts and generalizations so arranged as to explain and predict possible and probable relationships. Their intent is to explain human interaction.

    C. *Research*: The gathering of empirical data in support of a theory.

    D. *Variables*: Two or more factors among which researchers seek to determine relationships.

V. Sociological Research Methods

A. *Sample survey*: A portion of the population is surveyed.

B. *Case study*: An attempt to obtain a complete, detailed account of the behavior of the individual, group, or event under consideration.

C. *Participant-observation*: The researcher takes part in the lives of the members of the group being studied.

D. *Experiment*: One variable is held constant while others are changed; the results are then compared.

VI. Sociology and Sociologists

A. Sociology is a pure science that has practical application, thus it can be seen as an applied science because scientific knowledge is used in the effort to reduce or solve social problems.

B. Sociologists play three major roles: researchers, consultants and advisers, and teachers.

Learning Objectives

1. Contrast the social sciences with the natural sciences.

2. Define the term *sociology*.

3. List the four main tools used to gain knowledge in the past.

4. Briefly describe the four principles of the scientific spirit.

5. Define the term *scientific method* and describe the six steps of this method.

6. Define the terms *concept* and *theory* and give a sociological example of each term.

7. State the difference between dependent and independent variables.

8. Briefly describe how to conduct a sample survey, a case study, participant observation, and an experiment.

9. Name and briefly describe the major theoretical frameworks of sociology.

10. State the roles that sociologists play.

Self-Test

Select the best possible answer. If you miss any questions, go back to the text and find the correct answer.

Multiple-Choice

1. A basic definition of sociology is
   a. the scientific study of humans in groups.
   b. the study of human beings.
   c. the scientific study of individual behavior.
   d. the study of the relationships of humans and their environment.

2. Doubt, objectivity, and ethical neutrality are part of
   a. the scientific spirit.
   b. the commonsense approach.
   c. the method of sociology.
   d. the method of inquiry followed only by the natural sciences.

3. Generalized ideas about people, objects, and processes that are related to each other are
   a. abstractions.
   b. concepts.
   c. theories.
   d. research.

4. Attempts at predicting possible and probable relationships among data are
   a. theories.
   b. concepts.
   c. abstractions.
   d. research.

5. Which of the following is identified as a shortcoming of participant observation?
   a. There is a significant margin for error when testing the attitudes and opinions of a large population.
   b. Dependent variables often influence independent variables.
   c. The matched-pair technique is very difficult to use and is expensive.
   d. The researcher may become too involved with his subjects and therefore lose his objectivity.

6. The functionalist model of society states that
   a. stability and change are the dual characteristics of social systems.
   b. each system of society contributes to the maintenance and survival of the whole society.
   c. the structures of society help it survive and persist.
   d. All of the above.

7. The person associated with the conflict model in sociology discussed in the text is
   a. Comte.
   b. Durkheim.
   c. Marx.
   d. Mead.

8. The major roles that sociologists play include
   a. researchers.
   b. counselors.
   c. historians.
   d. all of the above.

True-False

_____ 1. Sociology can be defined as the scientific study of society.

_____ 2. The focus of sociology is the single individual and his or her development as a human being.

_____ 3. Theories are sets of concepts and generalizations so arranged as to explain and predict possible and probable relationships among phenomena.

_____ 4. Sample surveys are particularly effective when used to study a particular person, family, or neighborhood in depth.

_____ 5. Conflict sociologists feel that conflict is the most important and universal characteristic of social change.

_____ 6. The functional model views society as existing in a delicate balance; if something happens to one of the parts of the system, all other parts are affected.

Fill-in-the-Blank

1. One of the four main tools used to develop knowledge is _____, the acceptance of statements by people who are specialists in a field or who are thought to be divinely inspired. (intuition, authority)

2. All scientific research should go through the process of _____ to eliminate the possibility of error on the part of the researcher. (replication, generalization)

3. _____ are general statements made by the researcher defining the problem and stating the probable solution. (Theories, Hypotheses)

4. Social scientists try to show the relationship between independent and dependent variables. _____ always influence dependent variables, as in the attempt to determine if income affects child-raising methods. (Independent, Nondependent)

5. When a researcher actually joins a group he is studying to share its experiences and life-styles, he is conducting a _____ . (case study, participant observation)

6. The _____ model of society states that societies develop through a number of fixed stages, beginning with the simplest form and moving to the more complex. (evolutionary, functionalist)

Chapter 2
Society: People, the Social Animals

Goals

After you read the chapter, study the learning objectives, and take the self-test you will be able to:

1. Recognize why one needs to live in a society.
2. Construct a model of the social system of the United States.
3. Identify the relationship between status and role.
4. Be familiar with the various types of groups.
5. Compare and contrast Gemeinschaft and Gesellschaft societies.
6. Describe the three major social processes.

Synoptic Outline

I. **Humans must live in groups.** In order to become a full-fledged human being, one needs to be surrounded by, and interact with, other humans.

II. **Social System:** A model that illustrates how social relationships work in a society.

III. **Social Structure and Social Organization:** Interchangeable terms that refer to the network of organized relationships among the parts of the social system. They are the patterned and recurring ways in which individuals, groups, and institutions interact.

    A. *Microsocial or interpersonal level of social organization:* The study of interaction between individuals who occupy definite positions in relation to one another.

    B. *Macrosocial level of social organization:* The study of relationships between and among groups or organizations.

IV. **Elements of Social Structure: Statuses and Roles**

    A. *Status*: A position in a social group and a rank in the group.

    B. *Role*: The carrying out of the behavior expected for a given status.

C. *Ascribed and achieved status*

    1. Ascribed status involuntary: predetermined by biology, geography, or social structure.

    2. Achieved status voluntary: largely a result of individual will and effort.

    3. Preindustrial society marked by a high incidence of ascribed statuses. The individual is born not only with biological ascription but with an occupation and a socioeconomic position that is retained for life.

    4. Industrial society is marked by a high incidence of achieved statuses—society's permission for individual mobility from one occupation, pursuit, or socioeconomic class to another.

D. *The individual's multiple statuses and roles*

    1. Vary according to one's membership in various groups.

    2. *Master status:* The status by which one is evaluated and ranked by the greater society.

    3. Quality of performance of any given role is linked to the individual's self-image.

E. *Role conflict and stress results from*

    1. Discrepancy between the ideal role and the actual role.

    2. Multiple roles which conflict with each other's performance or value.

    3. Improperly learned roles.

    4. A single role which requires paradoxical behaviors, e.g., to be well liked and ultraefficient.

V. The Nature of Groups

A. *Aggregate*: Accidental assemblage of people in the same place at the same time.

B. *Category*: Accidental sharing of an attribute or behavior by a number of people. Noninteractive.

C. *Sociological definition of group:*

    1. Members share the communication system with other members through symbolic interaction.

    2. Membership in the group is mutually acknowledged by the individual member and by the other members of the group.

    3. Members are aware of and agree to adhere to an acceptable extent to the group behavioral norms—consensus.

    4. Members accept group statuses and roles—structure.

VI. Group Classifications: No fixed categories. A given group may share common features with a myriad of diverse groups. Any group may be multiply classified in accordance with that aspect of its structure. The researcher focuses on size, function, genesis, goal, type of interaction, conditions of entry, purpose, intergroup interaction, etc.

A. Size

    1. *Dyads*: The least stable since withdrawal of one member dissolves the group.

    2. *Triad*: Permits the coalition of the two weaker against the stronger member. Caplow believes the triad to be the preliminary structure of all social organization.

    3. *Small groups* are characterized by durability and face-to-face relationships between members who generally accept one another and share common values. Members perceive the group as a separate entity which strives to fulfill definite goals, with which members identify, and to which they feel loyalty.

    4. *Large groups,* the largest of which is society itself, are highly organized, formal, and bureaucratic.

VII. **Primary and Secondary Groups:** All-inclusive categories under which every other classification may be subsumed.

    A. Characteristics of primary groups

        1. Originally characterized by Charles Horton Cooley as groups whose members interact intimately, regard each other holistically rather than fractionally, and strongly influence each other's personality development.

        2. Additionally, primary groups are characterized by relatively small size, physical proximity of members, emotional interaction, relative durability, informality, and a wide range of spontaneous behavior.

        3. The family is the archetypal primary group.

        4. Primary group relationships are apparently indispensable for healthy personality development. However, because of the intensity and intimacy of primary group relationships, they may induce antisocial behavior and personality problems.

    B. *Characteristics of secondary groups:* Size may extend to millions; membership relatively short; formal interaction; constrains and limits varieties of behavior; membership motivated by mutual utility and expectation of benefit.

VIII. **Additional Classification of Groups**

    A. *In-groups and out-groups:* The in-group reinforces individual identity by strongly differentiating its members from nonmembers. As such it is exclusionary and socially divisive, promoting feelings of superiority in its members over other groups. It aids social cohesion, however, in that it supports its members and provides a nucleus.

    B. *Reference groups:* Those groups provide us with standards which we use to evaluate our own status against that of others.

    C. *Membership groups:* Either formal or informal organizations to which individuals belong.

D. Conditions of entry:

    1. *Involuntary:* Membership by accident or by enforcement. The individual's will has little or no effect on the fact of his or her membership.

    2. *Voluntary:* Membership by choice. The individual's will to join is a strong, though not the only, factor in admission to membership.

IX. Society: The largest group inhabiting a specific territory and sharing a common way of life.

    A. Gerhard Lenski's classification by *subsistence mode:* An evolutionary model—from less to more sophisticated exploitation of the environment.

        1. *Hunting and gathering societies:*

            a. Nomadic. Find rather than produce food.

            b. No specialization or institutionalization other than the family.

            c. Socioeconomic equality based on scarcity. No ranking.

        2. *Pastoral societies:*

            a. Nomadic. Herd driving.

            b. Family, economic, religio-political institutions.

            c. Rudimentary ranking based on accumulation of livestock. Ownership and nonownership classes.

        3. *Horticultural societies:*

            a. Seminomadic grain cultivators.

            b. Ranking based on specialization and wealth derived from food surpluses.

        4. *Agrarian societies:*

            a. Nonnomadic (settled). Technologically determined by the invention of the plow.

            b. Institutionalized and bureaucratized.

            c. Discrete social stratification based on specialization, land wealth, and goods owned.

        5. *Industrial societies:*

            a. Urbanized.

            b. Complex, interlocking institutions and bureaucracies supersede family and kinship ties in most functions.

            c. Extreme specialization, automation, and mechanization.

    B. Classification according to social organization:

        1. *Gemeinschaft or communal societies:* Small, homogeneous societies in which behavior is specified by tradition.

        2. *Gesellschaft or associational societies:* Large, heterogeneous societies in which institutions and secondary groups take over the function of kinship ties.

X. Social Interaction and Social Processes: Social processes are patterns of interaction between members of a group and between groups. Sociologists focus on three primary social processes:

A. *Cooperation*: A fundamental process which promotes harmony and prevents dissolution although individual members or groups within the larger society might not benefit equally from the cooperative effort.

B. *Competition*: Efforts by two or more individuals or groups to attain a limited resource or goal.

    1. Society's values indicate which goals are most desirable.

    2. Society's norms and rules govern competitive behavior, usually preventing it from becoming outright conflict.

    3. For certain of its goods and goals, society limits the types and numbers of competitors by requiring qualifications with respect to age, education, sex, etc.

C. *Conflict*: Open hostile struggle between opposing individuals or groups for a resource or goal. Its effects may be destructive or creative or both.

    1. Unlike cooperation or competition, which may be continuous, conflict is necessarily intermittent, ceasing upon victory or agreement.

    2. Intergroup conflict may have the effect of solidifying the memberships of opposing groups.

    3. It frequently leads to necessary change in the social structure.

Learning Objectives

1. State the major reasons why humans must live in groups.

2. Describe a social system.

3. State the definition of a social organization.

4. Name and define the two levels of social organization.

5. Define status and role.

6. Differentiate between status and role.

7. Explain the difference between ascribed and achieved status.

8. Describe how society may cause role confusion.

9. State the conditions under which role confusion is most likely to occur in individuals.

10. Define and give an example of an aggregate.

11. Define and give an example of a category.

12. List the conditions that sociologists use to define a group.

13. Identify the major group classifications.

14. Describe the characteristics of a primary group.

15. Explain how a secondary group differs from a primary group.

16. List the characteristics of societies in Lenski's classification system.

17. Describe the characteristics of Gemeinschaft (communal) societies.

18. Describe the characteristics of Gesellschaft (associational) societies.

19. Define and differentiate cooperation, competition, and conflict.

Self-Test

Select the best possible answer. If you miss any questions, go back to the text and find the correct answer.

Multiple-Choice

1. Role conflict and stress may occur because of
   a. discrepancy between ideal and real roles.
   b. multiple roles.
   c. a role that requires paradoxical behaviors.
   d. all of the above.

2. Role confusion is most likely to occur
   a. when one is satisfied with one's roles.
   b. when one's reference group and membership group is the same.
   c. when there is a lack of knowledge of the behavior associated with the role.
   d. none of the above.

3. Which of the following is a condition a number of people must meet in order to be considered a group by sociologists?
   a. Physical interaction among the people.
   b. Physical and symbolic interaction among the people.
   c. Individuals who share the same characteristics.
   d. A number of people gathered at the same time in the same place.

4. Groups may be classified according to
   a. size.
   b. interaction.
   c. condition of entry.
   d. all of the above.

5. Primary group membership is valuable to individuals because it
   a. provides emotional satisfaction.
   b. satisfies a particular goal.
   c. provides impersonal treatment to each member.
   d. uses rationality to reach organizational objectives.

6. When two groups that were formerly in conflict work together and arrive at an ultimate solution of the conflict, they exhibit the social process of
   a. accommodation.
   b. cooperation.
   c. conflict.
   d. assimilation.

7. Gerhard Lenski's classification of societies includes
   a. Gemeinschaft/Gesellschaft.
   b. communal/associational.
   c. simple/complex.
   d. agrarian/industrial.

8. In which of the following societies did social inequality emerge?
   a. Hunting and gathering.
   b. Horticultural.
   c. Agrarian.
   d. Industrial.

9. When classifying societies according to their basic patterns of social organization, one may divide them into
   a. Gesellschaft and Gemeinschaft.
   b. traditional and associational.
   c. none of the above.
   d. all of the above.

True-False

_____ 1. One can develop into a full-fledged human being without human interaction.

_____ 2. Social structure and social organization are interchangeable terms that refer to the network of organized relationships among the parts of the social system.

_____ 3. Each individual occupies but one status and role in society.

_____ 4. All people born on the Fourth of July form an aggregate.

_____ 5. A number of people who have some characteristic in common but who do not interact with one another form a category.

_____ 6. Primary groups are generally small in size, stable, and exist over long periods of time.

_____ 7. Cooperation is a basic social process because without it life at any level of social organization would be difficult.

_____ 8. Conflict is a hostile struggle between two or more persons or groups for an object of value that each prizes.

_____ 9. Society refers to the largest group of people inhabiting a specific territory and sharing a common culture.

_____ 10. Sociologist Gerhard Lenski analyzed and classified societies according to basic patterns of social organization.

_____ 11. The foundations for social inequity are laid in the pastoral society with the production of a surplus.

_____ 12. Gemeinschaft societies are large, heterogeneous societies.

_____ 13. Gesellschaft societies are small, homogeneous societies.

Fill-in-the-Blank

1. _____ is a model that illustrates how social relationships work in a society. (Social structure, Social system)

2. The _____ level of social organization concerns itself with the study of relationships between and among groups or organizations. (macrosocial, microsocial)

3. _____ is a position in a social group. (Status, Role)

4. The status one has at birth is _____ . (achieved, ascribed)

5. _____ groups are large, formal, and impersonal. (Primary, Secondary)

Chapter 3

Culture: The Blueprint for Life in Society

Goals

After you read the chapter, study the learning objectives, and take the self-test, you will be able to:

1. Define culture.
2. Identify the fundamental characteristics of culture.
3. Comprehend how language influences culture.
4. Name and give examples of the components of the normative system.
5. Understand the significance of the five major social institutions.
6. Differentiate between subculture and counterculture.

Synoptic Outline

I. **Universality of Culture:** There are significant differences among nations, societies, and groups of people, yet humans share a large number of similarities.

II. **Culture:** May be defined as the totality of what is learned, shared, and transmitted by the members of a society through their interaction.

III. **Fundamental Characteristics of Culture**

A. Culture is that product of social interaction that is uniquely human.

B. Culture includes all the accumulated knowledge, ideas, values, goals, and material objects of a society that are shared by all the members of the society and that have been passed from generation to generation by individual members.

C. Culture is learned by each member of a society during socialization—the process through which the individual learns to become human. Cultural learning takes place through symbolic interaction, a kind of communication in which language or gestures are used.

D. Culture provides each member of a society with ways of satisfying biological and emotional needs in a manner approved by the society. Culture does this by supplying people with systems, or patterns, of organized behavior.

E. Each human society develops a culture that is distinct from other cultures. Yet all cultures share similarities, because they deal with biological and emotional needs that are universal.

F. Culture, as well as society—of which culture is both a product and a guide—is in a constant state of flux. Changes occur either imperceptibly or rapidly, according to circumstances.

IV. **Symbolic Quality of Culture:** Distinct from the signals systems of animals, which are biologically determined and simple, human symbols systems are complex, i.e., ideational and emotional as well as functional, and meanings are arbitrary, i.e., agreed upon by members of the culture.

A. *Language*: the essential symbol system, both the product and the triggering mechanism of culture.

1. A vehicle for the continuation of the past and speculation about the future.

2. Sufficient to communicate all human activity and ideas, which in turn leads to an expansion of activity and ideas.

3. Enables the communication of abstractions: concepts, generalizations, theories, wishes, morals, values, etc.

4. Expansive: Capable of expressing changes in material and nonmaterial culture.

B. The *Whorf-Sapir hypothesis*: People perceive the world in terms of their linguistic symbols. Reality, as each culture sees it, is structured by the language of that culture (i.e., if you can't say it, it doesn't exist).

V. **The Effects of Biology on Culture:** Culture takes forms permitted by human biology, which is unique in having:

A. Hand and thumb construction which permits both gross and fine manipulation of objects.

B. Upright posture, which frees the hands.

C. Binocular vision.

D. A complex vocal mechanism that permits language.

E. A complex brain and nervous system that enables creative adaptation to environments for which humans are biologically unfit.

VI. **Material Culture:** All objects manufactured by humans to fill shared needs.

VII. **Nonmaterial Culture:** Composed of *cognitive* and *normative* components.

A. The *cognitive* category includes the definitions that people give to everything that exists, or to things that people think exist.

1. *Knowledge* refers to all the information about the physical world that can be objectively substantiated.

2. *Beliefs* may be defined as ideas and speculations about physical, social, and supernatural reality that are not easily supported by facts.

3. *Technology* is defined as the methods and techniques used to control the physical and social world.

B. The *normative* system includes rules or standards which designate good and bad, right and wrong; which channel behavior and thought; and which attach to them varying degrees of punishment and permissiveness.

1. *Values*: Abstract categories of the right and the good. The values of a society are usually expressed by its *norms*.

2. *Norms*: Standards of right action. Norms emerge when a group finds a particular act either harmful or beneficial. Norms are learned in the process of socialization.

VIII. Classification of Norms by Function and Importance

A. *Folkways*:

1. Rules for everyday behavior, i.e., behavior that is only vaguely linked to primary norms and that therefore elicits fewer and lighter sanctions than mores or laws.

2. In a complex society like America there are innumerable folkways.

3. Some are durable and become institutionalized or ritualized. Other are fads, fashions, transient manners.

B. *Mores*:

1. Rules which govern behavior in vital areas of life.

2. Usually observed by the whole society.

3. Elicit more rigid and more certain sanctions.

4. Deeply internalized and relatively permanent.

C. *Taboos*: Negative mores governing acts which are considered especially repellent and destructive.

D. *Laws*:

1. Codified rules of behavior.

2. Their breach incurs institutionalized (legal) processes and forms of punishment which are often physical.

3. Usually consistent with the most important mores. When they are not, enforcement is difficult.

IX. Norms and Social Control

A. *Sanctions*: May be positive—rewards—or negative—punishments. May be official or nonofficial. Official positive sanctions include such social responses as appointment to high office, election. Official negative sanctions include fines, imprisonment, death. Nonofficial positive sanctions take the form of social approval, prestige, acclaim. Nonofficial negative sanctions include social condemnation, ostracism, gossip, shunning.

B. The desire to belong accounts for the effectiveness of unofficial negative sanctions.

C. Real and ideal culture:

    1. *Ideal culture* consists of the formal, approved folkways, mores, and laws: the cultural norms.

    2. *Real culture* consists of what people actually do: the statistical norms.

    3. *Overt culture:* Public adherence to norms.

    4. *Covert culture:* Hidden or private behavior in breach of norms.

X. Culture as Structure

A. *Traits:* Single units of nonmaterial or material culture. A single act, object, manner, or idea.

B. *Culture complex:* An activity or idea to which a cluster of traits is attached or relevant.

C. *Institutions:* Made up of culture complexes related to an important activity at the societal level. Institutions primarily center on and help to fulfill universal human needs. Sociologists usually consider that there are five basic institutions. Although these basic institutions are common to all societies, the forms they assume vary from society to society. They arose from five fundamental human needs:

    1. The need to regulate sexual interaction and care for the helpless newborn human being gave rise to the *institution of the family.*

    2. The need to provide food, shelter, and clothing resulted in the emergence of the *economic institution.*

    3. The need to maintain peace and order within a society led to the formation of the *institution of government.*

    4. The need to transmit culture and train the young gave rise to the *institution of education.*

    5. The dread and fear of the unknown generated the *institution of religion.*

XI. Cultural Differences and Uniformities

A. *Ethnocentrism:* Conviction that one's own culture is superior, the "right" one. Occurs intraculturally as well as interculturally.

B. *Culture relativity:* A view that holds cultural differences to be appropriate and functional for the societies in which they occur. Judges diverse cultures by their own standards rather than by the imposition of the standards of the judging culture.

C. *Culture differences:* Sometimes erroneously attributed to race or biology, but no theory of cultural determinism by geography, climate, food supply, isolation, etc. fully accounts for cultural diversity.

D. *Cultural universals:* Abstract categories of behavior common to all cultures. Among them are the five institutions mentioned above, food taboos, self-adornment, age-grading, weather control, hospitality rituals, arts and crafts, forms of music and dance, and belief in supernatural phenomena.

XII. Subcultures and Countercultures

  A. *Subcultures:*

    1. More often marked by variant folkways than deviant mores.

    2. More often the variant norms are restricted to a few areas of life, the majority norms being observed in most areas.

  B. *Countercultures:*

    1. Behavioral norms which are in opposition to those of the greater society.

    2. May subscribe to the abstract values and goals of a society but deviate in the means of attaining them; or may reject both the means and the values of the majority culture.

    3. Though its folkways may also be different, the importance of its counteraction with society lies in its different mores and taboos.

    4. American countercultures that sprang up during the '60s have largely died out because of economic recession. Many of the countercultural ideas have been absorbed by the popular culture.

Learning Objectives

1. Define culture.
2. List the fundamental characteristics of culture.
3. Describe the relationship between language and culture.
4. Describe the differences between material and nonmaterial culture.
5. State the major components of the normative system.
6. Define norms, folkways, mores, taboos, and laws.
7. Explain why laws are necessary at some time in society.
8. State the reasons why norms and sanctions control individual human behavior so effectively.
9. Define cultural trait, cultural complex, and institution.
10. List the five basic institutions and indicate the human needs they satisfy.
11. Define ethnocentrism and list its functions and dysfunctions.
12. Define cultural relativity.
13. State the definition of cultural universal.
14. Describe the differences between subculture and counterculture.

Self-Test

Select the best possible answer. If you miss any questions, go back to the text and find the correct answer.

Multiple-Choice

1. Which of the following is true of culture?
   a. It is a unique product of human social interaction.
   b. It is learned by each member of society during socialization.
   c. It provides a way to satisfy biological and emotional needs in approved ways.
   d. All of the above.

2. Human's complex brain and nervous system allows
   a. for adaptation because we do not have instincts.
   b. for creative adaptation.
   c. for language development when coupled with the vocal system.
   d. all of the above.

3. One of the most important parts of nonmaterial culture is:
   a. tools.
   b. signals.
   c. the normative system.
   d. the sociological system.

4. The norms that guide human conduct in activities considered vital to society are
   a. folkways.
   b. mores.
   c. taboos.
   d. laws.

5. Which of the following is a positive sanction?
   a. Gossip.
   b. A smile.
   c. Ridicule.
   d. Disapproval.

6. Subcultures are
   a. inferior cultures within society.
   b. groups with distinctive features that set them apart from the wider culture but that retain general features of that culture.
   c. groups with distinctive features.
   d. groups that possess a value system and goals that are in direct opposition to those of the wider culture.

True-False

_____ 1. It does not seem possible that culture could be created without language.

_____ 2. American automobiles are examples of material culture.

_____ 3. Human behavior is guided to a great extent by the normative system of society.

_____ 4. Norms emerge when a society finds a particular act to be harmful or beneficial.

_____ 5. The celebration of holidays and fashions in clothes are both instances of folkways.

_____ 6. Laws become necessary in a complex, heterogeneous society undergoing rapid social change.

_____ 7. Conformity to societal norms is encouraged by a system of positive and negative sanctions.

_____ 8. The basic institutions, made up of cultural complexes, help fulfill universal human needs.

_____ 9. "America, love it or leave it," represents the attitude of cultural relativity.

Fill-in-the-Blank

1. Animals have been unable to produce culture because they communicate through a system of _____ . (symbols, signals)

2. _____ culture includes the ideas, values, knowledge, and beliefs of a people. (Nonmaterial, Popular)

3. The patterns that guide behavior which is extremely harmful or extremely vital to society are called _____ . (folkways, mores)

4. _____ is an attitude by which one assumes one's own culture is superior to all others. (Ethnocentrism, Culture)

5. To counter the subjectivity of an ethnocentric view of other societies and cultures, social scientists have suggested _____ . (cultural relativity, culture shock)

6. Abstract categories of behavior common to all cultures are called _____ . (norms, cultural universals)

7. _____ describes a group that possesses a value system and goals that are in direct opposition to those of the larger culture. (Counterculture, Subculture)

Chapter 4

Becoming Human: Socialization

Goals

After you read the chapter, study the learning objectives, and take the self-test, you will be able to:

1. Recognize the major factors that contribute to personality formation.

2. Be familiar with the means used by agents of socialization to accomplish the aims of socialization.

3. Understand the major theories of personality formation.

4. Recognize the types of socialization and that socialization is a lifelong process.

Synoptic Outline

I. **Personality:** The complex and dynamic system that includes all of an individual's behavioral and emotional traits. Personality refers to fairly consistent behavior and emotional traits characterizing a specific individual. Personality can change as a result of specific events and socialization.

II. **Personality Formation: The Biological Basis**

   A. In humans there is an absence of strong instinctual means with which to satisfy biological drives. Humans create the means of satisfying needs, and since all humans are born into society, they utilize the means their culture has evolved. This acceptance of society's means as one's own is socialization.

   B. Humans need "love"—emotional nurturing, comforting, security based on body contact. This need combined with the long period of caretaking of the infant empowers the primary group to be effective in the socialization process.

   C. Inheritance and environment: Personality is influenced by biological inheritance and the physical environment.

III. Socialization: Becoming Human

A. Goals of socialization:

1. Teaching the fundamentals of life in society.
2. Transmitting skills important in society.
3. Instilling societal aspirations.
4. Teaching societal members to fulfill social roles.
5. Providing each individual with an identity.

B. Socialization continues throughout life. Socialization is both conscious and unconscious and takes into consideration the emotions of love, anger, and anxiety.

IV. Theories of Socialization

A. *Cooley: The looking-glass self:* Theorizes that the self is developed in response to negative or positive reactions of others—:"I become how others see me."

1. The infant's self is differentiated from nonself by eliciting differential responses from others.
2. Behavior is reinforced when it appears to be what others find most desirable.
3. Guilt, shame, self-satisfaction, and self-esteem are based on the judgment of others.
4. Self-image changes as interactions and "others" change.

B. *Mead: Symbolic interactionism:* A theory that posits the following stages in the development of personality:

1. The infant becomes aware that cries and actions have meaning. To those that see and hear them they symbolize an idea and draw a specific response.
2. The child acquires language, a system of oral symbols which not only have referents in the physical world but ideational and emotional values.
3. The child, the subjective "I" is non-self-conceptualizing. As it acquires its society's symbols it can apply these symbols to the self in the same way it applies them to others, thus conceptualizing the self by objectifying it as "me."
4. Play the Game stages: Using linguistic and behavioral symbols, the child enacts another, at first confusing the symbols of one entity with the symbols of another, later delimiting roles with their normative symbols.
   a. *Significant others:* Primary group members with whom the child identifies, i.e., whose role the child can play.
   b. *Generalized other:* An entire group or all of society with which the child can identify. By imagining himself as the generalized other the child is able to accept its ideas of right and wrong on his or her own.
5. The internalization of cultural symbols which enables role-playing constructs the "me," and the values of society and the resultant conflict with the "I" produce feelings of guilt and anxiety.
6. *Minding or reflective thinking:* An ongoing dialogue between "I," the spontaneous, creative self, and "me," the conforming, socialized self.

C. *Psychodynamic theories of personality formation:* The most famous is Freud's psychoanalytic theory, developed in his treatment of personality disorders.

    1. Freud posits a personality model composed of the id, which is instinctual, pleasure seeking, and unconscious; the superego, which is the largely unconscious learning of parental injunctions; and the ego, the conscious self which directs the urgings of the id into safe channels. The ego acts as intermediary between the id and the superego and tests each against "reality."

    2. Arguments in opposition to psychoanalytic theory:

        a. Freud poses a conflict between biological drives and the external restraints of society. Such conflict is not necessarily present.

        b. Freud emphasizes the early years and terminates personality development with puberty. Sociologists maintain that socialization continues throughout life.

D. *Behaviorism or environmental determinism:*

    1. The opposite of psychodynamic theory in that it deemphasizes instinct, giving almost total weight to social conditioning.

    2. Not concerned with unconscious or perceptual processes but with overt behavior, which behaviorists believe is formed or modified through positive or negative reinforcement.

    3. George C. Homans's social learning theory emphasizes the importance of symbolic reinforcers as conditioning agents.

E. *Developmental theories:* Jean Piaget is the most famous exponent of a theory which stresses stages of physical and perceptual maturation that determine what the individual is capable of learning at any time.

V. Agents of Socialization

A. *Family:* Plays a most crucial role as it influences the child at an early stage of development and is the most constant influence in an individual's life.

B. *School:* Both in its formal academic and its informal "hidden" curriculum, i.e., subject matter as well as behavior and values.

C. *Peer Group:*

    1. Increasingly important in a heterogeneous society, where it rivals family as a primary group.

    2. Because it is a pleasure relationship rather than an authoritarian or dependency relationship, its culture is more readily and easily learned.

D. *Mass media:*

    1. Often criticized as an agent of antisocialization because of its emphasis on violence and sex.

    2. Distorts reality by displaying fantasy as reality and the exception as the norm.

E. *Occupation or specialized socialization:* Occurs as individuals internalize the values and manners peculiar to their choice of vocation and avocation.

VI. Socialization as a Life Process

    A. *Primary socialization:* Occurs early in life and centers on language and basic-skills acquisition.

    B. *Anticipatory socialization:* Learning in preparation for future roles.

    C. *Developmental socialization:* The continuous expansion of learning that occurs in primary socialization.

    D. *Reverse socialization:* The younger generation may transmit knowledge and skills to the older generation.

    E. *Resocialization:* Learning a totally new set of norms and values.

VII. Socialization: How Effective? Socialization is not always successfully accomplished because some people feel coerced; we are influenced by past experiences; socialization is often contradictory; and individual human will can influence behavior.

Learning Objectives

1. Define personality and socialization.
2. Describe the basic human biological characteristics that favor the process of socialization.
3. List the goals of socialization.
4. List the three elements that Cooley describes in the "looking-glass" theory.
5. Explain why Mead believed that symbolic interaction is the first prerequisite for personality formation.
6. Define *significant others* and *generalized others* and give examples of each.
7. Summarize the major points of the theories of personality development.
8. List the major agents of socialization and indicate the significance of each.
9. Define the major types of socialization.
10. List the major reasons why socializtion is not always effective.

Self-Test

Select the best possible answer. If you miss any questions, go back to the text and find the correct answer.

Multiple-Choice

1. The acquisition of personality occurs through
   a. learning in school.
   b. biology.
   c. socialization.
   d. maturation.

2. The goals of socialization include
   a. teaching the skills important in society.
   b. personality improvement.
   c. "looking-glass" self.
   d. "generalized other."

3. Charles Horton Cooley's explanation of the emergence of self is the
   a. symbolic-interactionist theory.
   b. anomie theory.
   c. labeling theory.
   d. looking-glass theory.

4. The major theories of personality development are
   a. primary, secondary, developmental.
   b. family, peers, mass media.
   c. psychodynamic, behaviorist, developmental.
   d. none of the above.

5. Socialization is not always effective because
   a. some peole feel coerced.
   b. we are influenced by past experiences.
   c. socialization is often contradictory.
   d. all of the above.

True-False

_____ 1. Personality changes as a result of socialization.

_____ 2. Socialization is a learning process during which members of society transmit to the new individual the social and cultural heritage of the group.

_____ 3. One of the biological characteristics that favors socialization is the lack of strong instinctual means to satisfy biological drives.

_____ 4. The family is not an important agent of socialization.

_____ **5.** George Herbert Mead maintains that the first prerequisite for personality formation is symbolic interaction.

_____ **6.** Primary socialization occurs only after one begins formal education.

Fill-in-the-Blank

1. _____ is a complex and dynamic system that includes all of an individual's behavioral and emotional traits, his attitudes, values, beliefs, habits, and goals. (Culture, Personality)

2. _____ is the learning process by which a biological organism becomes a human being. (Personality, Socialization)

3. Sociologists generally identify the _____ as the chief agent of socialization. (family, peers)

4. _____ are those primary group members with whom the child identifies and whose roles the child plays. (Significant others, Generalized others)

5. When the individual learns to take into account the role of society, she takes into account the _____ .(significant other, generalized other)

6. _____ socialization is learning in prepartion for roles. (Developmental, Anticipatory)

Chapter 5
Deviance and Deviants

Goals

After you read the chapter, study the learning objectives, and take the self-test, you will be able to:

1. Recognize the functions of deviance.
2. Explain why deviance is relative.
3. Gain insight into the theories of deviance.
4. Tell the difference between deviance and crime.
5. List the various types of crime.

Synoptic Outline

I. **Social Control:** Socialization is never perfect. To ensure social control, people must be subject to sanctions.

   A. *Positive sanctions:* Rewarding behavior considered good.

   B. *Negative sanctions:* Punishment of behavior that society considers undesirable.

   C. Sanctions may be *formal* or *informal*.

II. **Deviance:** The breaking of societal rules, particularly the important social norms, is called deviance. Those who break these rules are said to be deviant. Sociologists try to analyze why most people conform, why others become deviant, and the kinds and forms of deviance.

   A. *Deviance:* Behavior or traits that conflict with significant social norms and are judged negatively by a large number of people.

   B. The relative nature of deviance: Deviance means departure from social norms and such behavior is not all "bad." Deviance is relative to the circumstances, age, and mental and social status of the deviant and the definer.

   C. Kinds of deviance:

      1. *Nonconforming deviance* is prompted by ideological convictions.

      2. *Aberrant behavior* is prompted by greed or personal gain.

III. Functions of Deviance

A. Positive effects of deviance:

1. By contrast, deviance helps to set the boundaries of permissible behavior.

2. Deviance promotes solidarity as the group defends against the deviant or attempts to rehabilitate him or her.

3. The imposition of negative sanctions increases the value of positive sanctions for normal behavior.

4. Deviance may prove to be intrinsically beneficial — a new and better way — or it may stimulate necessary social changes.

IV. Explaining Deviance

A. *Biological explanations:* Body types and sex chromosomes form the basis for the two major biological theories.

B. *Psychological explanations:* Freud contends that an underdeveloped or overdeveloped superego accounts for deviance.

V. Sociological Theories of Deviance

A. *Anomie:* A state of normlessness produced by the frustration resulting from the conflict between societal goals and available means. Robert Merton lists modes of adaptation by means of which individuals cope with anomic conflict:

1. *Conformity:* Acceptance of the cultural goals and means of reaching them. This is the only *nondeviant* response.

2. *Innovation:* Acceptance of the cultural goals but rejection of the approved means of reaching them.

3. *Ritualism:* A substitution of the means for the goal. The goal becomes irrelevant as means are enacted for their own sake. Many bureaucratic functions typify ritualism.

4. *Retreatism:* The abandonment of both cultural means and goals. Retreatism is characterized by goallessness. Behavior has no desired end.

5. *Rebellion:* Active rejection of both cultural means and goals, and an attempt to replace with new ones.

B. *Differential association theory:* Holds that deviant behavior is acquired in precisely the same way as acceptable behavior, that is, through processes of socialization. The deviant, however, is socialized in association with a deviant subculture.

C. *Labeling:* A theory of deviance which proposes that all individuals act contrary to socially approved behavior at some time or other (primary deviance), but that only those who are discovered and labeled with their deviant act continue the behavior (secondary deviance). Others expect the individual to repeat the unconventional act, and the individual internalizes the expectation, i.e., fulfilling his social image, repeats the act.

D. *Symbolic interactionism:* Once one is labeled a deviant, other people's attitudes and expectations result in a self-fulfilling prophecy.

E. *Conflict persepective:* Those with power are able to enforce the rules that work to their advantage and those who deviate from the rules are labeled deviants. The powerful are far more able to avoid being labeled as deviant.

VI. **New Trends In Criminology:** Radical or "new" criminology is largely based on conflict theory. Radical criminologists contend that it is not the individual that needs reforming. The capitalistic system "creates" criminals and therefore needs reforming.

VII. **Crime: Deviance that Hurts**

A. Crime is any act the violates the law. Laws are differentiated from the unwritten societal norms in the following ways.

1. Laws are put into effect by political authority.

2. Laws are specific rules instead of informal understandings.

3. Laws are supposed to be applied uniformly to every deviant.

4. Laws carry specific punitive sanctions.

5. Laws are administered through official agencies of the society.

B. A distinction is made between criminal behavior on the part of adults and on the part of juveniles (those under 18).

C. It is not always easy to determine what type of deviant behavior is criminal because some patterns of behavior, though illegal, are not believed to be seriously deviant.

VIII. **Types of Crime**

A. *Juvenile delinquency:* Crimes committed by those under 18.

B. *Social order crimes:* Do not impose physical suffering on others. Classified as crimes because they are considered morally repugnant.

C. *White-collar crime:* Criminal acts committed by respectable persons in the performance of their occupational duties.

D. *Organized crime:* The criminal activity of rather large groups of individuals organized to maximize profits and minimize apprehension and punishment.

E. *Crimes against persons and property:* The most feared types of crime, as they usually involved violence.

IX. **Crime Statistics:** Interpreting crime statistics is quite difficult as most crimes go unreported and only the unsuccessful criminals are arrested.

X. **The Judicial System:** The police, the courts, and the prisons have many problems and often the intent of justice is not served.

Learning Objectives

1. State the reasons why positive and negative senctions are necessary to maintain social control.
2. Define deviance and state the functions of deviance.
3. Summarize the biological and psychological theories of deviance.
4. Define anomie and list Merton's five modes of adaptation, noting those that are termed deviant.
5. Summarize the major points of differential association theory.
6. Compare primary and secondary deviance in relation to labeling theory.
7. State the major thesis of the "new" criminology.
8. Define crime.
9. List the major types of crime.

Self-Test

Select the best possible answer. If you miss any questions, go back to the text and find the correct answer.

Multiple-Choice

1. Positive and negative sanctions are necessary because
   a. not everybody understands the law.
   b. socialization is never perfect.
   c. people are basically bad.
   d. none of the above.

2. The functions of deviance include
   a. setting the boundaries of permissible behavior.
   b. promoting solidarity.
   c. the possibility of stimulating necessary change.
   d. all of the above.

3. Which of the following is an example of a sociological explanation of deviant behavior?
   a. Freud's theory of anatomy.
   b. Merton's theory of anomie.
   c. Mead's theory of inherited criminality.
   d. The theory of original sin.

4. According to Sutherland's differential association theory, criminal acts are
   a. the works of the devil.
   b. caused by abnormal chromosomes.
   c. learned.
   d. the result of social deprivation.

5. Radical criminology contends that
   a. we need stiffer penalties to deter crime.
   b. the death penalty should be used more often.
   c. the capitalistic system needs reforming.
   d. longer sentences will reduce crime.

6. The major types of crimes include
   a. juvenile delinquency.
   b. white-collar crime.
   c. organized crime.
   d. all of the above.

True-False

_____   1. Freud advanced a biological theory of deviance.

_____   2. Howard Becker contends that once we label a person as deviant and treat him as such he usually comes to think of himself as deviant and acts accordingly.

Fill-in-the-Blank

1. _____ is behavior or personal characteristics at variance with significant social norms and expectations and therefore judged negatively. (Deviance, Negative sanctions)

2. _____ is an act that violates the legal code. (Deviance, Crime)

Chapter 6
Social Differentiation: Ranking and Stratification

Goals

After you read the chapter, study the learning objectives, and take the self-test, you will be able to:

1. Recognize that stratification is not necessarily based on "survival of the fittest" or the idea that "the cream always rises to the top."

2. Compare and contrast the theories of stratification.

3. Grasp the meaning of life chances and the resulting inequality of its distribution.

4. Understand the significance of the concepts of social power and personal power, and be able to relate them to life chances.

5. Identify the relationship between social class and life-style.

Synoptic Outline

I. **Social Differentiation:** Distinctions are made among various groups of people, both on the basis of biological and social factors. Various groups — women, the old, ethnics, the poor, and the non-Protestant — have unequal life experiences in the United States.

II. **Ranking and Stratification:** Ranking and stratification occur in all societies that produce a surplus. People are ranked according to

   A. *Wealth:* How much of the social resources they own.

   B. *Prestige:* The degree of societal honor their position evokes.

   C. *Power:* The degree to which one individual can direct others.

III. **Theories of Inequality**

   A. *The classical conservative position:* Maintains that ability and intelligence naturally find their own level. The resultant stratification is viewed positively as it eliminates the constant conflict which would erupt from humanity's innate greed and selfishness.

B. *The classical liberal view:* Maintains that social stratification is the result of social warfare. The victorious impose their system upon the others. The system itself corrupts the natural goodness of humans, forcing them to become greedy and selfish.

IV. **Structural-Functionalist Theory:** An outgrowth of the classical conservative view. The orderly conduct of society, or social equilibrium, takes precedence over the needs of the individual or any group. Such order requires:

   A. Rewards which will attract the best and the brightest to perform the most important functions.

   B. Lesser rewards on a downward scale proportionate to the special qualities, innate ability, or education needed to perform each of society's functions.

   C. *Criticisms of functionalism:* Center on the issue of just what is an essential function and the fact that stratification systems do not let some people develop their talents, while they reward some untalented people.

V. **Conflict Theory:** An outgrowth of the classical liberal view. Inequality is the product of conflict that originates in people's desire for power. Therefore, there will always be conflict in vying for position. Through such conflict, however, society remains dynamic and evolves toward the good.

   A. Marx believed that the fundamental single conflict was that between the haves and the have-nots — the owners of the means of production and the workers. This inequality, though intrinsically wrong, would prove to be the cause of the inevitable revolution which would bring about a classless society in which the means of production would be owned collectively and the proceeds of production distributed equally.

   B. Marx also believed that the major institutions — religion, family, economy, education, and government — as they were designed to function in stratified societies served the existing system of stratification.

   C. Criticisms of conflict theory:

      1. People are not equal in talent, intelligence, and drive.

      2. Inequality is a motivating force for people.

VI. **An Attempt at a Synthesis:** Functionalism and conflict theories are not mutually exclusive. Lenski contends that some inequality is inevitable, but the higher the level of productivity the less the need for inequality. Inequality is not likely to diminish unless the government intervenes.

VII. **Characteristics of Systems of Stratification:** All display the characteristics of differentiation, ranking, institutionalization, and influence on individual personalities. Sociologists examine the dimensions of class, status, and power.

A. *Class:* A stratum of people who stand in similar positions to each other, and, as a group, in a different position from others.

    1. Karl Marx's concept of class is essentially economic in nature.

    2. Max Weber argued that the Marxist view was overly simplistic. Weber added the concept of *life chances*—the opportunities that each individual has of fulfilling his or her potential. The higher the social class, the greater the life chances.

B. *Status:*

    1. Status is highly valued in American society. Much behavior may be viewed as the desire to achieve or display status—choice of mate, car, clothes, memberships, etc.

    2. An individual may have many statuses depending upon group memberships. Master status is the individual's rank at the societal level. Most often it is based on education and occupation.

    3. *Status determinants include:* Family status; wealth (often wealth, or class, automatically confers status); cultural values such as intelligence, efficiency, competitiveness; occupation; and, in the United States, other variables such as ethnic origin, age, religion, color, income, sex.

    4. *Status inconsistency:* Combinations of widely disparate status determinants, e.g., occupation and income inconsistency or race and achieved position.

C. *Power:* The third dimension of stratification.

    1. *Personal power:* Freedom of individuals to direct their own lives without much interference.

    2. *Social power:* Possession of the means to make decisions which affect groups or all of society. Control of some aspect of the social system.

    3. Some say power accrues to wealth. Others say wealth is equivalent to power. In either case they are so interwoven that it is rare for an individual to possess one without the other.

    4. The fact that wealth, prestige, and power are found in the upper classes and absent in the lower classes strongly supports the correlation between rank and life chances.

VIII. Systems of Stratification

A. *Caste:* A totally closed system of ascribed status. Exemplified by classical India.

B. *Estate:* A system in which certain estates are closed and others open. Greater mobility within each estate. Exemplified by feudal Europe.

C. *Class:* Varying degrees of openness or potential interclass mobility. An entirely open class system is an ideal. In actuality the following occurs:

    1. Classes are not prescribed by law or religion.

    2. Class structure at every level is not sharply delineated. Classes form a continuum.

    3. Ascribed status exists but achieved status also plays a part in rank.

    4. Social mobility occurs, particularly within various strata of the same class.

IX. Determining Social Class: Opinions differ as to what measurements should be used to determine class. Some sociologists hold that no static model reveals the flux and variance of ranking as it actually occurs. Any of the following measurements may be used: life-style, reputation, subjective ranking by objective criteria, occupational prestige.

X. Social Class and its Consequences

   A. *Family life:* Sex roles, divorce, child-rearing practices, etc., are markedly different in different classes.

   B. *Socialization:* Children of different classes acquire different behavioral and value norms.

   C. Health (mental and physical), life expectancy, participation in voluntary organizations, and arrests and convictions are all correlated with rank.

XI. Social Mobility

   A. *Horizontal mobility:* Changes in the way of life which do not alter one's stratum classification.

   B. *Vertical mobility:* Movement from one stratum to another.

   C. *The upwardly mobile individual:* Urban resident; only child or one of two children; influenced by ambitious parents; acquires more education than parents; marries late; waits to start a family; has no more than two children.

   D. *Intergenerational:* Movement to a stratum different from that occupied by one's family.

   E. *Intragenerational:* Movement to a stratum different from the peers in one's original class.

XII. Social Mobility in the United States

   A. Social mobility has occurred largely because our society places a great value on efficiency.

   B. A significant amount of social mobility has occurred because of *structural mobility*. Industrialization has resulted in the creation of high-status occupations that replace low-status jobs.

   C. Social mobility is influenced by increased education, nature of first job, and occupation of father.

Learning Objectives

1. Define social differentiation.
2. List the criteria sociologists concern themselves with in the study of ranking and stratification.
3. Summarize the classical liberal and conservative beliefs about inequality.
4. Give the functional explanation of the inevitability of social inequality.
5. State the conflict theorists' view of the purpose of stratification.
6. Outline the major points of Karl Marx's theory of inequality and stratification.
7. List the characteristics of stratification systems.
8. State Karl Marx's, Max Weber's and Gerhard Lenski's definitions of social class.
9. Define status and list the variables that determine social status.
10. Define power.
11. Explain the difference between social and personal power.
12. Describe the major research approaches to social class.
13. Compare open and closed stratification systems.
14. Distinguish between vertical and horizontal mobility.
15. Identify the traits of the upwardly mobile individual.

Self-Test

Select the best possible answer. If you miss any questions, go back to the text and find the correct answer.

Multiple-Choice

1. Social differentiation is
    a. based solely on biological differences.
    b. based solely on social differences.
    c. based on social and biological differences.
    d. none of the above.

2. People are ranked and stratified according to
    a. wealth, prestige, and power.
    b. class, status, and power.
    c. life chances.
    d. power only.

3. According to functionalist theory,
    a. change is the goal of societies.
    b. a system of rewards ensures that the important tasks of society are accomlished.
    c. society is evil.
    d. stratification is sinful.

4. Karl Marx believed that inequality was caused by
    a. the basic law of nature which was survival of the fittest.
    b. the struggle for scarce goods and services.
    c. a system of rewards which was needed to ensure that specific tasks were completed.
    d. the private ownership of the means of production.

5. The four characteristics shared by all stratification systems are
    a. caste, class, estate, and power.
    b. wealth, prestige, power, and class.
    c. differentiation, ranking, institutionalization, and influence on individual personality.
    d. none of the above.

6. Social status
    a. belongs to the rich.
    b. is a way of ranking according to the prestige of social roles.
    c. is less important to people than wealth.
    d. is seldom related to wealth.

7. The ability of one individual or group to control the actions of another individual or group is
   a. privilege.
   b. power.
   c. coercion.
   d. social ranking.

8. Horizontal mobility occurs when there is a (an)
   a. change of status without a change of class.
   b. change in social-class membership.
   c. downward movement in social-class membership.
   d. upward movement in social-class membership.

True-False

_____ 1. The view that humans are basically selfish and have to be controlled by society is at the bottom of conflict theory.

_____ 2. In the classical liberal view of inequality, inequality and the stratification of society are unavoidable.

_____ 3. The view of society as an organism in a perpetual attempt to attain balance is part of functionalist theory.

_____ 4. Karl Marx viewed history as a record of class struggles following the unequal distribution of rewards.

_____ 5. Karl Marx viewed social classes as resulting from unequal distribution of scarce resources in society.

_____ 6. Max Weber's definition of class did not include life chances.

_____ 7. Life chances refer to the opportunity of each individual to fulfill his or her potential in society.

_____ 8. Status is the position of an individual in relation to other individuals in the social system.

_____ 9. Income, education, family, and cultural values are determinants of status.

_____ 10. There is no significant difference between social and personal power.

_____ 11. The reputational approach to social class is the one most commonly used by sociologists.

_____ 12. Research indicates that upwardly mobile individuals come from large families and want to have many children of their own.

Fill-in-the-Blank

1. The classical _____ view holds that inequality is part of the law of nature, and that it is a product of human greed and selfishness. (conservative, liberal)

2. _____ theory maintains that inequality is fostered by the five basic institutions of society. (Functionalist, Conflict)

3. The term _____ refers to the opportunity of each individual to fulfill his or her potential in society. (life chances, status inconsistency)

4. _____ is an aggregate of persons in a society who stand in a similar position with respect to some form of power, privilege, or prestige. (Category, Social class)

5. _____ is the ability of an individual or a group of the population to control others with or without their conset. (Power, Force)

6. In the _____ approach to determining social class, researchers ask people to judge the rank of others in their community. (reputational, objective)

7. _____ stratification systems allow social mobility and the achievement of new status. (Open, Closed)

Chapter 7
Social Differentiation: Majority and Minorities

Goals

After you read the chapter, study the learning objectives, and take the self-test, you will be able to:

1. Comprehend why the sociological definition of minority is based on the concepts of personal and social power.
2. Identify the ways minorities cope with their status and describe the means by which the majority maintains its status.
3. List the obstacles to full integration.
4. Define and differentiate the following terms: race, racism, ethnicity, prejudice, and discrimination.
5. Trace the history of minorities in the United States.

Synoptic Outline

I. **Heterogeneity of the Human species:** Cultural and biological differences when brought into contact with each other, either between or within cultures, often result in conflict. The conflict leads to patterns of subordination and domination, superiority and inferiority.

   A. *Minorities:* Those categories of people denied power, prestige, and privilege based on ascribed characteristics. Minority status does not depend on numbers.

   B. *Kinds of minorities:*
      1. *Racial* minorities: differ biologically.
      2. *Ethnic* minorities: differ culturally.
      3. *Religious* minorites: those whose religious beliefs differ from the majority.
      4. *Sexual* minorities: women.
      5. *Age* minorities: the young or the elderly.

   C. *Defining minority status:* Minorities share some common features:
      1. They are recognizable by visible traits.
      2. They are treated differently because of these traits.

3. Their self-image and identity are centered on their minority-group relationship.

4. They are aware that they share a common identity with others in the group.

II. Race, Ethnicity, Religion

A. *Ethnicity* refers to a group's distinctiveness resulting from social and cultural factors that differ from those of the majority.

B. *Religion* refers to those whose religious practices differ from the majority's.

C. *Race* is the term that scientists use to describe biological differences that occur in humans.

III. E Pluribus Unum: Out of Many, One

A. *Anglo-conformity:* The attempt to impose WASP (white Anglo-Saxon Protestant) values and norms on all immigrants.

B. *Melting pot:* The ideal of unity based on the assimilation of diverse immigrant cultures into one. The United States has become a triple melting-pot nation.

C. *Cultural pluralism:* An ideal of peaceful cooperation and mutual respect among all culturally distinct groups.

IV. Majority and Minority: Processes of Coexistence

A. *Segregation* is the attempt to physically isolate a minority from the majority.

B. *Accommodation* is the situation in which a minority is conscious of the norms and values of the majority, accepts them, but chooses to retain its own ethnic norms and values.

C. *Acculturation,* or cultural assimilation, happens when a minority group accepts and makes its own the norms and values of the host culture.

D. *Assimilation* is a process by which minorities absorb completely the culture of the majority and enter the mainstream of the majority's culture.

E. *Amalgamation* takes place when all distinctions between majority and minorities are erased.

V. In the Way: Obstacles to Full Integration

A. *Racism* is the *incorrect* belief that both physical traits and behavior are inherited, inferior, and undesirable.

B. *Prejudice* infers that a person makes up his or her mind about something without any real knowledge about it.

1. *Stereotyping*: Uniform characteristics are assigned to an entire group without allowance for individual differences.

2. *Scapegoating* refers to the tendency of frustrated individuals to respond with aggression.

C. *Causes of prejudice:* Status inequality, competition, and authoritarian personality traits are factors in prejudice.

D. *Discrimination:* Actions taken as a result of prejudicial feelings.

    1. *Individual discrimination* is behavior prompted by personal prejudice of a member of a majority group.

    2. *Institutional discrimination* refers to the system of inequality existing within a society.

        a. *Structural discrimination* refers to discrimination built into social structures such as political and economic institutions.

        b. *Cultural discrimination* refers to the fact that the majority has the power to define its norms as the standard for an entire society.

VI. Prejudice and Discrimination: A Question of Economics

A. If two groups are of unequal status and there is economic competition, prejudice and discrimination appear.

B. As groups that are on the bottom of the stratification system gain in economic power, prejudice and discrimination are significantly reduced.

C. Concentration in specific neighborhoods aids in economic development.

D. For a minority to progress it must have a substantial middle class.

VII. Racial Minorities

A. *Native Americans:* The most disadvantaged of all minority groups. Their problems have been complicated by tribalism, as they think of themselves as separate tribes rather than Native Americans.

B. *Asian Americans:*

    1. *The Chinese:*

        a. Nineteenth-century immigrants, discriminated against to the point of persecution because of their availability as cheap labor.

        b. In the twentieth century they became upwardly mobile largely through the value they placed on education and as a result of small businesses.

    2. *The Japanese:*

        a. Prejudice flared during the Second World War.

        b. Their postwar geographical dispersal may have accelerated their upward mobility.

    3. *Other Asians:* 1.5 million in the United States. Significant resentment in areas of high concentration, though many enter the mainstream more easily than their predecessors.

C. *Black Americans:* Represent almost 12 percent of the population. They did not come to America voluntarily.

    1. Prejudice and discrimination supported by law and institutionalized discrimination have been slow to wane.

2. *The underclass:* Those forced to live a subsistence life-style with government help. Their problems include lack of skills, unemployment, and single-parent families.

VIII. Ethnic Minorities

A. *Hispanic Americans:* there are three major subdivisions:

1. *Mexican Americans* are the least upwardly mobile of the Spanish-speaking groups because of large extended families, close cultural ties to Mexico, and a higher rate of school dropouts resulting in low education and training.

2. *Puerto Ricans* are U.S. citizens. They are culturally and racially distinct from the Chicanos. There is some upward mobility but many are hampered by lack of language, low levels of education, and single-parent, female-headed families.

3. *Cubans* differ from other Spanish-speaking groups as the first wave of immigrants were older and well educated. The second wave (those who arrived in 1980) are not equally skilled and educated.

IX. Religious Minorites

A. *Catholics:* Represent 25 percent of the population of the United States. Anti-Catholic feelings have declined significantly.

B. *Jews:* Jewish Americans are more an ethnic than a religious minority but think of themselves as a religious minority.

Learning Objectives

1. Define a minority in sociological terms.
2. List the major kinds of minorities.
3. Define minority status.
4. List the processes of coexistence.
5. State the three major ideologies in regard to minorities.
6. Define and differentiate between race and racism.
7. Describe the ways racism is expressed.
8. Define prejudice.
9. Define discrimination and describe the differences between the major types of discrimination.
10. List the characteristics of Native Americans.
11. Compare the treatment and history of the major Asian American groups.
12. Sumarize the history of blacks in the United States.
13. Describe the similarities and differences among the three major Spanish-speaking minorities.
14. Name the two major religious minorites.

Self-Test

Select the best possible answer. If you miss any questions, go back to the text and find the correct answer.

Multiple-Choice

1. Minority groups are
   a. always smaller in number than is the majority group.
   b. always immigrants.
   c. categories of people who possess imperfect access to positions of equal power in society.
   d. native-born people who come under the subjection of another group.

2. The characteristics of ethnic subcultures do *not* include
   a. cultural difference from the dominant group.
   b. religious difference from the dominant group.
   c. values and beliefs different from those of the dominant group.
   d. definite physical features that set members apart.

3. The majority maintains status by
   a. branding minority behavior as deviant.
   b. obstructing assimilation by institutionalizing its prejudices.
   c. enforcing its norms.
   d. all of the above.

4. A sociological interpretation of "racism" is
   a. hatred towards persons of another race.
   b. belief in the inferiority of persons belonging to another race.
   c. belief that racial groups display behavioral differences which are genetically inherited.
   d. belief that racial groups display physical differences which are genetically inherited.

5. The basis of racist thinking is
   a. scientific.
   b. imperialist.
   c. stereotyping.
   d. cultural relativity.

6. Racial prejudice
   a. is generally directed toward groups, rather than individuals.
   b. is learned behavior.
   c. is all of the above.

7. Discrimination
    a. is the same as prejudice but is a stronger feeling.
    b. refers to the actions taken as a result of prejudice.
    c. does not exist when prejudice exists.
    d. is none of the above.

8. Which is *not* one of the three ideologies that prevailed in the United States regarding the best "solution" to the minority problem?
    a. Anglo-conformity.
    b. Melting pot.
    c. Ethnocentrism.
    d. Cultural pluralism.

9. The history of blacks in the United States
    a. is one of pluralism.
    b. is one of assimilation.
    c. is that of an unwilling minority.
    d. is all of the above.

10. The major religious minorities include
    a. Baptists and Methodists.
    b. Episcopalians and Congregationalists.
    c. Catholics and Jews.
    d. all of the above.
    e. none of the above.

True-False

_____ 1. Minorities are categories of people that possess imperfect access to positions of equal power, prestige, and privilege.

_____ 2. Ethnic minorities differ biologically from the dominant group in society.

_____ 3. All of mankind is descended from the same common stock, the species *Homo sapiens*.

_____ 4. In general, prejudice and discrimination are mutually reinforcing.

_____ 5. Anglo-conformity has had the greatest following historically in America.

_____ 6. Cuban immigrants in America have been unable to adjust beacuse their values and goals are so different from the majority of Americans.

_____ 7. Native Americans are a hidden minority, the most socioeconomically depressed of all minorities.

_____ 8. Asian Americans share a common history in the United States.

Fill-in-the-Blank

1. A (An) _____ is any group in society that is kept from attaining a high status on the basis of culture, race, religion, or sex. (ethnic group, minority group)

2. _____ minorities differ culturally from the dominant group in society. (Racial, Ethnic)

3. _____ is the belief that racial groups display both physical and behavioral differences that are inherited and are undesirable. (Ethnocentrism, Racism)

4. _____ refers to a group's distinctive social, rather than biological, factors. (Subculture, Ethnicity)

5. _____ is judgement of a group based on stereotype and hearsay. (Discrimination, Prejudice)

6. _____ discrimination is the most common form of discrimination in our society. (Attitudinal, Structural)

Chapter 8
Social Differentiation: Sex, Age, and Handicaps

Goals

After you read the chapter, study the learning objectives, and take the self-test, you will be able to:

1. Recognize the ways in which sex roles are learned.
2. Identify and indicate the significance of the major agents of sex-role socialization.
3. Comprehend that it is socialization to a greater extent than biology that accounts for sex-role differences.
4. State the reasons why the sexist ideology is false.
5. Gain insight into the reasons why the aged and the handicapped are minorities.

Synoptic Outline

I. **Social Differentiation:** Groups that are treated unequally because of characteristics they possess over which they have no control.

II. **Making of Men and Women**
   A. *Biological differences:*
      1. *Anatomical:* The reproductive system.
      2. *Genetic:* differentiation by *XX* and *XY* chromosomes.
      3. *Hormonal:* Development of primary and secondary sex traits.
   B. *Cultural differences:* If the behavior of males and females differed strictly on the basis of biology, all males would behave in the same way and all females would behave in the same way. Socialization (nurture) affects behavior more than biology.

III. **Sex Roles: Whys and Wherefores:** The functional division of labor made in hunting and gathering societies still persists in modern societies. Males have taken the powerful and decision-making positions.

A. *Gender-role socialization:* Begins at an early age and is largely accomplished by sex typing.

B. *Sex-typing:* Refinement of the process of socialization known as symbolic interaction.

    1. *Conditioning:* Rewards are given for correct behavior and wrong behavior is punished or at least discouraged.

    2. *Imitation or identification:* Older children and adults perceived as most like the individual are imitated.

    3. *Self-definition:* Putting oneself in the correct sexual category according to the norms learned through interaction as to what is considered male and female.

C. *Agents of socialization:*

    1. *The family:* The most important agent of socialization into sex roles.

    2. *Textbooks:* Until recently schoolbooks strongly reinforced sex stereotyping in their illustrations and contents.

    3. *Schools:* Stress traditional sex roles by segregating boys and girls and encouraging different academic subjects for boys and girls.

    4. *Mass media:* Rigid stereotyping is evident in both programming and commercials.

IV. Inequality and the Ideology of Sexism

A. The *sexist ideology* is based on the assumption that men and women are destined to play different roles because this is the natural order of things. The differences have acquired values of superiority and inferiority, with males being superior.

B. *Results of the sexist ideology:*

    1. All religions treat women as inferior.

    2. Women get the lower-paying jobs.

V. The Women's Movement:
Women's roles have undergone alterations in the past 20 years as demonstrated both by legislation and changes in norms. Equality has not been achieved. The goal of equality between the sexes should mean that each individual has the opportunity to be what she or he is inclined to be.

VI. Ageism

A. The ideology of *ageism* asserts that the very young and the old are inferior, and thus provides the justification for discrimination.

B. *Ageism and the young:* There is some justification in putting some constraints on the rights of the young. Sexual and physical abuse of the young indicate, however, that the young deserve some protection.

C. *Ageism and the elderly:*

    1. *Age discrimination:* The most obvious area of discrimination is in the area of employment.

2. *Disengagement:* The suggestion that the elderly willingly withdraw from social and occupational roles.

3. Problematic areas other than employment include the negative attitudes of society toward the process of growing old, widowhood, loneliness, and failing health.

VII. **Minority Status Based on Handicaps, Appearance, and Sexual Preference**

    A. The physically and mentally handicapped are denied equal access to education and public facilites.

    B. The unattractive (the ugly, the obese, short men, and tall women) are victims of discrimination both economically and socially.

    C. Homosexuals are viewed as deviants and are discriminated against legally and socially.

Learning Objectives

1. Define social differentiation.
2. Compare the sex-role socialization of males and females using the concepts of gender-role socialization and sex-typing.
3. Name and indicate the significance of the major agents of sex-role socialization.
4. State the reasons why women are a minority.
5. Repeat the major assumptions of the sexist ideology.
6. List the effects of the sexist ideology.
7. Summarize the history of the women's movement.
8. Summarize the ideology of ageism.
9. State why the aged are a minority.
10. List the reasons why those with handicaps, the unattractive, and homosexuals are minorities.

Self-Test

Select the best possible answer. If you miss any questions, go back to the text and find the correct answer.

Multiple-Choice

1. "Groups that are treated unequally because of characteristics they possess over which they have no control" is the definition of
   a. minority.
   b. sexist ideology.
   c. social differentiation.
   d. all of the above.

2. The major agent(s) of sex-role socialization is/are
   a. the family.
   b. schools.
   c. textbooks.
   d. all of the above.

3. The assumption that men and women are destined to play different roles because this is the natural order of things is the definition of
   a. sexism.
   b. social differentiation.
   c. sexist ideology.
   d. sex-typing.

4. The elderly are a minority because
   a. most of them are black.
   b. most of them are women.
   c. they lack power.
   d. none of the above.

5. Minority status is also based on
   a. physical handicaps and obesity.
   b. mental handicaps and height.
   c. handicaps, attractiveness, and homosexuality.
   d. all of the above.

True-False

_____ 1. Women are considered a minority because of their socially inferior treatment.

_____ 2. Sexism is an ideology based on factual, scientific evidence.

_____ 3. The sexist ideology has resulted in lower paying jobs for women.

_____ 4. As a result of the women's movement, equality has been achieved.

_____ 5. The ideology of ageism contends that youth is superior to age.

Fill-in-the-Blank

1. _____ begins at an early age and is largely accomplished by sex-typing. (Social differentiation, Gender-role socialization)

2. Women are numerically a _____ and socially a _____ . (minority, majority; majority, majority; majority, minority)

3. As a result of the sexist ideology, religions treat women as _____ . (superior, equal, inferior)

Chapter 9
The Making of Contemporary Society

Goals

After you read the chapter, study the learning objectives, and take the self-test, you will be able to:

1. Recognize that social change, gradual and/or dramatic, is going to continue to influence our lives.
2. Grasp the degree to which technology influences society.
3. Describe the process of social and cultural change.
4. Understand the meaning of the terms *demography* and the *demographic transition*.
5. Recognize the problems created by rapid population growth.
6. Appraise the reasons why the third stage of the demographic transition, if reached, will reduce the magnitude of the problems faced by developing nations.
7. Grasp the environmental consequences of overpopulation.
8. Understand the significance of zero population growth in reducing ecological and social problems.
9. Demonstrate how the urban crisis is intensified by suburbanization and metropolitanization.
10. Identify the relationship between population growth, environmental pollution, economic profit, and the global ecological imbalance.
11. List some possibilities in the search for the solutions to our population and ecological problems.

Synoptic Outline

I. **Statics and Dynamics:** *Statics* studies social phenomena as though they were frozen in time. *Dynamics* studies the source of change. Statics and dynamics are two dimensions of the same phenomenon.

II. **Modernization:** The process that involves the change from a preindustrial to an industrial mode of production and affects all areas of life.

   A. Problems of modernization: It destroys traditions and established ways of life.

   B. If the process of modernization occurs slowly, less turmoil is created.

   C. When modernization occurs rapidly, social disorganization tends to result.

III. **Social and Cultural Change**

   A. Social structure change occurs as a result of:

      1. *Planning:* Purposeful, goal-oriented change.

      2. *Reform:* Purposeful correction of flaws or dysfunctions.

      3. *Revolution:* Violent reaction to nonresponsive government for the purpose of substituting new structures for old ones.

   B. Cultural change occurs as a result of:

      1. *Innovation:*

         a. *Discovery:* A new perception or realization of an aspect of reality.

         b. *Invention:* A new combination of existing things or ideas.

      2. *Diffusion:* Dissemination of an idea or thing introduced from another society or known only to a small segment of a society.

   C. Other sources of change:

      1. *Physical environment:* Directs our cultural development and limits certain forms of social change.

      2. *Population:* Rapid population growth causes conflict, malnutrition, and even death.

      3. *Ideology:* Belief systems change as a result of social conditions and belief systems change social conditions.

      4. *Events and individuals:* Random events and acts of individuals can also lead to social change.

IV. **Technology:** Includes all the methods, devices, and artifacts made by humans that help people to manage and control their environment.

   A. *Technological revolutions:* From the invention of the plow (the first technological revolution), technology has caused restructuring of society's primary institutions—education, economy, government, religion, and family.

   B. *The industrial revolution:* The second technological revolution mechanized agriculture and manufacturing.

      1. *Automation:* A further development of mechanization in which machines run machines.

      2. *Industrialism:* Moved production from the home, in which members of families crafted each part of an item, to the impersonal factory site, where production was accomplished by large machines and miscellaneous work forces. Created the specialized function of merchant as middleman between maker and buyer.

C. *Technology and social change:* Technology has radically altered our lives, transforming both our social reality and our cultural values.

    1. *Technological determinism:* The idea that technology is so important that it determines a society's culture, social structure, and history.

    2. *Culture lag:* Results when material culture changes before social culture can catch up. This lag in values, ideas, and norms produces social problems and disorganization.

V. **Population:** Most societies suffer from population problems.

  A. Key demographic terms include:

    1. *Population density:* The number of people per square mile.

    2. *Birthrate:* The number of births per 1,000 women between the ages of 14 and 44 in a year.

    3. *Fertility rate:* The actual number of births per 1,000 women between the ages of 14 and 44 during their reproductive cycle.

    4. *Fecundity:* The biological potential for reproduction.

    5. *Death rate:* The number of deaths per 1,000 per year.

  B. *Population crisis:* Results from the shortened doubling times of the world's population. The world's population is doubling every 35 years without a corresponding increase in food and shelter.

  C. *The demographic transition:* The shift from high mortality and fertility (slow population growth) to low mortality and high fertility (rapid population growth) and finally to low mortality and low fertility (slow or no population growth) was the actual history of the Western World in the past 200 years. Demographers use this history as a predictive model for developing and undeveloped nations.

  D. *Zero population growth:*

    1. Part of the last stage of the demographic transition. Since Western, particularly American, exploitation of the environment far exceeds that of the rest of the world, stabilizing population will slow the depletion of the earth's resources.

    2. Zero population growth is a result of urban life, as city life does not favor large families.

VI. **Urbanization:** The population exodus from rural areas to areas of concentration of industry, business, and labor.

  A. It is a two-sided accommodation, as city factories require more labor while mechanized and chemical farming require less.

  B. Lower death rates, rising birthrates, and immigration, as well as urbanization, have contributed to the growth of cities.

  C. The U.S. Census Bureau defines a city as an area with a population of at least 2500. Sociologists refer to the *ecological* city, which includes the central city, suburbs, and satellite settlements that depend upon the city socially and economically.

VII. **Urbanism:** A set of attitudes and values along with a way of life distinct from rural life. Traditional rural values revolve around a close, secure, extended family life with relatively little change. The stereotype of rural people as honest, trustworthy, and helpful has been shown to be false.

VIII. **The Urban Transition:** In the transition from rural to urban dwellers there have been changes in mores; family life has changed from extended to nuclear; increased freedom has fostered anomie and alienation along with increased formal controls to replace the informal controls of the primary group.

IX. **Suburbanization and Metropolitanization**

    A. *Suburbanization*: Suburbs now house more people than the central cities. People move to the suburbs for a variety of reasons:

        1. Growth of the central areas.

        2. Increase in standard of living.

        3. Escape from city problems of dirt, crime, and noise.

    B. *Metropolitanization:* Ecological cities and SMSAs (Standard Metropolitan Statistical Areas), cities of 50,000 or more, have small areas. The problem of *megalopolis*—urban sprawl, with one city next to another—has resulted in a waste of money and resources as each metropolitan area maintains its own government.

    C. The *urban crisis* has resulted from suburbanization, with the loss of taxes and a population shift away from the older, larger cities of the Northeast and northcentral areas as a result of the loss of industrial jobs.

X. **Urban Ecology:** Three major models have been developed to explain the urban distribution of people and facilities.

    A. The *concentric-zone* model stresses the relationship between social status and distance from the center of the city. The higher their social class, the further individuals are likely to live from the central business district.

    B. The *sector* model focuses on the tendency of cities to grow outward from the center in wedge-shaped areas extending from the center to the outskirts or along main arteries of transportation such as rivers, lakes, canals, or railroads.

    C. The *multiple-nuclei* model suggests that there are a number of specialized centers in a city, not just one central business district.

XI. **Attempts to Reclaim the City**

    A. The flight to the suburbs, the growth of slums and ghettos, and the loss of a tax base have not totally defeated the central cities. Cities have many desirable features; therefore "gentrification" of many urban neighborhoods is occurring.

    B. *Urban renewal*, the provision of loans for slum clearance and low-cost housing, has not worked.

XII. The Natural Environment

A. The *ecosystem* is the way living things interact and interrelate with each other and the environment. The balance of the ecosystem is disturbed by overpopulation, pollution, and depletion.

B. *Overpopulation* results in 22 areas that negatively affect the environment.

C. *Environmental pollution* is the result of human tampering with the environment that has harmful consequences. Our water and soil have been polluted as a result.

D. *Environmental depletion:* We are depleting our nonrenewable resources at an alarming rate.

Learning Objectives

1. Differentiate social statics and social dynamics.
2. Define technology.
3. Summarize the effect of automation and industrialization in the industrial revolution.
4. Describe technological determinism.
5. Describe the results of cultural lag.
6. Summarize the major theories of sociocultural change.
7. State the process of social structure and cultural change.
8. List the ways in which each of the following may influence sociocultural change: physical environment, population, ideology, events, and individuals.
9. Indicate some of the ways in which rapid modernization may cause stress.
10. State the causes of the three stages of population growth.
11. Define the following terms: demography, population growth rate, birthrate, death rate, fertility rate.
12. List the relationship between population and food and population and income.
13. Define zero population growth, urbanization, and urbanism.
14. Summarize the major theories of the ecology of the city.
15. List the advantages and disadvantages of suburbanization and metropolitanization.
16. Describe the major elements in the urban crisis.
17. State the causes of the ecological imbalance and list the solutions.

Self-Test

Select the best possible answer. If you miss any questions, go back to the text and find the correct answer.

Multiple-Choice

1. The principal processes of cultural change include
   a. discovery.
   b. invention.
   c. diffusion.
   d. all of the above.

2. Factors that may influence sociocultural change include
   a. population and ideology.
   b. planning, reform, and revolution.
   c. discovery and invention.
   d. all of the above.

3. There have been _____ waves of population growth.
   a. four
   b. two
   c. three
   d. five

4. The science that studies population size, distribution, and composition is
   a. geography.
   b. topography.
   c. ecology.
   d. demography.

5. The stages of the demographic transition are
   a. high mortality and fertility to low mortality and high fertility to low mortality and fertility.
   b. high mortality and fertility to low mortality and fertility.
   c. low mortality and high fertility to low mortality and fertility.
   d. none of the above.

6. Zero population growth
   a. is the last stage of the demographic transition.
   b. will stabilize population.
   c. is a concomitant of urban life.
   d. is all of the above.

7. The ecology of the city is explained in part by
    a. concentric-zone theory.
    b. urbanism.
    c. suburbanization.
    d. functional theory.

8. Advantages of the suburbs include
    a. closeness to work.
    b. concentration of apartments.
    c. greater safety.
    d. large variety of cultural resources.

9. Factors in the urban crisis include
    a. the move of the middle class and industry to the suburbs.
    b. the inner city's declining tax base.
    c. a high percentage of deprived and trapped individuals.
    d. all of the above.

10. The major cause of the ecological imbalance is
    a. a decline in population.
    b. a decline in the population growth rate.
    c. rapid population growth.
    d. none of the above.

True-False

_____   1. Technology includes all the methods and devices that help humans manage and control their environment.

_____   2. Functionalists consider change to be the consequence of strains, tensions, and contradictions in the component parts of the social structure.

_____   3. Conflict theorists maintain that the cause of change is the conflict produced in society by the competing interests of social classes.

_____   4. Revolution is change obtained through violent means by the people of a nation whose government has not responded to their needs.

_____   5. Diffusion is a process of cultural change in which cultural traits are spread from one society to another and from one group in society to others.

_____   6. Rapid modernization is particularly stressful as it alters or destroys traditions and way of life.

_____   7. *Automation* and *industrialism* are interchangeable terms.

_____   8. The cause of the third wave of population growth was the improvement in medicine in underdeveloped countries.

_____ 9. Population growth rate and birthrate are terms associated with demography.

_____ 10. The second stage of the demographic transition consists of high mortality and high fertility.

_____ 11. Food production has grown much faster than population.

_____ 12. Urbanization and urbanism are interchangeable terms.

_____ 13. The sector theory is a theory of the ecology of the city.

_____ 14. Suburbanization is a significant factor in the urban crisis.

_____ 15. Urban renewal has been shown to be highly successful.

_____ 16. One of the solutions to the ecological imbalance is pollution control.

Fill-in-the-Blank

1. _____ studies structure and phenomena as though they were frozen in time. (Dynamics, Statics)

2. _____ studies processes of change, their causes and effects. (Dynamics, Statics)

3. _____ includes all the methods and devices that help humans manage and control their environment. (Material culture, Technology)

4. _____ is the process in which machines control other machines. (Automation, Mechanization)

5. _____ is the idea that technology is so important that it determines a society's culture, social structure, and history. (Material culture, Technological determinism)

6. _____ results as material culture changes and then a delay occurs before non-material culture changes. (Future shock, Cultural lag)

7. Combining the boat and the principle of the steam engine to produce the steamboat is an example of _____ . (discovery, invention)

8. In the _____ stage of population growth, population grew slowly but steadily. (second, agriculture)

9. The _____ stage in demographic transition is reflected by low fertility and mortality. (second, third)

10. A rise in income is usually accompanied by a rise in education and urbanization and the birthrate then tends to _____ . (fall, rise)

11. _____ is the shift of population to urban areas. (Urbanization, Urbanism)

12. _____ theory follows the growth of cities along the avenues of transportation. (Concentric zone, Sector)

13. _____ results in central-city degeneration and urban crisis. (Urbanism, Suburbanization)

14. The rapid growth in industrial technology has had _____ negative impact on the global ecosystem. (little, great)

Chapter 10

Collective Behavior and Formal Organizations in Mass Society

Goals

After you read the chapter, study the learning objectives, and take the self-test, you will be able to:

1. Recognize what is meant by mass society and mass communications.
2. Define and give examples of collective behavior.
3. Compare the theories of collective behavior.
4. Recognize other forms of collective behavior: rumors, fads, and crazes.
5. Grasp the difference between publics and public opinion.
6. Differentiate between propaganda and censorship.
7. Comprehend the conditions that promote social movements; who tends to join social movements; the forms that social movements take; and the stages that social movements go through.
8. Describe the functions of formal organizations and bureaucracies.

Synoptic Outline

I. **Mass Society:** A model society composed of an organized elite and an unorganized, diffused mass of people widely distributed and anonymous. The term is not interchangeable with modern society.

II. **Mass Communication:** Communication was broadened by the invention of writing and the printing press. The invention of the printing press significantly affected religion, politics, and culture. Mass communication differs from face-to-face communication in several ways:

   A. It exposes large audiences to impersonally transmitted symbols.

   B. It is one-sided, does not allow for normal interaction.

   C. It offers a superabundance of information.

III. **Collective Behavior:** Actions which take place without clear-cut direction of the norms. Spontaneous, relatively unstructured behavior engaged in by large numbers of people. Tends to occur in mass societies.

 A. *Types of crowds:* A crowd is a temporary collection of people who respond to the same stimulus.

  1. *Casual crowd:* Accidental gathering of people.

  2. *Organized crowd:* Come together for specific events.

  3. *Expressive crowd:* Gathers to express feelings.

  4. *Acting crowds:* Usually hostile acting out of feelings.

 B. *Characteristics of crowd behavior:*

  1. A stimulus evokes collective response.

  2. A common mood prevails.

  3. What constitutes acceptable behavior emerges at the moment.

  4. Individual identity merges into a common identity.

IV. **Others Types of Collective Behavior**

 A. Rumors: Unsupported reports of events that are not backed up by facts.

 B. *Fashions, fads, and crazes:*

  1. *Fashions* refer to manners of dress, architecture, or house decor of a given time.

  2. *Fads* and *crazes* are short-lived, minor fashions.

V. **Theories of Collective Behavior**

 A. *Contagion theory:* People in crowds respond emotionally and are infected by the behavior of others, forsaking reason and individuality.

 B. *Convergence theory:* People do not congregate by accident or "catch" formerly unfelt emotions. They are predisposed to the behavior. The gathering simply provides a setting for the release of latent feelings not expressible in other situations.

 C. *Emergent-norm theory:* The behavior of the crowd is not normless. In part it is controlled by conventional social norms, and new norms are established to fit the situation. Not all individuals in the crowd share these feelings, but those who believe they are in a minority remain silent or passive.

VI. **Publics and Public Opinion**

 A. A *public* is a scattered collection of people who share a common interest or concern about an issue.

 B. *Public opinion* refers to the attitude or judgment of a large number of people on a specific issue.

VII. Propaganda and Censorship

A. *Propaganda* is the deliberate effort to persuade people to accept a particular belief without question by giving only one side of an issue.

B. *Censorship* deletes all or parts of information.

VIII. Social Movements: Collective behavior which has as its goal social change of all or part of society.

A. Ideology in social movements: An *ideology* is a system of beliefs that provides a basis for collective action.

  1. Ideologies explain why things are the way they are.

  2. Ideologies reinforce the feelings of participants and make them a part of a program for action.

  3. Ideologies direct members' behavior to effect change.

  4. Ideologies educate members of a social movement and of society, justifying their actions.

  5. Ideologies often distort the truth.

B. Collective actions become social movements when:

  1. They have a specific ideology.

  2. They awaken a strong sense of idealism and solidarity.

  3. There is an orientation toward action.

  4. A significant number of people are involved.

C. Conditions for the rise of social movements:

  1. Social movements flourish in times of rapid social change.

  2. Individual feelings of *anomie* (lack of norms) or *alienation* (powerlessness and isolation).

  3. *Relative deprivation:* Desire for the benefits enjoyed by others.

  4. *Rising expectations:* Expectations that living standards will improve significantly.

D. Kinds of social movements:

  1. *Revolutionary* movements seek to overthrow the present system as they view it as beyond repair. A *nationalistic* revolutionary movement seeks to oust a foreign government.

  2. *Reform* movements seek to change some aspect of society without changing the entire order.

  3. *Change resistant* movements seek to slow, stop, or reverse change.

IX. Formal Organizations and Bureaucracy: As societies become larger, more complex, and more heterogeneous, bureaucracies develop to channel, regulate, and direct those activities which in simple societies are controlled by tradition and shared norms.

A. *Formal organizations:* Groups which exist for the purpose of achieving specific goals. Their methods and procedures are fixed so that they may be routinely repeated and performed by miscellaneous individuals. Characteristics of formal organization include:

  1. *Formal structure:* Systems and roles are fairly static and predetermined. The objective is stated and the organization establishes the means toward that objective.

  2. Relative permanency.

  3. *Stratification:* Hierarchical role structure.

  4. *Formal program:* The activities and interrelationships of members are systematic and conform to abstract guidelines.

B. *Voluntary associations:* Self-determined membership. They may be formal or informal in structure. The motive for membership is a common cause, interest, or goal.

C. *Bureaucracy:* A hierarchical system for rationally coordinating the work of many individuals through a division of labor and a chain of command.

  1. Max Weber's characterization of "pure" bureaucracies:

    a. *Specialization:* The most expert or skilled perform each discrete function.

    b. *Hierarchy:* A chain of command ensures the orderly flow of business and prevents power concentration or usurpation.

    c. *Body of rules:* These remain stable although individuals who fill each role may change.

    d. *Impersonality:* Detachment from both coworkers and clients prevents favoritism, collusion, preferential treatment.

    e. *Selection:* Based on merit and job tenure.

  2. Actual bureaucracies do not function in accordance with Weber's ideal:

    a. *Resistant to change:* Once the system is established it flows of its own accord and is not susceptible to the changing needs of society.

    b. *Rules become rigid:* No matter how unrelated to the particular case or inapplicable to the individual's problems, the rule is carried out as formally fixed.

  3. *Oligarchy:* Robert Michels observed that in large formal organizations, power falls into the hands of a few by default. The rank-and-file membership are unwilling to devote the time and energy necessary for equitable distribution of organizational power. The few who assume the major responsibility take control.

D. *The dynamic aspect of bureaucracy:* In spite of the problems noted, bureaucracies can respond to change because:

  1. Employees in developed countries are less economically dependent on their superiors.

  2. People are less willing to accept authority.

  3. The knowledge of technical specialists gives them an advantage over managers.

  4. Social innovation depends upon bureaucratic methods of administration.

E. *Informality in bureaucracy:* Informal networks are a means to get things done or to impede the organization. The informal structure humanizes the formal organization.

Learning Objectives

1. Define mass society and mass communication.
2. Define collective behavior.
3. Describe the major types of crowds.
4. List the characteristics of crowd behavior.
5. Define rumor and state its role in collective behavior.
6. Summarize the major theories of collective behavior.
7. Define the term *public* and identify the bond that holds it together.
8. Define the term *public opinion* and summarize the formation and measuring of public opinion.
9. Differentiate between propaganda and censorship.
10. Define social movements.
11. Summarize the ideological basis for social movements.
12. List the conditions which promote social movements.
13. Summarize the forms that social movements are likely to take.
14. Describe the purpose of formal organizations.
15. Define bureaucracy.
16. Compare "pure" bureaucracy and the operation of real bureaucracies.
17. Summarize Robert Michels's findings concerning oligarchies and state the implications of these findings for formal organizations.

Self-Test

Select the best possible answer. If you miss any questions, go back to the text and find the correct answer.

Multiple-Choice

1. Collective behavior is often precipitated by
   a. anomaly.
   b. rapid social change.
   c. deviant behavior.
   d. fear of the future.

2. Which is not a theory of collective behavior?
   a. Contagion.
   b. Alienation.
   c. Convergence.
   d. Emergent norm.

3. Which of the following would be identified as an "acting" crowd?
   a. People waiting for a red light.
   b. People at a football game.
   c. People at a rock concert.
   d. People at a riot.

4. Which of the following is not a characteristic of crowd behavior?
   a. Interaction as persons.
   b. A common mood prevails.
   c. Behaves according to previously established norms.
   d. Temporary.

5. Crowd behavior is limited by
   a. norms.
   b. leadership.
   c. external controls.
   d. all of the above.

6. Public opinion serves which of the following functions in society?
   a. It helps institutionalize new cultural norms.
   b. It persuades individuals to accept a particular belief uncritically.
   c. It provides the central ideology of social movements.
   d. It limits the effect of propaganda.

7. Collective efforts to change the present sociocultural order are
    a. mobs.
    b. crazes.
    c. social movements.
    d. crowds.

8. Expressive social movements
    a. solve discontent through geographic move.
    b. try to establish new societies with new standards and values.
    c. change the members' reactions to their environment.
    d. attempt to stem the tide of change.

9. Social movements flourish in an atmosphere of
    a. peace and harmony.
    b. totalitarian rigidity.
    c. relative deprivation and rising expectations.
    d. all of the above.

10. The purpose of social movements is to
    a. bring an end to injustice.
    b. institutionalize change.
    c. bring participatory democracy.
    d. give the younger generation an opportunity to lead.

11. Formal organizations are
    a. groups of people which you may join and have dealings with.
    b. a procedure.
    c. an established way of doing things.
    d. a pattern of customary behavior.

12. Which is a characteristic of pure bureaucracy?
    a. Informality.
    b. Automation.
    c. Concentration.
    d. Impersonality.

13. Real bureaucracies
    a. base promotion only on merit.
    b. are resistant to change.
    c. are humanistic.
    d. are all of the above.

14. Mass communication
    a. exposes large audiences to impersonally transmitted symbols.
    b. is one-sided.
    c. provides a superabundance of information.
    d. all of the above.

True-False

_____ 1. Collective behavior is relatively unpatterned and unstructured.

_____ 2. Collective behavior occurs in situations that are highly charged with emotion and in which the norms we use in ordinary interaction prove very useful.

_____ 3. Collective behavior is much more likely to occur during periods of rapid social change.

_____ 4. According to emergent norm theory, collective behavior merely brings out in the open feelings already present in the individual members of the collectivity.

_____ 5. A crowd is a collection of people who respond to a common stimulus.

_____ 6. The readers of _Time_ magazine constitute a public.

_____ 7. Public opinion has meaning especially in a mass society.

_____ 8. The mass media greatly influences, though they do not form, public opinion.

_____ 9. Reform social movements represent an attempt to remove the old social order and substitute it with a new one.

_____ 10. The last stage in the development of a social movement is dissolution.

_____ 11. Bureaucracy is a type of herarchical arrangement based on division of labor and a chain of authority for the purpose of coordinating rationally the activities of many individuals.

_____ 12. Bureaucratic organization in its ideal, or pure, form corresponds to bureaucracy as it really functions.

_____ 13. The "Iron Law of Oligarchy" suggests that a hierarchical arrangement based on division of labor produces apathetic leadership.

_____ 14. Mass society and modern society are interchangeable terms.

Fill-in-the-Blank

1. _____ is characteristic of a collectivity of people responding to a comon stimulus under conditions that are temporary, unstable, and unstructured. (Social movement, Collective behavior)

2. According to the _____ theory, collective behavior must be viewed as a process in which moods, attitudes, and behavior are communicated to a collectivity and are accepted by the collectivity. (contagion, convergence)

3. _____ is an unsupported report of an event or projected event. (Propaganda, Rumor)

4. _____ includes persons who are geographically dispersed but share a common interest, express it, and know others that are aware of this interest. (Public opinion, Public)

5. _____ is the attitude or judgment of a large number of people on a specific issue. (Propaganda, Public opinion)

6. _____ is a deliberate attempt to persuade an individual to uncritically accept a belief. (Censorship, Propaganda)

7. The Ku Klux Klan is an example of a _____ movement. (utopian, change resistant)

Chapter 11
The Family, Religion, Education

Goals

After you read the chapter, study the learning objectives, and take the self-test, you will be able to:

1. Comprehend the functions of the family.
2. Be aware of the influences of subcultural differences between the middle-class and the working/lower-class family.
3. Understand the reasons why the family is not disappearing but rather is undergoing significant change.
4. View religion from the sociological perspective.
5. Recognize the functions and dysfunctions (Marx's opiate) of religion.
6. Identify the relationship between religion and social class.
7. Recognize contemporary religious trends.
8. Describe the development of education into a formal organization.
9. Identify the goals and education in the United States.
10. Recognize the manifest and latent functions of education.
11. State the successes and failures of the educational system in the United States.

Synoptic Outline

Part A: The Family

I. **Pivotal Institutions:** Institutions are patterns of behavior, or traditional habits, that have accumulated around important human functions. All societies exhibit at least five pivotal institutions with their attendant functions:

    A. *Family*: Ensures a continuous supply of societal members and provides these new members with a nurturing environment.

    B. *Economy*: Provides the means for obtaining a livelihood for the members of society.

C. *Education*: Passes on important knowledge to the next generation.

D. *Religion*: Gives meaning to unanswerable questions.

E. *Government: Maintains order.*

II. **The Family:** The basic and universal institution. Some form of the family is found in all societies.

    A. Fundamental functions of the family are the regulation of sex, reproduction, economics, and education.

    B. All families share the following:

        1. They are social groups that originate in marriage.

        2. They consist, at minimum, of husband, wife, and children.

        3. Members are bound by legal, economic, and religious bonds, duties, and privileges.

        4. There is a network of sexual privileges and prohibitions.

        5. There is some degree of love, respect, and affection.

III. **Forms of the Family**

    A. *Extended or consanguine family:*

        1. Blood relatives of the parents reside with or in near proximity to the nuclear family.

        2. Child rearing is a shared responsibility.

        3. Family welfare takes precedence over individual welfare.

        4. Usually strongly hierarchical.

        5. All members contribute emotional, physical, and economic support.

        6. In patrilocal extended families, the daughter-in-law, who is not a blood relative, has the lowest status.

    B. *Nuclear or conjugal family:* Reproductive rather than kinship bonds. Typical of industrial societies where kinship ties are severed as a result of:

        1. Geographic mobility.

        2. Social mobility.

        3. Performance of traditional family functions by other groups.

        4. Emphasis on individual fulfillment rather than the welfare of the family.

IV. **Marriage**

    A. Traditionally the motive for marriage was the reproduction and care of offspring.

    B. In contemporary postindustrial society, emotional involvement, friendship, and companionship are increasingly important motives.

    C. *Marital forms:* Monogamy, polygamy (polyandry, polygyny).

D. Social restrictions on selection of mate:

    1. *Exogamy*: Requirements to marry outside of a specified group.

        a. All societies have exogamous requirements related to incest taboos, but what constitutes incest is culturally defined.

        b. Incest taboos are socially rather than biologically functional. They clarify relationships, eliminate confusion of family stratification or hierarchy, encourage the introduction of economically productive new adults, and encourage wider social interaction and alliances, thus bolstering the solidarity of the entire society.

    2. *Endogamy*: Requirements for marriage within a certain group.

V. Family Functions

    A. *Regulation of sex:* Societies attempt to channel sex into marriage and give high status to married people. Being single is usually discouraged.

    B. *Reproduction*: One of the fundamental functions of the family. Reproduction outside the family is discouraged.

    C. *Socialization of children*: Socialization has always largely been a function of the family. Other agents of socialization include schools and peer groups.

    D. *Affection and companionship:* One may find companionship outside of the family but affection is more likely to be found only within the family.

VI. Love and Marriage in America: Love as a prerequisite for marriage is a modern invention. Though there is free choice in our society, people tend to marry mates very much like themselves. This is called homogamy. Homogamous choices are based on age, proximity, race, ethnicity, education, religion, and social class.

VII. Changing Marital Patterns: Modernization, affluence, birth control, liberalized sexual norms, and the increased number of women in the work force have resulted in smaller or childless families and increased divorce rates.

    A. *Divorce*: The high rates of divorce reflect separation of marriage from religion, the emancipation of women, and the emphasis on individuality and personal happiness.

    B. *Divorce as the new norm:* Divorce has become an acceptable alternative to staying in an unhappy marriage. Liberalized divorce laws, particularly "no-fault" divorce, have made it much easier to end a marriage.

    C. *Consequences of divorce:* There is trauma for all in a divorce. Women experience greater trauma, possibly because of economic factors, while men find psychological adjustment more difficult. Children are traumatized more by years of parental fighting than divorce.

VIII. Alternatives to Traditional Marriage: Remaining single and living with a mate without marriage are alternatives to traditional marriage, particularly since the stigma of being single has declined.

IX. Forms of the New American Family: A majority of children grow up in the traditional family but a significant number grow up in one of the following:

A. *The single-parent family:* This form tends to be temporary. Most single-parent families are headed by women.

B. *The blended or reconstituted family:* This form is the result of remarriage where one or both partners have children from a previous marriage.

C. *The small, childless, or one-child family:* Contraceptives, economics, and careers for women are the major reasons for this form of the family.

X. Tomorrow's Family: The family institution will continue to exist, though in a variety of forms, in spite of all its problems.

Part B: Religion

I. Religion is found in all societies because it fulfills the need to give meaning and purpose to life.

II. Religion and the Social Sciences:

A. Early sociologists viewed religion as intellectual error or ignorance.

B. Karl Marx felt that religion was the result of man's fear of natural phenomena. He viewed religion as a mask for social class interest. The ruling class, according to Marx, used religion as an "opiate" to control the masses.

C. *Durkheim's view:*

1. Religion is society's way of differentiating the sacred and the profane.

2. The Divine is a projection of the image of society. It shares with society these attributes: It is greater than the individual. The individual depends upon it for his existence. It governs the right and wrong of behavior. It is authoritative and demands allegiance.

3. Deities are invented to explain forces over which humans have no control.

4. Religion creates social solidarity.

III. The Functions of Religion

A. *Establishment of identity:* Religion defines one's relationship with the universe and provides self-definition as a member of a group.

B. *Clarification of the world:* Religion presents a configuration of reality which makes it understandable.

C. *Support of societal norms and values:* It justifies society's demands upon the individual by connecting these demands to divine will.

D. *Aid in critical life stages:* Provides meaning for stressful biological and social life stages—birth, adulthood, marriage, death.

E. Helps people deal with guilt by offering a way back to a constructive life.

IV. The Conflict View of Religion

A. *Alienating*: Humans believe that supernatural powers regulate their condition in life. Religion causes them to give over their reins of control.

B. *Conflict causing:* Both between clergy and laity, and between various religious groups.

C. *Self-perpetuating:* Once created, religion takes on an objective identity which, because it is unchanging, supports the status quo.

D. *An "opiate of the people":* Supports social inequality by offering to the poor a justification for their condition and promises of otherworldly rewards.

V. Religion in America

A. *Common features of religion:* All religions have beliefs, ritual, and organization.

B. *Organization of religion:*

   1. *Church*: A church is a religious organization that is thoroughly institution-alized and integrated into the social and economic order of society. Churches are divided into:

      a. *Ecclesia*: An official state religion.

      b. *Denominations*: Not officially linked to the government and on an equal footing in the society.

   2. *Sects*: usually breakaway movements from an established church.

   3. *Cults*: the smallest, least durable, and least conventional religious organiza-tion. They tend to revolve around a charismatic leader.

C. Religion in the United States is atypical in that there has never been a state religion and the society has accommodated many different denominations.

D. *Religious affiliation and social class:* The relationship between church membership in particular denominations and social status is evident in America.

E. Participation in church activities is highest in the upper-lower and lower-middle classes and lowest in the lower and upper classes.

VI. Sanctification of the American Way of Life

A. Will Herberg found that Americans use religion for secular purposes. Church membership is a class and status, rather than a religious consideration.

B. Robert Bellah concludes that Americans share a "civil religion" that sanctifies the American political system.

VII. Contemporary Trends

A. The influence of established institutional religion has declined but religious influence is still significant in the family.

B. There has been a growth in evangelical and fundamentalist sects. They are problematic in that they propose simple solutions to complex social problems.

C. As long as people wonder about the meaning of life and experience disappointments, suffering, and death, they will need religion to still their fears.

Part C: Education

I. Education—Definition and Social Correlation

A. The accumulated knowledge of a society passed intergenerationally and intragenerationally.

B. Grows in proportion to the complexity of the society.

  1. Family centered in primitive societies.

  2. Humanist and elite in preindustrial societies.

  3. Technical and specialized in postindustrial societies.

II. Education in America: Open and universal for reasons of utility and ideology.

A. *Practical basis for open education:*

  1. Nineteenth-century need to mold a skilled work force.

  2. Current technology requires advanced and various technological knowledge and specialized skills.

B. *Ideological basis for open education:*

  1. *Melting pot:* Americanization of immigrants

  2. Democracy requires literate and well-informed citizens.

  3. Education is an asset to the entire society, not just to the individual.

C. *Local control* of schools has resulted in inequality of funding.

D. *Upward mobility:* People consider education to be the first step in upward mobility.

E. *Education as a cure-all:* Education is viewed as a cure-all for social problems.

III. Functionalist Perspective of Education: Education as it exists benefits the whole society.

A. *Manifest functions:*

  1. Transmission of cultural heritage.

  2. Recruitment and preparation for social roles.

  3. Cultural integration.

  4. *Innovation:* Generation of new knowledge.

B. *Latent functions:*

  1. *Schools allocate adult roles:* Schools help to create and maintain stratification.

  2. Because school structures reflect the structure of society they are instruments of status rather than of social change.

3. Schools are custodians of the young.

4. They stimulate the growth of youth subcultures.

5. They affect social attitudes: Higher education is correlated with greater broadmindedness.

IV. The Conflict View of Education

A. Conflict theorists assert that the educational system is used by the elite to manipulate the masses and maintain their power in the society. The real purpose of education is to allocate social status.

B. *Credentialism*, the practice of requiring degrees for high-paying and prestigious jobs, sets up barriers so that the lower classes and minorities are effectively eliminated from competition.

V. Education and Social Class

A. The bureaucratic structure of education tends to alienate lower-class and minority students.

B. The self-fulfilling prophecy with which teachers judge students usually comes true.

C. Lower-class students' cultural backgrounds do not prepare them for objective testing in the schools.

D. It is difficult for teachers to reach students whose background does not include reading of books, magazines, newspapers, or the belief that school is the key to success.

VI. The Role of the Family: The single most important determinant of scholastic success is the family. Middle- and upper-class families prepare their children for and expect academic success. Students from the lower classes are not exposed to the values and expectations of academic success from family or peers.

VII. Education, Race, and Ethnicity: Some racial and ethnic groups remain at the lower end of the stratification system and encounter less scholastic success.

A. The Coleman report found that the lower achievement of Hispanic and black students may be accounted for by family background and the feeling of minority students that they lack control over their environment. Minority students' performance improves when they attend a harmoniously integrated school.

B. A later study by Coleman found that private schools did a better job of education because they were safer, more disciplined, and had a well-ordered environment.

VIII. Education and Social Change: Education has been thought of as the primary way to gain upward mobility. Other factors such as family background have been shown to be of significance. School represents a way out of poverty for some, while at the same time reflecting and reinforcing social inequality.

IX. **Success and Failure of Education**

    A. A higher percentage of students finish school than ever before.

    B. SAT scores and literacy rates have declined.

    C. Schools have instituted a variety of reforms in response to criticism.

    D. Schools have attempted to deal with the lack of background and motivation of poor and minority students by lowering standards, but this has not been to the advantage of the students.

    E. Schools are still trying to solve the challenge of how to make universal mass education a reality.

Learning Objectives

1. Name the pivotal institutions and the essential functions performed by each, as well as the major theories associated with each institution.

2. Compare extended and nuclear families.

3. State the relationship betwen nuclear families and urban industrial societies.

4. Define the forms of marriage and the terms *exogamy* and *endogamy*.

5. Identify the major functions of the family.

6. Summarize the history of romantic love and marriage, including the concept of homogamy.

7. List the changing marital patterns in the United States and include the alternatives to traditional marriage.

8. Outline the forms of the new American family and speculate about the future of the family.

9. State the functions of religion.

10. Summarize the theoretical perspectives of religion, including those of Karl Marx and Émile Durkheim and the functional as well as conflict perspectives.

11. List the common features of religion.

12. Define and differentiate these terms: church, ecclesia, denomination, sect, and cult.

13. Summarize the characteristics of religion in America.

14. Summarize the relationship between religion and social class.

15. Explain what is meant by "sanctification of the American way of life."

16. Summarize the contemporary trends in religion.

17. Define education.

18. State the reasons why education is open and universal in the United States.

19. Outline the functional and conflict perspectives of education.

20. List the ways in which social class, race, ethnicity, and family influence academic success or failure.

21. State the relationship between social change and education.

22. List the major successes and failures of education.

Self-Test

Select the best possible answer. If you miss any questions, go back to the text and find the correct answer.

Multiple-Choice

1. The underlying reasons for the establishment of the family institution are
   a. to satisfy emotional needs.
   b. to provide for the biological needs of hunger and shelter.
   c. to assure the continuation of the species.
   d. to regulate sex.

2. Polyandry is
   a. group marriage.
   b. the union of one woman with several men.
   c. the union of one man with several women.
   d. common-law marriage.

3. The form of marriage which best fits into modern, urban, industrial societies is
   a. monogamy.
   b. polygamy.
   c. bigamy.
   d. polygyny.

4. The choice of mates for marriage is regulated in all societies by rules of
   a. endogamy and exogamy.
   b. homogamy and polygamy.
   c. homogeneity and heterogeneity.
   d. levirate and sororate.

5. The most prevalent form which the family has assumed in modern industrial societies is
   a. consanguine.
   b. procreational.
   c. extended.
   d. nuclear.

6. The American family has steadily decreased in size because
   a. we attach no stigma to children born out of wedlock.
   b. urban living severely reduces the male sex drive.
   c. the death rate has begun to increase significantly.
   d. many parents have decided to concentrate on upward mobility.

7. Religion
    a. serves no useful purpose.
    b. gives meaning and purpose to life.
    c. is an intellectual error.
    d. is none of the above.

8. The sociological perspective of religion includes
    a. the search for the one "true" religion.
    b. the examination of all creeds for validity.
    c. the belief that religion serves no useful purpose.
    d. the study of the function of religion.

9. Émile Durkheim believed
    a. that religion is a process dealing with the sacred.
    b. that people consider some things and events sacred and others profane.
    c. that religion was primitive people's explanation of events they could not understand.
    d. only a and b.

10. Of the following, who believed that religion is essentially the worship of society?
    a. Karl Marx.
    b. Émile Durkheim.
    c. J. G. Frazer.
    d. Auguste Comte.

11. Which is *not* a function of religion?
    a. It counteracts the rationalism of science.
    b. It offers comfort and solace to human suffering.
    c. It clarifies the physical world.
    d. It offers humans access to the beyond.

12. Religion
    a. establishes our identity.
    b. clarifies the world and aids in critical life stages.
    c. supports societal norms and values.
    d. is all of the above.

13. Karl Marx's statement that religion was the "opiate of the people" is an example of
    a. the world-maintaining force of religion.
    b. the world-shaking force of religion.
    c. religion's ability to subvert the status quo.
    d. religion's ability to give comfort in the critical stages of life.

14. Which is *not* a feature of religion?
    a. A set of beliefs.
    b. A body of ritual.
    c. Organization.
    d. Methodology.

15. In the United States, the link between religion and stratification is evident in the fact that
    a. the lower socioeconomic classes are all Protestant.
    b. the nation's elites have been consistently Protestant.
    c. the upper classes are made up of Jews.
    d. the lower classes are not religious.

16. Among modern religious trends are
    a. secularization.
    b. bureaucratization.
    c. evangelism and Pentecostalism.
    d. all of the above.

17. Education, the passing on of accumulated knowledge, is necessary because
    a. humans lack instinctual behavior.
    b. technology demands a trained worker.
    c. as societies become more complex, concrete knowledge is necessary.
    d. all of the above.

18. Education in America is open and universal because of
    a. the need for skilled workrs.
    b. the need to "Americanize" immigrants.
    c. the ideologies of self-fulfillment and social mobility.
    d. all of the above.

19. Which of the following is a manifest function of education?
    a. Cultural integration.
    b. Reinforcing the stratification system of society.
    c. The formation of a youth subculture.
    d. Custodial functions.

20. Identify a latent function of education in the following:
    a. Reinforcing the system of social stratification.
    b. Cultural integration.
    c. Reinforcing the values of the majority.
    d. Preparing students for their eventual role in society.

21. Among the successes of American education we find
    a. a higher percentage finishing high school.
    b. an increase in SAT scores.
    c. an increase in literacy.
    d. all of the above.

True-False

_____ 1. Institutions are the habits or traditional ways of doing things that eventually crystallize into patterns of behavior.

_____ 2. The pivotal institutions include the family, religion, education, the economy, and the government.

_____ 3. The function of providing affection and companionship has increased in the nuclear family.

_____ 4. The family in urban industrial society has become nuclear.

_____ 5. Historically, the most prevalent form of marriage has been polygamy.

_____ 6. In our society, endogamy means that the individual is encouraged to marry outside his subculture.

_____ 7. The extended family is typical of an agricultural society.

_____ 8. The high rate of divorce in urban industrial societies reflects the separation of marriage from religion, the emancipation of women, and a change in values.

_____ 9. Émile Durkheim's theories of religion stress the function of social integration.

_____ 10. One of the functions of religion is to help establish a sense of identity.

_____ 11. Ritualized behavior helps maintain the sacred.

_____ 12. A church is a religious association that is institutionalized, well integrated in socioeconomic life, and in which participation is routine.

_____ 13. Cults consist of groups of followers clustered around a leader whose teachings differ substantially from the accepted beliefs of a church or denomination.

_____ 14. Religion in America is atypical because there has never been a state religion.

_____ 15. Robert Bellah maintains that we have developed a kind of "civil religion" by making holy some of our political ideals, national heroes, and our common destiny.

_____ 16. Systems of social stratification have been tolerated by Christians because lower-class characteristics have been associated with sin.

_____ 17. Compulsory mass education came into being after the Revolutionary War when the need to educate backwoods frontiersmen was recognized.

_____ 18. According to the functionalist view, the transmission of knowledge from one generation to another is the latent function of education.

_____ 19. According to the conflict view, education perpetuates the stratification system of society.

Fill-in-the-Blank

1. _____ theorists contend that the well-being of males is attained at the expense of females. (Functional, Conflict)

2. _____ means marriage to someone who possesses characteristics similar to oneself. (Homogamy, Homogeneity)

3. The sociological term for a breakup of the family unit is _____ (divorce, family disorganization)

4. _____ divorce rates and _____ women in the work force are major changes in the American family. (Higher, Lower; more, fewer)

5. The families of the future will include more _____ (single-parent and blended families; stable and long-lasting marriages)

6. The least conventional and institutionalized form of religious organization is called a _____ (sect, cult)

7. Members of the _____ class are most likely to participate in church affairs. (lower-lower, lower-middle)

8. The institution which is primarily utilized to transmit the accumulated culture of a society from one generation to the next is _____ (socialization, education)

9. When schools act as babysitters, they are fulfilling one of the _____ functions of education. (manifest, latent)

Chapter 12

The Economy and Government

Goals

After you read the chapter, study the learning objectives, and take the self-test, you will be able to:

1. View economics from the sociological perspective.
2. Understand the major economic decisions and the ways that societies attempt to solve economic problems.
3. Comprehend the ideologies that underlie capitalism, socialism, and communism.
4. Recognize the major problems facing the American economy.
5. Use the sociological perspective in examining government and politics.
6. Name the functions of government.
7. Comprehend the meaning of the term *political power*.
8. Recognize the types of authority.
9. Describe the various political ideologies.
10. Identify the parts of the power structure in the United States.

Synoptic Outline

Part A: Economics

I. **The Economic Institution:** A system and process of production, distribution and consumption. The what and how of production is affected by geography, environment, and technology. Subsistence quantities are ordinarily equitably distributed. Surpluses lead to disproportionate accumulations, which correspond to social stratification. Consumption may be encouraged as a way of stimulating production or may be restricted due to scarcity.

A. *Economic decision making*
   1. *The issues:*
      a. What should be produced and in what quantities?
      b. What shall be the means of production?
      c. For which members of the society are the commodities produced?

    2. *Sources of decisions:*
        a. Custom and tradition.
        b. Command of a ruler or ruling body.
        c. Market fluctuations—supply and demand.
        d. In the United States, both government and private companies, as well as the market, exert control.
B. *Factors of production:* Labor, land, capital (society's resources).
C. *Additional resources:* Time, efficiency, technology.
    1. These factors of production become increasingly important as society becomes more complex.
    2. They are both causes and effects of complex industrial economies.

II. Contemporary Economic Systems

A. *Capitalism:*
    1. Rights of ownership: Private ownership of the means of production and distribution, land and natural resources.
    2. Philosophic base of the free enterprise system: Laissez Faire: Adam Smith's *The Wealth of Nations:*
        a. Pursuit of selfish interest works for the common good. Those who serve the demands of the market best become wealthiest.
        b. Laws of supply and demand and competition operate as controls on capitalist self-interest. Economic power originates in the consumer.

B. *Socialism:*
    1. Rights of ownership: Private ownership restricted to personal goods and relatively small companies. Crucial industries and resources publicly owned.
    2. Privately owned industry closely regulated by government.
    3. High taxes are the means of redistributing society's wealth.
    4. Central coordination and planning of production.
    5. No segment of the society suffers as a result of the benefits enjoyed by another segment.
    6. *Democratic socialism* occurs when a socialist economy is found within a democratic political system.

C. *Communism*
    1. No private ownership except of personal goods.
    2. Total equitable redistribution of the wealth of the society. A single standard of living.
    3. Government coordination of all aspects of the economy.

III. **Theoretical Perspectives on Economic Development**

    A. The *structural-functionalist* perspective contends that the economic system emerged to meet basic social needs and reflects the fundamental values of society. The freedom of the individual is emphasized. Criticism of this perspective revolves around the realization that capitalism denies some individuals and groups equal access to success.

    B. *Conflict* theorists start with Karl Marx's view of the rise of capitalism and its dysfunctions for the workers as they compete for limited jobs. His prediction of the revolt of the workers did not come about because of the rise of unions to protect the interests of the workers. Current conflict theorists focus on alienation, dehumanization, and the power of large corporations.

IV. **Western Economies in Historical Perspective:** The economies of the Western World are mostly modified capitalist, mixed-market economies. The transformation from agricultural to industrial societies caused fundamental changes in values and beliefs.

    A. Industrialization followed the growth of the middle class, the *bourgeoisie*, and the growth of the *Protestant ethic.*

    B. The new economic system greatly increased the production of goods and services. The working class, *the proletariat*, worked for wages in the largely family-owned factories (family capitalism).

V. **American Economy**

    A. *Corporations*:

        1. In a corporation, ownership is separated from management.

        Ideal structure:

            a. By vote, stockholders determine corporate policy, which is carried out by management.

            b. Since the public is both the consumer and the stockholder, consumer concerns will affect corporate policy.

        2. *Actual structure:*

            a. Corporate executives and directors own controlling stock.

            b. Corporate directors are often the corporate managers.

            c. Corporations own the controlling stock of other corporations.

            d. Interlocking directorates.

    B. *Oligopoly*: Concentration of the productive wealth of the society in a few corporations:

        1. .001 percent of the corporations own 50% of the manufacturing assets of the country.

        2. Because of their enormous economic power, corporations wield great political power.

C. *Corporate control of profits:*

   1. A few corporations divide vast markets. Virtual monopoly replaces free enterprise.

   2. Advertising replaces competition: Consumer choice is directed by advertising rather than by competitive prices or quality.

   3. Planned obsolescence.

   4. Artificial needs are created:

   a. Advertising creates demand for a product which is of little value to the society or the individual.

   b. Private affluence and public squalor: The consumer is primed to spend on unnecessary goods produced in the private sector rather than to pay taxes for public services.

D. *Diversification and multinational corporations:*

   1. Diversification refers to a corporation's acquisition of controlling interest in other, often dissimilar, industries.

   2. Multinational corporations often abuse their power, derived from their control over thousands of jobs.

VI. Work in Industrial Societies

A. Three sectors of employment:

   1. *Primary sector:* Extraction and processing of raw materials.

   2. *Secondary sector:* Manufacturing and construction.

   3. *Tertiary sector:* Services. Most workers in the United States ae employed in this sector.

B. Ten percent self-employed. 90% employed by others, for the most part in large bureaucratic organizations.

C. *Union membership:*

   1. Bureaucratization of unions.

   2. Similarity of union leadership and corporate management.

D. *Worker alienation:*

   1. *Marx:* Alienation results from the removal of the worker from the goals, purposes, and decision making of production.

   2. *Specialization and division of labor:* Intrinsically alienating since workers perform an action rather than creating a product.

E. *Anomie:* Durkheim's theory of the consequences of division of labor:

   1. *Mechanical solidarity:* In simple, preindustrial societies, the individual is set into social norms which have been fixed by tradition. Solidarity is the result of similarity.

   2. *Organic solidarity:* In complex, industrial societies, the individual is faced with conflicting, contrasting, and rapidly changing norms. Since the individual's function is specialized, solidarity is the result of interdependent differences.

VII. The Role of Government: Government intervention in the American economy keeps increasing. Some view the involvement of the government as a threat to personal and civil freedom while others welcome the expansion of government functions. The second group has noted the social problems that have arisen because of the "hands off" policy of government. Central planning has not been shown to be a panacea for social problems, either.

VIII. Future Trends of the American Economy: A restructuring of the economy is beginning to take place as we shift from a national to a global economy. Developing nations are becoming manufacturing nations while Western countries are losing industrial jobs and creating information jobs. Our nation is faced with the problem of what to do with the blue-collar workers that are displaced by the loss of industrial jobs.

Part B: Government

I. The Institution of Government: That pattern of statuses and roles that a society develops to fulfill the need for order within and defense against threats from external sources.

II. Purpose and Functions of Government

   A. A system of formal social control vested in a recognized entity.

   B. Manifest functions of government:

      1. Protection of citizenry.

      2. Arbitration and judgment of disputes.

      3. Planning and maintaining social services.

      4. Coordinating government sectors.

   C. Latent functions of government:

      1. Party machines.

      2. System of social stratification.

III. Political Power

   A. *Weber's definition:* "The probability that one actor within a social relationship will be in a position to carry out his own will despite resistance." There is always some measure of reciprocity, either overt or covert.

   B. *Types of power:*

      1. Control of the means of *reward*.

      2. *Coercion:* Control of the means of punishment.

      3. *Influence:* Control of the means of information and persuasion.

C. *Legitimate power:*

  1. That power which is exercised by *authority*—the institution recognized by the people as representative of their society.

  2. Based on popular will—people's belief that the system is appropriate—and on consensus—the agreement of the government's legitimacy by virtually all within the society.

  3. *Crisis of legitimacy:* The absence of authority in government and consensus among the people. Governments may resort to coercion. People may resort to revolution.

D. *Types of legitimate authority:* (Weber)

  1. *Traditional:* Culturally inherited norms, beliefs, and values.

  2. *Legal-rational:* Derives from public opinion that has been molded by persuasion or appeal to reason:

     a. Common to heterogeneous societies in which there is minimal sharing of traditional norms and beliefs.

     b. Responsive to change in the views of needs of society.

     c. Becomes formally organized in bureaucratic structures.

  3. *Charismatic:* The power of an individual personality. It lacks stability and endures only if the system advocated by the charismatic leader becomes institutionalized.

IV. The State

A. *Distinction between state and government:*

  1. State is an entity. Government is a process.

  2. State is permanent. Government, as the operational arm of the state, is temporary.

  3. Opposition to the policies of state is the basis of revolution. Opposition to the policies of government is the basis of politics.

B. *Components and powers of the state:*

  1. Membership is compulsory.

  2. Retains absolute power over the lives and property of its population.

  3. Composed of territory, population, government, and sovereignty.

C. *Theories of function and foundation:*

  1. Thomas Hobbes: Founded by social contract. The people relinquish individual liberty in return for protection and social order.

  2. *Functionalist:* Based on Hobbes. The state functions in the service of all members by providing:

     a. Ultimate source of arbitration.

     b. Orderly allocation of resources.

     c. Economic coordination.

     d. Vehicle for interaction with other states.

3. *Conflict*: Based on Rousseau. The state emerged from simple egalitarian societies to protect the position of the privileged.

4. *Marx's hypothesis*: State emerges as the arm of the dominant class.

   D. *The nation-state:*

1. Evolved through kinship, tribes, city-states, nation-states.

2. Factors of unification include territory, language, and economic interdependence.

3. *Nationalism*: Ethnocentrism on the societal level. A relatively late development following:

    a. Ruler identification with his population and territory rather than with other rulers.

    b. Popular awareness of and pride in cultural distinctiveness.

  V. **Political Ideology:** A philosophy of social order upon which the state, parties, or social movements are based.

   A. Members of a state share an ideology as a result of socialization.

   B. In heterogeneous societies ideologies are varied and often conflicting.

   C. *The ideology of democracy:* Derives from belief in the value of the individual. Democratic principles which follow from this premise:

1. Popular sovereignty.

2. Personal freedoms and the opportunity to pursue individual goals.

   D. *Political manifestations of democratic principles:*

1. The right to vote.

2. Freedom of information.

3. Freedom of social interaction and group membership.

4. Freedom to seek public office.

5. Freedom from persecution.

6. Freedom to critize the society and the government.

   E. *Autocracy:*

1. *Kingships, empires, military dictatorships:* Rule with or without consensus.

2. *Totalitarianism:* Modern autocracies which rule with apparent legitimation. Characterized by:

    a. Total control of all major social institutions. Ideology permeates education, religion, economy, media.

    b. Single political party to which the government bureaucracy answers.

    c. Pervasive secret police.

    d. Control mass media.

    e. Repository of all arms.

    f. Plans and coordinates all aspects of the economy.

3. *Authoritarianism:* Absolute power limited to the political sector.

VI. Power Structure in the United States

    A. *Democratic model:*

        1. Individual participation in political processes.

        2. Majority rule.

        3. Minority freedom and opportunity to become the majority.

        4. Equality before the law.

    B. *Pluralism:*

        1. Robert Dahl's "broker" theory: Neither the majority nore the minority control the government. Government decisions are made in appeasement of the demands of numerous small groups.

        2. Power is distributed among many groups which compromise certain of their interests in order to achieve others.

        3. Multigroups form a system of checks and balances on concentrations of power.

        4. The greater the diversity of the groups, the greater the equal distribution of power and the social benefits derived therefrom.

        5. Conflict and consensus: Consensus in regard to the fundamentals of democracy underlies conflict on specific issues.

    C. *Elitism: C. Wright Mills:*

        1. Complex, mass society reduces the possibility and effectiveness of popular participation.

        2. Power is centered in the top ranks of the corporate, military, and political directorates.

        3. Public opinion is manipulated through control of mass media.

        4. Multigroup interests do not distribute but instead reduce the power of the people.

        5. Analgous to an aristocracy, the elite is monolithic, sharing background, class, experiences. Primary allegiance and concern is with elite status rather than with the state (Domhoff).

        6. *Conflict and consensus:* Conflict is hidden by popular assent to the myth of democracy which is perpetuated by the elite.

VII. Political Processes in the United States

    A. *Interest groups:* The means by which individuals in voluntary associations attempt to affect public policy:

        1. Clarify and expose issues for the public.

        2. Lobby.

        3. Observe and constrain other interest groups.

    B. *Political parties:* Based on the right for organized opposition to the party in power.

1. *Purposes*:
   a. To gain control of the government in the name of the electorate.
   b. Watch and check the party in power.
   c. To present a platform of issues and ideologies and to "educate" the electorate.

C. *Participation in the political process:* Cynical lack of faith in democratic process and opposition to equality, political or civil rights.

1. Voter participation: Lower voter turnout due to political alienation.
2. Lowest participation occurs among the undereducated; those with unskilled jobs; rural residents; and underprivileged minorities.

VIII. **Political Opinion:** Totality of opinion expressed by members of a community on political issues. Political opinions are acquired through *political socialization*. The major agents of political socialization are family, peers, social class, race, and religion.

Learning Objectives

1. Define and list the human needs served by the economy.
2. Identify the three basic economic decisions served by the economy.
3. Give the three ways in which people in different societies solve their economic problems.
4. Define the factors of production.
5. Explain how technology influences production.
6. Summarize the changes in society which occur in the transformation from agricultural to industrial economies.
7. Summarize the differences between capitalism, socialism, and communism.
8. List the characteristics of the American economy.
9. Define alienation and anomie.
10. State the major issues in the American economy.
11. Define government.
12. Summarize the manifest and latent functions of government.
13. Give Max Weber's definition of power.
14. List the types of power.
15. Define legitimate power.
16. List the types of legitimate power.
17. Distinguish between state and government.
18. Define political ideology.
19. Summarize the assumptions and principles of democracy.
20. Describe and state the differences between the autocratic forms of government.
21. Summarize the democratic model of power in the United States.

22. Compare the pluralistic and the elitist model of the power structure in the United States.

23. State the purpose and functions of political parties.

24. Identify the reasons why voter participation is so poor in this country.

Self-Test

Select the best possible answer. If you miss any questions, go back to the text and find the correct answer.

Multiple-Choice

1. The economic institution supplies the human needs of
   a. goods, clothing, shelter.
   b. food, shelter.
   c. who gets what and why.
   d. all of the above.

2. The basic economic decisions made in every society can be summarized as
   a. capitalism, communism, socialism.
   b. food, clothing, shelter.
   c. who gets what and why.
   d. custom and tradition, command, supply and demand.

3. The problem of assuring human survival has been approached by societies through the method of
   a. custom and tradition.
   b. the command of a central authoritarian ruler.
   c. the market system.
   d. all of the above.

4. Labor, land, and capital are
   a. sources of decisions.
   b. factors of production.
   c. the economic institution.
   d. primary, secondary, and tertiary sectors.

5. The Industrial Revolution
   a. represented an overnight change in economy.
   b. was preceded and accompanied by revolutionary changes in ideology and economic motives.
   c. was based on the voyages of discovery.
   d. was a result of the decline of silver and gold as the definition of wealth.

6. The Protestant Reformation
   a. had no bearing on the emergence of capitalism.
   b. resulted in values which were helpful to the emergence of capitalism.
   c. originated as a protest movement against the emergence of capitalism.
   d. was a worldwide movement.

7. The American economy has not resolved the issues of
   a. underemployment or chronic unemployment for one segment of our population.
   b. poverty.
   c. erosion of purchasing power.
   d. all of the above.

8. Government may be defined as
   a. institutionalized social order.
   b. a system of law.
   c. orderly politics.
   d. a system in which some are rulers are some are ruled.

9. The manifest functions of government include
   a. creation of power elites.
   b. maintaining social classes.
   c. implementing social control.
   d. creation of party machines.

10. What is at the basis of power?
    a. Legitimacy.
    b. Authority.
    c. Charisma.
    d. The threat of force.

11. Legitimate authority
    a. depends on coercion
    b. is viewed as justified because the system it upholds contains values and beliefs shared by most of society.
    c. is needed in order for a government to survive.
    d. only b and c.

12. The most significant aim of the state is
    a. to protect its citizens.
    b. to impose organized political control over its citizens.
    c. to formulate and enforce laws.
    d. to plan, run, and regulate activities beneficial to its citizens.

13. A system of ideas, values, beliefs, and attitudes shared by members of a society and accepted as true by them is
    a. a doctrine.
    b. a religion.
    c. a philosophy.
    d. an ideology.

14. The democratic ideology contains all but one of the following beliefs:
    a. Importance and value of the individual.
    b. The good of society is to be considered before the good of the individual.
    c. Personal freedom.
    d. Opportunity to pursue individual goals.

15. The democratic model of power in the United States
    a. is based on government by elites.
    b. is based on majority rule, with respect for the rights of minorities.
    c. is based on apathy.
    d. none of the above.

16. The elitist view of political power in the United States holds that
    a. power is diffused among numerous interest groups.
    b. the stability of the political system is promoted by a great number of organized interest groups.
    c. decision making results from the steady appeasement of relatively small groups.
    d. the ultimate fate of all organizations is to be run by a small minority.

17. The pluralist view of political power in the United States maintains that
    a. power in society belongs to a limited number of individuals or groups.
    b. consensus results from manipulation of the mass media by the ruling elite.
    c. important decisions are made by the military-industrial complex.
    d. elites are responsive and accountable to the people through elections.

18. To gain *legal* control of government and to take on the responsibility for conducting its affairs is
    a. the purpose of communism.
    b. the purpose of authoritarianism.
    c. the purpose of political parties.
    d. the purpose of democracy.

19. Voter participation
    a. is high in the United States.
    b. is low, particularly among the young, the undereducated, the unskilled, and the underprivileged minorities.
    c. is high in the lower socioeconomic classes.
    d. is none of the above.

True-False

_____   1. In the transformation from an agricultural to an industrial society, status and power shifts to those who own most of the land.

_____   2. Karl Marx was one of the first to recognize that the decreasing responsibility of the factory worker for his work made that work meaningless.

_____   3. Our economy is shifting its work emphasis from production to service.

_____ 4. In a complex society, social control is maintained through moral control.

_____ 5. Max Weber's definition of power is "the probability that one actor within a social relationship will be in a position to carry out his own will despite resistance."

_____ 6. Regimes in which power is held by an absolute monarch or dictator, or by a small elite, but whose power is limited to the political sphere, are called authoritarian.

_____ 7. Pluralists maintain that we have "government by the people."

Fill-in-the-Blank

1. When economic decisions are made as the result of a market dependent on demand and supply, on prices, profits, and losses, society is following a _____ economic system. (command, private enterprise)

2. _____ is the entire stock of knowledge and skills that a society possesses at any given time. (Technology, Capital)

3. The religious ideas of the Protestant ethic prepared the emerging merchant classes of Holland and England for a new economic system called _____. (capitalism, socialism)

4. _____ is one of the factors of production which includes man-made things like machinery, shoes, and pencils. (Technology, Capital)

5. _____ is the economic system characterized by the possession of wealth by private individuals and production based on profits and supply and demand. (Socialism, Capitalism)

6. _____ is a term used to describe the feelings of powerlessness by factory workers. (Alienation, Anomie)

7. When a government has _____ its laws are followed and its officials are respected by the majority of people in society, regardless of their personal feelings. (power, legitimacy)

8. _____ authority is based on the personality of the leaders. (Legitimate, Charismatic)

9. The _____ is the formal counterpart of government that develops when government becomes complex and its functions increase. (political parties, state)

Answers to the Self-Test and Related Learning Objectives
Chapter 1

Multiple-Choice	Obj.	True-False	Obj.	Fill-in-the-Blank	Obj.
1. A	2	1. T	2	1. authority	3
2. A	4	2. F	2	2. replication	5
3. B	6	3. F	6	3. Hypotheses	5
4. A	6	4. F	8	4. Independent	7
5. D	8	5. T	9	5. participant observation	8
6. D	9	6. T	9	6. evolutionary	9
7. C	9				
8. A	10				

Chapter 2

Multiple-Choice	Obj.	True-False	Obj.	Fill-in-the-Blank	Obj.
1. D	8, 9	1. F	1	1. Social System	2
2. C	9	2. T	3	2. macrosocial	4
3. B	12	3. F	5, 6	3. Status	5
4. D	13	4. F	10, 11	4. ascribed	7
5. A	14	5. T	11	5. Secondary	15
6. B	19	6. T	14		
7. D	16	7. T	19		
8. B	16	8. T	19		
9. D	17, 18	9. T	16		
		10. F	16		
		11. F	16		
		12. F	17		
		13. F	18		

Chapter 3

Multiple-Choice	Obj.	True-False	Obj.	Fill-in-the-Blank	Obj.
1. D	2	1. T	3	1. signals	3
2. D	2	2. T	4	2. Nonmaterial	4
3. C	4	3. T	5	3. mores	6
4. B	6	4. T	6	4. Ethnocentrism	11
5. B	8	5. T	6	5. cultural relativity	11
6. B	14	6. T	7	6. cultural universals	13
		7. T	8	7. Counterculture	14
		8. T	9		
		9. F	11, 12		

Chapter 4

Multiple-Choice	Obj.	True-False	Obj.	Fill-in-the-Blank	Obj.
1. C	1	1. T	1	1. Personality	1
2. A	3	2. T	1	2. Socialization	1
3. D	4	3. T	2	3. family	8
4. C	7	4. F	8	4. Significant others	6
5. D	10	5. T	5	5. generalized other	6
		6. F	9	6. Anticipatory	9

Chapter 5

Multiple-Choice	Obj.	True-False	Obj.	Fill-in-the-Blank	Obj.
1. B	1	1. F	3	1. Deviance	2
2. D	2	2. T	6	2. Crime	8
3. B	4, 5, 6				
4. C	5				
5. C	7				
6. D	9				

Chapter 6

Multiple-Choice	Obj.	True-False	Obj.	Fill-in-the-Blank	Obj.
1. C	1, 2	1. F	3	1. conservative	4
2. A	2	2. F	4	2. Conflict	5
3. B	4	3. T	4	3. life chances	9
4. D	6	4. T	6	4. Social class	8
5. C	7	5. T	8	5. Power	10
6. B	9	6. F	8	6. reputational	12
7. B	10	7. T	11	7. Open	13
8. A	14	8. T	9		
		9. T	9		
		10. F	11		
		11. F	12		
		12. F	15		

Chapter 7

Multiple-Choice	Obj.	True-False	Obj.	Fill-in-the-Blank	Obj.
1. C	1	1. T	1	1. minority group	1, 3
2. D	2	2. F	2	2. Ethnic	2
3. D	3	3. T	6	3. Racism	6
4. C	6	4. T	8, 9	4. Ethnicity	2
5. C	6, 7	5. T	5	5. Prejudice	8
6. C	7, 8	6. F	13	6. Structural	9
7. B	9	7. T	10		
8. C	5	8. F	11		
9. C	12				
10. C	14				

Chapter 8

Multiple-Choice	Obj.	True-False	Obj.	Fill-in-the-Blank	Obj.
1. C	1	**1.** T	4	**1.** Gender–role socialization	2
2. D	3	**2.** F	5	**2.** majority, minority	4
3. C	5	**3.** T	6	**3.** inferior	6
4. C	9	**4.** F	7		
5. D	10	**5.** T	8		

Chapter 9

Multiple-Choice	Obj.	True-False	Obj.	Fill-in-the-Blank	Obj.
1. D	8	**1.** T	2	**1.** Statics	1
2. D	8	**2.** T	6	**2.** Dynamics	1
3. C	10	**3.** T	6	**3.** Technology	2
4. D	11	**4.** T	7	**4.** Automation	3
5. A	10	**5.** T	3	**5.** Technological determinism	4
6. D	13	**6.** T	9	**6.** cultural lag	5
7. A	14	**7.** F	3	**7.** invention	7
8. C	15	**8.** T	12	**8.** agriculture	10
9. D	16	**9.** T	11	**9.** third	10
10. C	17	**10.** F	10	**10.** fall	12, 13
		11. F	12	**11.** urbanization	13
		12. F	13	**12.** Sector	14
		13. T	14	**13.** Suburbanization	15
		14. T	16	**14.** great	17
		15. F	16		
		16. T	17		

Chapter 10

Multiple-Choice	Obj.	True-False	Obj.	Fill-in-the-Blank	Obj.
1. B	2	**1.** T	2	**1.** Collective behavior	2
2. B	6	**2.** F	4	**2.** contagion	6
3. D	3	**3.** T	4	**3.** Rumor	5
4. C	4	**4.** F	6	**4.** Public	7
5. A	4	**5.** T	3	**5.** Public opinion	8
6. A	8	**6.** T	8	**6.** Propaganda	9
7. C	10	**7.** T	1, 8	**7.** Change resistant	13
8. C	13	**8.** T	8		
9. C	12	**9.** F	13		
10. B	10, 11	**10.** T	13		
11. A	14	**11.** T	15		
12. D	16	**12.** F	16		
13. B	16	**13.** F	17		
14. D	1	**14.** F	1		

Chapter 11

Multiple-Choice	Obj.	True-False	Obj.	Fill-in-the-Blank	Obj.
1. D	1	1. T	1	1. Conflict	1
2. B	4	2. T	1	2. Homogamy	6
3. A	3	3. T	1	3. family disorganization	7
4. A	4	4. T	3	4. Higher; more	8
5. D	3	5. F	4	5. Single-parent and	
6. D	3, 7	6. F	4	blended families	8
7. B	9	7. T	2	6. cult	12
8. D	10	8. T	7	7. lower-middle	14
9. D	10	9. T	10	8. education	1
10. B	10	10. T	9	9. latent	1
11. A	9	11. T	10		
12. D	9	12. T	12		
13. A	10	13. T	12		
14. D	11	14. T	13		
15. B	14	15. T	15		
16. D	16	16. T	14		
17. D	1, 17	17. F	18, 19		
18. D	18	18. F	19		
19. A	19	19. T	19		
20. A	19				
21. A	22				

Chapter 12

Multiple-Choice	Obj.	True-False	Obj.	Fill-in-the-Blank	Obj.
1. A	1	1. F	6	1. private enterprise	3
2. C	2	2. T	7	2. Technology	5
3. D	3	3. T	8	3. capitalism	7
4. B	4	4. F	14	4. Capital	4
5. B	6	5. T	13	5. Capitalism	7
6. B	7	6. T	20	6. Alienation	9
7. D	10	7. F	22	7. legitimacy	15, 16
8. A	11			8. Charismatic	16
9. C	12			9. state	17
10. D	13, 14				
11. D	15, 16				
12. B	17				
13. D	18				
14. B	19				
15. B	21				
16. D	22				
17. D	22				
18. C	23				
19. B	24				